QUESTIONS OF IDENTITY

TMÁŘCE

QUESTIONS OF IDENTITY

Czech and Slovak Ideas of
Nationality and Personality

Robert B. Pynsent

CENTRAL EUROPEAN UNIVERSITY PRESS
BUDAPEST • LONDON • NEW YORK

© Robert B. Pynsent 1994

First published in Great Britain 1994 by
Central European University Press
25 Floral Street,
London WC2E 9DS

British Library Cataloguing in Publication Data

A CIP catalogue record for this book is available from the British Library.

ISBN 1 85866 005 X

Library of Congress Cataloging in Publication Data

A CIP catalog record for this book is available from the Library of Congress

Distributed by
Oxford University Press, Walton Street, Oxford OX2 6DP
Oxford New York Toronto
Delhi Bombay Calcutta Madras Karachi
Kuala Lumpur Singapore Hong Kong Tokyo
Nairobi Das es Salaam Cape Town
Melbourne Aukland Madrid
and associated companies in Berlin Ibadan
Distributed in the United States
by Oxford University Press Inc., New York

Typeset by Koinonia Limited, Manchester
Printed and bound in Great Britain by Biddles Ltd, Guildford, Surrey

CONTENTS

PREFACE

Problems of identity are particularly keenly felt by individuals or groups who find themselves left outside what is considered the norm in those parts of society or the world which appear to be the bearers of culture. Although one chapter in this book concerns notions of identity or non-identity in European literature as a whole, including Czech, the other three concern specific Czech or Slovak identity predicaments.

The very term 'identity' suggests problems: identity parade, identity crisis, ethnic identity. Indeed, I am not sure that, barring philosophers and psychiatrists, anyone who is at ease with him or herself gives much thought to identity. Furthermore, identity seems to me to be a fairly modern problem. I find it extremely difficult, indeed, impossible, to imagine a medieval Czech historian or theologian or literary artist asking 'What is a Czech?', or 'What is a German?' – or 'What am I?' Perceptions of the individual were, naturally enough, very different from today's or the nineteenth century's in a God-ordered world. One discursive novel from the first decade of the fifteenth century – that is from the end of the period in which Czech literature blossomed, *Tkadleček,* – might be anachronistically interpreted as the depiction of an identity crisis. The lengthy work consists of a lively dispute between Ludvík Tkadleček (*tkadleček* = weaver = *textor* = weaver of words), who has just been abandoned by the lady of his heart, and Misfortune. Tkadleček has gone to pieces, but his question is not 'What am I?' or even 'What is she?', but 'What have you done to me, Misfortune, and why?' Indeed, one may interpret *Tkadleček* as a Scholastic improvement on the old disputes centred on the dualistic nature of man, disputes between the Body and the Soul, where Tkadleček represents Emotion (or Sensuality, as in Lydgate) and Misfortune, Reason. Generally speaking, medieval man is what he does, not what he thinks or 'is'; that does not mean that mediaeval writers were not concerned with psychological motivation. On the contrary.

The first chapter in this volume addresses Václav Havel's conceptions of identity, as manifested throughout his writing career, from his earliest plays and essays in the 1960s to the speeches from the last year of his presidency of the Czech and Slovak Federative Republic. In the end, Havel's central conception of identity is that it consists in the sum of one's responsibilities. In other words, he comes close to the medieval perception: one is what one does.

Havel was writing mainly against a socialist régime which he saw as programmatically obliterating individual identity in favour of a collective pseudo-identity. My second chapter concerns nationalism, the creation of national identity, that is either the quest for a collective pseudo-identity or the rationalization of an emotional sense of belonging. The two writers I consider, Šafařík and Kollár, the former primarily a scholar, the latter primarily a poet, were Slovaks, that is members of 'a people with no history, just a past', as the saying goes. Inspired by Herder and German nationalism, these two writers, instead of fostering Slovak nationalism, attempted to create Slav nationalism. They wrote in Czech and German because Slovak barely existed: Slovak was not finally codified as a literary language until the mid 1840s.

European nations, in the sense that we understand the concept today, were invented in the last part of the eighteenth and the first part of the nineteenth centuries. A study of the writings of Šafařík and Kollár reveals a more or less perfect model of the way nations were created. Their enterprise failed, but had an enormous impact in central and eastern Europe. Indeed, after the Communist takeover in Czechoslovakia in 1948, one of the chief Czech ideologues, Zdeněk Nejedlý (1878–1962), saw the Red Army and the Soviet Communist Party as the fulfillers of Kollár's dream. And even Havel has spoken of the Poles as the Czechs' and Slovaks' Slav brothers.

The Swiss French Henri-Frédéric Amiel, one of the most important inspirers of the Decadent mood in the Austrian Lands, also puts all Slavs in the same basket. Where Šafařík and Kollár were unconsciously mythopoets (they thought of themselves more as discoverers), the Decadents were, generally, mythoclasts. The third chapter of this volume, which considers the background to a period of Czech literature more than Czech literature itself, discusses the Decadents' disillusion with the myth of the unity of personal identity. No doubt coincidentally, Max Stirner, whose egoist philosophy had a considerable impact on the 1890s, had an idea of 'living in truth' remarkably close in parts to Havel's and rejected rationalist objectivism in terms which foreshadow the writing of Havel's friend, Václav Bělohradský. The Decadents were individualists, usually intellectual anarchists, and the two main vigorous political currents of the last part of the nineteenth century, nationalism and socialism, were abhorrent to them. The individual, however fragmented, disintegrated, his personality, was cultivated as a fortress against the grey mediocrity of industrial society and its concomitant intellectual, architectural and social ugliness, against the disintegration of the old aristocratic order and the creation of mass political parties.

One of the most common expressions of the Decadent doubting of the existence of a stable identity lay, from Baudelaire onwards, in sadomasochistic fantasies. In Czech Decadent literature one thinks particularly of Zeyer, Karásek, and Marten, albeit such sadomasochism was most pronounced in writers who adhered to the Decadent creed only in part (for example, Lešehrad, Maria, Šarlih). The subject of the fourth chapter of this book might have been facetiously labelled 'Czech national masochism'. At least since the end of the National Revival (I think here particularly of Karel Havlíček [1821–56] and Karel Sabina [1813–77]), major Czech writers have frequently been outspoken critics of the 'Czech character', and during the National Revival itself innate Czech quarrelsomeness was repeatedly blamed for the people's having been subjugated to the Germans. As far as I have been able to ascertain, however, the first Czechoslovak president, T. G. Masaryk (1850–1937), was the first to point out the Czechs' 'unhealthy' cult of martyrs. The fourth chapter, after a summary study of Slovak and Czech myths, briefly considers six of these martyrs, each on the basis of one key work.

Identity, it will become clear, is a politically charged matter. Sometimes explicitly, sometimes implicitly, this book discusses the prickly relationship between individual persons and nations with the world surrounding them.

I am extremely grateful to colleagues for reading and criticizing the original drafts of the chapters contained in this volume, László Péter of the School of Slavonic Studies, chapter 2, and Anthony Savile of King's College, London, chapter 3. I have also had several discussions with my former teacher in Cambridge, Karel Brušák, on the subject of chapter 4. Without the enormous patience of Nicola Mooney, who has typed several versions of this book, I could have done nothing.

London   Robert B. Pynsent
October 1993

INTRODUCTION: QUESTIONS OF IDENTITY AND RESPONSIBILITY IN VÁCLAV HAVEL

The background to Havel's writing

In the West, Václav Havel is generally thought of primarily as a playwright. From the end of the 1970s, however, he became more important as a political essayist. Naturally enough, since he was made president of Czechoslovakia in December 1989, his writing was restricted to the composing of speeches. Even in these speeches, however, one will find ideas that have been occupying his mind since the beginning of the 1960s.

When Havel came to power, journalists were quick to make comparisons between him and the first president of Czechoslovakia, T. G. Masaryk. Masaryk had emerged from 'resistance abroad' against Austria–Hungary. Havel had emerged from 'dissident' 'resistance at home' against the socialist regime. Masaryk and Havel were both intellectuals and both essayists. However many brushes Masaryk may have had with the authorities, and even with his own students in the philosophy department of Prague University, he was essentially a member of the Austrian Establishment. Havel was not and never had been a member of the socialist Establishment. In that he was unlike most of the Czech 'dissident' and emigré community who have become well known in the West over the past twenty or thirty years; most of these had once been Communists, sometimes very active Communists, for example, Klíma, Kohout, Kundera, Vaculík. Masaryk was somewhat stodgy and unimaginative, which Havel has never been. No one has ever seriously doubted the political or personal probity of either (I do not count the defamatory articles about Havel published by Communist Party hacks in newspapers during the Soviet occupation of Czechoslovakia). Masaryk consciously, sometimes forcedly, followed what he conceived of as the main tradition of Czech nineteenth-century thinking, however strongly influenced he was by

English, French, German and Scottish thinkers. Havel, by contrast – however much he may, as he claims more than once, have learned from the Czech thinker Jan Patočka (1907–77), and other Czechs – is very much his own man and does not think of himself as having any specially Czech intellectual tradition behind him, in spite of the fact that he may have spoken of special Czechoslovak geographical and political experiences in his presidential speeches. He is not a man of grand theories as Masaryk was.

That does not mean that he is at all unconscious of his own people's cultural and political history. Indeed, in 1991 Havel made an emotional, even sentimental, declaration of his Czechness (1991, pp. 18–19):[1]

My home is the house in which I live, the parish or town where I was born or where I live; my home is my family, my friends, the social and spiritual environment in which I live, my occupation, firm or place of work. Naturally, my home is also the country in which I live, the language I speak … The historical experience, the Czech kinds of courage and cowardice, Czech humour – all these are inseparable components of the [spiritual] layer of my home. My home is, then, my Czechness, that is my nationality, and I see no reason whatsoever for not acknowledging this layer of my home; after all, it is as essentially self-evident for me as, for example, that layer of my home which I would call my masculine gender.

This book concerns modes of Czech and Slovak thinking in the three crucial periods of modern Czech and Czechoslovak cultural history. This section concerns mainly the period when Czechoslovakia was part of the Soviet Bloc. The second contains the middle part of the National Revival, when the new idea of nationhood was being formulated and when the notion of 'home' as Heimat was invented. The third period is that of the fin de siècle years when Czech culture had 'caught up' with Western European, when the Czech language was fully established as a language of high culture and as no longer threatened by German. The conclusion takes us through times of political crisis from St Wenceslas's treaty with the Germans and his establishing of Christianity as the rulers' religion in Bohemia in the early tenth century to the immediate aftermath of the Soviet occupation of 1968.

The section on the National Revival is concerned with the way in which subsidiary myths operated to support the central myth of nation. Kollár's notions of Slav Reciprocity (only scholars read Šafařík nowadays) and his form of nationalism, which a thinker who had some impact on Havel, Emanuel Rádl (1873–1942), considered racist, had a firm place in the Czechoslovak school curriculum. Very little indeed of Kollár's thinking can be found in Havel. Certainly he has exhibited 'Slav consciousness' on official occasions. In his address to the Pope at Prague Castle (21 April 1990) he declared (1990, p.97), 'I welcome you here, Your Holiness, also as a Slav who understands, and speaks, Czech. I welcome you as a great son of our fraternal Polish nation.' Furthermore, Havel's enumeration of the 'traditional' special qualities of Czechoslovak citizens (1992b, p.36) cannot but remind us of Herder's conception of the Slav character:

I count among these traditions: trust in the human spirit and its capacity to conquer violence without itself having to resort to violence; faith in suprapersonal values and in the better aspects of the human character; the citizen's responsibility for the community; understanding, tolerance and a capacity for forgiveness and repentance; a desire for a democratic order and the ability to conduct themselves democratically; a profound respect for human rights; the desire to live in a free and dignified manner in an independent state which acknowledges that it belongs to Europe; the ability to be impartial and not to fall into fanaticism; worldly wisdom, humour, imagination and a sense of community.

Slav consciousness need not have anything to do with Kollár, since it is evident in Czech writers from long before Kollár,[2] but the Stalinist cult of Kollár (Stalin had in 1944 and 1945 allegedly fulfilled Kollár's ideals) did lead Czechoslovaks automatically to link Slav consciousness with Kollár. National identity was of little concern to Havel until the explosion of Slovak national self-assertion in 1990. His habitual suspicion of national mythopoeia is evident in his condemnation of Milan Kundera's notion of 'the Czech lot' in history. In his condemnation of Kundera he implicitly rejected the passive element in not only Kollár's but also Masaryk's conception of a national vocation. In one of his most influential works *Česká otázka* (The Czech question, 1895), Masaryk wrote: 'With Kollár I believe that the histories of nations are not fortuitous, but that they reveal a definite plan of Providence and that it is thus the task of historians and philosophers, the task of every nation, to discern that universal plan.'[3] Historicist idealism is alien to Havel, not least because not only Kundera, but Marxist-Leninists altogether, had tended to 'demonize' history.

    The section of this book which considers the Decadent perception of the self demonstrates that Havel is a direct heir of the Decadents, although the only reference he has to the movement comes in his work on Josef Čapek (1887–1945), when he writes of the 'tuberose' atmosphere of Decadence (1963, p.13). This assertion may be defended in three ways. First, the Decadence was the first literary trend in which almost every writer was concerned with the self analytically (that is, not simply emotionally or superficially psychological like the Romantics), a trend in which the concerns of philosophers were not simply popularized but also consciously developed by writers of *belles lettres*. The philosophy of identity became the theme of literature. Secondly, the Decadents' sense of the threat posed to individual identity by a despiritualized industrial world resembles Havel's sense of the threat socialism after the 'scientific and technological revolution' posed to individual identity. Thirdly, the Decadence, which had initially been an elite and elitist trend, became a mass movement in the 1960s,[4] and Havel considers himself a child of the Beatles generation. In the 1970s he found the Western students' peace movements emotionally attractive, because he liked people who 'cared'. His mentor, Patočka, would no doubt have questioned him about that, since he was particularly suspicious of the 1960s student movements in the West; he finds them so entirely negative, for example 'even the [students'] breaking of taboos testifies only to a crisis , if it cannot be seen what direction is meant to be taken after the taboos are broken'.[5]

At the same time Havel displays a profound anxiety about the consumer mentality which overtook all Europe in the 1960s, and which appeared to be particularly dangerous, because manipulable, in socialist society. Like, for example, the novelist Vladimír Páral, he satirizes the non-communication arid socialist society seemed to impose on its subjects. The chief distinction between Havel and Páral, however, is that behind all his comedy one always senses serious concern in Havel, but, particularly in the late 1970s and in the 1980s, one senses sometimes frivolity, sometimes despair behind Páral's comedy. Furthermore, Páral is preoccupied with human sexuality and Havel hardly touches on the subject. The facts that Havel's plays are, generally speaking, dominated by men, and that the women in them tend to be accessories to or, sometimes, playthings of the men could in themselves be interpreted as social commentary. Though it may be simply a matter of decency – and one thinks of the muted manner in which he speaks of affection and their marriage in his letters from prison to his wife, Olga.[6]

Havel was born (1936) into the Prague patriciate,[7] and he was brought up and dressed as a patrician – which made his life embarrassing at school and which was a considerable practical disadvantage to him after the advent of socialism. On the other hand, it brought him into contact with philosophical thinking from his childhood on. His father was a friend of Rádl's, and Masaryk's complete works were in the family library. He first read some Patočka at the beginning of the 1950s, went to his first Patočka lecture at the end of the 1950s, but it was only in the 1960s, when Patočka started coming regularly to the Theatre on the Balustrade, where Havel was working, to discuss philosophy that he met the man. He did not become a friend of Patočka's, however, until the 1970s. He last met him when they were both being held for questioning in the Ruzyně prison just outside Prague, when, in the waiting room, Patočka held an improvised seminar on the immortality of the soul and 'human responsibility'.[8] Patočka's effulgent personality had inspired the spirit of Charter 77: 'I don't know what Charter 77 would have been if, in its beginnings, Patočka had not illuminated its path with the radiance of his great personality' (1988, p.153). From Patočka's private seminars and lectures, Havel informs us, he had 'derived education and hope' (1990, p.135).

The general points Havel takes from Masaryk are an apparent belief in a Czech humanist tradition (1990, p.14), and in the importance to present-day Czechoslovaks of the 'Bohemian Brethren' philosophers, Petr Chelčický (c.1390–c.1460) and Comenius (1592–1670), (1990, p.15). He also expands on the active side of Masaryk's notion of a Czech national vocation. Perhaps he is attempting to boost his countrymen's self-confidence, but possibly he is revealing his own missionary zeal,[9] a zeal which is more representative of Bolzano than of Masaryk: 'I am so bold as to say that we might be able … to introduce a new element into European and world politics. If we truly want it, from now on and always Czechoslovakia could radiate love, a desire to understand, the power of spirituality and thought'. Today's Czechoslovaks, he continues, should renew Masaryk's conception of a politics based on morality (1990, pp.15–16). He does, however, warn his audience against the Masaryk cult. After World War I, those who nurtured the cult of Masaryk had often been the very people who had previously considered him a traitor. We 'should adore Masaryk less and ponder more over the real meaning of his heritage' (1990, p.77).

I do not know whether Havel knows the Prague-based Austrian philosopher Bernard Bolzano, but since he clearly knows some Masaryk and most Patočka, and since both those men write about Bolzano, I can assume that he knows his basic ideas. It looks very much as if Havel feels that socialism had destroyed the Czechoslovaks' sense of community, just as, at the beginning of the nineteenth century Bolzano maintained that national friction had prevented or destroyed a sense of community in Bohemia. Lack of unity between Germans and Czechs had tempted the rulers (read: Communist Party leaders) to misuse their power and look to their own material enrichment rather than the well-being of the people.[10] And centuries of that lack of unity (read: forty years of Communist rule) has led the inhabitants of Bohemia to forget 'what citizens are capable of doing for themselves if they stick together.'[11] Havel's belief that love could shine forth into the world from Czechoslovakia may echo both Bolzano and Masaryk. Bolzano sees love not only as the cure for every social conflict, but also as the potential creator of a particularly prosperous Bohemia which the world would envy. For Masaryk one of the greatest failings of Marx is that he lacked love. Marx had been incapable of distinguishing between love and sentimentality and therefore had rejected the morality of love as essentially ideology. Masaryk, like Bolzano, conceives of love as Christian action, conscientious work against all the physical and moral poverty we are aware of, even if we cannot see it. Love is work undertaken to resist 'all the innumerable little, insignificant, everyday enemies, the microbes of physical and moral evil and misery'. Love is the force which creates democracy.[12]

Havel appears also to accept the notion that the Czechs have an ancient democratic tradition, the notion that formed much of the backbone of Masaryk's interpretation of Czech history. Well aware of the fact that especially over the previous twenty years the Communist Establishment had been flogging this 'tradition' to death in its promulgations, Havel said in his first New Year's Day address (1990), that he saw hope for the Czechoslovak future in 'the humanist and democratic traditions, about which so many empty words have been slumbering in the unconscious of the Czechs and Slovaks and national minorities and have quietly transmitted themselves from generation to generation' (1990, p.14). For all his intellectual cosmopolitanism, Havel is, then, not impervious to national and state myths. Patočka also appears to believe in the tradition, but he links it with the fact that modern Czechs are descended from peasants and smallholders who were liberated at the end of the eighteenth and beginning of the nineteenth centuries. The Czechs enjoy 'an elemental democratism that is derived from the fact that Czech society is basically composed of the common people'. The ruling class is, then, of essentially the same social background as the ruled, and so remains 'closely bound with the broad masses'.[13] That may be naive social historicism but, given Patočka's impact on Havel, it sheds some light on the behaviour of the patrician Havel.

It also renders less incongruous Havel's statements about his political intentions when he was a dissident.[14] When he was firmly established as the leader of Czechoslovak dissidents (he had been helped to that position by his own courageous personality, by the amount of time American and British broadcasting stations transmitting in Czech and Slovak devoted to him and not least because the Communist media spent more time and space defaming him than anyone else), he denied he had any political ambitions. Thus he writes to his wife from prison (1985a, p.288): 'I am essentially a social, indeed I would say political, man, but not, of course, in the sense that I should like to be a professional politician, but in the sense that I am interested in communal matters, i.e. the matters of the *polis*, community.' So too, in the interview held at long distance with the emigré journalist Karel Hvížďala, he declares, not entirely persuasively when one considers his activities in the Writers' Union in the 1950s and 1960s, 'I have never been a politician and never wanted to be one' (1988a, p.13). In another interview, held two years earlier, he states, 'I am not a politician, never have been, and have no ambition to be a politician, or a professional revolutionary, or a professional "dissident"' (1989, p.12). He repeats that as president: 'I never for one moment ever wanted to hold any political post' (1991, p.7).

Havel may be, and may have always been, a politician; he may subscribe to certain notions of Czechness, and he may have written mainly about socialism, but he has always striven to be universal. He is frequently said to be unhappy that his plays are seen as so political in the West, but, first, it has generally been the fate of literature from the Socialist Bloc to be read politically in the West and, secondly, he may have been genuinely unaware how many problems he put in his plays which are specific to socialist societies because of the language (jargon and so forth) and situations he employs. As a dramatist, he is primarily a satirist and satirists lampoon their own societies or other societies to which they have easy access. Even in the 1960s Havel did not have easy access to any societies but his own. In the typescript notes he had sent out of Czechoslovakia for translators and producers of his *Largo desolato* (1985),[15] Havel instructs them not to give the play a specifically Czech or socialist context. The trouble is that, though the philosophical problem of this play may be universal, its situation, a man expecting and receiving a visit from secret policemen, is not part of western experience – unless set in Europe during World War II – but typical of the Socialist Bloc or the Third World. Havel's essays, however, often are genuinely universal. His criticism and analyses are frequently directed as much at the West as at the Bloc. 'This Bloc', he writes in the most incisive of his essays, 'Moc bezmocných' (The power of the powerless, 1985, p.59), 'has not for a long time constituted an enclave, a world isolated from the rest of advanced civilisation … on the contrary, it is an integral part of that world, and shares and co-creates its global fate. That means in concrete terms that in Czechoslovakia essentially the same hierarchy of life values is inevitably promoted as in advanced Western countries.'. That constitutes, after all, the reasons for dissent: socialism consistently despoils Western liberal values. At the same time socialist governments usually claimed and still claim adherence to those values. Havel is critical of Western politics and of Western consumerism. He does not consider the manner in which party machineries in the West take over elections a constructive means of pursuing politics. And Western consumerism does not offer much better a path to true civilization than socialist anti-culture: 'the dictatorship of consumption, production, advertising, commerce, consumer culture and their whole great flood of information, all this (which has been described and analysed so often) can hardly be considered a hopeful path towards man's rediscovering his self' (1984, p.128). He is also horrified by the collective inanity inherent in the television culture which has afflicted both East and West: 'the herd mentality is, you see, a blood relation of manipulability and nothing can better conceal the reality of daytime inequality than the evening illusion of universal television equality and community' (1984, p.139).

Western consumerism and socialist dictatorships both constitute attacks on the identity of the individual. Both have the tendency to create uniformity and to limit the individual's expression of his or her self. Still, there is no doubt in my mind that it was Eastern Party dictatorship rather than consumerism (remember his love of jeans) that led Havel to write so much about the sanctity and the frailty of the self. In a 1980 letter from prison he states that, hitherto, all his plays had concerned the disintegration of human identity and continuity (1985a, p.75). Elsewhere he traces his interest in the nature of human identity back to 1956 (that is, the beginning of the Thaw, after the twentieth congress of the Soviet Communist Party). In what he says about this he links identity with truth and untruth, and thus addresses one of the central themes of 1970s Czech literature, dissident and publicly available. It was in 1956, he writes, 'that society and human minds were first stirred by that strange dialectical dance of truth and lie, of truth alienated by lie and of the deceitful manipulation of hopes, a dance which we today know so intimately and which gives such a vivid and original picture of one of the fundamental themes of modern art: the theme of human identity and existential schizophrenia' (1984, p.12).

Identity and responsibility

In an essay of 1987, Havel points out how totalitarianism has striven to obliterate identity and personal responsibility. The socialist state is a gross version of the centralized welfare state; the state is privy to all details of the individual, gives him his job (and denies him the right not to work), gives him free medical treatment (and makes it a criminal act to do anything that is detrimental to his health – I do not know how frequently that law was enforced), gives him free university education (as long as he passes exams on Marxism–Leninism and the history of the working-class movement, and as long as his parents have an acceptable sociopolitical pedigree), and so forth. Havel does not need to say all that; he gets straight down to the point that the State or the Party (or the Central Committee of the Party) had made itself the only true individual in the country (1989, p.119):

Having expelled all other comparable individual subjects from its world, the central subject finally deprived itself of individuality. It is from this that flows the strange amorphousness, transparency, indeed, even intangibility of power, the blandness of its language, the anonymity of its decision-making, and its non-responsibility. How can a subject with such a blurred identity be responsible? How can it, when it is in total isolation and so does not have anyone to be responsible to? ... The intention of totalitarianism is total homogenization, and its product is uniformity, a herd mentality, the abolition of differentials.[16]

The individual has no responsibility to the state that has no responsibility to him. But then the individual has no responsibility to his or her fellow individuals where all individuals have been made into a herd or, as Bělohradský would put it, have accepted the norm of impersonality. The leader of the herd has no responsibility for the herd, but if a member of the herd wanders out of line, the leader might punish him or her. Marxism–Leninism had by its doctrine of inheritable class-guilt not only whittled away at the individual's sense of responsibility, but also divorced guilt from responsibility.

When Havel is writing about the gross racist injustice of the expulsion of the Germans from Czechoslovakia after World War II he is no doubt bearing doctrinaire socialist conceptions of guilt in mind. Almost a hundred years previously Masaryk had written: 'Socialism altogether, Marxism, too, will always seek a collective element in every guilt ... Marxism represses personal responsibility too far.'[17] Very much in the spirit of Masaryk, Havel, speaking on the expulsion of the Germans, admonishes his audience thus: 'to accept the idea of collective guilt and collective responsibility means consciously or involuntarily to diminish individual guilt and responsibility. And that is a very dangerous thing. Let us just recall how, not long ago, many of us used to evade personal responsibility by claiming that we Czechs were just like that and would probably never be otherwise. Thinking of that sort is the imperceptible embryo of moral nihilism' (1990, p.84). Rádl, who follows Masaryk in viewing Leninist revolutionism as a form of dangerous Oriental moral anarchism, spends some time in his *Západ a Východ* (West and East, 1925) considering Oriental and Western ethics. The Oriental, he argues, finds Western ethics too harsh because it is an ethics based on the notion of individual responsibility and individual conscience. Patočka links the problem with the modern tendency of human beings to objectivize themselves. Objectivization is a form of alienation which involves escaping the burden of living. That escape may entail accepting a notion of collective guilt/responsibility or pursuing occultist fatalism where our guilt is predetermined and our responsibility is to a self outside this world or to some grand idea which will be fulfilled in the future and of which we are but a tool. There is, writes Patočka, 'an essential difference between responsibility, which *bears* and "exposes itself"', and lightening the burden, escaping'. The real self is identifiable with the burden; responsibility gives the individual's life its meaning.[18]

That makes for the central theme of Havel's letters to his wife from prison. A sense of responsibility makes the individual an individual and supplies the key to one individual's understanding of another ('the secret of man is the secret of his responsibility' (1985a, p.126)); except on a superficial level; there can be no direct communication between two human beings who do not have a compatible sense of responsibility. Following both Patočka and a work parts of which he studied closely in prison, Emmanuel Lévinas's *Humanisme de l'autre homme*, he writes in these letters of the notion that freedom from responsibility destroys freedom. Being is a matter of questioning Being and, thus, bringing one's self into existence by becoming aware of oneself. Havel puts his conclusion telegraphically: 'The secret of the self. Consciousness of oneself. Consciousness of the world. The enigma of freedom and responsibility' (1985a, p.377). Responsibility is the prime mover of identity and without responsibility there is no identity, for only responsibility can provide that form which we call identity. Responsibility is 'the basic cornerstone from which all identity grows and with which it stands and falls; as its foundation, root, centre of gravity, structural principle or axis; something like the "idea" which determines its extent and nature; like a sort of mortar which holds it together and if that mortar dries out, identity begins unrestrainably to crumble, disintegrate' (1985a, p.160). Responsibility consists in man's ability or decision to take the blame, to provide his own warranty, for everything he has done or will do under any circumstances. It provides the individual with his relationship to the world and the universe. It provides that combination of dependence and independence which constitutes full being. On the one hand, responsibility 'defines and gives meaning to his dependence on the world; on the other hand, however, it is only through responsibility that he definitively separates himself from the world in his sovereignty and independence' (1985a, pp.162–3). One is not born with responsibility; one has to learn it by experiencing trials and dilemmas, shocks and realizations. Only through the formation of responsibility can one 'found and confirm one's identity, does one's awareness or meta-experience of an absolute horizon grow and become firmly established'. Without that responsibility one becomes alienated from oneself, 'overcome by a feeling of absurdity and hopelessness' and 'falls victim to Nothingness' (1985a, p.311). At the end of the one-act, *Audience*,[19] Vaněk is close to a loss of identity as a result of the effects of alcohol. His boss, the maltster, has been asked by the authorities to write a weekly informer's report on him and he asks Vaněk to write the reports for him, in exchange for a cushy clerical job. Vaněk refuses, but at the end of the play either he will write the reports or he will join with the maltster in drinking away the responsibility laid on them by the police.

Havel's conception of responsibility extends beyond responsibility to self, friends or country; it is universal. As a human being one is responsible for humanity and for the environment that humanity has been given to inhabit. The socialist regime, because it was non-responsible, had as great an irresponsibility to Nature as it did to the human beings dwelling on its demesne. The cow, Havel writes in an essay from the 1970s, ' is no longer an animal: it is a machine, which has its "input" (coarse feed) and its "output" (milk); it has its production plan and its mechanic, whose job is the same as that of the whole Czechoslovak economy: to increase output with lower input' (1984, p.349). The conception suggested by the Book of Genesis and then promulgated by the Enlightenment that man had the right, nay more, the duty, to subjugate Nature, had been pursued to such a degree that man had begun not simply to subjugate, but to destroy. This had entailed a crisis of identity characterized by a crisis in mankind's 'experience of an absolute horizon'. That in turn 'leads to a crisis of the intrinsic responsibility of man towards and for the world, which means towards and for himself' (1984, p.349). Because everyone living under socialism was somehow dependent on the state and thus took part in the state's non-responsibility, after socialism everyone, whatever their active or passive attitude to the regime had been, is responsible for the state of Nature in Czechoslovakia.

So too, even if under socialism that country had played such a negligible role in world politics, now Czechs and Slovaks must show that they, too, are all responsible for the state of the world (1990, p.28). Havel propagates a form of Masaryk's practical philosophy, which the latter called 'humanitism'. Havel's thinking, however appears even more firmly rooted in Christianity than Masaryk's had been. Full responsibility requires humility (1990, pp.59–60):

We continue to be subject to the pernicious, thoroughly arrogant, impression that the human being is the master of creation and not just part of it and that therefore he is allowed to do anything ... We are still incapable of comprehending that the single real backbone of our actions – if they are to be ethical – is responsibility. Responsibility to something higher than my family, my country, my firm, my prosperity. Responsibility to the order of Being, where our every action is indelibly recorded and where it is first justly evaluated.

The interpreter between us and this higher authority is what is traditionally called conscience.

To be able to assume that responsibility to the higher authority, the Czechoslovaks must accept their guilt in helping to build socialism, the regime that had debased man into becoming 'a force of production' and Nature into becoming 'an instrument of production'. Everyone had accepted socialism as an irremovable fact 'and thus helped to sustain it'. Thus 'we were all, to varying degrees, of course, responsible for the functioning of the totalitarian machinery, and no one was only its victim; at the same time we were all its creators' (1990, p.12). One might link that with the responsibility Havel feels that, as a human being, he shares for the Germans' systematic murdering of Jews in World War II. His expansion of that, however, into a new meaning of 'Chosen People' is morally questionable. The Jews had been chosen by 'Fate' to make 'modern man stand face to face with his global responsibility' and thus by their sacrifices to cast man 'into the deepest depths of his metaphysical self-awareness'. (1992b, p.108).

The notion of global responsibility is not to be confused with that primitive, almost neurotic, feeling of responsibility which can overcome us, responsibility for something we are not responsible for. If one is sitting in one's office and the building collapses around one, one cannot be held responsible for it, except in some petty legalistic way, even if one has, in fact, supplied the stimulus for that collapse by knocking a picture-nail into the wall. Such a feeling of responsibility smacks of occultism or of the prehistoric state of man that Patočka analyses in his *Kacířské eseje* (Heretical essays), where men and the gods live together in this world and anything strange or unexpected that happens is a manifestation of the divine. Havel writes of the 'pre-self', the state one is in before one has achieved identity. The pre-self, like Patočka's prehistoric man, is not responsible, because it is not yet capable of completely answering for itself (1985a, p.395). The irrational feeling of being responsible for everything is 'the essential intention of the "pre-self"'. On the other hand, one needs to experience that feeling (as children often do) before one can be open to the 'voice of Being'. Therefore 'this "responsibility for everything" is not only the starting point for all future ("mature") responsibility, but also an inseparable, ever-present component or dimension of mature responsibility' (1985a pp.420–1). It constitutes a predisposition to responsibility, as well as a precondition. The trouble with Havel's argument is that it is like saying that superstition is a necessary precondition for religious belief. A superstitious person may well be particularly open to religious conversion, but one does not have to be superstitious to adopt a faith.

Havel's concept 'castness' (*vrženost*) is closely linked with his notion of a pre-self. The term, which recalls the Jewish image of the expulsion from Eden, signifies one's being cast into life and into responsibility. One is cast into life before one acquires a self. Since one acquires a self by learning responsibility, responsibility must exist before one is cast into it. Havel explains his point thus (1985a, p.381):

This authentic responsibility, as yet not filtered by anything, free of all speculation, and preceding all deliberate 'taking upon oneself', responsibility which is not negotiable for anything else and not explainable by any psychological schemes is, so to speak, there before the I itself: first, I find myself in it and only then, having somehow or other accepted or rejected this castness, do I institute myself as the person that I am.

Havel may simply be saying in a complicated way that a metaphysical entity, responsibility, exists before we are aware of it, and that, when we do first become aware of it, it has a traumatic effect, such as one might link with being cast down or out from a height. A reader of Havel will, however, be inveigled into seeing a personal element in the concept 'castness'. He had from childhood had a sense of not belonging, which the Stalinists' treatment of offspring of the patriciate had intensified. At the same time, Havel had in his youth been vigorously 'anti-bourgeois', and for a long time he had thought of himself as a socialist. Becoming a dissident could, superficially perhaps, be seen as the institutionalization of his sense of not belonging. Not belonging had led his life to be accompanied by a feeling that he had done something wrong, that he was at fault in not belonging. He expands on that in the speech he gave on receiving an honorary degree at the Hebrew University of Jerusalem (1990, p.102): ' my inner feelings of exclusion or non-inclusion, of a sort of disinheritedness and essential ineptitude … are the hidden motor of all my persistent endeavours. … Indeed, I would be so bold as to say that anything good I have ever done, I possibly did only to try to conceal my well-nigh metaphysical feeling of guilt.'

The responsibility of being a dissident

One might feel guilt at not being like one's fellows or at not fulfilling one's role as a member of the intelligentsia. The intelligentsia's role was always to criticize the Establishment, to provide the impulse for reform and, in some geographical areas, revolution. Havel certainly fulfilled the role of a member of the intelligent-sia, at least according to the rules he laid down for himself. One would expect that feeling of guilt to increase – and in a speech in Copenhagen (28 May 91) he does speak of 'becoming constantly suspicious' of himself (1992, p.82), when as the leader of a dissident intelligentsia he became the leader of an Establishment.

Masaryk's position after World War I was similar, but not the same. In his pamphlet, *Krise inteligence* (The crisis of the intelligentsia, 1928), Emanuel Rádl states that the Czech intelligentsia had forgotten that it was their job to lead the nation. They had simply handed their role over to the politicians and had thus surrendered to the postwar slogan that every ideal must submit to the interests of nation and state. Instead of occupying themselves with ideals, the 1920s intelli-gentsia had, claims Rádl, allowed their interests to merge with those of the state: they had taken bureaucratic posts, joined in the condemnation of Austria, hatred of Germans, praise of the Czech past, praise of democracy, and attacks on Roman Catholicism. In general terms, the position of the Czech intelligentsia in the first years of the new Republic was, then, certainly comparable with the position of the intelligentsia after November 1989. But only in general terms. The new Re-public had inherited the richest, most developed part of Austria–Hungary; the new leaders of postsocialist Czechoslovakia inherited an economic backwater.

One may, however, conceive of the role of the intelligentsia according to Patočka's perception: not to be critics of the Establishment, but to be permanently aware that truth is problematical. By acting in accordance with their knowledge of problematicality 'they do not surrender to certain inclinations and temptations, and by distancing themselves from them they create "authenticity", a new self which puts aside its private interest and situation and, in this sense, "transcends" both.'[20] According to Patočka, the intelligentsia is always bound up with a moral view of things, the choice between right and wrong, in other words, between gaining and losing the spiritual self. So too, Bělohradský saw the dissidents as reflecting the notion that conscience was not just a private matter, as making it possible for the objectivistic state to be 'guilty in face of a personal conscious-ness'.[21] That perception allows a former dissident to become a member of a new Establishment.

Patočka saw the state of Czechoslovakia under socialism as a warlike peace. He compared the situation of the Eastern Bloc intellectual with that of men who had been through trench warfare. That experience was and is superable only by what he calls the solidarity of the shocked (*solidarita otřesených*), which is *eo ipso* built by people who are in a state of uncertainty, by dissidence:

The solidarity of the shocked is the solidarity of those who understand. In today's circumstances, however, that concerns not only the basic plane of a servile or liberated approach to life, but in addition it involves an understanding of the significance of science and technology, of the Force that we are releasing ... The solidarity of the shocked will not construct positive programmes, but will express itself, like Socrates' *daimonion* in warnings and prohibitions. ... The solidarity of the shocked is built on persecution and uncertainty: that is its battle-front, a quiet front that goes without advertisement and sensationalism, even when the ruling Forces try to wrest their section of the front from them.[22]

The term 'solidarity of the shocked' became a catchword of Czechoslovak dissident circles. Later, Patočka came to the view that every responsible Czechoslovak had to become to some degree a dissident. That was because: 'Essentially human rights concern every member of society, the *responsible individual*, the human being in his or her essence.'[23]

Havel writes about the moral predicaments of the dissident in most of his plays of the 1970s and 1980s. Dissident society was the mirror image of socialist society. Where socialism demanded non-responsibility and created non-responsibility even in private life, being a dissident was an expression of responsibility. Socialist society demanded conformity, uniformity, strove for the diminution of individual identity; dissidence, however, called for the expression of that identity. (At least this was the theory; naturally, dissident groups attracted many sorts of exhibitionists and no doubt also servants of the State. For example, the leader of the 'Jazz Section' of the Musicians' Union, whose prohibition in the summer of 1986 created such a fuss, allegedly turned out to have been a police informer all the time.) Dissident society certainly was a mirror image of socialist society in another way. Being an ex-Communist let alone being the son or daughter of a Communist did not bar one from it. Havel considers that aspect in his one-acter, *Protest* (1979). The apparatchik Staněk, who has left his friends from the 1960s, taken the course of serving the regime for the sake of his career or a comfortable life, wonders that the dissident Vaněk can have anything to do with the ex-*nomenklatura* Pavel Kohout (called just Pavel in the play). Staněk takes his dog-in-the-manger (or sour-grapes?) attitude as a cowardly attempt to apply some whitewash to himself as an ex-reformer who had joined the lower echelons of the Establishment. Staněk certainly feels guilty at having his job, and feebly tries to justify himself with the untenable 'what-about-my-flat?' argument and the understandable 'what-about-my-family?' argument.

Havel is fully aware of the advantages that being a dissident brings, however uncomfortable it might sometimes make life (one notices the idea of power here). 'Since he finds himself outside the whole universe of actual power and traditional political practice, i.e. outside the co-ordinate system of efficiency, tactics, success, compromises and necessary manipulation by half-truth and deceit, the dissident can be wonderfully himself and still make fun of himself without running the risk of becoming ridiculous for everybody' (1989, p.82). He discusses the luxury of living according to one's principles as against being a normal or normalized socialist citizen in *Audience*. Vaněk more or less represents Havel, who spent a brief period in 1974 as a manual worker in a provincial brewery. The first exchange concerning the advantages of dissident life is the following (1977, p.260):

MALTSTER Hey, Ferdinand –
VANĚK Yes?
MALTSTER Everything's a load of shit –
VANĚK I know –
MALTSTER You know fuck all! You've got it made. You write your plays – roll your barrels – and you don't give a damn about anyone. You've got everything you want, haven't you? Come on, they're scared of you!
VANĚK I doubt that –
MALTSTER Honest! But what about me? Nobody's interested in me! Nobody sends any reports anywhere about me! They can shout at men as much as they like! They've got me where they want me! They'd squash me like a worm if they decided to! Like a worm! But you – you've got it made!

Perhaps clearer still is the Maltster's near monologue (1977, p.265); I quote it in extracts, omitting also Vaněk's interspersed remarks:

And what about me? You'll leave me in the shit, won't you? You couldn't care less about me! I can be a swine! I can wallow in this filth; it doesn't matter about me; I'm just an ordinary idiot in a brewery – but sir, sir can have no part in it! I can get my hands dirty – as long as sir keeps clean! With sir it's a matter of principle … Principles are more important for him than people! That's just like you lot! … Lots of fine words, and you can afford it, because nothing can happen to you; somebody's always interested in you; you can always fix it; you're on top, even if you're down … Principles! Principles! Of course, you defend those principles of yours – they're really worth something, you'll get a very good price for them, make quite a bit on them. Those principles earn you your living – but what about me? … I'm just good for making the manure those principles of yours grow on …!

The maltster's argument is actually false, and no less refined than his desire to have Vaněk invite a pretty actress to the brewery so that he can ogle her. A principle is a luxury only to the unprincipled. Furthermore, a man in Vaněk's position can theoretically only survive at all if he retains his principles; a man with principles who then betrays his principles, say by becoming a police informer, does not become unprincipled, but a man with suppressed or stifled principles, a man with an impaired identity who is fully aware that his identity is impaired. In betraying his principles he would betray his responsibility to himself and the world. Keeping within Havel's conceptual framework, one sees the vacuity of the maltster's argument, if one translates the maltster's words as 'you'll get quite a good price for your identity' or 'This responsibility earns you your living'.

Principles, responsibility, identity can take a dissident to prison. By being in prison the principled man may still serve, not least because he might awaken something like a conscience in fellow-citizens who are in some way supporting

the regime. Perhaps that is what Plechanov in saying when he states of the impris-
oned Albert in *Asanace* (Redevelopment): 'I am afraid that the only grounds we
have for pride is at the moment in the dungeon.' One aspect of the play Havel
published immediately before this, *Pokoušení* (Temptation, 1986), concerns the
destruction of personality, identity, which takes place if one tries to compromise
between one's responsibility as (however mild) a dissident and service to the
socialist State. Havel conceived *Pokoušení* in prison.

Dissident responsibility and the work ethic

One of the chief methods of Czechoslovak opposition intellectuals during socialism was embodied in the term 'small-scale work' (*drobná práce*). The best way
of defeating socialism was whittling away at it rather than indulging in spectacu-
lar happenings, preparing for an uprising, infiltrating the working classes and
such more glamorous methods of resistance. Such methods were dangerous to
those whom one involved in them and were not, anyway, in the Czechoslovak
tradition, the Masaryk tradition. Small-scale work was the best method of fulfilling one's dissident responsibility.

In the section on Charter 77 and its offshoot, the Committee for the Defence
of the Unjustly Persecuted (VONS), in the essay, 'The Power of the Powerless',
Havel speaks of small-scale work as the method of the Charter movement. And in
an essay on the seventieth anniversary of the founding of Czechoslovakia (September, 1988), Havel answers his own rhetorical question on what Czechoslovaks
could do to achieve more democratic freedom thus: 'In this matter I think we can
learn from Masaryk and take up his conception of small-scale educational and
instructive work, whose significance for the nation's political future he sensed so
clearly' (1989, p.206). Havel satirizes his own adoption of the Masaryk idea in
Asanace (Redevelopment). He is making fun of himself, as he claims only a dissident can, in 'normalized' Czechoslovakia. The weak-spined Dubčekite, Bergman, who is not concerned with humanity, but with his own sentimentalization of
himself and his dead love-affair with Luisa, declares, 'There is more point in persistent small-scale work than in loud-mouthed manifestos' (1988b, p.70). 'Humanity', Masaryk had written, 'is not sentimentality, but work and, again,
work.'[14] And Bergman's words echo a statement of Masaryk's in *Naše nynější
krise* (The present Czech crisis, 1895):

The educated modern Czech ... is, then, against all revolution, revolution from below
and from above. Revolutionary tactics is old-fashioned tactics, is bourgeois
philistinism. A realistic, concrete conception of state and society excludes political
romanticism; realism and (violent) revolution are absolute opposites. Anyone who believes in revolution does not take life seriously ... The world is and has always been

based on work, not on mood; the world is maintained only by work, by small-scale work, constant work.[25]

The irony of Havel's choice of this particular slogan lies in Masaryk's source. 'Marx's greatest contribution', writes Masaryk, 'is that he revealed the world of small-scale work to us. I acknowledge that other people before him had referred to this sort of work, but no one had done so as effectively as he'.[26]

The amount of space Masaryk devoted to work in his writings made the concept of work a major theme of Czech thinking in the twentieth century. Havel's resumption of the theme in his essays cannot be said, then, to derive solely from Masaryk. It may, however, be significant that Masaryk saw work as the very antithesis of Marxism–Leninism. Bolsheviks, he informs us, 'know how to force people to labour (their régime has introduced the slavery of the bourgeoisie – where "bourgeoisie" is defined quite arbitrarily, but also the slavery of the workers); they know how to fight, to kill and to die, but they do not know how to work with application and tenacity.'[27] In *Světová revoluce* (The world revolution, 1925) Masaryk suggests, however, that the Bolsheviks' incapacity to work (and to administer) was not so much the product of Marxism–Leninism as part of the legacy of Tsarism.

In contrast, the Czechs had always achieved everything by quiet work. That constitutes the key element in the Czech national mythology: the Czech tradition of 'humanitism' had been founded on work. 'Life is served not by violence, but by conciliation, not by the sword, but by the share, not by blood, but by work, not by death, but by life itself – that is the answer of the Czech genius; that is the meaning of Czech history and the inheritance of our great forebears.'[28] 'Humanitism' demands reformation and not revolution; revolution is philistine or aristocratic whereas reformation is truly of the people: 'Popular politics is persistent, unceasing reformation – popular politics is enthusiasm for work, and work itself.'[29] Work makes the path to democracy, and 'he who wields the sword never has been, can and will never be a democrat. I am for equality and fraternity; that is why I am for work.'[30] Work is Masaryk's answer to all political extremism: 'The radical likes agitating and the conservative likes doing nothing. Realistic activity, work, challenges radical agitation and conservative stagnation.'[31]

Rádl accepts that work is of primary importance for a democracy, but what he does not indulge is a cult of work like Masaryk. He was not as impressed by the American Protestant 'work ethic' as Masaryk. On the other hand, he did, like Masaryk, consider that the perception of work revealed a fundamental distinction between East and West. In his discussion of Nirvana (*Západ a Východ*) he maintains that the concept Nirvana involves a highly refined sort of suicide which demands no action, and he compares that with what he takes to be the Western ideal, to work and never to despair.

The most highly regarded Czech thinker of the 1960s, Karel Kosík, also takes up the notion of work. For him working is being human; work is ontological. Man creates himself through work, and that self-creation involves a serious struggle. Havel's conception of responsibility may, then, be at least loosely connected with Kosík's conception of work. The conception of work Patočka produces in *Kacířské eseje* is avowedly in part derived from Hannah Arendt. It is clear from this conception that Havel's understanding of the role of 'small-scale work' in the prosecution of useful dissidence is not as entirely Masarykian as he has led one to believe. Patočka points out that work makes one sensible to one's freedom. The fact that work is by nature 'weight' or a burden indicates a previous sensation of 'weight', the 'weight' of life itself. A weight has to be borne, is not something one can be indifferent to. One feels responsibility to the 'weight' of life. If one consciously transfers, as mankind had, the 'weight' of life to the 'weight' of working, then work is necessarily founded on a 'free existence in this world'. At the same time, however, Patočka continues, work has the capacity to slow down, indeed even repress, the development of that freedom. The notion of 'weight' itself might suggest involuntariness, but it is based on a decision whether or not to live. That decision involves 'weight'. That weight is then manifested in necessary work. For to be part of a community, one has to work. In the very acceptance of a fellow human being one is, avers Patočka, stating that one is working not only for one's own needs, but also for his or hers.[32] Working, then, expresses not only the burden that one acquires by living, but also a relationship towards the community in which one is working. Though one may initially believe that one is working just as an assertion of one's own identity, through work one becomes aware that this identity is also dependent on those for whom one has accepted responsibility. 'Work is always personal,' writes Havel (1991, p.82), 'and one only does it well when one knows what it is for, what it will change into, when one knows that it is noticed – and only then can one like work.'

The importance of that for Havel (and other active dissidents) is evident when one remembers that socialist society was a society where one did as little work as possible, unless it was private work. Such private work was generally undertaken only with the aim of increasing one's material prosperity. Such work was essentially as non-responsible as the legally enforced work one did for the anonymous state. To work as a dissident gave one that sensation of freedom concomitant with working for a community.

Truth and identity

That community characterized itself as living in truth – in contrast to living in the lie which socialist society constituted. Havel's concern for truth does not reflect only the Czechs' preoccupation with truth in their writing, nor only 'truth' as an opposition to Party lies; it also reflects or reacts against the role the word or concept played in Communist ideology. Communist newspapers were as commonly called 'Truth' as Anglo-Saxon newspapers are called 'Times' or 'Post'. For decades in Czechoslovakia the 'true' meaning of a literary text was said to be found in its Marxist-Leninist (which often meant Stalinist) class interpretation. One of Havel's earliest essays, 'O dialektické metafyzice' (Concerning dialectical metaphysics, 1964), demonstrates that his perception of truth has always involved a denial of the Marxist-Leninist truth. He appeals here for a new dialectic to replace the circular, narcissistic, dialectic of modern Marxism–Leninism. He expresses himself as something of an 'angry young man', but his basic approach is the same as it is almost thirty years later, for example (1966, pp.75–6):

With an original, new, deliberately one-sided view, working possibly from even – yes, really! – a new concept, a concept – one-sidedly – chosen for a given situation, with such a view, a bold, penetrating, fresh, original and provocative view, it is more possible to touch on the truth – even if only from one side – than with a view which tries to register the truth from all sides and does not succeed in registering it from any.

I doubt that Havel's perceptions of lie, truth, and living in truth are directly derived from Masaryk. The notion of living in truth is, anyway, a commonplace of Ancient philosophy and of Christian teaching, a commonplace vigorously and originally employed by one of those figures whom Masaryk saw as demonstrating the Czech 'humanitist' tradition, the radical Church Reform philosopher, Chelčický. Nevertheless, Masaryk did use the concept 'lie' in a manner which foreshadows Havel. Masaryk saw everyday Austrian society as a lie; the origins of that lie, however, were not socialism, but divorce, free love and the general sexualization of life at the end of the nineteenth century: 'Impurity – that is the death of real ideals; impurity – that is the source of the lie on which modern society rests.'[33] It may also be significant that Masaryk saw Communism as a fundamentally mendacious doctrine which preached unbearable uniformity: 'The basic lie of Communism rests in the fact that everyone is to want to have what his neighbour has and everyone is to be what the next man is'.[34]

The lie of communism is more complex, because it touches everything, in a Leninist 'normalized' state. Because it is forced by its own ideology to call untruth truth, the socialist ruling class finds itself in a vicious circle from which it does not have the slightest inclination to escape. 'Power', writes Havel in 'The Power of the Powerless,' 'is in the captivity of its own lies, and therefore it has to falsify. ... One does not have to believe all the mystification. One does, however, have to behave as if one believed; or at least one has to tolerate it in silence, or at least get on reasonably well with those who operate it' (1984, p.63). In such a society man does not simply allow his identity to be removed from him; whether he is fully conscious of it or not, he actively helps in its removal (1984, p.71):

One is forced to live in a lie, but one can be forced to live in a lie only because one is capable of such a life. So it is not only that the system alienates the man, but, at the same time, the alienated man supports the system as his own involuntary project. As a corrupt image of his own corruption. As a document of his weakness ... It is by no means a matter of a conflict of two identities.

It is something else: *a crisis of identity itself.*

To put it in a very simplified way, one could say that the posttotalitarian[35] system ripened on the soil of an *historic meeting of dictatorship with consumer society.*

In the 'posttotalitarian' system, the citizen is both the subject and object of ruling, both the victim and the instrument of the system. 'Posttotalitarianism' consists in a communal self-imposition of totalitarianism. The individual loses his or her identity in a dour game of bondage. If one breaks the rules, one will be trying to 'live in truth'. 'Posttotalitarian' socialist living is living in untruth. '"Life in un-truth" can function as a constitutive support of the system only on the presump-tion of its own universality; it must encompass and permeate everything; it cannot endure any coexistence whatsoever with "Life in truth": any divergence from it *denies it as a principle and threatens it as a whole'* (1984, p.73).

Havel's concept, 'life in truth', is no doubt influenced by Patočka's inter-pretation of Husserl and Heidegger. However distracting Patočka's phenomeno-logical terminology and ambiguous syntax, his meaning is clear, as is the attraction such an interpretation of truth linked with freedom and the very essence of conscious, thinking living would have for such as Havel:

The revelation of Being is the experience from which philosophy grows, the con-stantly renewed attempt at life in truth. Finally, freedom is the freedom of truth, and this in the form of the revealedness of Being itself, of the truth of being and not just existences (in the form of open behaviour and in the correctness of statements). Freedom ... means ... that Being itself is finite, that it lies in the jolting of all naive 'certainties' which seek to find their home in existences so that they do not have to acknowledge that man has no home except this all-revealing and free state.[26]

Thus dissident living in truth is living the philosopher's life. That does not sound so grand if one links it with Patočka's version of Husserl's definition of living in truth: regulating opinions by insights, not regulating insights by opinions.[37] Chris-tianity, to which Havel moves closer and closer in what he writes, adds a special dimension to this truth. This dimension, in Patočka's rendering of it, is evidently central to Havel's conception of identity. Christianity gives the soul a content which expands Platonic thinking: 'the truth which the soul struggles for is not a truth of view, but the truth of its own fate, truth linked with eternal responsibility, which can never be revoked'.[38] Charter 77 was an attempt at living in truth. Havel states that journalistically: 'As we all know, complete and utter truth lies in the realm of the unattainable. If Charter 77 is determined to follow the entirely unpractical and untactical path of seeking unprejudiced truth, it is only an expression of its moral orientation and the essential endlessness of the goals which issue from that orientation' (1989, p.100). Perhaps he sounds more grandiose than he wishes when, still with regard to Charter 77, he proclaims, 'even where institutionalized untruth rules, a citizen can tell the truth' (1989, p.102).

It is often deliberately unclear in the plays where Havel is making fun of his own ideas and where not. The semantic tension of particularly his later plays is supplied by such potential irony. In *Pokoušení* (Temptation), the secret policeman, Fistula (Mephistopheles), while he is acting the adept in the esoteric arts, makes a statement on truth which the audience understands, first, as a potentially political statement on the relativity of verity and, second, as devilish irony directed at the Czech preoccupation with truth: 'My dear sirs, the truth is, after all, not only what we think, but also why, to whom and in what circumstances we say it' (1986, pp.66–7). In his interview-autobiography, however, when he is talking about the play, he gives as his own opinion that 'the truth is not only what one thinks, but also in what circumstances, to whom, why and how one states it' (1988a, p.79). The slight change of words does not remove the relativism. The irony is, however, no longer there. We are left with a truism pointing out the distinction between, say, 'Daddy has gone to Heaven, darling' and 'Old Joe has popped it.'

The sense of crisis

A sense of crisis is always likely to lead to an individual's seeking 'the truth', and to make indifference appear morally wrong. For Masaryk liberalism had brought about a crisis and demonstrated that it was incapable of dealing with it. For Havel socialism had brought about a crisis which it did not want to deal with, even if it had been capable of doing so.

At least in Czech, the very term, perhaps even concept, crisis, is largely an invention of the end of the nineteenth century. Even today the word bears a greater sense of urgency or disaster in Czech than it does in English. Therefore to link Havel's perception of crisis with the chain Masaryk – Rádl – Patočka (one might add Bělohradský) is not as gratuitous as it might seem. All the more so, when both Masaryk and Havel saw their crises as not only a matter of the Czechs, but of the whole world, even if the Czechs were the starting point for both of them.

Masaryk perceived a student crisis in the mid 1890s because students could no longer perform the political role they had earlier in the century. The more general crisis in the Bohemian Lands was, he thought, linked with the failure of the Old Czech and Young Czech parties – and particularly the Old Czechs had been guilty of a 'chauvinism of indolence and ignorance.'[39] In the introduction to his lengthy work on Engels and Marx he maintains that his studies have demonstrated to him that 'contemporary Marxism is in a state of scientific and philosophical crisis'.[40] And after World War I, when the Social Democratic Party was splitting into right and left wings, in other words, when the Czechoslovak Communist Party was in its birth throes, he declares: 'The crisis we are now going through is the crisis of all nations, of the whole universe.'[41]

Rádl saw a more general crisis of the Czech intelligentsia in the 1920s, a crisis which had arisen from intellectuals' lack of faith in the spiritual and from the politicization of culture. Politics had ousted education. Like Masaryk, or Bělohradský later, he sees the Czech crisis to be just a part of a world crisis: the decay of Czech literature was, he claimed, paralleled and influenced by an 'international decay of literature'.[42] Later, he saw that crisis as deriving from the aestheticization of literature.[43]

Patočka saw a world student crisis, a crisis of what he calls the mass intelligentsia, at the end of the 1960s (*O smysl dneška*). Otherwise, he certainly describes in the 1960s and the 1970s what Masaryk or Rádl – or Havel – would call crises (in technological civilization, in modern man's unspirituality, for example), but he generally avoids the term. It is, after all, a trifle melodramatic.

Havel employs it as liberally as Masaryk. In his 1975 letter to Gustáv Husák the term appears to Havel tactically apposite for putting across a political point, but it still sounds melodramatic: 'in spite of all the pretty-looking external facts, *internally this society is not only not consolidated at all*,[44] but it is sinking into an ever more profound crisis, a crisis that is, in many respects, more dangerous than all the crises we remember in our modern history' (1984, p.20). More than ten years later he uses the term in a manner even more reminiscent of Masaryk, this time in connection with socialist consumerism (1989, p.92): 'the desolate silence of totalitarian consumer hopelessness has settled over the country ... People have quietly accepted the schizophrenic solution to the equation of life that was offered them: on the outside they began to pretend loyalty and inside they ceased to believe in anything. It was not only a political crisis. It was a moral crisis.'

Elsewhere he extends this crisis over the whole world, for the moral crisis is a crisis of responsibility. Humanity is, he claims, passing through a crisis of responsibility for itself and for everything on the surface on the Earth. Like a Man of the Nineties, he blames this to a large degree on advances in science and technology (1985a, pp.424–5). A crisis of responsibility is equivalent, in Havel's thinking, to an identity crisis. Again somewhat grandiosely, he maintains that the whole world is going through just that: 'all the classical certainties, from the concreteness of the human face to the immutability of space, right to the continuity of time, are in a state of disintegration. Nothing is really true any longer because the human identity as the single source and measure of truth is dissolving' (1989, p. 228).

Again like Masaryk, Havel considers that a major cause of the present crisis is indifference. Masaryk consistently linked that with liberalism, which led to 'indifferentism in religious, philosophical and moral matters,'[45] for liberalism's tenet of tolerance all too easily meant indifference rather than positive tolerance. Indifference could be interpreted as a lack of identity or, at least, a failure to project identity. Havel conceives of indifference as arising from the situation in which ordinary citizens find themselves in 'normalized' Czechoslovakia, where self-defence against a society ruled by fear combines with the aggressive pursuit of personal prosperity. Indifference contributes greatly to the creation of 'the moral climate of today's 'unified society'. People 'have lost their faith in the future ...; they fall into apathy, uninterestedness in suprapersonal values and in their neighbours, into spiritual passivity and depression' (1984, p.25). He considers 'indifference and resignation to be the gravest version of humanity's fall into nothingness' (1985a, p.190), where nothingness is 'the modern face of the Devil' (1985a, p.200). Together with hard-heartedness and spiritual laziness, indifference and resignation combine to express modern man's unfaith. Thus, 'the tragedy of modern man does not lie in the fact that he knows ever less about the meaning of his life, but that that is of ever less concern to him' (1985a, p.273). Once more one notices how close Havel is to a Christian perception of living.

Consumerism and identity

In a socialist country consumersim can easily be seen as a mockery of Marxist materialism. When a socialist state encourages the consumer mentality to keep its citizens under control, it shows its own disregard for Marxian idealism, but also the necessary failure of an ideology based on hatred, envy and social manipulation. If Czechoslovaks began to be interested in matters beyond their country cottages, their cars, themselves, they might well begin to indulge in active criticism of the system. Instead of political choice, the Husák regime had given people choice in washing machines and refrigerators (1984, p.26ff).

Consumerism is closely linked with careerism, for in a socialist country, making a career for oneself has nothing to do with gaining more responsibility; it is a matter of being able to live more comfortably. 'If fear lies behind man's self-defensive endeavour to preserve what he has, *selfishness and careerism* become the chief motor of his aggressive endeavour to obtain what he does not have' (1984, p.23). Consumerism affects the highest reaches of socialist society. Those in public or otherwise powerful positions tend (in the 1970s) to be 'well-known careerists, opportunists, adventurers and people with a bad conscience' (1984, p.24).

As for Páral, for Havel television and living in prefabricated high-rise blocks emblemize and epitomize socialist consumerism's link with the disintegration of identity. The television culture is anti-individualist of itself; it also encourages the lulling of consciousness into indifference. A disintegrated identity can be nothing but indifferent. 'Apt expressions of the herd mentality involved in the consumer life are the modern high-rise estate and that wonderful machine, *the television*; *man's disintegration into his individual* anonymized functions (producer, consumer, patient, elector, etc.) …; man finds himself in a sort of anonymous "non-space" if, for example, he lives on a high-rise estate; after all, it does not matter where the estate is; they are all the same' (1984, p.350). That statement is repeated almost word for word in Havel's letters from prison. Here he does, however, expand on his conception of consumerism (frequently through television) as levelling individuals down into an amorphous mass; 'man is rendered totally powerless, faced with anonymous social macrostructures; in all his complexity he adapts to the general "moral" norm which consists in surrendering everything that extends beyond the horizons of herd life – thus does human identity fall into an ever more profound and comprehensive crisis' (1985a, p.343). At one point in these letters he puts that in Patočka terms. The main temptation of the consumer age, he says, is 'to exchange one's identity for "a world of existences"' (1985a, p.60). He defines that 'world of existences', the world of a self fallen victim to mere existing, thus: 'it is a world of functions, purpose and efficiency, a world directed at itself and enclosed in itself, empty in its outward colourfulness and illusory richness, unconscious in its submergence in information, cold, alienated and, finally, meaningless' (1985a, p.400). Havel waxes sentimental when he envisages a world without this consumerism. Man will no longer simply have somewhere to live; he will have 'a home'. His world will have its own 'order, culture, style'; instead of being subject to the 'stereotypedness of production and consumption', he will be offered a variety of ways of life. He will no longer be a member of 'a herd, manipulated and homogenized by the range of consumer goods and by consumer television culture, whether he is offered this range by three competing capitalist giants or a single non-competing socialist giant' (1988a, p.21).

Like so many malcontents, since, at the latest, the second half of the nineteenth century, Havel blames technology for much of modern aridity. Still, for someone living under socialism that blaming has a political dimension because Marxism–Leninism involves the worship of science and technology. Socialism scientifies everything. Masaryk had nothing but scorn for what he saw as Marx and Engels's one-sided Positivist cult of science. Indeed, he maintains, 'often it is not just a cult; it is idolatry.'[46] Patočka's view of technology is based on his experience of socialism. His vision of the modern technological world's destruction of individual identity constitutes an old-fashioned catastrophist model, which appeals to Havel:

[Modern technological society] alienates man from himself, removes from him the occupation of the world, immerses him in an everyday alternative, no longer of toil, but of boredom or cheap surrogates for living, and, finally, of brutal orgiasm ... It forms a scheme of omnipotent strength and mobilizes the whole of reality for the release of pent-up forces, for a rule of might which is realized by means of global conflict. Man is thus being destroyed externally and beggared internally, deprived of his 'oneness', his irreplaceable self; he is identified with his role; he stands and falls with his role.[47]

Right at the beginning of his career as an essayist, Havel had conceived of technological society similarly. In his 1963 essay on the gag as a comic device, he states that the technological age involves 'a hitherto unheard-of atomization of knowledge and the destruction of all the integral spiritual structures of the past' (1966, p.138). In *Pokoušení* (Temptation) he also comments on the way in which those who are powerful misuse science in order to eliminate anything that threatens their power (1986, p.108). Then, in a speech marking the anniversary of the Communist takeover in Czechoslovakia, he talks of the way in which the 'scientificness' of socialism had depleted human identity. As in his 1963 essay he had seen the Chaplinesque gag as a cathartic device to awaken us to revolt at the tyranny of technological rationalism, so he sees humour as one of the ways in which man can assert his identity in the face of 'scientificness' (1990, p.63):

Science has no conscience. It is, to be sure, an important, wonderful thing, a great fruit of the history of human reason, but the human spirit is not only reason. It is also thoughtfulness. And consideration. And conscience. And decency. And taste. And loving one's neighbour. And responsibility. And courage. And distancing oneself from one's self. And doubting. And even humour.

Havel satirizes Marxist-Leninist 'scientificness' in his plays – a scientificness which Masaryk had called 'inquisitorial and marked by infallibility', a world-view 'which has nothing in common with science or scientific philosophy.'[48] It had helped create the sterile society depicted in *Ztížená možnost soustředění* (The increased difficulty of concentration, 1969), where love, too, has become the subject of scientific study and where emotional immediacy has been exiled from life. That sterility increased during the Husák period, and was typified by the socialist new class which Havel depicts in the one-acter, *Vernisáž* (Private view, first performed in Vienna, 1976). The couple he portrays here are tasteless, tactless and trendily open about sex. Their child is just another charming piece of furniture who fuses with their Gothic Madonna, Baroque cherub and hypermodern drawing-room suite and hi-fi. Their expensive furniture, clothes and food express not a love of *bons viveurs* at ease with the world, but the frenetic attempt of the spiritually empty to prove that they are not empty. Their vulgarian sexuality and food fetishism express their lack of elemental sensuality and emotional warmth – and perhaps also guilt at collaborating with the regime through consumerism. Their life is just as planned as the economy of the state whose citizens they are.

They also embody that lack of privacy, sense of the private, which characterizes or characterised all socialist societies. In *Vernisáž* that is exemplified by the couple's prying into the life of their dissident visitor and his wife. In *Protest* Havel employs names to emblemize the socialist lack of privacy. Whereas in Anglo-Saxon countries, especially the United Kingdom, the use of Christian names has become a statement of anonymity or false palliness (as when insurance agents or Social Security clerks address one by one's Christian name), in Czechoslovakia the use of Christian names still indicates some level of actual friendliness; indeed it still involves a prior ritual (a drink together or a kiss or a hand-shake). The official Staněk calls the dissident Vaněk by his Christian name, where Vaněk calls Staněk 'Mr Staněk'. Staněk calls Kohout 'Pavel', whereas Vaněk uses only the surname, Landovský, when he refers to his actor-dramatist friend. Staněk is consciously attacking the identity of his erstwhile friends by using their Christian names.

Havel takes this idea to an absurd, but believable, extreme in *Largo desolato*, when the secret police demand that the main character, Leopold, deny his name, that is his authorship of an essay on the ontology of the self (1985b, pp.52–3):

FIRST FELLOW In short: if you sign here and now a brief statement that you are not Dr Leopold Kopřiva, the author of the piece of writing in question, the whole matter will be judged null and void and the earlier decision will be quashed –
LEOPOLD If I understand you correctly, you want me to declare that I am not me –
FIRST FELLOW That interpretation may be apt for a philosopher, but legally it is nonsense. It is not a question of your declaring that you are not you, but only of your declaring that you are not identifiable with the author of this document – essentially it is a mere formality.
SECOND FELLOW A name's just a name.

This exchange contains an extra irony, for, especially in two scenes, Leopold is not the same man as the Dr Kopřiva who wrote the essay. That is clear in the scene where he argues with his mistress, Lucy, about whether he loves her and whether he has in her case fulfilled what he has written about love. It is even more clear, however, in the scene where the philosophy undergraduate, Markéta, comes to visit him, flatters him by using the language of his essays, so that he also begins to speak in quotations or paraphrases of passages from his essays – and, meanwhile, tries to get her drunk on rum so that she will go to bed with him.

Identity and the erotic

As far as Havel writes about the erotic at all, he writes about its failure. What erotic life he describes tends to be vulgarized. There is so little of it that one is wary of interpreting his descriptions just as symptoms of arid socialist society, or even as hints at sexual consumerism. Certainly, however, these descriptions do reflect his concern with identity.

The fact that the leader of the putsch which forms the subject matter of *Spiklenci* (The conspirators, first performed in Baden-Baden, 1974), Mohér, indulges in sadomasochistic cavortings with the would-be *grande dame*, Helga, constitutes a trite comment on power politics. On the other hand, one could understand it as a reference to the way in which personal relationships become perverted once every aspect of life is politicized, as in a socialist society. One would then make a link between this sadomasochism and the arid sexual experimentation of the 'normalized' *nouveau riche* couple in *Vernisáž* (Private view).

Havel satirizes the aridity of modern sexual relationships in *Ztížená možnost soustředění* (The increased difficulty of concentration). The main character, the philosopher-cum-sociologist Eduard Huml, is having an affair with Renata, about which his wife knows all. Huml uses the same or similar terms of endearment to both women; his communication with them is based on little more than phatic gestures. The two women have also lost their identities for him, have become interchangeable. He is aware that he has been a double failure, though that does not remove his warm coldness; he will not now commit himself except by gestures to any woman – hence the manner of his flirting with his secretary and with the leader of the crackpot sociologists, Balcárková. As in most of Vladimír Páral's works, sex, instead of liberating man, increases his imprisonment, his stress.

In *Largo desolato* also, Leopold's common-law marriage with Zuzana has broken down, and his mistress, Lucy, comes openly to their flat and sleeps with him there. In this case, however, Zuzana also appears to have a lover, Olda. Love, if Leopold knew it, does not liberate his identity any more than it had Huml's. Huml had theorized in essays about happiness and Leopold theorizes about love. One might understand that as jolly satire on the Marxist-Leninist scientification of all life, as well as on the tendency of intellectuals to theorize themselves into a state of emotional inadequacy. Leopold is intended to represent a man going through his own identity crisis and so one should not take his uneasiness at Lucy's quoting to him what he has said and written on love just as satire on the gap between theory and practice in would-be philosophers. The vocabulary Lucy attributes to Leopold is the vocabulary of Havel (or Patočka) as an essayist, for example: love is 'the essential dimension of Being – the living well-spring of its fullness and meaning' (1985b, p.31), or: 'Only through closeness to another do we attain our own identity' (1985b, p.44).

Havel links erotic banality with political banality in the figure of the opportunist Luisa in *Asanace* (Redevelopment). She speaks in erotic clichés, just as after 'liberalization' she calls out in echo of the slogan, 'Workers of all lands, unite', 'People of all lands, love all lands!' (1988b, p.50). For all his apparent affection for Western peace-freaks, one cannot but imagine that Havel is ironically alluding to the fatuous slogan, 'Make love, not war'.

Homosexual love occurs only in *Pokoušení* (Temptation). The police chief or high Party functionary known as Primář (who could also represent the Devil) has a homosexual lover, Kotrlý. It looks, however, as if Kotrlý has assumed this sexual inclination simply as a component of his toadying. Havel says very little indeed, in his plays or his essays, about the place of the toady in socialist society. It is remarkable but, I presume, entirely coincidental that in his analysis of the political function of toadies Bolzano could have been characterizing Kotrlý:

He places not only himself and the power his job gives him as low as possible in the power hierarchy of higher officials, but he also works ever more at destroying or consigning to oblivion *the rights of the whole people*. Then in such a people, the spirit of *defamation and false denunciation* rules in the end. Out of mutual hatred, one part of the people endeavours to belittle the other and to put its intentions in a dangerous light with the government ... Is it to be wondered at, my friends, if, after all this, the authorities themselves then become corrupt?[49]

The centralization of emotions

Awareness that the socialist regime could remove the privacy of any citizen at any moment, and even did so apparently unintentionally with the uninsulated walls of prefabricated tower blocks, gave Havel juicy subjects for ripe satire. Privacy has no part to play in socialist society, if man no longer has his human identity and becomes simply his role in society, as Patočka and Havel suggest, when 'a man is what he produces', as Masaryk puts it.[50] (Havel has spoken of socialism turning the human being into 'a means of production'.) And, as Rádl argues in *Západ a Východ*, socialism and communism are systems for protecting state and society from the individual.

What counts as the most intimate of human relationships, love, would ideally come under state control in a perfectly organized centralized state. In the words of the bureaucrat, Plzák, from his first independent play, *Zahradní slavnost* (The garden party, 1964),[51] Havel is satirizing words that were actually frequently said and written in the Stalin period, and by a few old hacks like Jiří Taufer in the 1970s. Socialist love was claimed to be a higher kind of love. Havel is also satirizing state-imposed optimism (1964, pp.24–5):

And the human being of today has a rich emotional life, far richer than any previous human being. But because of that an increased degree of attention must be paid to ascertain that love does not extend beyond a certain optimum limit of tolerability – the fact is that, should this occur, it might happen that love would awaken temporary sadness in people!

In *Pokoušení* (Temptation) one might view the relationship between Foustka (Faust) and Markéta (Gretchen) as a sour satire on the way the Party may organize and disorganize citizens', especially intellectuals', love-lives. And in the sometimes violent erotic relationship between Foustka and Vilma, it appears in the end that Vilma might have been part of the general conspiracy against Foustka.

As totalitarian politics might try to control love, it comes close to destroying compassion. For most of *Spiklenci* (The Conspirators, 1974), the ministerial private secretary, Alfred Stein (presumably a Jew?), is being tortured in the background (his 'Ow!' provides the play with its refrain), but no one takes any notice. In his address to the nations of Czechoslovakia on New Year's Day, 1990, Havel characterizes the moral state of socialist citizens, their attitude to love and compassion, in a manner which only apparently verges on the hyperbolic (1990, p.12):

The worst of it is that we live in a corrupt moral environment ... We have learnt to believe in nothing, not to take any notice of each other, to look after only ourselves. Concepts like love, friendship, compassion, humility or forgiveness have lost their depth and breadth, and for many of us they signify only some psychological peculiarity or are a faded memento of times past, somewhat ridiculous in an age of computers and space-probes.

Socialism's attempt to prescribe happiness for its citizens, in the shape of the formulaic ideals in the Stalin era (which corresponds to centrally fostered consumerism in the aftermath of the fall of Dubček) led to sterility and unhappiness. In *Ztížená možnost soustředění* (The increased difficulty of concentration) the alienated Huml and his treatise on happiness embody satire on centralized happiness and a parody of Sixties writings on the individual and society. Their authors speak and write in platitudes partly to protect themselves against their own emotional sterility and partly to project a Utopian self. The emotions Huml expresses in his tirade at the end are old-fashionedly romantic, utterly acceptable as that, but his language is pompous and clumsy. Furthermore, the audience knows nothing of Huml's 'heart'; that seems to have been entirely repressed by his flatulent 'brain'. The simple meaning of his words is the same as Havel's in the New Year address:

The unique, personal human relationship which arises between two human selves is, at the moment, the only thing that can, at least partially, mutually reveal the mystery of these two selves. In such a case values like love, friendship, caring, compassion and unrepeatable, irreplaceable human understanding – or indeed conflict – are the only instruments this human contact has at its disposal. With all other instruments we can more or less explain the human being, but never, even a little, know him or her. Thus the fundamental key to the human being is not situated in the brain, but in the heart.

The artificial language *ptydepe* whose introduction and abolition provides the story-line of Havel's second play, *Vyrozumění* (The memorandum, 1966), is the vehicle for a grotesque satire on the centralization or bureaucratization of emotions. As the propagators of *ptydepe* declare, the trouble with natural languages is that they are unscientific. *Ptydepe* has no homonyms or homophones and no words where the substitution, addition or subtraction of a single letter would change their meaning. Thus typing errors will not lead to any ridiculous situations or the appearance that the bureaucracy is incompetent. Havel satirizes the foolishness of socialism's attempt to scientify society and to impose emotions, as well as the Eastern Bloc's predilection for well-organized applause, in the *ptydepe* word for 'Hooray!' – which even the brilliant student of *ptydepe*, Kalous, has trouble with (1966, p.191):

PERINA … The *ptydepe* expression for our important word Hooray is *frnygko jefr*
    dabux altep dy savarub goz terexes. And now a little memory test …. Hooray!
KALOUS *Frnygko jefr dabux altep dy savarub gop terexes.*
PERINA Wrong again! *Goz terexes*!

Analogously, in *Zahradní slavnost* (The garden party) Havel satirizes the centralized suppression of immediacy and censorship in the way the joke session of the Fifth Division of the Office of Liquidation is organized. The female secretary explains the rules: 'you may take part if you have submitted to the humour secretariat and the idea-regulation committee the exact text of your joke, supplied with a medical certificate and the section chief's approval at the latest two months before the date of the garden party' (1985a, pp.16–17).

In his letters from prison (1985a, pp. 214–15) Havel characterizes the centralization of emotions as the system's attempt to make man in the image of the Devil, not the first time he has seen socialism as infernal:

The chilling work of man in 'the Devil's image': a system of violent levelling to sameness, of perfectly organized impotence and centrally planned desolation and tedium, a system with a conception of man as a cybernetical unit without free will, without his own mind and unique life, a system with that monstrous ideal of 'good order' as a euphemism for graveyard.

Identity and history

This system was also notoriously economical with the past. The force of 'History' was a manipulable force. If the force of History was manipulable, so was the history of the individual. Since individual identity arguably consists in individual history, and one's own perception of one's history relies to a large degree on one's memory (one's own selective ordering of that history), anyone concerned with the notion of identity must consider memory. When Havel speaks about the system's 'conception of man as a cybernetical unit without free will', he is referring to Marxist-Leninist determinism. Masaryk had rejected that determinism, especially in Engels, as a species of 'scientific' prophecy, and according to Masaryk, prophecy is not action, derives from cognition, not will. Like Havel, he asserts the right of moral will against Engelsian determinism: 'It is not just a matter of what will be, of what will happen to me, but also of what should be, what should happen to me. I, too, I, with my consciousness and conscience, am history!'[52] Because, like the true liberal that he denied he was, he believes in the perfectability of man, Masaryk sees history in that light: 'Our eagerness, our longing for perfection is realized in history'.[53]

Havel's perception is similar, but his idea of progress does not consist of the Enlightenment idea of Masaryk's, but more that of spiritual progress, a development further into spiritual awareness. In both Masaryk and Havel activity is essential (1984, p.38):

The basic law of the cosmos may be increasing entropy, but the basic law of life is increasing structuredness and the fight against entropy: life resists all uniformity and sameness; its perspective is not homogenization, but variegation; it is the restlessness of transcendence, the adventure of the new, resistance against the status quo ; the essential dimension … is a constantly actualized mystery.

A major element in the socialist system, he says, which attacks life, the possibility of living fully like this, is the creation of pseudohistory, for full life involves memory. 'As we know,' he writes in a later piece, 'man is the history of man' (1989, p.145). A life without memory (history) is one which makes a man a machine, or the instrument of production that the system desires: 'A private life without an historical horizon is sheer fiction, window-dressing, finally, actually a lie' (1989, p.125).

One aspect of *Zahradní slavnost* (The garden party) concerns just this. On the purely comic side we have the main character, Hugo's, father and mother, bourgeois who want to change their history to show they, and thus also their children, have a sociopolitical pedigree of the right sort. Havel is here satirizing the sociopolitical-pedigree (*kádr*) system altogether, but also the weakspined has-beens who support it with their own diminished identity. At one point the father,

Pludek, declares, 'I have five poor great-uncles' (1964, p.7) and a little later he says something with the same intention, and is here supported by his wife (Havel here satirizes also the then recent campaigns against *kulaks* (1964, p.10)):

PLUDEK We used to go around smashing windows!
PLUDKOVÁ Rich farmers' windows!

Where the parents have a diminished identity, Hugo is a man of no identity. At the beginning of the play he is having a chess match against himself. It does not matter whether he is black or white. Chess also emblemizes his capacity to manipulate others in a system run on the ideal of non-identity. By chance he appears at a garden party held by the Office of Liquidation, makes the acquaintance of some functionaries, soon learns bureaucratic behaviour, and by the end of the play he is a senior state functionary, estranged from his family, and perhaps even more estranged from human life than he had been at the beginning. Though I am always suspicious of authors' words about their own works, Havel's interpretation of the ending of *Zahradní slavnost* (The garden party) twenty years later is worth noting. He says that in the end Hugo visits Hugo and thus definitively loses his identity (1988a, p.219).

Havel develops his theme further in *Ztížená možnost* where ideal socialist non-identity is embodied in a picture of the total interchangeability of roles. Here that is, however, seen largely in private rather than public life: the interchangeability of women for Huml. Huml has memory only for the words of affection not for the objects of attention. The computer, Puzuk, has a fuller identity than the human characters, its operators; he has a greater capacity for commitment than they. The notion of interchangeability of roles suggests that the people here have no individual history, or that their history can change with circumstances. To a degree, the roles of the conspirators, with the exception of Mohér, are interchangeable in *Spiklenci*; their interchangeability is manifested by the fact that each of them uses the same meaningless, would-be personal, phrases.

In the slightly Schnitzleresque *Horský hotel* (Mountain hotel, written 1976) role changing (which here includes the transposition of memory) is taken to a somewhat tedious extreme. The role changing is based on language. All the characters in this absurd microcosm are without identity, and the fabulous pasts they claim appear to be based on episodes they have picked up from *Trivialliteratur*. All attempts of one character to impress another fail because no one is conditioned to expect sincerity; the attempts themselves are generally based on a lie and express nothing but the self-evident insecurity of alienated man. Again these are characters without histories.

Language and identity

Because he is a playwright (because of the role of language in drama) and because of the bastardization of language Havel saw around him, in the press, political speeches, even in literature, language serves him as a signal of identity and
non-identity. Among his plays, *Largo desolato* is the least language-based, even
though it constitutes a picture of a so-called identity crisis. Once more I shall
quote Havel on his own work, but this time, not on the grounds that it helps us
understand *Largo desolato* any better, but on the grounds that what he says about
the play puts a great deal of what he considers the problem of identity in a nut-
shell (1989, pp.284–5):

It is a 'musical essay' on the weight of being human; on the difficulty of man's struggle for his identity with an impersonal force which wants to take it away from him; on
the strange discrepancy between man's actual possibilities and the role adjudged him
by milieu, Fate and his own work ; on how easy it is to know theoretically how to live,
but how difficult it is really to live like that; on the eternal 'remorse of reason'; on the
tragic incapacity even of people who wish each other well to understand one another;
on human loneliness, fear, and cowardice.

Language does have some function in the play as representative of the different
types of people who want to help the depressed Leopold Kopřiva. Apart from the
student, Markéta, and not counting the episode where all return together, all the
characters appear to Leopold twice. Most of them have a stereotypical manner of
speech which typifies their social background or their function in Leopold's life.
Markéta's language, in which she largely quotes Leopold, also expresses her relationship to him – or another kind of pressure on him. Still, psychology is more
important than language in *Largo desolato*. Indeed, Havel has presented here a
state of mind in far greater detail than in any of his other plays. His description of
the symptoms attending Leopold's depression is based on convincingly conventional verisimilitude: his feeling of physical weakness, his unwillingness to leave
his flat, his lack of appetite, his tendency to drink, even his clumsy inchoate seduction of Markéta.

   Havel makes the link between language and identity from his first play onwards. The chief element of behaviour Hugo, in *Zahradní slavnost*, has to learn to
ensure his career as a high-flying official is bureaucratic language. He gains his
position and non-identity to a large degree on account of his inextinguishable
capacity to parrot. Political success here depends on uttering the right phrase or
right slogan at the right moment. When he has learnt what he needs, he is able to
speak of the rival bureaucratic organization, the Office of Inauguration, with the
anonymous high-handedness of an apparatchik who had done particularly well at
the Party University – the incongruities of syntax and imagery belong to Havel's
parody (1964, p.43):

The pseudo-familiar Inaugurator phraseology concealing profound ideational vapidity behind a well-practised veneer of professional humanism, which has of necessity finally led the Office of Inauguration into the situation of an underminer of the positive consolidational endeavours of the Office of Liquidation, whose historically absolutely inevitable expression is the wise act of its liquidation!

In *Vyrozumění* Havel extends nonsense to an absolute with the artificial language *ptydepe*. The memorandum of the title is written in *ptydepe*. The director of the anonymous state office, Gross, tries to have it translated into Czech, but the bureaucratic system makes that impossible – though, in the end, a typist does translate it for him, and forthwith loses her job. The memorandum turns out to be a directive ordering the dissolution of the *ptydepe* programme. At the end of the play another artificial language is being introduced, *chorukor*. Havel satirizes the inhumanity of the totalitarian attitude to language with the creation of totalitarian languages. The introduction of the second, and the former *ptydepe*-instructor's subsequent attack on *ptydepe* also constitutes satire on the conduct of changes in the Party line (1966, p.213):

The fundamental error of *ptydepe* was that it uncritically overrated the significance of redundance. Redundance became a campaigning device, the latest slogan, and meanwhile it was quite forgotten that, apart from useful redundance, which lessens the danger of incorrect interpretations of texts and thus increases their reliability, there is also useless redundance which simply consists of the mechanical lengthening of texts.

Ptydepe, like *chorukor*, is a language of non-communication. Since identity must always be communicated before it can exist in any meaningful sense, and since the most common form of communication is verbal, *ptydepe* might be called an expression of non-identity.

The primary interpretation of 'Bariéra' (Barrier) in Havel's collection of concrete poetry, *Antikódy* (Anticodes) concerns the difficulty or impossibility of communication. A loop of 'I's to the left is separated from a loop of 'you's to the right by a wall of 'words', and this wall is double the height of the loops. The secondary interpretation is sexual. The penis is a barrier to communication between me (or a man) and women (or a woman); seduction may consist in true words rising above the two people involved, but those words, like the seduction itself, act as a barrier to communication (1966, p.104). The linguistic idea of the poem is later echoed in *Ztížená možnost* when the computer manifests a greater capacity for genuine communication than human beings.

Non-communication can occur simply as a result of different levels of education. That can occur even within the ranks of the socialist bureaucracy, where the identity-free senior official is less educated than the junior official. The book chosen by the junior official, the male secretary, in the following exchange from *Zahradní slavnost* (The garden party (1964, p.26)), may be intended to demonstrate that he is puerile, even retarded, and therefore is also nearly identity-free:

PLZÁK Technology – that's what I call a hot word! You see, it's my opinion that we're living in a technological century: the magnet – the telephone – the magnet – not even Vernon ever dreamt of that!

SECRETARY I was recently reading *Twenty Thousand Leagues Under the Sea.*

PLZÁK And we'll soon be able to read even further under the sea!

(That joke is also directed at the Münchhausenesque claims of some Soviet propaganda in the first ten years or so of the Cold War.)

Non-communication is sometimes expressed by the depiction of characters speaking to each other only apparently. The most obvious examples of that are the repeated phatic exchanges between the maltster and Vaněk in *Audience.* 'Official' Czech, political jargon and journalese usually consist of this apparent speaking. It is not simply that the function of language is debased in 'official' Czech, but that it more or less ceases to be language at all. Havel puts that rather melodramatically in his prison letters: 'the word which is not guaranteed by a life, loses its significance; one can silence a word in two ways. Either one gives it such significance that no one dares say it aloud, or one can remove all its significance so that it turns into air' (1985a, p.359).

Language is often abused by becoming the instrument of bullying or manipulation, but then, also, collaboration. Havel makes fun of language as a bullying device, when in *Zahradní slavnost* (1964, p.43) Hugo is grinding down the Director, whose post he intends to take:

DIRECTOR I'm sorry, but –

HUGO I really don't know what 'but' you're going on about –

DIRECTOR I'm not going on about 'but', but I meant –

HUGO So you even meant 'but'?

DIRECTOR I don't mean 'but', but –

HUGO Perhaps you don't mean 'but, but', but you mean 'but', and that's quite enough. But I tell you, you won't outbut me with any 'but'.

One might see the maltster as using language to bully or to manipulate Vaněk in *Audience.* He speaks colloquial-to-vulgar Czech, while Vaněk speaks educated literary Czech – until the end, that is. The ending is ambiguous but it looks as if the maltster has got Vaněk where he wanted him. Furthermore, their roles appear to be exchanged, and so both have potentially lost their identities. Bullying to deprive a person of his identity also forms the central episode of *Chyba* (Mistake, first performed, Stockholm, 1983); here (1992a, p.318) the not entirely insensitive Third Prisoner feebly tries to defend the new, non-conformist prisoner, by suggesting that he might be 'some Hungarian or something'. The cell boss's response is 'That's his mistake.'

In 'The power of the powerless' Havel demonstrates how a phrase in the form of a slogan hung up in a greengrocer's shop, however little the greengrocer or his customers notice it, is a fundamental way of supporting the regime. If he deliberately took the slogan down, however, he would lose his job, and he knows that. The display of the slogan is non-communicative on a verbal semantic level, but it does communicate as a gesture of support for an ideology. Ideology is a set of phrases which are not directly concerned with the real life of the individual. Ideology, however, in giving the specious appearance of relating to the living world, may function as an alibi for all society, 'from the greengrocer, who can conceal his fear for his job in the veil of his alleged concern for the unity of the workers of the world, to the highest functionary, who can clothe his concern for retaining his power in words about serving the working class' (1984, p.61). The greengrocer 'has accepted the prescribed *ritual*, has accepted "appearance" as reality, has adhered to the given "rules of the game". Naturally, by adhering to the rules, he has joined the game, become a player, made it possible for the game to continue' (1984, p.64).

Individual words may have the same function, may also actively contribute to uniformity and conformity, that is: lack or diminution of identity: 'The word "peace" – like the words "socialism", "mother-country" or "the people" – is just one of the rungs on which clever people climb higher up the ladder, but at the same time it is one of the truncheons used to beat those who "opt out"' (1989, p.59). One might put that another way. Conventionally the cliché conceals identity in language performance, though, in Havel's terms, it might be said to reveal non-identity or to express submission to the norm.[54] In his first play Havel satirizes cliché in the form of old-guard political mythology. In an exchange between the female and male secretaries (1964, p.18), this brand of cliché is used as an expression of loyalty and mutual recognition of or identification with the Establishment.

FEMALE SECRETARY Or do you have no confidence in the decisions of the steering committee?
MALE SECRETARY The committee made up of the leading executives of the Office of Liquidation?
FEMALE SECRETARY Old, experienced colleagues who were already liquidating before you were born?
MALE SECRETARY In conditions your generation cannot even imagine.

In the same play a much-fostered Lenin 'quotation' which had become part of the Communist verbal-myth arsenal is satirized in Pludek's statement: 'Jaroš kept his future in mind, and learned and learned and learned' (1964, p.19). The clichés of pseudopatriotism and of propaganda are satirized in the following words Pludek addresses to Hugo: 'My dear son! Life's a struggle and you're a rat! I mean, a Czech' (1964, p.14). Bergman's speech at the end of *Asanace* (Redevelopment (1988b, p.95)), after the honourable Plechanov's suicide, constitutes satire on collaborators who pretended to be liberal, parody of Establishment automatic (clichéd) speechifying, but also a seriously anti-totalitarian statement – which actually foreshadows Havel's own words on his share in the shame for the Germans' treatment of the Jews:

We are all deeply shocked by what has happened … We are shocked primarily because, faced with his death, we realise that we must bear our portion of guilt for it, for we, too, are responsible for the sad state of this world … This bitter awareness of our share of the guilt does, however, have its positive side … Therefore, in this difficult time, let us promise that we shall never again allow human stupidity to prevail and to spread nihilism … Let us promise that we shall never again allow our souls to be redeveloped and that we shall never again – redevelop the souls of others.

That last promise also indicates Havel's constant concern with the socialist regime's use of language for social organisation or manipulation – like the Stalinist instruction to writers that they should become engineers of human souls. If a human soul is engineered by language, it is being deprived of its identity.

One way in which, in the 1950s, the Czechoslovak regime produced linguistically manipulative new social ideals was by producing arid portmanteau words, usually borrowings from or imitations of the Russian. The words themselves were plangent with inhumanity. Havel barely mentions this practice, because it was in desuetude by the time he was writing his published works. He does parody such words in *The Garden Party* (1964, p.36) and simultaneously ridicules the manpower wastage involved in bureaucratization (in the word *kolklemp*, the *kol* is from 'collective' as in the Russian *kolkhoz* and the *klemp* is from *klempíř*, 'plumber'):

SECRETARY Evidently *kolklemp*s will be established; these are complex collectives composed of one plumber and eight inaugurators.
DIRECTOR And will these *kolklemp*s inaugurate or plumb?
SECRETARY Plumb, of course!

Especially if one understands *Spiklenci* (The conspirators) to constitute, to some degree, a reflection of events in early 1969 leading to the final fall of Dubček and the installation of Husák, one may see in the jargon used by Mohér an example of language being used to manipulate history. Such manipulation is cynically self-serving, since the public does not believe one word of it, any more than those who bombard the public with such jargon. Both those who use the jargon and those who are its audience, however, understand it as a statement of impending oppression (1977, p.95): 'A few *ultraleftists and anarchists controlled* by Zionist circles have succeeded in fanaticizing almost all *students and now they intend abusing the population's justified* discontent with the present situation in the country, and with the aid of various superficially appealing slogans, they intend establishing general anarchy.' Havel makes a similar use of oppressive jargon in *Pokoušení*, especially through the character of the Deputy; Foustka himself, when he is being submissive, also uses the language of Party directives. The artificial language, *ptydepe*, in *Vyrozumění,* on the other hand, suggests a ruling technocracy's attempt to impose mechanical thought on ordinary citizens and to impose a Utopia through desensitization.

The rule of fear in socialist society also perverts the communicative function of language. Language has to be used to say nothing, in other words, to conceal identity. If one allows oneself to be driven into the habit of using language to say nothing, one loses one's identity. The following example of language used to that goal may also constitute satire on the dialectic. The faceless Hugo is speaking to his parents: 'Me? Well, I'd say he ought not to accept and not to refuse, accept and refuse and, at the same time, refuse, not accept, not refuse and accept. Or the other way round' (1964, p.52).

Identity is expressed by communication and may be defined by one's relationship to others. Hugo has no relationships except those generated by fear or power. The identity crisis of Leopold in *Largo desolato* consists in his questioning the validity of his relationships with other human beings. This questioning may be interpreted as representing that sense of being persecuted by everyone one knows which frequently attends depression. The crisis is also exemplified by Leopold's incapacity, or by his realization of his incapacity, to act in accordance with his own words. Language has failed him. His one false hope of regaining an integrated identity is provided by the girl who quotes his own earlier (pre-crisis) words to him. He morally abuses his earlier whole self by attempting to turn them into a means of seducing her. Thus he makes his words, which had been written in reaction to the callous manipulativeness of socialist society, into a means of manipulation.

In his 1985–6 long-distance interview with Karel Hvížďala, when he describes the society he would like to see instead of anonymous socialist society, Havel speaks of just such relationships as Leopold has lost or suspects he has lost or never had. One is, once more, vaguely reminded of Masaryk's humanitism when Havel states the necessity of a new anti-totalitarian society centred on human beings (1988a, pp.18–19):

First and foremost, it is a matter of man's being the measure of all structures, including economic structures, and not of the structures' being the measure of man. That means that the most important thing is that personal relationships should not be lost, i.e. relationships between a man and his fellow-workers, between superiors and juniors, between man and his work, between this work and the fate of its results, etc., etc. … Now everything falls into the immense pit of impersonal, anonymous economic mechanicality, from the work of the lowest unskilled labourer right up to the decisions of the bureaucrat in the central planning office.

Identity, the transcendental and religion

One wonders whether the forty-year experience of socialist anonymity fostered Havel's notion that a sense of paradise lost or of a lost home forms a necessary constituent of the self. When man is cast into the world, he maintains, man is alienated from Being, but burns with a longing for integrity, meaning: for a fusion with the total transcendence of the self (see 1985a, pp.378–9). This recalls the less positive Freudian notion of the longing to return to the womb (to the home of the amniotic fluid) or, indeed, the Czech Romantic, Mácha's (1810–36), conception of the lost paradise of ignorance. Except that Havel's notion of a sense of loss drives one on into active working on oneself, not into existential nihilism.

Havel's notion, like Mácha's, presupposes some previous existence. Mácha imagines a prenatal (and posthumous) non-existence. Havel appears to imagine a previous spiritual existence. His is Platonic thinking which may have as much to do with Rádl as with Patočka (leaving aside his other reading, which he does not mention). Rádl perceived the Czech intellectuals of the 1920s as having abandoned the spiritual, of which he writes; 'The realm of the spirit is of its essence a kingdom which is not of this world; it is the realm of the ideal that should be, but is not; the spirit of a power which, though it intervenes in the world, is not a part of the temporal and spatial world'.[55] Awareness of the transcendental or of the absolute involves responsibility to the realm of the spirit, or to God, as well as to one's fellow human beings, who, consciously or not, are in the same relationship to the absolute as oneself. Spiritual awareness, then, demands commitment from one. (In *O naší nynější filosofii* (The present state of Czech philosophy, 1922), Rádl attacks, for example, Josef Durdík (1837–1902), for not making philosophy and public commitment one and the same thing.) Patočka views the link between spiritual awareness and responsibility as being at the core of Christian ethics, in which responsibility to the absolute actually dominates responsibility to one's fellow human beings; one does, however, express one's responsibility to the absolute through commitment to man. The core of Patočka's statement runs as follows: 'Christianity understands good differently from Plato – as self-forgetting goodness and self-denying (not orgiastic) love. Not orgiasm ... but *mysterium tremendum. Tremendum*, because responsibility is now placed not into a humanly scrutable essence of goodness and unity, but into an inscrutable relationship to the absolute, supreme existence'.[56] According to Patočka, the scientification of all aspects of life had been a major factor in producing modern nihilism, that is: the loss of a sense of meaning in life. That itself leads man to ask whether all meaning is not man-centred. If the meaning of life were only man-centred, one would finally be faced with a denial of meaning and the concomitant stagnation of life. Nihilism should be replaced by the conscious unveiling of meaning – and meaning itself is present only 'in the search for Being'.[57] Havel might be echoing that when he writes to his wife, 'The search for the meaning of life is actually the search for the absolute horizon. This absolute horizon is a matter of subconscious presumption, essential experience, and faith' (1985a, p.279). The search for the meaning of life is the only sufficient action in the antimetaphysical modern world which denies 'the obligatory significance of personal experience – including the experience of mystery and the absolute – and which, in place of the personally experienced absolute, lays down as the measure of the world a new absolute, created by people and in no manner mysterious, an absolute liberated from the "dimensions" of subjectivity and, thus, impersonal and inhuman; that is the absolute of so-called objectivity, of objective rational cognition, of the scientific scheme of the world' (1989, p.35). Modern man's great self-delusion lies in his belief that science can or will reveal everything. Good hides away in nooks and crannies, and Evil has taken over the world. 'The demons have been released from the stables of the myths and now grotesquely disguise themselves as men of the twentieth century who do not believe in ghosts' (1989, p.56).

Transcendence, which is the essence of the spiritual, is 'the endeavour to cross all horizons' (1985a, p.388), but any total understanding or happiness means the death of the self. Havel probably has Patočka's discussions of ecstasy and orgiasm in mind: 'Joy is coloured by terror, calm by anxiety, and happiness has a fatally tragic tinge. This experience reveals to us that unqualified identification, total insight, complete happiness are the end of the self, death' (1985a, p.392). On that basis it appears that Havel is wary of ecstasy, being out of his senses, beyond the selfness which is fundamentally defined by responsibility – or flight from responsibility.

Such an attitude to ecstasy would be borne out by Havel's apparent temptation to indulge in the esoteric arts. Occultists normally seek absolute self-control in order to approach knowledge. The attraction of occultism to socialist man is clear; unlike religion, occultism provides a system to replace the Marxist-Leninist system; occultism can explain everything, however airy-fairy some of those explanations might appear. Occultism also, however, provides neat mechanical models of identity, and essentially denies or destroys individual identity altogether: either because one's abiding identity is one's astral self or because one is an essentially passive transient self, a stage in a metempsychotic chain, or because the ideal is to fuse with some other self. In *Pokoušení*, Havel makes fun of trendy occultism, but also of state-run psychotronics,[58] while at the same time treating Foustka's dabbling in the occult as a metaphor for dabbling in the evil of compromise with the infernal machine of socialism. Still, we learn from Havel's 1984 essay, 'Thriller' (*Do různých stran*), that he has been reading Heinrich Cornelius Agrippa of Nettersheim. Something of occultist passivity attends the beginning of his longest stay in prison, when he declares to his wife that he believes Fate had long ago decided he should have a long spell in prison (1985a, p.13). His attitude to astrology is ambiguous. In the first of his prison letters he says that astrologers had rightly predicted he would be incarcerated in 1979, and much later on (9 January 1982), he writes to his wife that he is pleased the astrologers have some positive predictions (1985a, p.310). His understanding of astrology is not such as one would expect from someone seriously interested in the occult. That is clear when he writes: 'I am beginning to have a rather sceptical view on astrologers. It seems to me that their predictions relate too frequently to alternatives, events which could have happened, but did not happen' (1985a, p.64).

Religion, however, becomes ever more important in Havel's writing. To have a full identity, one must have a faith. Faith can cure the modern crisis. In other words, he is thinking again very much like Masaryk. In *Der Selbstmord als sociale Massenerscheinung der modernen Civilisation* (Suicide as a mass social phenomenon in modern civilization, 1881), the latter proclaims religion to be the cure for the suicide pandemic he observed in the contemporary world. Monotheistic religions work against suicidality and the Christian idea of a love that binds man to both Heaven and Earth necessarily preempts any urge to kill oneself. And in *Jan Hus. Naše obrození a naše reformace* (Jan Hus: The Czech National Revival and the Czech Reformation, 1896) Masaryk claims that the whole 'Czech question' was a religious question. Havel bewails modern man's loss of God because that entails a loss of an absolute by which he can measure his self (1984, p.238):

With the loss of God man has lost an absolute and universal system of co-ordinates to which he could relate anything and, primarily, himself. Man's world and personality gradually started to split into separate and mutually independent fragments which corresponded to various relative co-ordinate systems. And because of this man began to lose his inner identity, that is: his identity with himself. And with that identity he began to lose many other things, including his own continuity, his hierarchy of experiences and values, and so forth.

What man needs is a faith in a supreme being, not a materialist faith such as socialism tried to impose with its dogmatic optimism; such optimism can easily turn into hysterical scepticism. Faith has nothing to do with believing that everything will turn out all right or with visions of catastrophe, and it 'is not dependent on what the reality appears to be at any given moment' (1985a, p.168).

Lack of faith involves the loss of metaphysical values which necessarily results from arrogant anthropocentrism. What is needed is 'a spiritual revival' (1988a, p.17) to balance the results of modern advances in science and technology. The God-less world is a morally arid world: 'the spiritual state of contemporary civilization is characterized by the loss of metaphysical certainties, the experience of the transcendental, and by the loss of all suprapersonal moral authority, the loss of altogether any higher horizon … The great abandoning of

God which the modern age is going through has no parallel in history (as far as I know, we are living in the midst of the first atheist civilisation) (1988a, p.16).

Havel denies he is a true Roman Catholic Christian, since he does not go to Mass, and he is not utterly convinced of the divinity of Christ. He is, however, not a materialist, believes in the Christian morality and does believe there is some grand design: 'I believe that nothing disappears irrevocably, least of all our deeds. That is how I explain my conviction that it is worth striving for something in life, for something more than what has some visible return or reward' (1988a, p.212). And he has a pretty clear perception of God (1985a, pp.106–7):

I am not a child of the age of mythical, but of conceptual thinking, and because of that my God appears to be something terribly abstract, vague and, actually, not very attractive (all the more so because my relationship with Him is so difficult to describe) ... my experience of Him is vivid, intimate and concrete, perhaps ... more vivid than in the case of someone who has a 'normal' God properly endowed with all the appropriate attributes ... And what is also characteristic of my God is that He is a master of waiting, which sometimes makes me rather nervous. It is as if he arranged various possibilities for me and then silently waited to see what I do. If I fail in something, He punishes me – naturally, through me (for example with a bad conscience); if I do not fail, He rewards me (with my relief or joy) – and often He even just leaves me in uncertainty. His last judgement is taking place now, continuously, ceaselessly – and yet it is the last over and over again: nothing that has been done can ever be undone; everything remains in the 'memory of Being' – I shall remain there, too – condemned to be by myself for ever – I shall remain there the person I am and the person I make of myself.

Havel also believes that God 'holds in His hands the mysterious course of everything' (1990, p.96).

His God appears to be primarily conscience, that is an exhortation to responsibility, and thus to an integrated identity (1995a, p.405):

I do not know whether there is or is not a God in the way that Christians conceive of Him, and nor do I know whether it is appropriate for me to call the summons to responsibility which I hear, God. I know only this: that in the sphere of our inner experience I am writing about, Being (which is, after all, easier to assume than the existence of God) in its integrity, fullness and unendingness, as the principle, direction and meaning of everything that exists, and as the profoundest and, at the same time, the most comprehensive 'innerness' of all existence ... acquires distinctly personal features.

When he is welcoming the Pope in Prague, Havel brings together the main elements of his conception of responsibility and God that I have attempted to trace in this Introduction: 'With your visit, you will remind us all ... about the real source of truly human responsibility, its metaphysical source ... Yes, today the future of mankind lies in a civilization of the spirit, of responsibility and love' (1990, pp.98–9).

2

THE MYTH OF SLAVNESS:
PAVEL JOSEF ŠAFAŘÍK
AND JAN KOLLÁR

Introduction: myth, nation, nationalism

A myth is not true or false. It is a normally narrative expression of concern for the society of which the mythopoet is or deems himself to be a member. Its aim is to illuminate its recipients' awareness of the human condition or of the special situation of an individual community.[1] It suggests or seeks to establish a value which will help individuals orientate themselves 'in the midst of things, [seek] an answer in the quest for self.'[2] Myth usually has to do with creations, beginnings, matrices, models, and as it reveals permanent values in these beginnings or models, it binds a group morally and historically (mnemically). It draws 'a circumference around a human community and looks inward toward that community',[3] and purports to express a collective experience. A myth is a primary cultural phenomenon: it may be created by a culture and may create (a) culture. A myth explains origins: of the world, of a community, of values. In Kołakowski's conception, a myth derives from a cultural or human 'need to make the empirical realities understandable; that is, to grasp the world of experience as intelligible by relating it to the the unconditioned reality which binds phenomena teleologically.'[4] A myth is normally rational (according to the understanding of reason at the time of its creation or in the eyes of the mythopoet), and it is an active force: it explains, but it also constitutes 'a pragmatic charter' of faith and moral wisdom.[5] A myth is an authority and, as such, codifies obligations. New myths or new variants of old myths may always be created, and Šafařík (1795–1861) and Kollár (1793–1852) together created a complex new myth of Slav nationalist deliverance. Like any myth it looked to the future as well as the past, and like any nationalist myth it had a utopia as its goal.

Their myth concerned the Slav nation, was based on a conception whereby the nation was not linked with any past, present or future political state. Šafařík was the son of a Slovak Lutheran clergyman and Kollár was himself a Slovak Lutheran clergyman; they both, then, grew up in a tradition which had Czech as its literary language. Because of the Czech literary tradition, not only because of Herder, then Fichte, the late eighteenth and nineteenth-century notion of nation was, in most of Europe, co-extensive with language. In the 'Dalimil' chronicle of c.1314 (republished, for the first time since 1620, in 1786) *český jazyk* (Czech tongue, language) was used to mean 'Czech people', as it was in the fourteenth-century romance *Štilfrid* and in the radical religious philosopher, Petr Chelčický's (*c.* 1390–*c.*1460) *Siet' viery* (Net of faith), and indeed, by Sixt z Ottersdorfu (1500s–1583). Clearly, however, for the two Slovaks the Czech language could not mean only Czech (Bohemian and Moravian) nation. They sought to obliterate this problem with the idea of a Slav nation. In its use during their life-time the idea of nation (*národ*) was itself a myth. Both were Hungarians,[6] and the Hungarian *nemzet* meant only those Hungarians who shared in the four cardinal privileges, i.e., magnates and the petty nobility. Certainly the Kantian notion of self-determination combined with the Fichtean vision of linguistic struggle will have played a major role in Šafařík and Kollár's conception of nation.[7]

Still, to understand what they meant by nation it is useful to look at definitions drawn up over the last few years – really as a guideline to the study of my subjects' complex myth. Leslie Spencer takes for granted 'nations' as more or less existing today, thus the author no longer considers nation a myth; myth is a constituent element of nation: a nation is 'a human grouping, the members of which share an intuitive sense of sameness, based on a myth of common descent, and a shared sense of future.'[8] Gellner perhaps accepts that nations are still fundamentally products of mythopoeia:

1. Two men are of the same nation if and only if they share the same culture, where culture in turn means a system of ideas and signs and associations and ways of behaving and communicating.
2. Two men are of the same nation only if they *recognize* each other as belonging to the same nation. … nations are the artefacts of men's convictions and loyalties and solidarities.[9]

Both Spencer and Gellner speak of 'sameness', and Šafařík and Kollár had to create that sameness, which suggests that, at least in their case, Kedourie is right when he says that nation got its meaning from nationalism.[10] Hroch dismisses such assertions as 'subjectivist'. For him nationalism derived from the actual existence of nations. The terms 'cultural' and 'people' might not be clear in his text, but still Hroch's nation is something which perforce has to exist; his definition is dialectical: 'a large social group characterized by a combination of several kinds of relation (economic, territorial, political, religious, cultural, linguistic and so on) which arise on the one hand from the solution found to the fundamental antagonism between man and nature on a specific compact land-area, and on the other hand from the reflection of these relations in the consciousness of the people.'[11] In the term, 'kinds of relation', one presumes Hroch is deliberately avoiding the notion of a 'shared' culture which both Kedourie and Gellner find useful in defining nation. Though Gellner argues that peoples who consider themselves to belong to different 'nations' may share a culture. Even if we limit any attempt at definition to the Habsburg Monarchy, if we limit that further to the 1820s and 1830s, when our two writers produced their most influential works, we would still find that no definition of nation would contain exactly the same elements for the younger Croat, Magyar, Czech, Slovak, Galician and Austrian-German intellectuals. Certainly they would all include language as a major part of what they understood as defining nation for them. They would probably all think of the French and English (not the British) as nations. But I do not think one could say much more than that.

Their nationalisms are, however, more or less the same, for nationalism is a matter of ideology, or metaphysic.[12] Plamenatz's analysis of nationalism as a purely cultural matter suits my purposes very well, indeed might lead one to suggest that in the fundamental elements of their Slav nationalism Šafařík and Kollár propounded the purest quiddity of nationalism. Plamenatz's division of nationalism into two types, Western and Eastern, is at first sight appealing. In Western (German and Italian) nationalism, a people (its elite) feels disadvantaged but equipped to succeed in doing what its models (England and France) are doing, and so the nationalists pursue a policy which ensures they do just that. In Eastern nationalism, a people that has recognized its own backwardness, and that it is living or has until recently been living in a civilization which is alien to it, feels the need to re-equip itself in order culturally to raise itself (the Slavs, the Third World). Western nationalism 'is normally liberal, but can turn extreme; Eastern nationalism is apt to be illiberal. Both Western and Eastern nationalisms are imitative, but Western nationalists tend to be friendly towards their models, whereas Eastern nationalists tend to be hostile.' Šafařík and Kollár try hard to be Western nationalists. Plamenatz's more general definition will certainly fit them and help us see what they were up to: 'Nationalism ... is the desire to preserve or enhance a people's ... cultural identity when that identity is threatened, or the desire to transform or even create it where it is felt to be inadequate or lacking.'[13]

The nationalist does not necessarily work for independent statehood, but he does aim for a unification of cultural forces within what he chooses to call his nation. He is rebellious in the sense that he casts doubt on the status quo in customs and some institutions, but he is by no means necessarily revolutionary. The nationalist wishes the members of the nation (of his dream or plan) to be the sole bearers and purveyors of high culture on the territory he designates as appropriated (by history or theory or geography). It is difficult to believe in

Gellner's position that nationalism is necessary concomitant with modern industrial development and the need for efficient communication which that development entails (take for example, Slovak or Hungarian nationalism). On the other hand, in general the fact is that nationalism could not come about as anything but a movement of a small group of intellectuals unless communications in general (roads, newspapers, soon railways) created (by joining) an audience ready to be converted to belief in its nationhood and national goal. To use Gellner's terms, work remained mainly 'the manipulation of things' in Slovakia; it did not become the 'manipulation of meanings.' That remained the preserve of a small body of intellectuals.[14] Kedourie distinguishes between patriotism, xenophobia and nationalism, saying that the first two are age-old matters of emotion, whereas nationalism is an intellectual matter, a 'comprehensive doctrine which leads to a distinctive style of politics.'[15] In fact, nationalism appears to need xenophobia. Xenophobia may exist without nationalism, but hardly nationalism without xenophobia. A nationalist cannot have a lickspittle approach to his model (think, for example, of Herder's attitude to France).

Šafařík and Kollár's lives and works

Both Šafařík and Kollár spent most of their working lives outside their native linguistic area, and so were nationalists from abroad. Both of them also spent some time at the University of Jena, the mainspring of the *Burschenschaft*. From 1819 to 1833 Šafařík was a master at an Orthodox school in Novi Sad (Neusaatz); he spent the rest of his life in Prague, as editor, censor, librarian and university teacher. From 1819 to 1849 Kollár was a Lutheran priest in Pest; his parishioners were German (Pest was a German town at the time) and Slovak. In 1849 he was appointed government adviser on Slovak affairs in Vienna, where he was also given a chair of Slavonic Archaeology at the University. He used his advisership to work against the wishes of the majority of Slovak intellectuals. I do not think one can be certain that Šafařík was, as Brock states, intellectually superior to Kollár.[16] Šafařík was a scholar, a gluttonous reader, whose interests in life were academic, though he gave a fiery speech at the Prague Slav Congress in 1848 and did noble work as state censor. He was an extremely pleasant man, which Kollár was not. Both were enthusiasts for the Slav cause (initially certainly Šafařík was inspired by Kollár), but Šafařík channelled his enthusiasm into scholarship, Kollár into poetry, semi-political theory, and wild romancing about the noble Slav origins of place-names, religions and civilizations all over Eurasia. Kollár had no rigour, but he certainly had imagination, and instead of looking at the two men in terms of intellect, it would probably be wiser to look at them in terms of the application of intellect; Šmatlák states that Šafařík worked at the academic level expected at the time on depicting the variety of Slavonic histories and cultures, where Kollár devoted himself 'mainly to the psychological and philosophical interpretation and rationale of the "Slav" idea.'[17]

The Czech historian, Palacký (who was also Protestant and, because of that, had a Hungarian education), wrote in 1846: 'there is not a *single* educated Slav who would be indifferent to Šafařík's name and position'.[18] Although he became slightly *engagé* in the year of revolutions, previously to that Šafařík was politically a careful man; in the first of his two chief works, his *Geschichte der slawischen Sprache und Literatur nach allen Mundarten* (History of Slavonic language and literature in all dialects, Buda, 1826), he writes for example, that, after much spilling of blood, Croatia is now 'enjoying felicitous peace under the gentle sceptre of her Austrian rulers'[19] or that Bohemia had begun to flourish under 'the moderate, bliss-endowing reigns of Maria Theresa, Joseph II, Leopold II and Francis I' (G 291). When dealing with Poland he consistently sees the Russians (or Tsar Alexander) having the very best intentions towards the Poles and Polish culture (for example, G 385). The *Geschichte* does not aim to be an original work; Šafařík wanted as his audience the educated public of Europe which, he felt, had been biased against the Slavs. It is, then, a defensive work as well as the work of an enthusiastic promoter of the notion of true Slav scholarship, a man whose ideas were considered plain dotty by his Orthodox employers and colleagues in Novi Sad. He attempted with this work (which often consists of not much more than lists of institutions or barely glossed bibliographies) to follow the precepts of the Breslau general literary historian, Johann Friedrich Wachler, whose innovative term 'literary culture' Šafařík employed, although he proved unable to treat the development of literary culture within the general development of culture.[20] The *Geschichte* is a dull compilation, but Šafařík's lively partiality often phosphoresces through the forest of sources, references and demonstrations of truths. It does, indeed, offer more of an *Aggregat* than a system, as he says, but he preferred to present an accurate account of the development of Slav culture in his sources' words than an inaccurate account on his own (G 42–3). No doubt exaggerating a little, Kollár wrote: 'Delighted, astonished and now clearly aware, the Slavs saw themselves for the first time systematically ordered in Šafařík's *Geschichte* as in a great mirror, publicly displayed before the whole of Europe as one nation.'[21]

Šafařík's other main work is the two-volume *Slovanské starožitnosti. Oddíl dějepisný* (Slav antiquities. Historical section, Prague, 1837); he intended writing a second part, a 'cultural section', but he did not even start it. *Slovanské starožitnosti* is an augmentation of the *Geschichte*. Most of the material up to the tenth century in the *Geschichte* is here, but reconsidered, often completely reinterpreted. The author introduces more of his own emotions into this work and, more important, many more of his own constructions on history and culture. It is

written in ponderous Germanic Czech with a sprinkling of Slovak lexical items.
He labels it himself an account of 'our native history',[22] thus emphasizing his
Slav nationalist intention. With this work he did what Kollár had constantly been
hoping to do.[23] Šafařík is determined to demonstrate better than he had in the
Geschichte that the Slavs were culturally equal to the Germans. As Niederle
writes, almost all 'the fundamental theses of *Slovanské starožitnosti* are today
questionable, in some cases have been dismissed forever from scholarly knowledge. Nevertheless Šafařík did achieve his main goal: to demonstrate the
antiquity and the equality of the Slavs in Europe.'[24] Again, none of the fundamental theses is completely of his own invention (his precursors are the Czech
Dobrovský, the Slovene Kopitar and the Pole Surowiecki, quite apart from older
scholars of things Slav like Schlözer), and he does not claim they are. The ar-
rangement of his theses, however, the pursuit of detail, and the amount of substantiating material he has gathered are new.[25] He used literally every source at
the disposal of scholars in the 1830s and 'every fact, every important word, every
significant detail is for him positively sacred.'[26] The work was translated into
German (1843–4) and Polish (1844) and parts of it were published in Serbian and
Russian. It also brought Šafařík honours: he was elected to learned societies or
academies in Berlin, Moscow, Munich, Odessa, St Petersburg and Washington.[27]
It was also largely because of Šafařík that the academic notion of *Slavistik* spread
over most of the world except the British Empire.

Kollár was more of a publicist than a scholar and so he could not expect such
honours. His contribution to the creation of the myth of Slavness was, however,
greater. It was more due to Kollár than to Šafařík that the notion of Slav cultural
unity and Reciprocity (*Wechselseitigkeit*) survived well into the 1950s and, indeed, still survives today in pockets of eastern Europe. In this essay I shall be
dealing primarily with his essays on Slav Reciprocity and on his travel writings,
but it was his huge cycle of sonnets, *Slávy dcera* (The daughter of Sláva)[28] which
made his name, and which indeed contained, albeit in an emotional form, many of
the Slav or panslav ideas he elaborated in his prose. With *Slávy dcera* he turned
both dominant trends of Czech and Czecho-Slovak verse upside down: 'the
Anacreontic autostylization of the poet who besings love as a game with a fixed
set of rules and the convention of patriotic verse without social content or active
ideology.'[29] *Slávy dcera*, furthermore, provided the profoundest ideological
experience its young readership had ever had with its statement of positive
values, national pride, loyalty, belonging to an almost boundless Slav family
where anything was possible.[30] In addition to that, he was the first modern author
of Czech verse to write of direct erotic experience and many of the erotic sonnets
still today retain their sensualist impact. Because the prophetic visionary nationalism of the cycle was combined with this true-to-life eroticism, the national message acquired a realistic, authentic quality around which young Czech and Slovak

patriots could rally. The language of *Slávy dcera* was new (a combination of Czech, sometimes revived words, neologisms, Slovakisms and words taken over from other Slavonic languages) and its freshness was so influential that, in Jakubec's view, 'All later [nineteenth-century] Czech poets took Kollár as their starting point; they were so enthusiastic about his language that as far as they possibly could they tried to adopt it as their own.'[31] Elsewhere Jakubec compares its contemporary importance with that of Šafařík's *Geschichte*; both, he says, were written under the influence of Herder's notion of *Humanität* and both set down what at the time appeared to be the fundamental problems of Slavness.[32] There is, however, nothing mystical about Šafařík, as there is about Kollár. Mickiewicz recognizes *Slávy dcera* as something quite new in literature and acknowledges the quite extraordinary enthusiasm with which Kollár burned: 'Kollár really does have tears in his eyes when he speaks of the misfortune and sufferings of Czechs, Poles, Serbs. He bears all these nations in his heart and loves them all equally with the impartiality of a Czech scholar. Wherever he goes, day and night, he holds the entire Slavonic race in the embrace of his mind.' The only trouble is, Mickiewicz writes at the end of his piece, that no one will sing his sonnets, since they do not make for 'a true image of the hopes and desires of the Slav nation.'[33]

Kollár's enthusiasm may look like automythicization, as if he were making sure he fitted the myth he had created. One might see that, for example, in his autobiography, published posthumously, in 1863, in his account of his meeting with his best friend during his studies in Pressburg (today's Bratislava), Pantaleon Živković. One notices in the following a motivation which persistently recurs in Kollár's writing, that Slav feeling is part of his natural make-up, is innate though not immediately discovered: 'Unconsciously, of natural instinct, I at that time became, quite sincerely, friendlier with this Serbian Slavobrother than with any German or Magyar. As early as this a dark inkling, emotion, passed through my heart that things had to be different in Slavdom, that we were all one nation.' [34] Naturally, one must remember this was *ex post*, but I have no reason to believe that Kollár did not believe he was writing the truth. The same goes for his account of his first arrival in Jena – which a sceptic might take as an authentication of the elegiac 'Předzpěv' (Prelude) to *Slávy dcera*: 'Hardly had I … looked at the surroundings of the River Saale than previously unknown feelings, unimagined pains, began to penetrate my heart, such as take hold of us in graveyards, but in a far more elevated and awe-inspiring form. Those feelings concerned the death of the Slav nation here, the graves of dear ancestors and tribes, the Sorbs, who had been oppressed then destroyed here' (P 276). In his lively first travel book, the *Cestopis* (Pest, 1843), he appears often simply crazy in his divagations, but that very craziness draws the reader to him, for it makes him or her respect Kollár's Slavism as a serious religion and esteem his personal qualities of imagination and pride. For example, one might take his admiration of the Slavonic Italian painter, Schiavone, an admiration which evinces a passion as great and pure as any religious or erotic passion:

Perhaps pictures by old members of other nations are more beautiful, but Schiavoni's are more Slav: we are closer to these colours, feel more akin to these figures; it is a Slav heart that beats out to meet us, Slav lips which here call out with such penetrating tones these words: 'What a pity that you Slavs do not love and cultivate your nation! What you could become! What excellent painters, what famous artists of all kinds you could have!'[35]

In the same *Cestopis*, when he is introduced to King Ludwig of Bavaria's African slaves by their Czech tutor and he has them sing songs, one of the most remarkable aspects of their language that he notices is that it has hard and soft consonants like Slavonic.

The Slavomystic bears out Plamenatz's view that there is nothing incongruent between liberalism and nationalism. For all his near racism, for all his hostile remarks, for all his prejudices and obsessiveness, Kollár was a man of firm libertarian, and often liberal, principles. Kollár's fundamental political thinking had a strong impact on T. G. Masaryk's conception of the Czech national mission in the last two decades of the nineteenth-century and, thus, indirectly on Czech and Slovak politics for the first half of the twentieth century. It may be significant that, as Kollár tells us in his autobiography, his reading of Montesquieu's *Esprit des lois* as a schoolboy in Bystrica had a considerable influence on the course of his education (P 180). His conception of government and state is evident in the sermon he preached on returning from Saxony finally to marry his beloved of nearly twenty years' standing, Friederike Schmidt. He speaks of Saxon schoolmasters and clergy all being 'in the fair-dealing [*rovnou*] paternal care of the government of the land.'[36] Then, in *Wechselseitigkeit*, he defines the state as follows, and he appears to be thinking particularly of an ideal Austria (W 37): 'The state is an association [*Verein*] of several lands and various peoples under a common head [*Oberhaupt*]; its role is protection, justice and the promotion of culture among the peoples entrusted to it.' In *Nábožný pohled,* he calls for religious tolerance and for equal social and political rights to adherents of all confessions. He also calls for the industrialisation of Hungary. With industrialisation Hungary will cease to be a child and become an independent adult. Industry will, he believes, reduce poverty, increase the economic and moral wellbeing of all her inhabitants (N 6–8).

The aim of education should not be to create conformity, but naturally to further individuality, special features of the individual human being and the individual nation (W 90). The state may not interfere with this individuality. There are four aspects of life which law-givers may not touch: a man's religion, a man's language and nationality, a man's (nation's) customs and, fourthly, 'old laws' (*starých zákonův*) (C 15). I am not at all sure what the last means; I can only guess one is to understand 'customary law' – it is highly unlikely that he is thinking in an Augustinian manner. Kollár puts these rules into the mouth of a fellow pastor he meets, but embraces them as his rules as well. Every individual is entirely responsible for his own actions: 'One cannot live without individual consciousness; destroying that is the grave of all morality.' (C 133–4) Kollár was, throughout his career, particularly concerned with responsibility. One of the reasons he wanted his readers to think of a Slav and not a Czecho-Slovak (let alone a Czech or Slovak) nation was that he considered a large nation to have great responsibility and a small nation to have little responsibilty (W 61). In his autobiography he elaborates thirteen arguments against capital punishment which he had apparently worked out in 1815. The ninth of these seems to me to contradict the notion of individual responsibility and consciousness; an essentially liberal attitude is supported by an illiberal determinist argument (incidentally, both Lavater and Gall figure in *Slávy dcera*): 'Nature herself and the constitution of the human body inject into many the tendency to certain delinquent acts … The phrenologist, Gall, and others have discovered a particular place in skulls which serves as an instrument of stealing. If a condemned man has this place marked, he is punished for a gift endowed to him by Nature, thus for Nature's guilt' (P 226). As his assertion of individual consciousness reacts against the post-Kantians' notion of a universal consciousness, so his conception of freedom reacts against their notion of freedom as self-realization and self-realization as a complete fusing with the universal consciousness.[37] The independence of the individual lies in the 'wise' limiting of his own freedom for the sake of the common weal. Kollár then links the freedom of the nation, the freedom of the individual, and his own linguistic politics: 'only that nation is truly free which operates and administers in literature and writing with only one language; the nation makes other numerous, often coarse, dialects and regional variants subservient to this one language so that the whole does not suffer through the multiplication of free communities [*obci*] and the foundation of new thrones and does not finally break up into little pieces, fragment … The freest man is he who does not serve himself.'[38] Kollár also purveys a libertarian, anti-élitist view of literature such as Masaryk would purvey later on in the century. Kollár's ideal is 'no writers' and scholars' aristocratism, no monopoly over literature and ideas …: a true national and spiritual free community [*obec*]' (C 46).

One may easily miss the democrat in Kollár's prose because he does have the habit of the totalitarian either-or manner of arguing. A typical example is the following didactic, propagandistic question, which epitomizes an argument at the centre of his whole life's *oeuvre*: 'Which is the more meritorius contribution to humanity: fighting, shedding blood, enslaving, oppressing, death and destruction, the German way? Or: peace and hard work, farming and trade, the home and hospitality, freedom and life, the Slav way?' (C 256).

The Slav nation, Slav reciprocity

The germ of that question, like the germ of so many of Šafařík and Kollár's ideas on the Slavs, lies in the brief chapter on the Slavs in Herder's *Ideen zur Philosophie der Geschichte der Menschheit* (Ideas towards a philosophy of the history of mankind, 1784–91). Herder begins that chapter with the phrase, 'The Slav peoples take up more space on the Earth than they do in history.'[39] The very size of the Slav nation, population (70 or 80 million depending on which of our authors' works we go by), and geographical extent are emphasized by both Kollár and Šafařík. This serves two purposes; first, to present the Slav question as by nature globally important; secondly, to help to foster pride and self-confidence in the Slav audience. In his first published prose work, the sermon *Dobré vlastnosti národu slovanského* (The fine qualities of the Slav nation, Pest, 1822), which greatly inspired Šafařík, Kollár makes the point straight away: the Slavs form the greatest and most extensive nation in Europe.[40] Šafařík is a little more careful and says in his *Geschichte*, citing Schlözer, that no nation except the Arab has spread as widely over the Earth as the Slav (G 46).

In his writings on the Slav idea Kollár divides Slavonic into four dialects: Russian, Illyrian, Czechoslovak and Polish. In the *Geschichte* Šafařík follows Dobrovský in dividing the Slav tribes into two groups of four. The South Eastern group contains: (i) the Russians, including the Ukrainians; (ii) the Serbs, including Bulgarians, the Serbs themselves, Bosnians, Montenegrins, Slavonians and Dalmatians; (iii) the Croats, (iv) the Slovenes (*Vindi*). The North Western group contains: (i) the Bohemians, including the Moravians; (ii) the Slovaks; (iii) the Poles, and (iv) the Sorbs. Now he comes to language and, following Dobrovský's usage in *Institutiones linguae slavicae dialecti veteris* (1822), he speaks of Slavonic dialects. (In the 1810s Dobrovský had still been calling them languages.) Šafařík divides the dialects into two groups of five, thus; the first group has (i) and (ii) Church Slavonic and Russian, which together have the subdialects, Russian, Ukrainian and Byelorussian; (iii) Serbian, which has two subdialects, Bulgarian and Serbian; (iv), Croat, and (v) Slovene. The second group has (i) Czech, (ii) Slovak, (iii) Upper Lusatian Sorbian, (iv) Lower Lusatian Sorbian, and (v) Polish. Three important things arise from this taxonomy. First, in the interests of balance, he gives enormous weight to the Slav tribes and languages of the Monarchy. Only those Russians who are not Ukrainians (in the South Eastern group (i)) and the Sorbs (in the North West group (iv)) do not to some degree belong to the Monarchy. Secondly, he achieves that by having the Bulgarians and Bulgarian belong to the Serbs (actually, largely because he knows very little indeed about the Bulgarians at this stage in his career). Thirdly, he achieves it by considering Slovak a separate dialect (an idea very few would have adhered to

since the failure of Anton Bernolák adequately to codify a literary language between 1787 and 1790). Emphasizing, only apparently distorting, the sheer number of Slavs in the Monarchy was probably intended to boost the confidence of
those Slavs. In *Slovanské starožitnosti* his taxonomy is greatly simplified. Tribes
and dialects are not separated and he presents two groups of three. The first group
is still called the South Eastern, and that contains: (i) the Russians, (ii) the Bulgarians, and (iii) the Illyrians, which comprise Transdanubian Serbs, Croats and
Slovenes. The second group is now called the Western and includes: (i) the Poles,
who comprise Poles themselves, Silesians and Pomeranians; (ii) the Czechoslovaks, who comprise Bohemians, Moravians and Slovaks, and (iii) the Polabian
Slavs, who comprise the Sorbs and various now extinct tribes like the Veleti and
Bodrici. The new taxonomy is partly necessary because he is dealing with the
history of the Slavs only up to the end of the first millennium A.D. He does, however, now know much more about the Bulgarians (and indeed no longer speaks of
Old Church Slavonic, but of 'Cyrillic or Old Bulgarian'). Furthermore, he is pay-
ing at least lip-service to the 'Czechoslovak' idea, in which he never believed as
passionately and dogmatically as Kollár. In *Slovanské starožitnosti* Šafařík does,
however, certainly try to demonstrate the cultural unity of the Slavs.

That the idea of some Slav cultural unity is far older than Kollár and Šafařík
forms a stock rider to nearly all discussions of Kollár's notion of Slav Reciprocity. Kollár, however, not only formulated an idea which appealed to intellectuals
(and in some countries, politicians) throughout the Slav world, but he also provided a programme of action. It also seems that none of Kollár's so-called predecessors created anything like the Kollár–Šafařík myth. With one exception,
Antonín Marek, I am not aware that any of these predecessors contributed to
Kollár's thought incisively. As Štefánek points out, the strongest (and most pre-
dictable) expressions of Slav consciousness concerned the Czechs and the Poles.
Among those this critic lists are the Polish King Casimir, who in 1438 (*sic*) informed German envoys that the Poles and Czechs were of the same origin and
tongue, and in 1433 the Polish Jan Czapek of Sany had some Czechs burnt at the
stake for selling themselves to Germans against the interests of the Slav nation;
most important seems to be a Polish bishop, Jan Nepomuk Kossakowski, who
'developed an idea of Slav reciprocity'.[41] Vlček mentions a seventeenth-century
Croatian priest, Jura Križanović, the Slovene Majar (who was younger than
Kollár) and the Slovak Johann Herkel[42] (who was concerned particularly with the
idea of a panslav language, an idea with which the Czech lexicographer
Jungmann also briefly toyed). Another critic suggests that Kossakowski and two
other Poles, Staszic and Woronicz, may have had a direct influence not only on
Kollár's notion of Reciprocity, but also on his verse.[43] Staszic and Woronicz were,
however, Russophils, who like Stanisław Trembecki at the end of the eighteenth
century, conceived of a union of Slavs led by Russia.[44]

There is absolute proof that Marek's Slavophil ideas influenced Kollár, since the latter paraphrased an article of Marek's in a poem which he published as an appendix to his first essay entirely devoted to Slav Reciprocity, published in Czech in the Slovak poet, Kuzmány's, periodical, *Hronka*, in 1836, 'O literárnej vzájemnosti mezi kmeny a narečími slávskými' (On literary reciprocity between the Slav tribes and dialects). On the other hand, Marek's essay was published after *Slávy dcera* and after Kollár's first definition of Reciprocity. (The poem actually appeared first in Serbo-Croat in the *Danica illyrska* in 1835.) Marek's Slavism was, like Trembecki's, Russocentric in the poem 'Marek Jungmannovi' (Marek to Jungmann, 1814); the spirit of the Slavs wafts from the East, for there the strong Slavs live. Still, even there he speaks of Czechs' gaining pride by becoming Slavs, and in that he is approaching the Šafařík–Kollár idea. In the essay, however, one finds Slav awareness, passionate love of fellow Slavs, and the hint of a belief in the Slavs as the proto-Europeans. Thus one has most of the ingredients of the myth of Slavness. It was first published in the periodical *Jindy a nyní* (Then and now) in 1833. I quote the key passages:

Those whom language hath joined together let no man put asunder. It joined us Bohemians, Moravians, Slovaks and Silesians with our brethren, the Poles, Russians [*Rossianiny*], with our southern brethren, on the Danube, the Morava, the Drava and Sava, with our brethren on this side of the Balkan Range and with our brethren beyond the Range who give life to Constantinople with the work of their hands, and with those who occupy the rocky shores of the Adriatic. I shall also not forget the Sorb … The all-embracing love of the Slavs forgot old rancours and enmities. – Let us no longer pay heed to the voices of foreigners who endeavour to defame one of us in the eyes of another so that we should be rent apart, so that we should soon fall, as our forebears fell in the German Empire, in Britain and France, for, there too, a tongue related to ours resounded. … No matter how you are clad, there is always but one nation; no matter what alphabet you use, there is always and will always remain one nation, as long as the mother tongue is not adulterated or extirpated. I shall not be like that shortsighted troglodyte who constantly looks only into and under himself; I feel that I belong to all Slavdom and that all Slavdom belongs to me![45]

Marek's panslavism is, however, merely emotional. It is sentimental Slav patriotism rather than programmatic Slav nationalism. It is also entirely linguocentric, which Kollár's Slav nationalism is not. In Kollár's conception the bonds are biological. In *Wechselseitigkeit* that biological bond is mysticized. Kollár's language here is that of ritual and, while it is still redolent of the Communion service, it also looks forward to the language of extremist nationalist movements like Hitler's: 'all Slavs are One Blood, One Body, One People [*Ein Blut, Ein Körper, Ein Volk*]; all their dialects are homogenous; the differences of cultivation [*Bildung*] within the Slav tribes are only differences of *degree* not *kind*' (W 119). So what may look like Marekesque emotionalism is not, for blood is really different from language. When he writes, 'What is Slav, wherever it is, is ours'[46] or his Terentian

'*Slavus sum nihil Slavici a me alienum esse puto*' (W 47), he is thinking biologically. On the other hand, he combines this biological nationalism with a convinced pursuit of Herderian *Humanität*. The epigram 'Horlič' (Enthusiast)
expresses that: 'Consider the nation only as a vessel of humanity/ and always
when you cry "Slav", let the echo of your cry be "human being"'.[47]

Herder gave Kollár a universalist ideal, but it was Turnvater Jahn, whose hatred for the French was of quite a different sort from Herder's emulative hostility,
and Moritz Arndt, and, in particular, the transmission of ideas such as theirs at the
Wartburgfest, that provided the primary impulse to Kollár's Slav nationalism. His
conception of the Slavs as one nation is strongly influenced by the
Burschenschaft's conception of the single German nation. Kollár attended the
Wartburg celebrations, which were held on 18 October 1817 to commemorate
three hundred years of Protestantism. He was impressed by the burning of anti-
nationalist and anti-*Turnverein* books, which hardly comports with his nascent
liberalism, and by the way religion and patriotism and young and old were all
united at the celebrations. But he was mainly impressed by the students' programme. For the sake of organised writing he summarizes that programme as issuing from the lips of a particular student by the bonfires on the Wartburg (P 261):

Every student must be not only a human being and an educated man, but also a German. He must free himself of egoism, provincialism, dialectism, and elevate himself
to the level of a whole nation. It is a disgrace for an educated student to be nothing but
a Saxon, a Hessian, a Franconian, a Swabian, a Prussian, an Austrian, a Bavarian, a
Hanoverian, a Swiss and so forth. May all our national dissection cease and let us be
one body, one German nation.

In 'O literárnej vzájemnosti' Kollár writes of that egoism. Egoism, he states, may
be personal, tribal, dialectal or national, and as egoism can blind an individual, so
it can social groups. That blindness is arrogance, arrogance such as he sees in
Germans and Magyars; Slav nationalism does not suffer from egoism, which does
not mean that it does not have benefits for the individual and for the dialect.

Belonging to a large nation will protect tribes; in other words, Czech or
Slovene culture is safer as a component of Slav culture than it would be if it were
a self-contained entity. Slav nationalism will protect individual dialects, will give
those dialects the responsibility that adheres to membership of a large nation. If a
large nation neglects its language, it is committing a sin against humanity because
it is concealing a large aspect of humanity – and, therefore, leaving it unculti-
vated. If, however, a small nation neglects its language, that is more forgivable,
since as a small nation, 'it cannot progress far in knowledge and art; indeed, in its
narrow confines, it must needs soon wither away. Thus a small nation would do
better, if it attached itself to the language of some larger nation, for only in a large
… nation can printed knowledge and art flourish … Only in a large nation can the
learned work successfully' (DV 14). The Slav nation is, then, a practical concept

which will ensure that all Slav tribes will be in a position to have a 'modern culture'. Only large, united nations, as homogenous as Kollár imagines the Slavs, are 'creators of new ages, teachers and bearers of culture' (W 82). Through cultural unity, Slav writers will be in a position to be 'national architects involved in the building of the temple of human culture' (W 85).

He takes the need for unity further in his contribution to *Hlasové*, which highlights the fact that Kollár fostered his Slav feeling and his notion of Reciprocity because he was a Slovak who found himself in a geopolitical situation where his own subdialect (his term) might be annihilated by the Magyars. Though by 1846 he may have been hanging on to his idea out of stubbornness as much as out of conviction, actually nothing had happened which might have made him imagine the Slovaks had a rosier future. What he writes in *Hlasové* also comports with Šafařík's reduction of the number of Slav tribes in his 1837 taxonomy, and because everything 'all-Slav' was sacred to Kollár, there is no reason to believe that is a coincidence: 'the more educated a nation, the fewer tribes it has or tolerates; a man or a tribe that sacrifices his or its life to a whole, lives and works in a whole and for a whole, has the greatest and finest life' (H 139). Slav cultural unity, Slav Reciprocity, will allow all Slavs full participation in European culture. One whole will be working within and for a greater whole.

Kollár first defines Reciprocity in his wild would-be scholarly work of 1830, *Rozpravy o jménech, počátkách i starožitnostech národu slávského a jeho kmenů* (Essays on the names, beginnings and antiquities of the Slav nation and its tribes). If Slavs, he writes there, wish to have a national literature and education or culture, they must dispense with atomization and instead cultivate 'national reciprocity'. He takes care to state immediately that Reciprocity has nothing to do with politics. Reciprocity means 'not a political, but a literary joining of all four chief Slav tribes; each Slav tribe would retain its dialect, but it would know of, buy and read the books and literature of other Slav tribes.'[48] He makes Reciprocity into a programme in 'O literárnej vzájemnosti'. The definition of Reciprocity here is the same as in *Rozpravy o jménech*, but now it has acquired a tinge of mysticality because of the liturgical term he uses in part of the definition: 'Reciprocity is, then, a communal taking unto oneself [the word used in *přijímanie*, Communion or accepting], a communal bestowal and consumption [*užívanie*]' (LV 36). Again here, the libertarian, anti-revolutionary Kollár emphasizes that he is concerned with cultural, not political, communion. Reciprocity, he writes, 'does not consist in the political unification of all Slavs or in any turbulent demagogical undertakings directed against governments or administrations; such undertakings result only in confusion and misfortune' (LV 38). The idea may not be political, but he is thinking politically. He does see benefits for existing governments issuing from his idea. He at least claims that Reciprocity will function as a political sop: 'risings and rebellions of Slavs against the foreign rulers under whose sceptre they live will cease, for with Reciprocity the desire for [political] association or unification with other Slavs will be quelled or weakened. They will have no reason for breaking away from their rulers, for everything that they could receive from a neighbour they will have at home' (LV 134).

In the longer German essay on Reciprocity Kollár makes the sop sound more positive for the smaller Slav tribes; on the other hand, he does suggest that not all rulers might be such that the products of Reciprocity could flourish under them. He also appears to be warning his readers of the danger of Russian hegemony (W 135):

under foreign, non-Slav, rulers, as long as they are tolerant, the weaker Slav tribes find a greater guarantee and security for the individual independence and perpetuance of their dialects, which, under a ruler of a different, mightier Slav dialect might, in accordance with the laws of attraction, be swallowed up by that dialect; or at least, the weaker dialect might fuse with it and, in the end, disappear.

The epigram 'Budoucnost' (The future), which states that when in the lifetime of the poet's grandchildren, people will not write in Polish, Russian, Czech or Serbian, but in Slavonic, may be interpreted, as it is by Vodička,[49] as looking forward to a time when there will be no more Slav dialects. On the other hand, the phrase 'po slovansky'[50] (either 'in Slavonic' or 'in the Slav manner') more probably means 'as conscious members of the Slav nation' and not as narrowly ('egoistically') Polish, Russian and so forth. Certainly, Kollár normally emphasizes that the individual literary dialects should and will be preserved. The last thing his Reciprocity should lead to is the creation of a single Slav literary language 'such as some people have started dreaming about' (LV 38). He points out that, when he uses the term Panslav, which he uses only in German, he means 'concerning and embracing all Slavs' (W 49). Elsewhere he writes: 'Each tribe will be a planet spinning around one sun, Slavia, following its own path, and yet Slavia will influence each tribe as the tribes will influence one other' (LV 136). The result will be that a Pole will not be just a Pole, but a 'Slavopole', every Russian a 'Slavorussian' and so on (LV 160).

The liturgical element in Slav Reciprocity is no doubt already visible in the sonnet of *Slávy dcera* where the poet constructs an all-Slav idol, where the head is Russia, the torso the Poles, the arms the Czechs and so forth. The whole of Europe might kneel before that idol. In one aspect of the Reciprocity programme in particular, however, the religious element consists not in pagan or pseudo-Christian ideals, but rather in esoteric ritual, or, perhaps more accurate, the sort of ritual associated with secret societies – of which there were several in Enlightenment Austria. The conscious Slav may undergo three degrees of initiation. A Slav in the first degree will know the four main living Slavonic dialects: Russian, Illyrian, Polish and Czechoslovak. In the second degree he will also take on smaller dialects, for example, Ukrainian on top of Russian or Slovene on top of Illyrian. In the third degree, the degree of the true Slav mystics, he will know all Slav dialects, living and dead. Since Kollár might well have been influenced by esoteric thinking, one might construe his conception of the Slav nation along the lines of the Spanish Cabalists, for whom the ten Sephiroth are 'the ten names most common to God and in their entirety they form his one great Name.'[51] Certainly a nation is sacred for Kollár.

What he, or indeed Šafařík, means by nation, *národ*, is not always at all clear. The Czech word itself was even less precise in the early nineteenth century than today. Certainly the nation (*národ*) is for Kollár a God-given institution or grouping (N 8). In *Dobré vlastnosti* Kollár defines *národ* as a 'community of people who are linked by the bond of one language and one set of customs and habits' (D 8), but since he is there referring to the Slav nation, that probably must be seen either as an historicising or utopian definition. His definition of the spirit of a nation appears to imply folk or collective memory: 'the spirit of a nation is nothing but the sum of all thoughts, knowledge, intentions, behaviours, customs and deeds which may be found among its various sons and daughters' (D 24). When he speaks of the need to belong to a large nation, because a small nation cannot be culturally successful (D 14), he uses *národ* for both the large and the small, but when he is discussing various groups of Slavs he writes of the Slav *národ* and each group he calls a *kmen* (tribe). Perhaps it should be the aim of every small *národ* to become a conscious *kmen*. In German (W), he generally uses *Nation* for *národ*, but he also uses *Volk*.

Šafařík uses *národ* like Kollár when he means the Slav nation, and also like Kollár , he sometimes uses it to mean the speakers of individual Slav dialects.[52] Once he uses the diminutive *národek* (SSI 7) for 'tribe', but normally he uses *kmen*, like Kollár. Given Romantic ideology and the Romantics' promotion of the oral tradition, it may not be inconsistent when Šafařík uses the adjective *národní* for 'of the common people' (SSI 27 or SSII 374). On the other hand, he does elsewhere use the then more normal term for 'folk', *prostonárodní* (SSI 264). Šafařík is, then, a little sloppier than Kollár in his use of *národ*. That is probably because, however strongly he believed in the Slav nation, he was not an ideologue like Kollár.

The nation is for Kollár not only a practical solution to the language problems of the Slavs in the Habsburg Monarchy; it is also an object of a highly civilized form of love. Nationalism (creative love of the goodness or specialness of one's nation) is a sign of high culture for Kollár, where patriotism (love of one's country) is typical of low culture. Slavness is a high culture, even if the Slav tribes have been slow to realize this. Slav Reciprocity will teach them that this is so. Kollár's logical point of departure in his discussion of nationalism is, 'One can always find a mother-country again, if she were lost: but one can never, anywhere, find one's nation and language again' (W 77). His words speak for themselves (W77–9):

The mother-country herself is dead soil, an alien object, a non-human being [Nicht-Mensch]: the nation is our blood, life, spirit, subjectivity. Love of one's mother-country is something instinctual, a blind natural drive. Love of one's nation and nationality is more a product of reason and cultivation [*Bildung*]. One may find love of mother-country even in plants and animals …. The coarse savage clings to his wretched, reeking, stinking, smoke-filled hut and his inhospitable wilderness more than an educated man is attached to his country house and park. … One should beware of dull, intolerant, hate-filled patriotism; it is often merely an excuse for the blackest deeds; beyond his fellow-countrymen the patriot knows only enemies; patriotism often serves only for the ostensible justification of injured human rights and for misused violence against weaker neighbours or fellow countrymen who belong to other peoples. In writing this I do not on any account wish to damn love of one's mother-country, but only to express a desire that love should abandon its Ancient character and assume the character of *Humanität* … Anyone who scorns his nation, fails to honour and love its language, neglects its spirit and character, can in any case not be receptive to any true patriotism. The smaller must be subordinate to the greater, nobler, love of one's country to love of one's nation.

Kollár certainly did love the Slav nation, but he had to instruct (as a hierophant in *Slávy dcera* and as a teacher in most of the prose I am dealing with here) his audience on what this nation was and, then, on how to love it.

He had to create a nation. He had to use a device which seems to be inherent in Central and East European nationalisms, that is: active atavism. By active atavism I mean a seeking out and even inventing of ancestors and ancestral characteristics. It consists in deriving remote history from the present, rather than deriving the present from history. At the beginning of *Wechselseitigkeit* (W 33), Kollár claims that this is happening naturally anyway: 'The Slav nation is striving to return to its original unity, as the plant which has flowered and borne fruit returns to its germ.' Šafařík had set about finding that germ in his two main works. The Slavs, Šafařík maintains, had entered Europe a few hundred years, perhaps even a thousand years, before Christ – and the reason they had left India was probably that it had been overpopulated (G 46). That is deriving history from the present and, at the same time, Šafařík has managed to sneak in an idea that, at the very beginning, circumstances *forced* Slavs to do things. They had reached the Danube by the fifth century b.c., although in the *Geschichte* Šafařík is not yet quite certain that Herodotus mentions the Slavs. The southern Slavs had probably been *forced* to go south by the Goths who had settled in Dacia in 250 a.d. (G 49). Thus does Šafařík provide a mood at the beginning of the *Geschichte* which will itself become a tool of interpretation (with a little help from Herder). Šafařík, however, always tries to be as scholarly as possible in his enthusiastic derivations.

One cannot say that of Kollár. Kollár uses common sense, but the common sense of a man with a goal rather than of an inquirer. For example, the Frankish ruler of the first Slav state, Samo (*reg.* 623?–658?), cannot have been a Frank, because his name sounds Slavonic to Kollár (it might, he suggests, be a hypocoristic form of Samoslav), because all twelve of his wives were clearly Slavs, because Dagobert's emissary, Sicharius, had not dared to appear before Samo in Frankish dress, and because no Frank could possibly have fought against the Franks.[53] Perhaps more interesting, as far as active atavism is concerned, is the way he calls patterns on the stone remains of an allegedly Great Moravian church 'slavesques' (C 25).

Slovak and Slav

Deriving remote history from the present using the emotional skills of active atavism, was a method encouraged by Kollár's and, indeed, Šafařík's status as a Slovak. Both had been brought up on Hungarian history and, through their religion, a certain amount of Czech history. Both were highly conscious that they were different from Magyars and from Czechs. For both the first solution seemed to be the Slav idea, since the Slavs must have a history. It is also significant that, in Hungary, Slovaks were frequently called simply Slavs. Indeed, at the beginning of Šafařík and Kollár's writing lives *slovenský* could mean Slav or Slovak. Kollár eventually used the word *slavjanský* for Slav, partly in the spirit of Slav Reciprocity, but partly to distinguish between Slav and Slovak. One of the two poems on the bandit hero, Jánošík, in Šafařík's one collection of verse, *Tatranská Múza s lírou Slovanskou* (Muse of the Tatras with Slavonic [?] lyre, Leutscha [Levoča], 1814) is called 'Slavení slovanských paholků' (In praise of Slav lads). Šafařík does seem to be celebrating their Slavness rather than their Slovakness, though, again, that is probably the same thing. There are occasionally indications in the *Geschichte* that Slav and Slovak are sometimes interchangeable or that Slovaks represent what is essentially Slav about the Slavs – at least at the back of the author's mind. An illuminating example of that is when he writes of the Slavs' 'thousand-year suffering' (G 92), a concept that, years later, would become a cliché of Slovak nationalists (see the Conclusion of this book).

Further support to the idea that Slovak and Slav would have been synonyms to our two authors in their early lives lies in the usage of the Hungarian word *tót*, which for most of the nineteenth century meant Slovak – and which socialism in Hungary expunged from dictionaries as a pejorative. Šafařík complains in a footnote that Magyar Piarist of Dalmatian parentage, András Dugonics (1740–1818), asserts that 'in Slavonic' means the same thing as 'in Romany' (and Slavonic is *tót*): '*tótosan vagy-is cigányosan esik*' (G 82). Similarly Kollár, as part of a diatribe against Magyars' disrespect for other nationalities, quotes a German work from 1799 where *tót* is translated as Slav. The quotation provides a source for the now infamous saying, *Tót nem ember*, a Slovak is not human: 'Tót nem ember: Bot nem fegyver, Kasa nem etel'. (The Slav is not a man; a cudgel is not a weapon; millet-pap is not food (V 429).) There is actually no serious evidence that this saying was used by Magyars of the time. In *Dobré vlastnosti* Kollár alludes to the same saying when he writes that there are people who do not consider Slavs human (DV 19). Twenty years later, however, Kollár translates *tót* as Slovak; again he is talking of Magyar calumny, this time in their ditties: 'El Magyar, all Buda meg – Haldogklik a buta Tót [The Magyar still lives; Buda still stands; the stupid Slovak is dying] etc.'; or 'Én szegény Tót legény, Mindeg krumpli etc.' [I'm a poor Slovak lad, Always potatoes …]' (C 52). There were, then, linguistic matters of fact which could draw Šafařík and Kollár to call themselves Slavs rather than Slovaks.

As Magyar politicians pressed more and more loudly for Hungarian to be the sole language of the administration, the judiciary and, rarely, all schooling, a nationally conscious Slovak intellectual might justly have seen himself as wedged between two threats of 'cultural imperialism', Magyar and Czech. Going for Slav could have appeared a sensible move. In Kollár's *Hlasové*, Šafařík describes the Slovaks and their language in a situation which would lend further support to the Slav idea, albeit he is here arguing against the new Slovak literary language and describing Slovakia thirty years after he had become a 'Slav'. He depicts the Slovaks as a collection of disparate settlements separated by mountains, which results in their language's being broken up into subdialects. Furthermore, they have practically no industry, and there is no Slovak capital city which could to some degree unify separate groups (H 86). The Slovaks themselves had clearly not been at all interested in their language. In his 1829 article on the Slovaks, Palacký quotes Jan Čaplovič (Johann Csaplovits, 1780–1847), who became a very active anti-Magyarizer: 'No people in Hungary is as indifferent to its mother tongue as the Slovaks. [The first Slovak novelist, Bajza, had said this some years earlier.] More intelligent Slovaks are ashamed of speaking Slovak and always use Latin or German. This is much less the case with Magyars, Rumanians and Serbs.' What is happening, Palacký writes, is that, once Slovaks have had a few years at school, they immediately want some white-collar job and so they join the Magyars and become the worst persecutors of their mother tongue. He says that the Slovak gentry had always sided with the Magyars, even when they had not known a word of Hungarian.[54] Vodička, perhaps rather dismissively, sees Kollár's adoption of the Slav idea as compensation for the state of his people and language, for the lack of a home-based nationalism.[55] Šmatlák sees the Slav idea as a means for Slovaks to overcome a sense of isolation and weakness and to join in not only Slav, but also European literary and philosophical activity.[56] No doubt Vodička and Šmatlák are right, but our two pan-Slavists were more active in their approach to the Slovaks than that. They created in their minds ideal Slovaks and an ideal Slovak language and made them models for other Slavs.

Kollár attributes the idea of Slav Reciprocity to Slovaks. Though he nowhere claims his ideas are original, he does have the habit of referring back to himself (or to a close fellow like Šafařík) in his writings, even of substantiating arguments on the basis of allusions to his own writings (as he is probably doing here). In this habit he reminds one of a later mythopoet, Sigmund Freud. 'Someone who already has something', states Kollár (LV 62), 'is usually content with what he has and does not consider expanding; when someone does not yet have anything, he wants a great deal, everything. At that time the Tatra Slovaks had almost nothing of their own in literature; that is why they were the first to open their arms to embrace all Slavs.' Just as they had nothing from a literary point of view, so they had nothing politically. He speaks of the Slovaks as having no political representation, though the context is the blight of 'Magyaromania'. In so doing he suggests that either (a) the Slav idea contained in itself a more or less hidden political element, or (b) that he hoped for political gains for the Slovaks through Slav Reciprocity. That point is supported by the anomalous, for him, use of the word *národ*: 'Anyone who knows the circumstances of the Slovaks in Hungary will understand that one can do nothing through the Diet, since the Slovaks have no deputies there. A nation [*národ*] which does not have the right to have a national will or the opportunity to express that will is not yet a nation' (C 51). Kollár does not blame only the Magyars. It is partly the Slovaks' own fault. In the following wistfully sarcastic remark one might see frustration or despair and interpret that as a further reason for his (and Šafařík's) looking outside Hungary for a cause to espouse. Though, here again, one could understand this as the, historically, typical Slav lot – in Kollár's eyes. 'Any bold national or human[57] consciousness seems sinful to us Slovaks, born and brought up in servitude as we are. To put ourselves in one and the same class with other human beings or nations and to ask for equal rights seem to us to be turning life and the world upside down. A human being is capable of dehumanizing himself that far!' (C 71) Even that could be changed. What could not be changed was the Slovaks' lack of history. 'The life of the Slovaks', Kollár writes (H 108), 'is without history …; a numbing emptiness and a spirit-destroying wasteland prevail in their past.' To create a history for the Slovaks, one has to find a history of the Slavs. Because the Slovaks are so backward, however, one might find some stage of the history of the Slavs in them.

In Šafařík's (actively atavistic) conception, Slovak was a language (dialect) which had, in Great Moravia, been a language of country houses and princely palaces. When, however, the Slovaks had lost their independence to the Magyars, their language had been relegated to peasant cottages (G 365). When one connects that with his attraction to the idea that Slovak is the sole remaining direct descendant of the Old Church Slavonic dialect (G 125) (and Šafařík maintains that there are words in Slovak which are in no other dialect than Church Slavonic and that the grammatical structures of the two dialects are remarkably similar [G 127]), one is faced with a major element of a myth which will make Slovakhood a very special Slavness. By *Slovanské starožitnosti* the implication is that proto-Slavonic survived longer in Slovakia than anywhere else, because, for geographical reasons, the Slavs who settled there during the *Völkerwanderung* remained out of contact with other European nations for longer than other Slav tribes (SSI 488). That was an important theory because it could help give the Slovaks self-confidence (since it came from as eminent a scholar as Šafařík), but also because it could be used in the argument against Slovak linguistic separatism. Since 'the Czech language ... is the daughter of Slovak' (H 124), there could not be any point in trying to recreate the mother; that would be, to use a Šafařík simile, like starting from the *Iliad* to get to the ABC. Linguistic active atavism was, then, unacceptable.

Once one begins to imagine Slovak as the oldest existing Slavonic dialect, one has to begin thinking of the Slovaks as the original Slavs, of Slovakia as the fountainhead of the Slav nation. The notion that the Slovaks were the only indigenous inhabitants of Upper Hungary (more or less today's Slovakia), that they had been there since the fourth century BC, and that all Slavs are descended from them appears to be the brain-child of the Slovak, Juraj Papánek (1738–1802), first made public in his *Historia gentis Slavae: De regno regibusque Slavorum* (1780); it stands to reason, by the way, that here again the terms Slav and Slovak are interchangeable. In the *Geschichte*, Šafařík writes of the Slovaks as 'these worthy descendants of the Carpathian and Danubian proto-Slavs' (G 358). He is initially a trifle more cautious in *Slovanské starožitnosti*. He does not go much further than to say that he considers that the Slavs were in the Carpathian area very early. The very name Carpathian comes from Slavonic *khrbet*, back, spine, thence ridge (G 77). The Russian chronicler, Nestor, maintains that the Slavs had been settled in the north of Europe, but that they also had a homeland south of the Tatras, from where they had been expelled by the Celts (Šafařík's interpretation of Nestor's *Volokh*), when they reunited with their compatriots in the North. Šafařík is delighted by Nestor's account, for it proved that the Tatras had been inhabited by proto-Slavs (SSI 259–62). A little later (SSI 271) he lends weight to the idea with vague onomastics: 'in ancient times, long before the arrival of the newer Slavs in today's Hungary and the neighbouring regions, Slavs had inhabited these lands [which we see from] the names of mountains, rivers, lakes and towns and from the remnants of Slavonic nations [*sic*] which were in evidence in the foothills of the Tatras under the names Satags and ... Sarmatians in the fourth and fifth centuries.' Then he begins rationally to speculate on that and, concerning the Celts' driving the Slavs back over the Tatras: 'as is always the case in such population movements, some Slavs remained, settled on the southern slopes of the Tatras, then in the basins of the Vaag, Hron, Ipeľ, Sajava, Hernad, Torisa, Ondava and upper Tisza, in these Arcadian vales' (SSI 283).

Šafařík is a great patriot as well as a Slav nationalist, though his patriotism, is based on increasing nostalgia and the fact that he had virtually completely forgotten his Gömör County dialect. Predictably enough, Kollár fully embraced the notion that the Tatras were the primal European homeland of the Slavs, and he appended his own frills (LV 62): 'From a grammatical and geographical viewpoint, their dialects lie at the central point of all Slav dialects: for the Tatras are the birthplace and cradle of all Slavs. That is why the idea of Reciprocity, if it did not arise there first, at least set down the fastest and deepest roots among the Slovaks of Hungary.'

It is clear that the linguistic Czechoslovakism Kollár and, to a far lesser degree, Šafařík pursued was Reciprocity in miniature: or it was a model for Reciprocity. For the history-less, language-less Slovaks becoming a Czechoslovak and not remaining mere Slovaks (cf. becoming a Slavopole and not remaining a mere Pole) made a Slovak part of an established literary community and thus theoretically gave him access to Czech books and libraries and publishers and, thus, easier access to the rest of the Slav world *via* Prague. (There was no Slovak [Czechoslovak] public library in Hungary in the period I am concerned with.) Czechoslovakism also made the Slovak part of a culture which did have a history and part of a nation which fewer than two centuries earlier had, even in the grimmest Revivalist accounts of the recent past, had its own high culture. If Czechoslovakism could work there was no reason why the vaster Slav Reciprocity should not work. If linguistic Czechoslovakism failed, there was not much hope for Reciprocity. Hence the ire with which Kollár conducted his campaign in *Hlasové* against the linguistic separatist Štúr and his fellows. Šafařík, who had in the *Geschichte* recognized Slovak as a separate dialect of Slavonic, began talking of Czechoslovak in *Slovanské starožitnosti*.

Kollár reports a semi-fictional conversation held in Padua where the advantages of Slovak declensions and the disadvantages of colloquial Czech were discussed. Kollár's point is that Czechoslovak will ensure the survival of Czech and Slovak literary culture: 'the main question is Reciprocity and unity, for, if our dialects and literatures continue to fragment, what will become of us? What will become of the Czechs? What of the Slovaks? I would be the first to sense the logical and aesthetic priority of Slovak over Czech, but I should rather have *something* than *nothing*' (C 157–58). The 'logical' alludes to the primacy of Slovak among Slav languages. Kollár constantly complains about the superabundance of *i* sounds in Czech (*iikání*), dislikes the Czech long *u* (*uukání*), and the indistinctness of gender-markers in certain noun and adjective types. When he reads a Czech translation of the *Iliad* he is so shocked by all the *i* sounds that he declares the translator, Jan B. Josef Vlček (Vlčkovský), 'an enemy of the nation'

(C 245). Kollár sees a single Czechoslovak language as a means of protection for the Slovaks against the Magyars as he sees the Slavonic cultural union as a protection against the dominance of German culture – and against English philistinism. In his conception of Czechoslovak he advocates Reciprocity (C 246): 'Slovak also has its disorders, its cacophonies and endless variants, but we want a *Slovak Czech* and a *Czech Slovak* which would interpenetrate each other, enrich and adorn each other.' Šafařík points out that a Slovak, Jesenský (Pavel Iessenius), had worked on the Bohemian Brethren translation of the Bible, and holds up the Czech of that Bible as the model for modern writers, 'that artistically polished, supple, most noble, resonant, rich, precious and delightful literary language' (H 70–1). Kollár pleads the same, in *Hlasové* and elsewhere. Another argument is that, during the Counter-Reformation, the Slovaks had kept Czech going by printing and reading Czech books. There is some truth in that, though the notion contains the myth necessary to most National Revivals: that before the Revivalists had got to work there had been a period of literary or linguistic stagnation. Kollár and Šafařík's conviction as Protestants that the Czech literary language had served Slovaks well for several hundred years played a role in their battle. It did not help their cause in Slovakia itself that Štúr and his confederates were also Protestant.

The origins and extent of Slavdom

Whether or not the Slovaks were the original Slavs was irrelevant to an important aspect of Šafařík and Kollár's enterprise, that is: the proving of the historical re-spectability of the Slav nation. Not much more about the origins of the Slavonic tribe of the Indo-European group is known today than in the time of Kollár and Šafařík. Today's scholars accept Procopius's account (*De bello Gothico*) that Slavs had been involved in Belisarius's military operations against Rome and Jordanis's counting of the Veneti among the Slavs (*Gethica*), only that it is now thought that Slavs were not called Veneti until round about AD 500. It does seem that the Slavs moved to the Ukraine from the West and crossed the Danube from the North. In all probability they formed themselves as a distinct Slav tribe some-where South East of the Baltic. There does not seem to have been a recognizable cultural unit which one could call Old Slav much before the fifth century AD. What was Czechoslovakia seems to have been settled at the end of the fifth or beginning of the sixth centuries from the South East, from the Eastern Carpathians and from the Danube Basin.[58] This account is a sober account which does not mean that Šafařík's more glamorous version does not still have its adher-ents. The patriotic Czecho-American, Francis Dvornik, still largely follows Šafařík. He still hopes that Herodotus's Scythian ploughmen were Slavs, and he believes the Budini in the Driester, Bug, Dnieper area were probably Slavs;[59] Šafařík doubted that in his *Geschichte*, but was certain of it in *Slovanské starožitnosti*.

With his *Slovanské starožitnosti* Šafařík intended to create a shield for the Slavs against the Germans.[60] Šafařík believes that the Slavs came from India, while their constant neighbours, the Germans, came from Iran. One can, he avers, easily recognize that by comparing Slavonic with Sanscrit and German with Persian (G 46). This forms an essential starting point for Šafařík and Kollár's myth of the Slavs. By the time they were writing a great deal was known in Europe about Indian culture (though at the time of the *Geschichte*, Šafařík had not read much about it; he relied on Polish scholars), and Indian religion, because it was so sophisticated, seemed to our mythopoets the ideal sort of paganism for the Slavs to have had, since it was civilised paganism. Šafařík and Kollár did not know anything about the prehistorical unity of Indo-European religions; they espoused a belief because it appealed to them emotionally and because it seemed to comport with the scholars' establishment of an Indo-European (Indo-Germanic) group of languages. Apart from early mentions of the Slavs as Veneti or Heneti, Šafařík does not in his *Geschichte* speculate on the various possible testimonies to Slav culture. He writes that what is clear is that the Slavs had spread over the whole of northern and eastern Europe in the sixth and seventh centuries AD, and that they had frequently waged war with their neighbours (G 47). That last statement will later be revised; war-like Slavs do not accord with the myth. The Slavs, Šafařík continues, have always been split up into little tribes and had therefore had various names. There we notice active atavism, deriving the historical state from the present state of affairs. Kollár, as one would by now expect, goes to town on the links between Indian and Old Slavonic religion. For example, the black dress of the inhabitants of the island of Velja (that is, Krk) is linked with the worship of the Slavonic god Veles, and the Indian Krishna with *černý* (black); Krishna is further linked with *krásný* (beautiful).

When he is writing *Slovanské starožitnosti*, Šafařík is no longer so concerned with the Slavs' Indian origins. He seeks primarily to show that they were proto-Europeans of the North. If they came from the East, they must have come at the same time as other European nations. If they are not known to Greek and Latin writers by the name Slav or by any of the names of the subtribes, one cannot assume that they came from their Asian home later than the other Indo-Europeans. If they had, the invasion of a large nation like the Slavs would have caused such a commotion that it would have been recorded by Ancient writers. The number of Celtic words in Slavonic and the number of Slavonic words in Gothic prove the Slavs' prehistoric inhabitation of Europe (SSI 63). Kollár takes Šafařík's assertions further and makes the Slavs the autochthonous inhabitants of central Europe (C 256): 'history and geography, language and customs and

thousands of other circumstances prove incontravertibly that in the most ancient
of times, before the Romans and Celts, the Wendo-Slavs inhabited not only all
upper Italy, Venetia and Lombardy, but also Switzerland, the Tyrol, part of
Bavaria, Raetia and Noricum, and that the Italian tree of life has its roots in Slav
soil.' Later he contradicts this somewhat by saying that the Slavs and Celts were
joint original inhabitants of Switzerland.[61]

The assertion that the Venedi, Vinidi, Vilti, were Slavs is essential to
Šafařík's argument. (Dobrovský had denied the Venedi were Slavs.) In the
Geschichte he says that the Veneti or Vindi inhabited the same areas as the Slavs,
but were not racially the same as the Slavs, and he maintains that Vindi is the
same word as Hindi or Hindu (G 47–8). Only a few pages later, however, he asserts that the area between the Vistula and the Elbe was inhabited by a Slav tribe
called the Vinidi or Vendi (G 52). In *Slovanské starožitnosti* they are completely
identified with the Slavs. Even Tacitus wrote 'about our forebears, the Venedi'
(SSI 138). For Kollár, the Slav Venedi had founded and named Venice and
Venetia (C 82). Šafařík asserts that the Veneti had settled in areas of the Low
Countries and England between AD 450 and 550 (SSII 588). Kollár quotes from
an article, 'De Slavis et Lecho', by one J. T. Seger (1772), who had found a good
number of what he considered Slav names in Holland (Hunna, Zwolle, Wilta and
so forth). And Kollár himself links *Belge, Belgium* with *Volga, Bolgar*, in other
words asserts a blood relationship between the Belgians and Bulgarians (V 150-
52). Šafařík demonstrates, on the basis of place-names, the presence of the Slav
Venedi from the Ganges to Wales. Gwent and Gwyneth are names which clearly
reveal their original Slav inhabitants (SSI 184). The Venedi/Veleti are also responsible for the names Wilton and Wiltshire (SSII 574) – here I am reminded of
the sixteenth-century Czech traveller in England, Šašek z Bířkova, who noted in
the area around Salisbury that the inhabitants had frequently reverted to paganism. Kollár asserts that one could tell by the name of that ancient Mercian
streaker, Lady Godiva, that she was a Slav and, referring to Šafařík, speaks of
Windermere and Windsor as originally Slav settlements (V 48).

On the other tribes sometimes linked with the Slavs I shall just summarize
Šafařík's contentions. The Anti were Slavs, but not the Alani. The Slavs fought in
league with the Romans against the Huns but, on the other hand, some writers
confuse the Huns with the Slavs. Sometimes the Slavs were allies of the Huns
and, involuntarily, of the Avars. (That last point is probably true.) In the
Geschichte the Jazygs are, at one point, Slavs and, at another, the same as
Sarmatians and Alani. One has to go into a little more detail with the Sarmatians.
Šafařík never asserts that they were Slavs, but that they were allies of the Slavs in
the third century AD (G 49). By innuendo he identifies the Sarmatians and
Scythians with the Magyars. At the beginning of the sixth century the Slavs, he
states, lived a settled life like Greeks, Romans, Celts or Germans, that their way

of life had nothing to do with nomadic tribes like the Sarmatians and Scythians (he usually refers to Magyars as nomads or simply as Asiatics), 'who constantly crouched under felt tents or wandered about from pasture to pasture on carts or horseback, not desiring anything but pillage and plunder' (SSI 73–4). The Sarmatians had in AD 359 attacked the Emperor Constantine's forces in Peterwardein and their battle-cry had been *mar ha, mar ha*, which Šafařík imagines is the Slavonic *mor ho, mor ho* (G 51), which did, indeed, become a Slovak battle cry in the nineteenth and twentieth centuries largely because of a poem by Samo Chalupka (1812–83). Later, Šafařík inveighs against Dugonics for vilifying the Slavs in asserting that the Hungarian words *Morva* (Moravia) and *marha* (cow, cattle) were cognate, indeed fundamentally the same (G 82). Then, to add to the irony of it, Šafařík suggests that *Morrha* might be the other Moravia, an area in Thrace around the Rhodope Mountains (SSII 656). I do not want to draw any conclusion, but I would add that in the oral tradition of interwar Slovak intellectuals the battle-cry *mor ho* was simply a version of Hungarian *marha*. (My colleague, László Péter, informs me that a Hungarian verb exists, *lemarházni*, to call someone a *marha*.)

A truly serious verbal problem for Šafařík was the derivation of the appellation, Slav (*Slovan, Slavjan*). For Kollár there was no problem. It was quite clear to him as mythopoet that it was cognate and synonymous with *sláva*, glory, fame.[62] That is asserted in *Slávy dcera* and *Rozpravy o jménech* and he devoted a whole study to the question, *Sláva bohyně a původní jméno Slávů čili Slavjanů* (The goddess Slava and the original name of the Slavs, Pest, 1839). Šafařík's starting point is that it is clear that the Slavs had always called themselves Slavs, and he cites the Slovenes (*Slovenci*) and Slovaks (*Slováci*) (G 49), and later he mentions that the Danube between Pressburg and Komárom marked the frontier between the Slovaks and vestiges of Slovenes. He is fascinated by the apparent coincidence that only these two tribes had retained this name (G 286). His argument for the antiquity of the name could have been supported by the facts that both Slovaks and Slovenes had been for centuries primarily inhabitants of isolated mountainous or hilly areas, and that they were both on the frontiers of the Roman Empire. Šafařík does not believe that the name is derived from *sláva* or from *slove/slouti* (to be called), although he recognises that this derivation has been common since the fourteenth-century chronicler, Přibík Pulkava z Radenína (SSII 46). He admits that the names of conquered peoples often acquired pejorative meanings and so it is just possible that the Greeks or Romans had called the Slavs slaves. In other words, since the Greeks and Romans had made Slavs their slaves, they had adopted the name the conquered people had given themselves. 'Slave' might, then, be derived from 'Slav' (SSI 64). Šafařík's own idea is based on an analogy with the names of Slav tribes; Poles take their name from *pole* (field) and Croats (*Hrvati*) from mountains or ridges. Thus the appellation Slav might well be cognate with Lithuanian *sallava* or Latvian *sala* (island, holm) (SSII 46). The derivation remains unsolved. Though still today the folk derivation *slovo*, (word, thus speaker of our language) in contrast to *Němec* (German) from *němý* (mute) obtains among scholars. Šafařík repeats this folk etymology, *Němec-Slovan*, in the *Geschichte*, but adds that *Němec* could mean either 'the mute one' or the nameless (*beze jména*) one (G 49). In *Slovanské starožitnosti* he links it with a tribe called Nemetes mentioned by Julius Caesar and Tacitus (SSI 65, 44). He was no doubt encouraged to suggest that largely because it would help attest the antiquity of the Slavs (they used such an old label), but partly because the Hungarian word of Slavonic origin for a German is *német*.

Šafařík's derivation of *Vlach* as an old word for 'stranger' (G 49) is probably more or less correct; he asserts that the word originally meant 'Celt' in Slavonic and only later meant 'Romance' (and much later, Italian). The label survives in toponyms like Wales, the Valais and Wallachia, and its origin may lie in an Indo-European word denoting practitioners of transhumance. (Actually, *Vlach/Valach* simply means stranger from the South, as *tót*, Dutch, *deutsch* means stranger from the North.) Again, Šafařík's assertion that it originally meant Celt in Slavonic serves propagandistically to attest to the antiquity of Slav settlements in Europe.

In the change of meaning of *Vlach* we have a narrative element in the myth. More important for the myth is to show that the ancient, pre-Christian Slavs were not savages. This had already been demonstrated by the 'ancient' manuscripts forged and 'discovered' by Václav Hanka (1791–1861) and others (from 1816 to 1819), in which both Kollár and Šafařík (but also the far more sceptical Palacký) firmly believed. One of the 'discoverers', and possibly co-forgers, Josef Linda (1789–1834), had written a novel depicting the glorious bucolic life of the pagan Slavs, *Záře nad pohanstvem* (Dawn over heathendom, 1818) and, though it went virtually unnoticed by patriots, its existence documents the Czechs' sense that they needed to demonstrate the non-savagery of their ancestors for the sake of national pride. Untouched by Chateaubriand's depictions of Red Indians' life of bliss, Šafařík denies that, before they had been converted to Christianity, the Slavs had been mere animals indistinguishable 'from American and African savages' (SSI 583). 'They were never', Šafařík writes in the *Geschichte*, 'so savage that one could count them among the barbarian nations' (G 54). Furthermore, 'as constant neighbours of the Greeks, whose colonies spread as far as the Black Sea, the Slavs achieved their degree of civilization more or less contemporaneously with the Greeks, even if in their own individual fashion (G 56)'. The Forged Manuscripts, the Russian Igor lay, the folk songs collected by Vuk Karadžić and the immense vocabulary of the first Slav translations of the Bible manifest a literary culture which it must have taken centuries to create (G 60).

One of the key proofs of the antiquity of Slav civilization is the fact that it had towns. Both Šafařík and Kollár mention these towns frequently. Like so many other elements in their myth, they derive the importance of these towns in the first place from Herder, who wrote: 'On the Baltic from Lübeck upwards they built sea-trading towns, among which was the Slav Amsterdam, Vineta on the island of Rügen. ... On the Dnieper they built Kiev, on the Volchov Novgorod, which both soon became flourishing centres of trade.'[63] For our two Slovak authors this was important because it contrasted the Slavs with the nomadic Magyars. Its mythic significance was further increased by the fact that there were virtually no Slovak towns in Hungary; towns in Upper Hungary tended to be German or, at best, inhabited by *Handrburci*, speakers of Germanized Slovak. Given that both our Slovaks write in Czech, it may also have mattered that Prague was at the time largely German and many other large towns in the Bohemian Lands almost entirely German, for example, Brno (Brünn), Ústí (Aussig) or Jihlava (Iglau). Šafařík and Kollár's Protestantism also led them, particularly Kollár, to see the industrial town as the manufacturer of decent, hard-working, civilized human bliss.

To prove the antiquity of the Slavs our mythopoets had also to prove the antiquity of Slavonic and, if possible, to demonstrate its superiority to other languages. The most evident way to do that was to compare Slavonic with Ancient Greek. Šafařík compares the way Greek was split into various dialects with the present state of Slavonic (G 98). That becomes a central element in Kollár's 'O literárnej vzájemnosti', where he speaks of the Ionian, Aeolian, Doric and Attic dialects all deriving from the proto-Greek of Phthiotis in Thessaly – four dialects, like the four dialects he sees in Slavonic. In Homer, he claims, traces of all four dialects are to be found (LV 50–4); therefore Homer had practised Hellenic linguistic Reciprocity. Thus Kollár can demonstrate the correctness of his programme on the basis of the older Western culture. For Kollár there are signs that ancient and present-day Slav culture are close to the Greek (W 59): 'The correspondence and similarity between the Slavs and the Greeks is altogether remarkable, and that is not only with respect to the dialects, but also to other matters, for example in the *music* of their folksongs ...; in the *names* of persons, for example, *Heracles* = Jaroslav; *Charicles* = Miloslav; *Kleopatra* = Vlastislava, and so on. ... Someone as early as Ulrich von Hutten remarked in his *App. ad Tacit. Germ.*: "Ingenia Slavorum habent sane Graecum quiddam referentia."' Šafařík even adapts the Greek meaning of the term barbarian in *Slovanské starožitnosti* to mean non-Slavonic, thus implicitly aligning Slavonic with Greek (*barbarské čili cizojazyčné*, SSI 26).

Slavonic is, however, also better than Greek. Šafařík indulges in philological mythopoeia when he declares Slavonic more fully developed than Greek or German. What he writes manifests a confusion unusual for Šafařík: 'Slav declensions, because they do not use the article, but replace it by attaching inflexional suffixes, are more complete than Greek or German.' (G 76) Perhaps not entirely consistently, he goes on: 'from its declension without articles and conjugation without stem-changes, its pure, stable vocalic endings and precisely established quantity, independent of any logical word-stress, from all this one perceives the suitability of Slavonic for opera and for Classical metres' (G 78). I do not know whether it is conscious mythopoeia when Šafařík writes of Slavonic as particularly 'old, precise and rich' (SSI 27), or when he claims that the fact that Slavonic is so 'neat and rich' is a persuasive witness to the length of time the Slavs had been in Europe (SSI 62). He is neither consciously mythopoeic nor, indeed, really aware of what he is maintaining when he writes that Russian has a completely free word-order or that one can place a word wherever it is most natural for the word-order (*sic*); a few sentences later he claims that word order is only 'more or less free' (G 163–4).

If they are setting about creating a Slav nation (or asserting that such a thing exists) mainly on the basis of language, it is clear that Šafařík and Kollár have to take a position on purism. Purism may play an important role in Reciprocity, and it might be a useful instrument for ensuring the purity of the myth-base and as a teaching aid in the educative mission of their 'Slavism'. In the *Geschichte*, Šafařík praises the achievements of purism in Russian, Polish and Czech; the least pure Slav dialects are for him those whose speakers have been longest under non-Slav domination (G 78). He finds it hard, however, to be an out-and-out purist, even in the *Geschichte*. Thus he writes (G 407) of Polish in the sixteenth century, that it 'imported many Italian and some Turkish words, which, however, since they were single, scattered loan words, did not at all alter the general character of the language; in part, these words suppressed better native words.' When he does not yet know anything about Bulgarian, he states the only Slavonic dialect to have the definite article is Germanified Sorbian (G 76). Later on in the book, when his knowledge about Bulgarian has increased through his reading, he disapproves. For the myth it is important that Šafařík regards change as suffering (G 231):

Over the years [Bulgarian] has suffered in its grammatical structure, in its fundamentals, the greatest changes and transformations of any Slavonic language. It has, for example, an article which it places at the end of words, like Romanian or Albanian. ... This de-Slavicization finds its most natural explanation in the normal view: that the Bulgarians are a mixture of Slavs, Romanians and Tatars and that the language of the Slavs separated [sic] from Romanian and Tatar and assumed foreign elements.

Bulgarian contrasts strongly with Slovak which had retained its pure Slavness. In *Slovanské starožitnosti* (SSI 488–9) Šafařík formulates a justification for purist doctrine: one notices that it is based on the idea of naturalness, for language constituted for the Romantic thinker the expression of those natural configurations of people they called nations:

Many examples confirm that, when one language mixes with others, its free flow stops and all its forms become as if dead and petrified and cease to burst into flower in the same manner as they had done previously. On the other hand, if a precise language follows its natural course in its forms or grammatical structure, it changes faster and more frequently … Slavonic has gone its own way, has freely developed from itself and, like a fresh, vigorous tree, it has sprouted many branches, leaves, blossoms and fruit.

If Slavonic has an impact on other languages, that can have only a positive result. Thus, claims Šafařík, Slavonic softened German of the Saxon dialect and made the language of Luther's Bible so superior to other forms of German (an idea he has from Kopitar) (G 452). Similarly, when he is talking about Finno-Ugric languages, and thinking mainly of Hungarian, he suddenly maintains: 'as today, so from the earliest of times, human languages have always enriched themselves by taking words from foreign languages' (SSI 330). He cannot be an out-and-out purist, for 'only the poor languages of savages are free of all foreign material' (SSI 528). Kollár advocates a panslav purism which is in keeping with his own linguistic practice. It is part of Slav Reciprocity. 'Each dialect will thus receive pure-Slav cultivation and true-Slav form; it will be all the more active in avoiding barbarisms [cizomluv], riddling out foreign words and turns of phrase, in shedding Latinisms, Germanisms, Tatarisms, Gallicisms, etc., and enriching itself from true Slav sources' (LV 130). For him a truly panslav language is one which any other Slav could understand; to achieve that each Slav dialect must use only Slav words. 'Foreign words alienate Slav from Slav, push tribe away from tribe, separate dialect from dialect' (LV 154).

Practical Slavness

Where one could understand what Šafařík and Kollár understood by the Slav language, the notion of a Slav literature was, on the surface, problematical. In the case of Šafařík it was a matter of theoretical appropriation; thus, Nestor was 'our' writer (G 47). Kollár saw the need for a Slav literature because he considered the Slavs aesthetically backward (W 97): 'We Slavs are giants in geographical analysis and on maps, but dwarfs in art and literature.' He does not doubt that the Slavs have artistic talent, as he ascertains when he sees Schiavone's pictures; he recognizes 'the capacity of our nation to work not only with the plough in agriculture, but also with the brush in painting' (C 12). The talent may be there, but, without Slav Reciprocity, he is afraid for the future of Slav art. In literature as in all culture, the Slavs must abandon their tribalism. Czech or Polish literature is not enough by itself, however fervently written. 'Those one-sided days are past; the spirit of today's Slavdom entrusts us with another, greater duty, that is to create a reciprocal panslav literature' (LV 44). In *Weschselseitigkeit* he speaks of a 'communal national literature' (W 37), and he reproaches Pushkin, Mickiewicz and Milutinović for being Slav poets who had, unfortunately, failed to be inspired by Slav Reciprocity. Kollár points mockingly to the Magyars, who, he claims, are in need of just such Reciprocity (LV 128): 'the Magyars, being a small nation, even go to other continents, into Asia, to Mongols, Tibetans and so forth, in order to find their ancestors and brothers or a nation on a par with them, and thus to gain a greater terrain and public for their literature.'

To recreate the cultural unity of the past it was necessary to establish panslav institutions. In Chapter 7 of his *Geschichte* Šafařík calls for more schools, libraries, museums, learned societies and literary critical journals as vital for the support of Slav literature. Kollár goes into far more detail. Bookshops containing works in Slav dialects other than the local should be set up in all large Slav cities: Prague, Vienna (*sic*), Pest (*sic*), Brno (*sic*), Belgrade, Zagreb, Lemberg (Lwów, Lviv), Cracow, Warsaw, St Petersburg. Public and private libraries should be established containing books in all Slav dialects, particularly grammars and dictionaries. Comparative grammars and dictionaries of all dialects should be compiled. Folk-songs and proverbs should be collected and published, since in the oral tradition, he imagined, the distinctions between Slav dialects are not as great as in literary dialects. Books should be translated from one dialect into another. Chairs of Slav dialects should be set up at universities, and departments at schools. Learned Slavs should travel to areas inhabited by speakers of other Slav dialects and, ideally, they should publish accounts of their travels. A literary periodical should be founded, which would publish in all dialects. Only with such institutions can a Slav literature be promoted.

It is certainly thinkable that Kollár was particularly keen on 'literary reciprocity', not so much because of Enlightenment ideology as of his Protestant faith in the benefit that the written word (the Scriptures) has for the moral welfare of the common people. Certainly Šafařík also looks Protestant when he writes (SSII 496) the following of the Bulgarian Slavs who had abandoned the Christianity that they had been brought by Greek missionaries: 'on account of a lack of reading and teaching in Slavonic they were slipping back into heathen blindness and, on top of that, moaning under the yoke of the heathen rulers of Bulgaria.'

Herder's picture of the Slavs and its impact on Šafařík and Kollár

Almost everything Šafařík and Kollár write about the Slav character can be derived directly or indirectly from Herder's account in *Ideen zur Philosophie der Geschichte*. When Šafařík first gives a general characterization in his *Geschichte*, he acknowledges Herder as his source (G 58). First, I shall take the characteristics which Herder places in history, and then I shall deal with permanent character traits. Even in the historical part, he makes Slavs the embodiments of Christian suffering humanity.

When the Slavs had gone to war with the Goths, Huns or Bulgars (Bugri), they had 'for the most part' done so only as auxiliaries or servants (*mitgezogene helfende oder dienende Völker*). The Slavs had never been a nation of warfarers and adventurers 'like the Germans', who had wronged them more than any other nation. They were enemies of robbery and pillage. They had suffered from 'wars of oppression' ever since Charlemagne, and what the Franks had begun, the Saxons completed. The Germanic tribes of the North had annihilated their Baltic trade and the Danes had destroyed their city of Vineta. The remnants of the Slavs in Germany resemble what 'the Spaniards made out of the Peruvians'. The Slavs only settled in areas which had been abandoned by other peoples. In Germany, Herder says, mainly they were miners, smelters and casters of metals, salt producers, linen makers (*verfertigten Leinwand*), mead-brewers and fruit-growers.[64]

The more general charactertistics Herder attributes to the Slavs are essentially those attributable to any peasant group. He tells us that they had been herdsmen and farmers. They loved agriculture (*liebten die Landwirtschaft*), and domestic work, loved to lay in plenty of stock in corn and animals; they were also fond of various crafts (*häusliche Künste*), and they traded successfully with what they produced. They were quiet, industrious, peace-loving, munificent (*mildtätig*), hospitable to the point of recklessness, lovers of the freedom of country living, and they led a merry musical life. They were also submissive and obedient. All their virtues, however, had not preserved them from oppression, but rather had contributed to their being oppressed. When they had been forced to fight, the Slavs had shown no lack of courage. What Herder has done, then, is provide the model for a Slav nationalist myth.

Herder does not consider the Slavs one nation. He talks of the Slav peoples (*Völker*) and nations (*Nationen*). One can see, however, how Herder's characterization would have appealed especially to two Slovaks, whose compatriots really were almost only peasants. In *Dobré vlastnosti*, Kollár distils Herder's picture into five fundamental virtues, two of which are not mentioned by Herder and one of which (tolerance) is an interpretation, such as one would expect of an 'enlightened' Protestant – even if he did loathe Voltaire. In the manner by which he introduces the five Slav virtues one notices straightaway that he states (like Herder) that these were their virtues in the past, as they are now. In other words, he is again practising active atavism, to which, however, Herder's little essay had encouraged him. Herder actually makes a point of saying that one would have thought that, after so many years of oppression, the Slav character would have changed, the Slavs would have become base, cunning curs. But they had not, maintains Herder; they retain the virtues they had had since the days of Charlemagne. Kollár's words run as follows (DV 9):

And what, then, are the pleasant things and the characteristics which particularly distinguish the Slav nation from all other nations, which we see in the Slavs at least to a higher degree than in the others, and which we may consider their hereditary adornments and treasures? They are the following five characteristics: *piety, diligence, innocent merriness, love of their language and tolerance towards other nations.*

The quality of piety, which is alien to Herder's picture, could also be seen as a typical Slovak peasant quality. On top of that, we have Kollár's apparently automatic tendency to make things religious; that has nothing to do with his being a parson. It does comport with the fact that his betrothed was the apparently pious daughter of a parson and with his verse devotion to her and the Slav idea. Even 'love of their language' could be taken as an interpretation of 'love of rustic freedom' or 'the freedom of the countryside', and not simply as a product of Kollár's nationalist propaganda. The addition of 'innocent' to the concept merriness accords with the piety but, more important, with his perception of his Friederike Schmidt (whom he, for some reason, called Wilhemine or Mína, although she was baptized Johanna Augusta Friederike) and, then, of Slav girls in general. It also accords with Kollár's didacticism. Šafařík takes over unacknowledged (in the text (G 86), but they had corresponded about it) Kollár's first distillation of Herder: 'Amongst the *basic characteristics* of the Slav nation as a whole are: *a religious frame of mind, a love of work, simple, sincere merriness, love of their native language* and *tolerance.*' The two minor differences are the replacing of 'innocent' with the less straightlaced and more neo-Classically or even Romantically bucolic 'simple, sincere' and the omission of 'towards other nations' after 'tolerance', which serves to make the Slavs more generally libertarian or liberal. Later on in *Dobré vlastnosti*, Kollár increases the number of Slav characteristics (for him less important traits than the first five) and the following, with the exception of the last (friendship), also essentially reflects Herder's picture: 'their renowned hospitality ... chastity [*čistotu*] and sense of shame ... moderation, modesty, domesticity and simplicity of manners; ... profound respect and esteem for old age; ... faithfully and loyally they preserve unto death the bond of friendship, which is publicly blessed in church like matrimony' (DV 16–17). I believe the last element to be a complete invention, unless Kollár is making South Slav blood-brotherhood general. The 'respect for old age' is not in Herder, but again may be a general peasant characteristic.

Apart from the direct quotation in Šafařík's *Geschichte*, the closest one comes to a comprehensive distillation of Herder appears in *Slovanské starožitnosti*, when the author is comparing the Slavs with the Sarmatians. The only element not in Herder is the characterization of the Slav manner of fighting (SSI 407–8):

The Slavs had resided in Europe from the very beginning of their history; they were gentle, peace-loving people who inhabited permanent settlements, houses, villages and towns; they earned their living by agriculture, husbandry [*hospodářstvím*] and trade; they fought on foot and used shields. ... The Slavs were sons of their European primal motherland; they loved their country and cultivated it in peace and quiet; therefore, too, in all the terrible tempests of time, in the persistent teeming and surging of Eastern and Western nations over their land, the Slavs remained in their country and multiplied.

Šafařík's emphasis on the permanence of their settlements fits in with his general implied contrasts of the Slovaks with the bedouin Magyars. In this passage one also notices the urgency of his message that the Slavs were proto-Europeans.

An essential element of the myth of Slavness in Šafařík and Kollár lies in the perception of the Slavs as northern Europeans. (The fact that this could be said to be true is irrelevant to the myth.) This perception is probably based on fundamentally racist grounds. Kollár, however, links even this with Slav piety, for it was when the Slavs were in Northern lands, before the Slavs were Christians, that they were known among foreigners for their great piety (DV 9). In his discussion of Slav piety in *Dobré vlastnosti*, the reader can see his active atavism at work. He spends longest on the present piety of the Slavs and what he puts before the reader is an idealized memory of Slovak village or small-town life. From this memory-picture one also gathers that Slav pacificness might be understood as belonging to, or produced by, their natural piety (DV 10):

Sundays and holy days are not defiled here, that is, in Slav areas, to the extent that they are in other regions; the Holy Scriptures are more earnestly read than elsewhere and family prayers more often conducted; quietness and orderliness at church prevail more than elsewhere; praying, the Sacraments and divine service are liked more here; talk about sacred matters is more restrained; words of cursing, swearing and blaspheming are almost all borrowed from foreign languages; robbery, banditry, manslaughter, murder and the spilling of blood are rare, almost unheard-of in this nation.

Since Kollár's father sometimes acted as a Justice of the Peace and sometimes as notary, however puritanical he was, the young Kollár must have heard of, even if he did not see, brawls and worse. In his autobiography he describes a particularly violent robbery, and if the highwayman had not been Slovak, he would certainly have told us. In other words, in his enthusiastic lucubrations on Slav piety, he is consciously mythopoeic. The last section, on the uncriminality of the Slavs, constitutes an expansion of Herder's statement that the Slavs were 'enemies of robbery and pillage'. Kollár (DV) and Šafařík (G) have similar, rather unimaginative and brief, lists of Slav saints to prove their piety point; one is only surprised that the scholarly Šafařík should have taken over from Kollár the thoroughly unSlav Rozvita (G 88), but there was no place for self-criticism of that kind in the mythic passages of the *Geschichte*. Furthermore, Lutherans are unlikely to want to think too much about saints. Šafařík also takes from Kollár the assertion that, even before the spread of Christianity among the Slavs, they were renowned for their piety (G 86–7). When in Italy, Kollár finds he has slightly to moderate this part of his Slav myth: 'No nation is more pious and, mind you, more inclined to superstition, than the Indians, the Slavs and the Italians' (C 243). Again, one hears the Protestant voice here – not wanting to be ungracious, but feeling somewhat glutted by Italian churches.

The second attribute Kollár gives the Slavs, diligence, may also be linked with Protestantism. Actually, Kollár finds it more difficult to argue Slav industry than he does Slav piety. He has to admit that there may be people who are harder-working than the Slavs, but, he says somewhat ambiguously, for the Slavs diligence is 'almost the closest to them, the most usual and most widespread' (DV 11). Šafařík is more certain; he informs his reader that the diligence of the Slavs is known everywhere; his rider is that, by saying that, he does not wish to imply that other nations are lazy or less skilful than the Slavs (G 88). Again paraphrasing Herder, he says that, because they had no lust for war, 'they enjoyed the fruits of their freedom in peace, devoting themselves to crafts and trade in the cities and to agriculture and herding in the country' (G 155). Only Kollár takes up Herder's *häuslicher Fleiss* (domestic diligence, hard work looking after their households), when he exclaims with pathos, at the sight of hard-working Croat market-women (C 53): 'Oh, profound, ardent sense of toilsome domestic work and domestic happiness – thy name is Slav.' Again that is consciously mythopoeic, since, shortly beforehand, he had contrasted these women's busyness with the slackness of market women back home.

The third virtue, merriness, is linked specifically with Protestantism, Saxon Protestant tolerance and support for manufacturing only in *Nábožný pohled*, but that is no doubt unimportant, since merriness is a stock contemporaneous intellectual's assessment of peasant behaviour. Since singing goes together with folk poetry, our authors may consciously be making a virtue out of necessity. In a non-literary culture there is only oral tradition. That is good because it is natural. Slav merriness is linked with Slav (and here certainly, ideal Slovak) naturalness, and this leads the staid sensualist Kollár to indulge in some of his biological mythopoeia (DV 12):

The people of this nation seem to be by nature more inclined to joy than to sadness; their blood is healthy and fresh; their nerves and veins are so lively and sensitive, their limbs so supple and agile, their eyes so bright and grateful, their faces so affable and amiable, indeed, their tongues so talkative and fluent, that, wherever they go, joy and merriment bustle around them … an artless, natural, innocent, relaxed joy which lends the whole world a pleasant colour and all life sweet pleasure.

Like Kollár, Šafařík compares Slav merriness with Ancient Greek merriness, and he speaks of the Slavs' lively, fresh blood. Slav merriness is the work of Nature –

so Slavs naturally avoid melancholy (G 88). In the *Výklad*, having quoted several German sources on Slav merriness and musicality, Kollár indulges his predilection for linguistic mythopoeia (V 209): 'This merriness is so much part of our nation's character that the whole Slav language does not even have a word appropriate for denoting what is called *Ernst* in German and *seriositas* in Latin.' Though in his initial list Kollár omitted the 'musical' epithet to merriness that is in Herder, he introduces it in his expansion of the virtue of 'innocent merriness'. 'Where there is a Slav woman, there is song', he writes, and, wherever Slav lips go, the whole countryside rings with singing and joy (DV 12). He also draws a wise moral from this fact, which constitutes a purely artificial device. On the one hand, it introduces another element from the Herder picture; on the other, it provides an explanation, which is what is expected not only of complete myths, but also of individual elements in a complex myth: 'where there is an abundance of singing, the inhabitants are usually sincere, trusting, helpful, and amiable towards guests and visitors' (DV 13).

Again one visualizes the Slovak village. Šafařík makes the close connection between singing and folk poetry. He takes from Kollár, 'Where there is a Slav, there is singing'; he talks of the hills, forests and farmsteads ringing with song, and then informs us that folk poetry is purer and more widespread among the Slavs than among all other nations (G 89). He abides by this myth element when he has ceased to be under the more or less direct influence of Kollár: 'The Slavs are the most philharmonic nation and, as far as folk poetry is concerned, the leading nation in Europe' (SSI 264). Kollár, however, soon gets fed up with the Czechs and their veritable cult of music. His words dimly look forward to the Czech popular historian, Antonín Žalud-Vysokomýtský's, dismissal of the cult. Žalud was, however, in no way influenced by Kollár's *Cestopis*.

In this work Kollár writes: 'The deep immersion, nay more, submersion, of the Czech nation [*národu*] in a sea of music, which is so praised by others, I cannot praise. The Czechs' love of music has degenerated almost into melomania' (C 291). On the basis of his experience of the Gipsies of Hungary, Kollár considers that musicking can make people servile (what Herder maintained the Slavs had, almost miraculously, managed not to become), and he worries lest the Czechs become servile. He is afraid (C 292) that the Czechs might lose their patriotism (*sic*) and nationality through playing and listening to music;[65] 'as things are now, all their newspapers, conversations, meetings and clubs swarm with news about music, about concerti, academies, quartets and the like: enough to make you sick.' The Czechs have, in fact, perverted innocent, merry folk-music into towny, foreign social occasions. In Kollár and Šafařík's conception of folk, one notices that they acknowledge no dirges or mournful songs of lost love.

If one is a nationalist, indeed a propagandist of any sort, one has to 'think positively' – about one's own people. Slavs must be jolly because that sounds positive and it would not be a sensible way to recruit Slavs to the panslav cause if you promised them the threnodes of thralls. The propagandist fourth virtue in Kollár's list, love of the language,[66] is such a case of positive thinking. If he states that this love of language exists, his audience may believe it. If they do not harbour it themselves, they may feel guilt at their lack and so cultivate such a love. Kollár's aim in stating this existence is also political; if his audience believes him, that will help in the battle against Hungarian. Still, however propagandistic Kollár's statement is, once more it constitutes an interpretation of the state of affairs in isolated Slovak villages and little market-towns where only Slovak was spoken. Kollár's starting point is again, then, a reality of a sort. This time, however, the 'love' has no basis in anything but his own subjective perception of reality. One might go so far as to say that in this case and, actually, elsewhere, Kollár is describing himself as the typification of the Slavs. Once again Freud comes to mind. Both authors make their own predicaments or genuinely believe their own predicaments to be those of a large group of mankind. (I am not denying Freud's competence as a psychologist and psychiatrist.) They then impose their model on others. The politicality of the virtue of love of one's language becomes clearer still when Kollár expands on it and speaks of its naturalness in contrast to the unnaturalness (blindness or blinkeredness) of the implied Germans and Magyars (DV 13):

It is not that they have always preferred to use and speak their language, but they also do their best to conserve and enhance it ... I do not wish here to remind you of those painful, unfortunate memorials which the past has left on this matter; I do not wish to speak about the hatred and blindness which other, neighbouring, nations visited on this quiet, pleasing nation, and by which they sinned [Herder's *versündigt*] against it .... But the greater the blindness of those pitiable adversaries, the more fervent the Slavs' love for their nation and their dear mother tongue.

On this matter Šafařík emphasizes the intellectual need for love of one's native language, since one 'can achieve true perfection of language and intellect only in one's mother tongue' (G 40). Proof of the Slavs' innate love of their language lies in the fact that they had translations of the Bible so early (DV 13 and G 90). Thus love of language may be linked with the Enlightenment belief in the value of (universal) education.

Kollár speaks of the Enlightenment virtues of tolerance in *Slávy dcera* where we learn that the Slavs were not even cruel to murderers (one remembers Kollár's horror at a schoolboy's being executed for stealing some money from an army-officer – mind you, the soldier was a German). Slav tolerance is evident in the Russians' treatment of their Finnish and German populations. In *Dobré vlastnosti* the Slavs' tolerance is inextricable from their pacificness (that notion is expressed also by Šafařík). Neither author perceives a need to define tolerance itself. In all history there is no sign of cruelty or savagery among the Slavs at war (G 90).

When Kollár sees the Croatian Revivalist, Ljudevit Gaj's, library, which contains publications in Hungarian as well as the Slav dialects, he considers it a demonstration of Slav tolerance; here, however, he links tolerance with intellectual versatility and, thus, open-mindedness (C 46) – which one might, I suppose, see as the beginning of a definition of tolerance. Šafařík conceives of a different active tolerance in the Slavs. Historically, they look after underdogs. For example, they help the Letts and Lithuanians against the marauding Germanic tribes (SSI 145).

The peace-loving aspect of the Slav character is, however, what attracts Kollár and Šafařík most. Its importance in the complex myth is that it explains positively why all Slavs, with the exception of the Russians and Montenegrins, are subject nations. It also helps explain how the Slav nation allowed itself to be fragmented. In *Dobré vlastnosti* the love of peace is linked with their diligence and with the success the Slavs had in making wasteland fertile (Herder has this, too); the Slavs' intolerance towards sloth perhaps renders their tolerance and their pacificness especially Protestant; in the following quotation (DV 11) the 'excellent writer' is Herder, and one notices how the almost teetotal Kollár changes Herder's mead-brewing into bee-keeping:[67]

Since they are by nature greater lovers of peace than warring (a certain excellent writer speaks thus about them), they occupied themselves with agriculture, with the rearing of cattle and bee-keeping; they converted deserts into fertile fields … they led a very industrious, hard-working life and so they would not even suffer lazy ne'er-do-wells and idlers amongst them, and condemned them to death or exile.

Kollár employs what became a Revivalist cliché about the Czechs, the notion of the Slavs as a dove-like nation (*holubičí národ*), a characterisation coined, I believe, by the Czech Protestant émigré, Adam Hartman (*Historia persecutionum ecclesiae Bohemiae*, 1647; Czech version, 1655; the work is usually attributed to Comenius, as it is elsewhere by Kollár, because Comenius aided Hartman with the Latin text). Kollár (DV 15) writes that everywhere among the unaggressive Slavs one will find:

a special sort of kindliness, gentleness, peacefulness, so that some people [notice Kollár's propaganda method], not without cause, give them the name, '*dove-like nation*'; in other words, a nation as gentle and innocent as a dove. Although from time to time their deeds were valiant and heroic, they never engaged in bloody wars [*sic*] or wars whose purpose was gain; they knew only how to defend themselves and never intentionally harmed others; they did not subjugate foreign nations, but only occupied empty, deserted land abandoned by others; they never bore … swords or other weapons in time of peace, and wherever they went, they tamed other, savage, nations with their quiet, peaceable presence.

According to his autobiography Kollár had had a passion for doves when he had been a schoolboy. He had used all his pocket money to buy them and had trained them to follow him about (P 110-11). He does not expressly state that this craze revealed his Slav ardour as a child, but one cannot imagine he did not think that was so. When he is contemplating Schiavone's work, he decides that the artist paints women much better than men because of his Slavness: 'Perhaps that was a result, an expression of his natural Slav national character; after all, they are sons of a *dove-like nation*' (C 113). The pigeons in St Mark's Square in Venice (C 95) remind him of the ultimate Slavness of the bird (the Czech for pigeon or dove is *holub, holubice*):

Here, too, Venice betrays its Slav origins and character, its blood relationship with our *dove-like nation*, all the tribes of which have particularly loved these birds from times of yore; they used to keep them in their farmsteads and looked after them with great care .... The name 'holub' (*columba palumba*) passed from the Slavs to the rest of the European nations, and, with the name, doubtless the object.

In *Wechselseitigkeit*, Kollár examines Slav peaceableness again, and he again follows Herder, but a different passage in the German's essay; he also gives the characterization a didactic loading. Kollár says the Slavs had never tried to rule the world, had never made the subjugation of nations or the shedding of blood their business, because they loved the freedom of their enemies as much as their own. And now the Slavs should cultivate that gentleness of theirs, foster the plough rather than the sword, and then they will attain the crown of *Humanität*. Šafařík follows Herder and Kollár exactly on the question of the Slav love of peace and unwillingness to subjugate other nations (G 58 and 90). He adds that they paid barbarian usurpers an annual tax rather than fighting in order to secure their peaceful manner of life (G 155). In both the *Geschichte* and *Slovanské starožitnosti,* he speaks of their fighting only to defend themselves, but in the latter he adds that they also sometimes fought to avenge themselves; in that case, however, they bridled their revenge with moderation (SSI 589).

Both our writers have to explain why the pacific Slavs sometimes waged wars of aggression. Even in a myth there has to be consistency, for an irrational myth is a contradiction in terms. In one argument Šafařík suggests that, because they were so industrious, their population grew, and so they needed *Lebensraum* and were compelled to push back the 'belligerent Franks, Thuringians and Saxons' (SSII 16). He passes over the inconsistency with the myth inherent in the Russian Ivan IV's conquest of Kazan, Astrakhan and part of Siberia (G 156) or Igor's son, Svatoslav's, conquest of the Khazars, Ossetians and Cherkeses (SSII 90), or Oleg's particularly violent invasion of the Bosporus (SSII 88). On the Slavs' taking of Greece he claims that they may have invaded involuntarily with the Avars, but then he is mightily inconsistent when he tells us that between AD 802 and 811 the poor Peleponesian Slavs had tried in vain to throw off the Greek yoke (SSII 244).

Herder's point that the Slavs occupied only abandoned land emphasizes the Slavs' pacific nature, but it may also be used, as part of the explanatory myth, to reveal yet another reason why the Slavs are not mentioned earlier in Greek and Latin texts. In Šafařík's general version of this aspect of Slav pacificness, he points out that Germanic tribes had made incursions into Africa, Celts into Asia, Mongols into Europe, but Slavs, when they moved, went only into 'immediately neighbouring areas which were for the most part empty' (SSI 439). The 'fact' that the Slavs only moved peacefully into virgin or abandoned territories serves Šafařík well to explain the present German population of the Bohemian frontier territories. Bohemia had been deserted by the Marcomans by the time the Slavs arrived there, and there is 'no indication that the German spirit in any way influenced the Czechs immediately after their entry into Bohemia. The remnants of the Germanic nations the Czechs encountered there must have been ... a wretched little remnant which was immediately absorbed in the Slav nationality; the stronger Germans probably withdrew into lonely mountain ranges' (G 300). That constitutes active atavism (i.e. population of Giant Mountains).

If circumstances had driven Slavs to war in the past, the 'positive thinking' of propaganda demands that they had been valiant. Furthermore, statements of Slav valour constitute statements that most Slav tribes are not subject-nations now because they are cowards or had been inept warriors. (I emphasize again that I am considering two nationalist mythopoets; the fact that all peoples produce brave men and cowards has nothing to do with my analysis of this model of cultural nationalism.) Šafařík reiterates the Slavs' capacity for valour (for example, G 57 and 90). In *Slovanské starožitnosti*, he informs his audience that Slavs had fought as gallant mercenaries for Byzantium and for Arab princes (SSII 17). Šafařík may be demonstrating Slav sophistication or equality to other Europeans when he informs us that in the earliest times the Slavs fought with javelins, shields, bows and arrows (G 57). That comports with a later statement that the early Slavs were only foot-soldiers (SSI 407). Elsewhere, however, he writes that they had both infantry and cavalry (SSI 73). This is, however, probably of no importance to the myth.

Herder's praise of Slav farming certainly is important to it. For the Slovaks Šafařík and Kollár it explains why the Slavs are nearly all peasants now, explains that this is their natural state or vocation and that it is a hallowed tradition (that is: not simply the result of an alien feudal system). Farming is, moreover, the 'foundation of life', as Kollár writes (N 5). He experienced the Slavness of it in his childhood (P 114): 'My parents had an attractive holding and, in the summer, like all Slavs, they loved work in the fields and brought us up to that, too.' The 'loved' refers back to the Herder picture. More significant, however, is the deliberate suggestion that it is only among the Slavs that people other than labourers help with the harvest. Another brief extract from the same passage (P 115) reveals two other sides to the mythic aspect of Slav peasanthood: 'To this very day the harvest is a truly national celebration among the Slovaks. Life is as in Arcadia.' That emphasizes, first, some particularly Slav ancient ritual, secondly, the ideal, idyllic nature of peasant life. The comparison with Greece may not be just a cliché, when we remember that in Arcady the peasants were particularly fond of music and dancing. The Slavs' tranquil peasanthood was also their undoing, Kollár maintains; he quotes Kopitar, who is himself echoing Herder: 'The real misfortune for the Slavs and their beautiful language was that these peaceful tillers of the soil ... in their innocence had forgotten to prepare for war' and so they had been subjugated (V 38–9). Of all the occasions on which Šafařík mentions the Slavs as farmers the most telling is the following rationalization (SSI 584):

The Slavs' invincible predilection for farming is the work of Nature herself, a natural result of their lengthy inhabiting of the best arable land in Europe, the plains around the Vistula and the Dnieper ... if some of them, in the process of migrating, took up weapons, they did so only to take control of nearby wasteland and, having taken it over, they turned its overgrown grassland into fertile fields. Everything in them ... suited this occupation: the natural pleasantness of their character and manners and their predilection for a free life could find satisfaction only in farming ... the prime element in the Slavs, from which all other elements developed, was agriculture and animal husbandry.

The hospitality with which Herder, Kollár and Šafařík fame the Slavs is a typical peasant characteristic. Within the myth, however, it serves to emphasise that the Slavs were natural givers (as the Germans, Magyars and Tatars were natural takers). Šafařík, reasonably enough, puts their hospitality together with their 'unusual' amiability (G 57); later he modifies that: he appears to be lending their hospitality more dignity, lest hospitality be taken as a synonym for exploitability: they were 'pleasant and no threat to reasonably civilized foreigners; indeed they were amenable and hospitable' (SSI 585). In the *Výklad* (V 26) Kollár quotes Csaplovits (1818) on this Slav trait: 'Hospitality is the national virtue [*Nationaltugend*] of the Slovaks in Hungary.'

For Herder the Slavs' love of peasant life was motivated by their love of the freedom that life in the country gave them. In the Šafařík–Kollár myth of Slavness this love of freedom has two fundamentally opposed sides. First, it is quietist; it corresponds to Kollár's assertion that Slav Reciprocity will prevent rebellions against foreign rulers. Secondly, it suggests to the contemporary that love of freedom proclaimed by the French Revolution, which Kollár so greatly disapproved of. It embodies, then, that tension between neo-Classical orderly bucolic and Romantic liberty which Kollár's verse works betray. According to Šafařík the Germans who came to Bohemia were certainly priests and colonists, but also prisoners of war. In Bohemia, however, prisoners were allowed to live in accordance with their own laws; they were declared free and even given privileges (G 303). If a Slav was taken prisoner, no matter what power's prisoner he was, he became free immediately he stepped on Slav soil and no one had any right to his person (SSI 586). It does not apparently sully the myth for Šafařík that, when Oleg takes up his seat in Preslav, the freedom-loving Russians send as tribute to him furs, wax, honey – and serfs (SSII 91). The clearest indication of the Slavs' love of freedom is not their treatment of prisoners, however, but the fact that they never subjugated foreign nations (SSI 589).

The Slavs' natural democratic feeling appears to be a manifestation of their love of freedom. This aspect of Kollár and Šafařík's myth reflects contemporary political thinking and it serves to demonstrate the topicality of the natural Slav way of life. They based much of their conception of the Slavs as democrats on one of the Forged Manuscripts, *Libušin soud* (Libussa's judgement). Myth feeds on myth. In his interpretation of Procopius' *De bello Gothico*, Šafařík states that from the beginning the Slavs had had a society which was organized democrati-cally (G 57). When they were only in northern Europe, he tells us elsewhere, they had formed small states, each governed by councils made up of the common peo-ple and each with an elected chieftain (G 155). That seems to have developed into something like a constitutional monarchy with a nobility; the limits to a totally egalitarian regime resulted from German influence (SSI 586):

In the earliest of times all Slavs were, to be sure, equal before the law and free men. It seems, however, that class differences and the hereditariness of the highest rank in the land laid down roots very early, without impairing democracy; that occurred particu-larly in societies which had Germans as their neighbours or which were mixed with Germans.

The main point is that the 'administration of communal matters was in the hands of the nation itself' (SSI 585). When he deals with later times, in Russia, Šafařík is careful not to sound republican; he also gives members of a Germanic tribe some credit, for the only change the Norsemen wrought in Russia was to trans-form 'unbridled democracy into strong autocracy' (SSII 81). Russian autocrats still retained democratic principles: when Vladimir had ordered his subjects to become Christian, he used no coercion; they were persuaded by his example (SSII 96). Šafařík is inconsistent about the creation of estates in Slav lands. Within a page he says German influence introduced social ranks and that the Slavs had their own original ranks of nobility (SSI 585–6). Perhaps he imagines that ranks of nobility gave their holders honour, authority, but no material bene-fits; he summarizes the situation thus (SSI 586): 'non-noble Slavs remained free ... Servitude and serfdom came only later, to the western Slavs from the Ger-mans, and to the southern from the Greeks and Italians.' Kollár is at least certain that feudalism is German, because that comports with the myth (CD 31): 'The old Germanic principle of aggression, subjugation, feudalism, the destruction of foreign nationality and language shames mankind, and the history of the world is forced to turn its face away, blushing.' In contrast, Kollár sees the Saxons of his day as model democrats. There they have learned what Kollár implies the Hungarians have not yet fully learned: that 'civil life limits but does not try to destroy the equality of men, that servitude and vassaldom do not comport with the spirit of the Christian religion.' In Saxony, 'prince and subject, lord and servant, burgher and shepherd are equal before the law, even though socially different. Farmer is not an insulting or pejorative, but an honourable, appellation' (N 5–6). The Slav language is democratic, because it permits literary dialects – and here Kollár is speaking against his own fear of fragmentation and disunity. The contrast of Slavonic with Latin probably has political meaning, but it alludes to Latin as still the most common language of administration in Hungary, rather than to Latin as the language of the Roman Catholic Church (as might have been the case, if he had been a Czech): 'Latin is an aristocratically formed central language of Romans, while Greek and Slavonic deserve to be called democratic, periphery-based, dialect-based languages ... Latin has only one centre, the city of Rome; Greek and Slavonic have several centres' (W 51).

Connected with the notion of Slavs (and even their language) as democratic is a notion I find in Šafařík, but not in Kollár: that Slavs are naturally liberal. This, theoretically speaking, is necessary to the myth to make the Slavs representative of the finest aims of Western society (see Plamenatz's notion of liberal Western nationalism). The one statement that can be interpreted as demonstrating liberalism is an extension of the Herder picture or of our two authors' versions of it. The most convincing word is 'considerate': the Slavs are 'well-behaved, gentle; they love peace, the laws of the community, national customs and, particularly, providing hospitality and free passage to well-intentioned guests; they are immensely considerate' (SSII 71).

Their love of law no doubt has something to do with the Forged Manuscript, *Libušin soud*, as well, but it would also comport with contemporary libertarian ideals. Once more in his interpretation of Procopius, Šafařík writes (G 57), 'Justice without deception or evil was the chief feature of their character.' Later on in the *Geschichte*, he writes that a Slav is far more willing to suffer injustice than to inflict it (G 91). Thus Šafařík is particularly impressed by the Serbian Dušan the Strong's code of laws from 1349; in this code he finds a noble, sophisticated spirit of *Humanität* (G 218). He also points out that the Emperor Justinian I was a Slav (G 138), whose real name he says was Upravda or Vpravda (*pravda*, law, truth); he had been born in Vederiana near today's Kyustendil (SSII 171); it does not greatly concern Šafařík that Justinian led or ordered several attacks on the Bulgarian Slavs, for that is external to the main body of the myth. Kollár calls Justinian Upravda in *Slávy dcera* and he spends quite some time on him in the *Výklad*. Then in the *Cestopis* he makes the Slavs the main codifiers of European law. Upravda had founded the Western legal system and another Slav, Basil of Macedonia, had founded the Eastern. The English jury system also has Slav origins and it had arrived in the British Isles either with the Wilts of Wiltshire or with the Saxons who had previously had Slavs as their neighbours (C 198–9). Within the myth a central point is that Europe's law-givers had suffered so greatly (according to Kollár's rules on what may and may not be touched by laws: illegally) at the hands of the non-Slav Europeans. As far as Herder's picture is concerned, the love of law may be interpreted from the Slavs' obedience, their hostility to robbery and pillage and their respect for freedom.

Šafařík and Kollár make very little of Herder's assertions about the Slavs as great traders and as miners and craftsmen. Kollár in *Dobré vlastnosti* and Šafařík in the *Geschichte* mention their opening up land and sea trade. When Kollár arrives by the sea in his *Cestopis*, he considers how relatively little open sea the Slavs have. This landlocked state had prevented their developing trade and industry. Of course, it had been the Germans who had cut the Slavs off from the sea and merchant life (C 78). He mentions skill in mining among Slav virtues in *Wechselseitigkeit* (W 98). The reason these aspects are not of great concern to our two writers is that it has nothing to do with bucolic (Slav or Slovak) peasants and can help very little in active atavism. There is nothing in the present to derive that part of history from. Indeed, purely practically, the mining towns in Upper Hungary were almost entirely German.

Herder says nothing exclusively about Slav women, but the few things Šafařík and Kollár write about them (I necessarily forget *Slávy dcera*, for the best parts of that are about Slav women) do comport with their interpretation of Herder. For Šafařík Slav women were extraordinarily faithful to their men (G 57). One does not know whether Šafařík was deliberately reacting to the mediaeval chroniclers' pictures of the early Slavs living in a state of sexual communism. Kollár claims Slav women are more modest than other women (V 20). The most imaginative passage on Slav women in Kollár's prose is the following (V 456–7):

Bělohlava [whitehead] or even *bjela pohlava* [the white sex], *bjela osoba* [white person], or, indeed just *Bjela is* a generic name for women among the Slovaks; the Poles call women *biala plec* [the white complexion]. These appellations bear fine witness to the purity of Slav women, for the name doubtless comes from the whiteness of their bodies and their clothing ... And Slav women, living as they did in northern regions and in the Tatras, were for the most part so-called blondes with reddish-straw hair and a white head; they covered their hair with white kerchiefs; it is from this that they were called *Bělohlava* ... To this very day a particular predilection for the colour white prevails among Slav women; nearly all ethnographers have noticed this in Slav tribes.

The physical characteristics of the Slavs in the Šafařík–Kollár myth

To create a mythic structure strong enough to withstand German (and Magyar) criticism, to persuade fellow-Slavs that the Slav cause should be supported, and, most important, strong enough to help give the Slavs self-confidence, an ideal physical model Slav had to be moulded. That had first, to match the 'inner' features of the Slavs and, second, to help 'prove' that the Slav was a proto-European. Here we are entering a dogmatic ideology which has very little to do with Herder's picture. We are firmly in the realm of biological mythopoeia.

Because both Šafařík and Kollár have in their origin myth established that the Slavs are a northern European people, they may have the Slavs comport with the chivalrous ideal. Thus Šafařík writes, in his interpretation of Procopius again, that the Slavs were 'tall, strong and fair' (G 57). He explains that fairness later (G 86): 'Fair hair is the feature common to almost all Slavs. Even in the case of southern Slavs this feature is concealed less by Nature than by artifice. This fair hair, together with the fact that they have a far whiter skin than other nations, recalls their original, or at least long-standing, settlements in the North.' In this second description of the typical Slav, which may well include at least an element of competition with the north Germans, the Slavs are, however, no longer tall. Now they have something more like a decent Slovak peasant physique: 'Generally speaking, Slavs are of middling height, well-built, with a strong frame and unusually supple and firm muscles' (G 86). Still here Šafařík compares and contrasts the typical facial features of the Slavs with those of the Germans.

In *Slávy dcera* Kollár had maintained that the round faces of the Slavs manifest joy in life, innocence and virtue, whereas the Germans' long faces manifest cruelty, sadness and anger. Šafařík rationalizes that, as a mythopoet or propagandist rather than a philosopher, but there is only the barest hint of Teutonophobia here: 'The principle of heightened perception or subjectivity, which is physically and psychologically thoroughly valid for the Slavs, may be seen in that all sharp features have disappeared, especially in the face; the Slavs' facial features are incomparably more rounded, more delicate and softer than the Germans'; externally the Germans are endowed with penetrating incisiveness' (G 86). Kollár uses facial comparison to support another aspect of the complex myth, the Slavness of Venice: 'These prototypes are present in all Venetian heads and faces; one is Roman: long-necked, high-minded, melancholy, domineering, taciturn; the second is Slavonic: round-faced, amiable, merry, talkative, melodious; the third is some sort of hodgepodge of Germanic and Arab blood' (C 94–95). In *Slovanské starožit-nosti*, when he has decided that Herodotus is speaking about Slavs when he describes the Budini, Šafařík again compares the typically Slav with the typically Germanic, but the colour of Slav hair has changed now. The type remains northern, however, and so the myth-aspect remains intact: 'Grey or blue (*glaucon*) eyes and light-brown or brownish (*pyrron*) hair are unmistakable, natural signs of members of the Slav tribe. As early as Procopius it was noted that Germanic tribes had red or reddish (*hyperidos, subrufus*) hair' (SSI 220). It does not matter how suspect you might consider the translations from the Greek; the myth depends on the Czech words; the function of the Greek words in the text is to demonstrate scholarly authenticity. When in the town of Thun in Switzerland in 1844, Kollár immediately believes there is a clear link between the town and the Bohemian patriot, Count Thun, and so biological mythopoeia enters at the town gate (CD 23): 'In the town of Thun the people are quite different from anything I have so far seen in Switzerland. Not only the faces and figures, but even the clothes seem to have something Slav in them.' Šafařík approaches this type of biological mythopoeia when he tells us that 600,000 of Bavaria's 3,660,000 inhabitants are Slavs if one goes by surname and physique (SSII 355). Since the destruction of the Polabian Slavs forms the centrepiece of *Slávy dcera* and thence of the racial aspect of the Šafařík–Kollár myth, the report we receive of the citizens of Saxony (including Lower Franconia) from Kollár (N 7) will not astonish us:

But these enemies and oppressors have still today not succeeded in wiping away, erasing absolutely, all national signs and characteristics from our Slav brethren here. Our language has, indeed, fallen silent …, but faces, figures, clothes and customs, particularly in Lusatia and the Oldenburg and Bamberg regions, still remain so unchanged that, more than once, I was tempted to greet or address those I met in our mother tongue.

Kollár is always keen to separate the Slavs from the Germanic races as clearly as possible, and that can mean finding similarities with Romance nations – as he compares the Slavonic and Italian languages. He is, then, delighted when he hears of French doctors' latest findings: that Germanic, English or Norman blood is black, thick and heavy, whereas French, Italian and Slav blood is whitish, thin and light (C 183). He does not interpret that for his readers, leaves it up to them to comprehend the apparently obvious meaning.

Finally, as far as Slav physical features are concerned, Kollár invents one particular Slav gesture in *Slávy dcera*, the Slav kiss, which his readers are intended to take in earnest. His goal is no doubt honourable, to emphasise the nobility, innocence, natural love of religiousness, and the gentleness of the Slavs. The Slav kiss is ritual – and myth is 'inseparable from *dromena*, things to be done or specified actions. The ritual actions that accompany the rehearsing of myth point in the direction of the original context of the myth.'[68] This kiss is *pravoslávský*,[69] 'true Slav', a word which echoes and alludes to *pravoslavný*, 'Orthodox', in the ecclesiastical sense. Unlike salacious Greek, Roman and German kisses, the Slav kiss is chaste (*čisté*). One kisses down one's sweetheart's face from brow to chin, then across it from ear to ear, and both times the lips meet, soul meets soul. Eroticism fuses with the sign of the Cross.

It might have been too twentieth-century to say that Kollár was Slavicizing Nature, if he had not called his Mína's lips a *růžoplotná zahrádka*, little rose-fenced garden. Nature influences natural Slavs, but natural Slavs also influence Nature; because what Šafařík writes sounds so normal today, I cannot be entirely convinced that the following (SSI 529) is part of the mythopoeia: 'As the earth and its climates form here one, and there another, image of the nation's body and soul, so the nation leaves on the earth it has inhabited and cultivated a seal embossed with indelible signs of its own special way of life.' It is, however, not a large step from that thought to a Kollárian conception of how race can affect climate. In *Slávy dcera* he tells us that where Czechs live it is bright weather but that where Germanized Czechs or Germans live the sky is full of black clouds. It works the other way round, too. In *Wechselseitigkeit* Kollár opines that one reason why Slavs do not suffer from the dichotomy of head and heart from which other nations suffer is that the race, the nation, has such a wide geographical, and thus climatic, experience. The Slavs live in all climates and therefore have a complete experience of the world that others cannot have, thus: simultaneity of thought and emotion.

One Nature myth Kollár creates before our eyes in the *Výklad* after hinting at it in *Slávy dcera* is the notion that the linden tree is specially beloved of the Slavs. Indeed, he claims it is sacred to the Slavs. He supports his invention (which is based on auto-mythopoeia since he fell in love with Mína under a linden tree) with a huge list of place names which include the tree. Otherwise he quotes just three lines of nineteenth-century Polish verse to substantiate his assertion. Macura's wary suggestion in his scintillating account of National Revival cults that Kollár is not the inventor of this part of the Slav myth, since one finds in Václav Stach the lime as a symbol of Czechness as against the oak of Germanness and, in folk customs, the lime as the female and oak as the male principle does not convince me.[70] Kollár also uses the linden in connection with Slav honey-making, in other words, reinforces his perversion of Herder's mead-brewing as well as reinforcing the myth he has created out of himself for himself and then for his nation (V 15): 'It appears that the Slavs as great lovers of bee-keeping and honey-making were led by this occupation to a special love of this tree which bees like so much, the linden.'

The Slavs' naturalness and traditional closeness to Nature by virtue of their occupations mean that renegades from Slavdom were unnatural, more or less perverted. For all the pleasant things he says about the Saxons he, when he goes to Saxony to marry his Mína, conceives of these ex-Slavs as national zombies. This is a new, perhaps monitory, element in nationalist ideology, and in the myth which belongs to it (N 7):

These denaturalized people do not really belong to any nation now. A certain distrust and defiance brood on their brows; a certain secret regret and pain at a lost natural treasure cloud their eyes ... their national disfigurement and distortion will through the history of the world heap everlasting shame and disgrace on these otherwise venerable regions and cast a shadow on the brightness of their fame.

The bastards produced by voluntary or involuntary abandonment of one's nationality should constitute a warning to Kollár's congregation not to allow themselves to be Magyarized. Losing one's nationality will lead to total alienation, even from oneself. This is a sound nationalist argument (N 8): 'as denaturalized issue of adultery, we shall be scum for our neighbours, objects of pity for our descendants, victims of disgrace to ourselves.' When Kollár describes the inhabitants of Čates in Carniola, he describes a population deformed by being linguistically and nationally mixed. His description comes close to an extreme nationalist call for pure blood (C 42): 'The little town of Čates, which lies on a small hill, is prettier than its two-faced, two-tongued inhabitants by whose looks it is hard to tell whether more of the German or of the Slav element is left in their state of bastardization.'

Slavs and foreigners

The whole of Herder's little essay up to the message of hope can be seen as a picture of the Slavs as victims. Šafařík and Kollár embraced this vision. It served their myth well, for it introduced another religious element. It is not always clear whether we have before us something like the Christian cult of victory over suffering or some obscurantist cult of suffering itself. According to Šafařík (G 81–2), Slav victimhood had begun a millennium and a half ago and still persisted: 'Ever since the Huns, the Goths, the Avars, the Franks, the Magyars and the rest began attacking and partly exterminating the Slav nations, who had been peacefully farming and trading, hatred and persecution have passed from life into writing and from writing into life.' The Russians had been particularly piteous victims, he writes at the beginning of the second volume of *Slovanské starožitnosti*; the Russians are historic sufferers, victims of Tatars, Avars, Bugri, Khazars (filthy Judaeomoslem rabble he calls them elsewhere), Magyars, Pechenegs, Kumans, Turkmens and so forth (SSII 70). The Avars are the worst, as they nearly always are in Šafařík; he usually endows them with the epithet 'repulsive'. It may be important that in the Slovak oral tradition Avars and Magyars are often confused.

Herder had written that the Slavs' peaceful, industrious, generous, obedient way of life had contributed to the ease with which others had oppressed them. So too, Šafařík writes (G 56) that, because they had towns and led a 'patriarchal manner of life', they had become 'easy prey for savage, barbarian nomadic nations like the Goths, the Huns and the Avars.' In *Slovanské starožitnosti*, that triad changes to Scythians, Sarmatians and Goths (SSI 193). He is repeating Herder when he describes Slavs as 'gentle, pacific, loving farming, and, for that reason, oppressed and despoiled from all sides' (SSI 55).

When one considers Šafařík and Kollár's perception of Slavs as victims or as an exploited nation, one remembers that, in spite of the reforms of Maria Theresa and Joseph II, serfdom was largely still in place in Hungary during most of their writing life. Furthermore, those feudal institutions which had been dismantled were very much still within living memory. The peasants in Hungary, whether Magyar, Romanian or Slovak, could easily be conceived of as the victims of exploitation. Kollár is most certainly thinking of Slovak peasant labourers when he describes the Slavs as a nation of toilers for others. He appears to see a positive side to this circumstance, since it, at least ideally, preserves these peasants' Christian souls or Slav nature – perhaps Slav capacity for toil. He is not writing angrily, and in the dramatic urgency of the long period a tone of wistful reproach remains (DV 11–12):

Other nations usually work for and on behalf of themselves: Slav callouses work both for and on behalf of others; it is mostly Slav hands that cultivate our gardens and vineyards, mostly Slav hands that carry the scythe to the meadow and, at harvest time, the sickle to the field; it is mostly sweat from their brows that flows in the building of houses and bridges, in labouring in mountains and in valleys, on roads and elsewhere; it is mostly their hands that prepare man's everyday needs, bread, milk, cheese, honey, clothes and shoes.

In Šafařík's conception, the hordes of Sarmatians, Avars, Bugri, Burgundians, Vandals and so forth did not work on the land they conquered but lived off the toil of the Slavs. Often the Sarmatian or Finno-Ugric or Germanic adventurers would simply arrive in a Slav region 'like locusts to devour the fruits of other people's sweat, if they could produce enough; then, having consumed, they moved on' (SSI 286–7). The Celts were just as bad: 'they looked out to live and grow rich on the callouses of industrious Slavs' (SSII 8).

'Let us be just and love our nation without hatred towards any other nation,' Šafařík writes hopefully in his *Geschichte*. Later he is not so careful with his own emotions towards other nations, though he never experiences anything like Kollár's frenzied dislikes. Other nations were not as just towards the Slavs as Šafařík wanted his fellow-Slavs to be towards them. The myth of Slav victimhood comprises being conquered, then suffering physical exploitation and, on top of that, being disparaged or despised. Kollár writes that it was as if for some reason calumniators (Germans and Magyars) had sworn eternal hatred of the Slav nation. Others make fun of the Slavs' language, dress or customs, and these are nations whom the Slavs had previously civilized, whose 'lion or bear-skins had been removed by Slav industry and manners' (DV 19). That refers primarily to the Magyars. The notion of the Slavs as civilizers is based partly on the type of Slavonic vocabulary Hungarian contains and partly on Herder's belief in the Slav future. The mild Šafařík senses 'some kind of outmoded dislike of and distaste for Slavdom' (SSI 3) among non-Slav scholars. The unmild Kollár writes, probably not unjustly, for one remembers how Jews are sometimes blamed for having been persecuted by the Germans (V 107): 'It is strange that historians usually attribute the subjection of the Slavs in German regions only to the strength, toughness and courage of the Germans; they pass over in silence manifold examples of lies and deception, base tricks and snares; indeed they often attach the blame to these Slavs, to their national character.' In the *Cestopis*, Kollár complains (with the Croats) about the foul things the Magyars print and sing about the Slavs; if the Slavs wrote anything even vaguely similar about the Magyars, indeed, if they defended themselves against Magyar calumny, there would be a terrible row (C 52).

Some of the worst enemies of the Slavs are for Kollár the English, whom he sometimes lumps together with the Germans. He comes utterly to detest the English – as a major threat to Slav survival. While he is in the Mediterranean Kollár meets some Bulgarians on board a ship and they start moaning about the English (C 78–9):

These poor Bulgarians complained bitterly about the English and their ambassador in Constantinople, through whose influence, they told me, all education is suppressed and many cruelties are perpetrated, which are destroying the nation. The Turks themselves, they said, are stupid, sloppy people; if the Bulgarians want to open a school with teachers, the Turks let them get on with it, but the English immediately go to court and protest to the pasha. 'Why on earth do they do that?' I asked. They answered that they were afraid lest the Slavs should grow too prosperous, that, if the Slavs were educated, their sea trade might suffer. These good people related to me many more examples of educated barbarism from those selfish shopkeepers. ... when Mr Andelko Palashov ... tried to open a school ... he had to suffer a hundredfold bastinado from the Turks at the instigation of the English and then he had to go into exile.

Kollár tells his readers that he had once been a great admirer of the English but on this journey he had learnt better, not from stories, but from personal experience. The English are, he finds out, 'impolite, inconsiderate, downright rude at mealtimes.' Some mercantile lord he meets is 'red-haired, freckled, with protruding eyes, and a high-pitched voice, and gabbles away nineteen to the dozen in a mixture of English, French and German' (C 131). The English are haters of the Slav nation because of the Russians. The Englishman tells him that the Opium Wars have a great deal to do with preventing Russia gaining too much power in Asia. Kollár answers this with words that manifest his sincere belief in the peaceful, dove-like mission of the Slavs (C 131–2):

I, dear sirs, am myself a Slav and therefore I can safely say that Europe's fear of the Slavs, especially the Germans' and the English, is the fruit of sick minds and ill-willed hearts which want to make the quiet and peaceful Slavs who have German rulers look suspicious, because under some guise or other they want to lead to the oppression of their nationality.

Here Kollár seems to be reverting to his old hatred of Sir John Bowring who had had the temerity to write in the *Foreign Quarterly Review* that the Slav nations of the Monarchy were restless under the Habsburgs. He puts the English and Germans together again later (C 260) in some sort of conspiracy: 'Anglo-German philanthropy works simultaneously for the emancipation of Jews and negroes and the subjugation, possibly the spoliation, of the Slavs, so that afterwards they can John-Bullify or Deutschmichelify the scattered remnants.' He writes also about an Englishman called Paget (i.e. John Paget) who had married a Magyar (i.e. Polixena Wesselényi) and this brings him to his concern at the way these two oppressor nations were coming closer together. Young Englishmen were now coming to Hungary, especially Transylvania, to learn the Magyar language. Kollár is also particularly concerned about a fanatically anti-Slav English novelist called Miss Pardoe (i.e. Julia Pardoe [1806–62]) (C 299). The English he meets on his travels are 'impertinent' (C 115), 'puffed up' (C 193), souvenir-hunting vandals (C 177). Both the Englishmen he meets in Brescia have ginger hair (C 192); this seems to be the villainous characteristic of Kollár's Englishmen altogether. On his second journey he joins a young American businessman in attacking an elderly English retired naval officer, 'a real John Bull, taciturn, puffed-up, in love with his English nation and all its faults and virtues' (CD 34). As a student Kollár had seen Wellington in Pressburg and, two or three short decades later, he remembers him thus: 'an altogether English man, short, fat, with broad shoulders and a big face; his fundamental character traits appeared to be arrogance and conceit' (P 199). The English become for Kollár one of the types of the devil in his myth of the angelic Slavs.

Perhaps for Kollár they are worse than the Germans, who had been the evilest of his devils up to the publication of the *Cestopis*. Šafařík talks of the Germans or Germanic tribes as the Slavs' enemies from time immemorial, but Kollár is more precise. Twenty-three German emperors from Charlemagne to Henry IV had worked at the 'denaturalization' of the Slavs (W 95). Kollár claims he is not anti-German at all, but only dislikes what the Germans had done to the Slavs in history. Still, however, he does not trust them: he shares the view of some elderly Croats who compare the German menace with the Magyar menace thus (C 66): 'the Magyar element is not as dangerous to the Slavs as the German; … the former undermines our language and nationality publicly and coarsely, whereas the latter does it in a secret, gentle manner.'

The Magyar devils are the devils of the East: 'Asiatic hordes' (W 95), 'an Asiatic tribe of nomads, fishermen and hunters' (G 359). Šafařík links them directly with the Scythians and Mongols: 'felt tents, swinish filth, the dough which the women cased themselves in to clean off from time to time their engrained mud and dirt, idleness and, apart from robbery and war, apathy' (SSI 317–18). The Magyars are also arrogant; one of them had said that the Magyar is 'a masterpiece of creation' (LV 68 and W 69). Part of the complex myth for Kollár (and for Šafařík) is that the Slavs were converted to Christianity very early, at least in Moesia. Probably because of that, Kollár tries to make St (King) Stephen of Hungary almost a Slav: he is known as Vojík; his mother had been called Beloknegini; he had cousins called Ladislav and Vazilej, and Ladislav's wife had had the name Primislava (C 29). On the whole, however, Šafařík and Kollár slightly despise the 'Asiatic' Magyars and they certainly do not despise the Germans. The Hungarian language is rather unsophisticated (G195) and it seems to be made for swearing (V 430 and CD 32); Kollár avers that the Magyars excel in pejoratives for other nationalities (V 43). He writes a fair amount about Magyarization right up to the end of his life; early in his career he had published an article, 'Etwas über die Magyarisirung der Slaven in Ungarn' (Something on the Magyarization of the Slavs in Hungary, 1821).[71] Magyarization has, however, little to do with the myth, except insofar as it was a force driving Šafařík and Kollár to create their myth.

Obstacles to Slav reciprocity

Even for such as our two authors, the Slavs did have failings, which made their movement towards cultural unity pedetentous. The Slavs tend always to be trying to catch up and, thus, suffer from some sort of cultural indolence: 'We always arrive late,' writes Kollár (C 54), 'we are always last; we are too weak for anything.' They are also passive and expect things to be done for them: 'Slavs … expect everything from the government or leave everything to chance' (C 112). A similar mentality is manifested by the fact that the Slavs do not organize themselves schools, hotels or clubs abroad like other nations, however many Slavs may be working in a city. Their passivity does not allow them to: 'wherever they went, they disappeared in a sea of foreigners' (C 144).

That might also have something to do with the lack of self-respect both writers see in the Slavs. Šafařík urges his Muse not to conceal her Slavness in the introductory poem to *Tatranská Múza*. Some Slavs know five dead languages, but would have trouble even getting into Heaven in their own language (DV 23). Kollár speaks of Slav lack of self-respect in his discussion of Slav virtues and failings in *Wechselseitigkeit* (W 98). Here too, he maintains that the Slavs admire only non-Slav writers. Elsewhere he writes, 'we should all be ashamed … that we neglect our own fields and yearn, long for foreign things. If someone does not respect himself and his own, how can others respect him?' (DV 23). 'For centuries', Šafařík writes, 'Slav hearts have clung to an uncontrolled love of foreign things'

(SSI 590). Šafařík almost paraphrases the early fourteenth-century 'Dalimil' chronicle on the Czech upper classes' liking for foreign manners, clothes and foot-wear (G 306).

The main obstacle to Slav Reciprocity is Slav disunity and discord. This and the love of foreign things are negative peasant qualities and so they reflect the same reality as the main alleged virtues of the Slavs. The inquisitive peasant (Kollár complains about them in Switzerland), like village quarrels, is the stuff of literature, especially comic literature. One might also say that 'love of foreign things' as a Slav failing could help explain the Slav 'brain drain' and thus work as active atavism: the contemporary tendency of educated people to abandon their Slavness goes back to the old Slav failing. The division of Slavonic into dialects reflects ancient Slav quarrelsomeness. Slav disunity forms a theme of Šafařík's *Geschichte* (for example, G 47 and 92). *Hlasové* opens with a quotation from Šafařík and Kollár's much-loved source, Constantine Porphyrogennetos (*reg.* 913–59), who reports the words of Prince Svatopluk of Great Moravia on the need for love and unity to avoid destruction by the foes of the Slavs. That is actu-ally cheating a little, since essentially he is speaking about the danger of splitting up the Empire among one's sons. One of the refrains in the *Cestopis* is a German quotation from a 1794 letter of Dobrovský's to Jiří Rybai (Juraj Ribai): 'wir uneinigen Slawen' (H 9; C, for example, 55), 'we quarrelsome Slavs'. Slav disunity results partly from ignorance; with hyperbole of the sort he sometimes enjoys, Kollár states (DV 30): 'For example, the Serb considered the Czech closer to the Hottentots than to himself, and the Czech considered the Muscovites to be some Mongol race.' The Poles are a different matter. They are anti-Slav Francophiles (W 71); he is pleased for them when they are given money for a Polish school in Paris, but finds it selfish of them that they do not intend setting up an all-Slav school (C 145).

There is another, practical, obstacle to cultural unity, the alphabet. In the Preface to his *Geschichte* Šafařík regrets the communication difficulties between Slav dialects caused by the use of different alphabets (G 43). At this stage in his life he believes all dialects should be written in Cyrillic (G 98). In *Wechsel-seitigkeit* Kollár suggests that one achievement of Reciprocity would be a uni-form orthography, though, he adds, uniformity might mean one uniform Latin script and one uniform Cyrillic (W 155). In other words, neither Šafařík nor Kollár was seriously worried by the alphabet. Although Cyrillic could be made to play a significant role in the myth, both authors were sensible enough to know that to change the orthography of the 'Roman Catholic' Slav languages into Cyrillic made no sense, historically or internationally.

The mission of the Slav myth

If myth has to be narrative (other than narrative as a people's history), then *Slávy dcera* is the myth which supports the rest. 'Myth', Pettazzoni writes, 'is true history because it is sacred history, not only by reason of its contents but also because of the concrete sacral forces which it sets going.'[72] That fits with *Slávy dcera*, as does Kołakowski's assertion that myth 'must give an account of death and of love.'[73] *Slávy dcera* explains nearly everything about Kollár, about the Slav idea, about Slav history – and, rather feebly, it shows us Slav Heaven and Hell. Within seven years of its 1832 'complete' edition *Slávy dcera* had become an untouchable sacred text.[74] Even Šafařík quotes from the poem to support and lend pathos to his argument (SSII 159). The complex myth I have been considering in this section all ultimately stems from *Slávy dcera* (where Kollár had already reworked Herder). One might justly say that Šafařík had shown Slav consciousness long before the publication of Kollár's sonnet cycle, but Šafařík would not have written his *Geschichte* as he did, if it had not been for Kollár's work.

Kollár and Šafařík's Slav nationalism plays almost the opposite role to that Kedourie expects from nationalism. He states that nationalism looks 'away from and beyond the imperfect world,' which our two authors' nationalism essentially does not, even if its ultimate, woolly, message does. It does condemn the way things are, as Kedourie says such authors should, but on no account does it ultimately become 'a rejection of life, and a love of death';[75] if one condemned all antiquarianism as love of death, one would have half an argument; and if one were convinced that all messianism was a love of death, not just a rejection of this world, or hope for a better world, then even love itself would cease to have any meaning.

Factual history may certainly require myth, as Kołakowski insists,[76] but myth also requires factual history and, when that has been accomplished and things do not look any better, one ought to look to the future. Herder, when he has related the history and the present state of the Slavs, decides they have a great future:

Meanwhile the wheel of changing time ceaselessly turns; and, since for the most part these nations inhabit the most beautiful stretch of land in Europe, since one probably cannot imagine anything else, but that in Europe law-giving and politics, instead of the warrior spirit, have to and will promote ever more quiet hard work and the peaceful intercourse of peoples: at that time you once industrious and happy people who have sunk so deep, you, finally awakened from your long, indolent sleep, liberated from your slaves' shackles, you will be allowed to use as your own property your beautiful countryside from the Adriatic to the Carpathians, from the Don to the Mulda and to celebrate in this countryside ancient feasts of peaceful hard work and trade.

The important part of this message or quasi-prophecy is that the age of the Teu-
tonic belligerent spirit must die and the Slavs gain their liberty in a new age of
peaceful farming and trade. Herder says nothing of how this will happen; the
wheel of time will just somehow set this in motion. That was clearly not enough
for Kollár. The age will come for him now when the Slavs will save mankind.
Kollár's thought foreshadows French mysticizers half a century or more later, for,
actually, Kollár is saying that the outcasts, the victims, shall become the saviours.

Kollár's belief that his love for the Slavs would be good for the whole of
humanity was now based on historical experience, for myth is also experience.
With their patience, gentleness and industry the Slavs had honed off the Vandal
and Goth rough edges of the Germans (W 94). The Slavs had left innumerable
nations in peace, and had taught innumerable nations how to work and tend the
land, how to be happy (DV 15). Possibly most important, the Slavs had led to the
purification of the Christian Church: 'The Slavs ploughed and sowed; Luther and
the Germans only reaped' (C 207). The Reformation had begun with the
'Slavobulgarian' Bogomils; then it had moved across the southern Slav lands to
northern Italy, then to France. The name of the Cathars does not come from the
Greek for pure, clean, but from the Slav town of Cataro (Kotar) (C 200); the
Paulicians (actually their origins were in Armenia) were named after their leader,
Peter Pavlich; the founder of the Waldensians, Waldo, was actually a Bulgarian,
Vlad (C 201). Bogomil himself (Kollár calls him Basil) or at least his apostles had
taken his ideas to England, where they inspired in 1320 a Waldensian preacher
called Lollard and Lollard's followers had given Wyclif his ideas (*sic*).

In *Dobré vlastnosti* (DV 25) he has already adapted Herder's vision a little:
'It is certainly true that very recently new life has been starting to stir in the whole
Slav nation, a new fervour and efficiency which will perhaps soon attract the eyes
of the whole world and create a new age in the history of mankind.' Behind his
wish culturally to unite the Slavs lies Kollár's belief that only the Slavs can save
the West. The Slavs are not simply gaining their own history; they are going to
make the history of the world (W 95–6):

The history of the world has another, higher, meaning and vocation than to tell us
about battles, campaigns, bloodshed, conquests and subjugations. It should present a
divine rule over the world; that is, it should show how, under the eternal will of the
Godhead, man must always progress to the better, that is the good .... Certainly we
shall gain a deeper knowledge of the nations in useful occupations and quiet crafts, in
laws and manners, in playing and singing than on the bleak battlefield or the deceptive
path of political history.

The Slavs are to become the creators of a new principle of culture, a civilized
principle (W 96):

According to the Classical-Germanic principle of culture fame was earned by making many people slaves and servants; such an oppressor became a hero or knight …; the servant or slave who had been robbed of his freedom was despised, mocked, laden with ignominy. Now it is the reverse. According to the present, if you will, the Slav world view and cultural maxim, ignominy is not as likely to befall the slave as the enslaver, not the oppressed, but the oppressor and robber of freedom.

The Slavs' vocation is to bring on the third stage of civilization. Kollár's idea here probably lies under the influence of the Joachite belief that, first there was the Age of the Father, the Old Testament age, then the Age of the Son, the New Testament age up to the present, but the new age, the Age of the Spirit, or the Age of Love (which does not have a testament), is nigh. The works of Joachim of Fiore and his disciples were fairly widely read at the time Kollár was writing. In Kollár's conception two ages/principles have outlived their usefulness: the principle of antiquity, art, scholarship and education [*Bildung*], is pagan-national and always one-sided. The second principle, the modern (*das Moderne*), romantic chivalrous, sentimental is Germanic-Christian. The third (thoroughly Herderian) age/principle is universal and pure-human. Only a nation like the Slav, would have the power to bring on the third age (W 102). Kollár believes in syntheses (as almost everyone would for the rest of the nineteenth century), and he believed that the Slav simultaneity of thought and emotion which is a prerequisite for being able to give birth to an age where the ideals of humanity will be realized. Even when Kollár is writing on a far narrower basis the ideal of synthesis remains, for example, the following (H 113), which looks forward to Masaryk: 'It is now almost two thousand years that work on the fields of our nation has been done only in accordance with the *analytical* method. Now it is truly high time for us to choose and pursue the *synthetical* method.'

   Slav Reciprocity is a synthetical method and it is Kollár's chief contribution to the securing of the new age. He believes it can lead the Slavs, then the world, to health, provide a way out of degenerate Byronism. Xenophilia, the love of the foreign in art and language, is a sign of degeneration. His view that moral degeneration reflects the idea that linguistic degeneration reflects moral degeneration, that would become popular towards the end of the century in Austria, not because people read Kollár, but because of Karl Kraus. Kollár writes (W 73):

One should first know one's own blood and descent and only then someone else's. It is always a sign of the degeneration of a nation when it despises and forgets what is its own and nearby, dallies with the alien, foreign, distant and thus falls into an unnatural contradiction in itself, into hybridity and self-destruction, which the language is then forced to feel bitterly, for as soon as a people goes bad, the mirror of its inner self, language, must go bad, too.

Byron represents all that is negative about Romanticism; Kollár seems to forget that he was not inconsiderably indebted to *Childe Harold* in his *Slávy dcera*. Byron is 'the most romantic-modern antipode of the Classical-Ancient culture element' (W 90). The romantic-modern principle had been dominant for centuries and, in its fostering of chivalry, humility, piety, love, tenderness, hope and longing, it had borne some good fruit, but now with Byron that fruit is bitter indeed. The earlier virtues have degenerated into savage naturalness, sentimentality, oversensitivity, wild enthusiasm, over-excitement, feverishness, overrefinement and satedness. That last resulted in dulled intellects and dulled feelings. Byron represents the culmination of 'das moderne krankhafte Prinzip', the morbid modern principle (W 104). Kollár's language and approach foreshadow Masaryk and, indeed, Max Nordau. The modern *Zeitgeist*, according to Kollár, is at its most horrific in English literature (W 106); Byron's Muse cares only for despair and horror (C 237). Byron's influence has led normal people to dwell long gazing at instruments of torture and so forth (C 105), and the poet himself had shown his utter disrespect for human suffering and indifference to human baseness by having himself locked up for a time in a Venetian dungeon, so that he could the better write *The Prisoner of Chillon* (C 106).

Finally, I take Kollár's total rejection of the modern because the modern is unnatural. The passage here from *Wechselseitigkeit* was written at almost the same time as Musset's *Confession d'un enfant du siècle*. Musset, however, had no answers, where Kollár has his new age of *Humanität* ushered in by the Slav nation. With the modern in the state that it is, Kollár and Šafařík's complex myth will help put mankind on a healthy, natural, farming, trading, tolerant, innocently merry path (W 106):

The swing of modernism [*Modernismus*][77] has reached its goal, and now one must return to the centre. The old forms of culture are sinking, and must sink; they are too narrow and brittle; new approaches and forms are coming to life: new channels of education [*Bildung*] are opening, and nothing can restrain the flow of cultural rejuvenation and a new worldview. Every extreme, every bizarrerie and grotesquery that emerges out of satiety and a superabundance of better things and that abandons the forms prescribed by Nature, is a sign of sinking taste and of the autumn of a culture.

Kollár remained an optimist.

3

THE DECADENT SELF

Introduction

The Decadent self is a fluid self, a dissolved or fragmented self. A philosopher might say that at least since Descartes,[1] who conceived of the self as a subject of consciousness which does not need a body to exist, the self has been fluid. And a cultural historian might assert that the mediaeval disputes between Body and Soul where the Body is predisposed to damaging the soul, also points to a changing self. I am not suggesting that Christian mystic dualism is the same thing as Cartesian dualism; indeed, in the Middle Ages the human being seemed to have little problems with his or her identity; broadly speaking, one was what one did. Descartes's view, however, is clearly that of a man with no such sense of unproblematicality. Still, Descartes's view of the self is not as important for the Decadents as Hume's (Czech Decadents came to Hume through Masaryk), let alone Schopenhauer's.

Although the literary dissection of the self begins before Romanticism (one thinks of *Tristram Shandy* or, in Czech literature, Mácha's *Krkonošská pout'* [Giant Mountains journey]), Romanticism stimulates it further, but it is not, I argue in this section, before the Decadents and their immediate precursors that the analysis of the self, of the *persona* of consciousness, becomes the central concern of literature. That happened, at least to some degree, because philosophy itself had become the reading matter not only of an educated elite, but of the whole intelligentsia. That was probably largely the result of the impact of Nietzsche. And because of the Czech Decadents' determined rejection of the conventional national and social concerns of vernacular literature, they could indulge in such self-analysis with particular delight.

Some would say that for the Decadents the self had become god.

Remembering that *persona* is the Latin for 'mask', one is not surprised that Decadent studies of the fluid or fragmented self often constituted studies of a fluid or fragmenting mask. One may understand Wilde's Dorian Gray as an ironic depiction of a man separated from his mask, or Hlaváček's Manon in *Mstivá kantiléna* as a woman unmasked to reveal the melodious, fragrant can of worms that she was.

As the Decadents' view on life was ambivalent, on the one hand, vitalist, on the other, exhibiting a delight in decay, so their view on the self was ambivalent. On the one hand, they appeared to see the self as in as great a state of decay as European civilization and, on the other, they imagined an intensely aware self might survive, or at least, rise above the decay, indeed even join in a new civilization brought by the new barbarians (for example, S. K. Neumann, even Růžena Jesenská). *Fin-de-siècle* literature's concern with the self was one of Max Nordau's main targets; Book III of *Entartung* (Degeneration) is entitled simply 'Die Ich-Sucht', but then, as Shaw writes, Nordau 'is so utterly mad on the subject of degeneration that he finds the symptoms of it in the loftiest geniuses as plainly as in the lowest jailbirds, the exceptions being himself, Lombroso, Krafft-Ebing, Dr Maudsley, Goethe, Shakespear [*sic*], and Beethoven.'[2] For Nordau (who was greatly admired by Masaryk), as for all populists, what the self is, is clear. Indeed, one might claim that for non-philosopher *littérateurs*, generally before the second half of the nineteenth century, the self was the soul/psyche and essentially immutable. For the Decadent, the boundaries of self are not at all clear – and, indeed, the very existence of the self is questioned. On the other hand the Decadents generally denied the mythic distinction between inner and outer selves (cf. their theories of dandyhood, in Czech literature particularly Arthur Breisky's, but also Karásek's tentative analysis in *Scarabaeus* [1908]), even though so much of their writing concentrated on the depiction of states of mind. States of mind are states of body.

I am primarily concerned here with impulses which led to the formation and realization of the Decadent self in central Europe, for Austria, claims Broch, was 'the actual centre of decadence' where 'the maximum limit of the European value-vacuum was achieved.'[3] Schorske put it so boldly that his words have since acquired a redolence of cliché: 'Not only Vienna's finest writers, but its painters and psychologists, even its art historians, were preoccupied with the problem of the nature of the individual in a disintegrating society' – and one could say the same of Prague.[4] At the same time, however, artists and thinkers were finding a way of making themselves whole within this decay; psychiatrists, like painters and poets, were consciously striving to 'exploit contradictory psychological forces to create a synthesis of the lived and the dreamt.'[5]

Stirner, Amiel and the Decadent self

The fact that I concentrate on the impulses to Decadent conceptions of the self which came from a minor German philosopher, Max Stirner, and a major Swiss diarist, Henri-Frédéric Amiel, does not mean that I reject the normal notion that Schopenhauer, Baudelaire and Nietzsche formed the foundations of central European Decadence. Stirner and Amiel are, however, not accorded the attention they deserve, given their place in the 1890s mind. It may be that they expressed a few key ideas well rather than that they exerted sustained influence like the other three. The satirist, Viktor Dyk, who was himself well into the 1900s essentially a Decadent, ironizes Czech Decadents' individualism, hedonism, and anarchism, but also their veneration for the ideas first of Stirner, then of Nietzsche.[6] The Czechs came to Stirner partly directly via John Henry Mackay's editions of his works and partly indirectly via Paris. In the Paris of the 1890s Stirner provided a philosophy of intellectual individualist anarchism. Translations did not appear in Paris until 1900, in the *Revue blanche*,[7] though Stirner had been discussed in French periodicals since the beginning of the 1890s. When the Paris Decadent anarchist theatre troupe the Oeuvre put on Hauptmann's *Einsame Menschen* in 1893, the police stopped the staging after the dress rehearsal; the anarchists protested, but the French government introduced their law against 'associations of malefactors'. Two representatives of the anarchist Decadents, Charles Chatel and René Chaughi, reacted to the law in the *Revue libertaire* (1.January 1894) and in their article they informed the security forces of the names of 'malefactors', i.e. people who had the audacity to express thoughts in literature; apart from Tolstoy, Ibsen, Herbert Spencer and Nietzsche, they name Stirner.[8]

Stirner is, as far as the Decadents are concerned, the author of one work, *Der Einziger und seine Eigentum* (The ego and its own, 1845), just as Amiel was the author of one work, the *Fragments d'un journal intime* (Fragments of an intimate diary). Amiel's *Journal* was not written for publication; but it was published, initially incompletely by the author's friend Edmond Scherer (1883–84); the Decadents, obviously enough, knew only the 'Fragments'. Its posthumous publication was something of a sensation. Sober Lanson was as impressed as any Decadent; Amiel was, he says, a remarkable 'type', impotent in practical affairs and inwardly active, a mind entirely occupied with the analysis of itself (what Matthew Arnold considered the nineteenth-century disease), using up his time and his ability to act in studying himself, subtle, penetrating, sad and with an acute clarity of vision.[9] To be sure, Amiel does get on Lanson's nerves a little, because of his 'manic' complication of everything in order to analyse it. In his wide-ranging essay on contemporary literature, 'Synthetism v novém umění' (Synthetism in the new art, 1892), the man who was to become god among Czech literary critics, F. X. Šalda, placed Amiel among 'the artists who dominate our age, the true princes of the last quarter of this century', together with such as Spinoza, Pascal, Poe, Stendhal, Baudelaire and Beethoven.[10] The English Decadent and precursor of the Decadents, Pater, particularly notes Amiel's statement that every landscape is a state of the soul. Pater implies that what he finds enchanting in Amiel is that he appears to be imbued with the modern spirit, but that his modernity does not arise from cultural satedness. Pater's assessment of Amiel reminds one of Masaryk's or F. V. Krejčí's assessments of Czech Decadent literature as being born of cultural hunger rather than of satedness like contemporaneous French or English literature. There is in Amiel, Pater writes, the man 'who would be "the man of desires"; and who seems, therefore, to have a double weariness about him'. The expression of modern sensitivity and mood – 'the culture of *ennui* for its own sake – is certainly carried to its ideal of negation by Amiel. But the complete, the positive, soul, which will merely take that mood into its service ... is also certainly in evidence in Amiel.' That service, Pater maintains in accordance with the Decadent code, 'is in counteraction to the vulgarity of purely positive nature.'[11] And particularly in Austria, the sheer empty vulgarity of liberalism and its failure created an especially eloquent revulsion to anything that smacked of Positivism and modern science.

Hofmannsthal's slightly pert 1891 review of Amiel's *Journal*, 'Das Tagebuch eines Willenskranken' (The diary of a man with a sick will), begins with a dogmatic statement that exhibits an appreciation akin to Pater's: 'They are few who suffer the sufferings of the age and think the thoughts of the age. And books from which such a pain of the age speaks, are the saddest, and become renowned because they are the only books which we can almost completely understand.'[12] The young critic finds depicted in the work a return to a lost naivety that reflects the two chief moods of the present two generations of hesitators: homesickness (which Hofmannsthal from his Viennese point of view sees typified as *Nationalitätenfieber*), and religious nostalgia. That contrasts strongly with Pater, who considers Amiel's religious feeling part of his sound sensitivity to the role of religion in educated life. Hofmannsthal ascribes the intensity of the book's expression of the *maladie du siècle* to its author's Swissness, which may be understood as a fusion of Frenchness and Germanness or an intermediate state blending the Roman Catholic yearning for the mystical and cult of compassion with the Protestant tendency to pious pose, the Protestant predilection for big words: in Amiel he sees a Roman Catholic dreamer combined with a Protestant Hamlet. Furthermore, Amiel embodies the 'completest exemplification' of Schopenhauer's 'fourth book', since that reveals the battle between the will to affirmation and the will to negation. Here Hofmannsthal is unwittingly pointing out one of the aspects of Amiel that attracted the Decadents to him so strongly, for this dichotomy (the ambivalence mentioned in the beginning of this chapter), life-affirmation *versus* luxuriance in decay, characterizes the whole European Decadent trend. It is partly on account of this that Hofmannsthal finds fault with Amiel because he had not achieved: 'The art of suggestion, *l'art d'évoquer*, the great master art ... ; he lets himself be mastered, is a stringed instrument and photosensitive plate.' He is 'Almost an artist's soul; one thing is lacking; ability.'[13] His wishing to embrace everything is, claims Hofmannsthal, nothing more than an incapacity to limit himself. He lacks the discipline of commanding art.

Hofmannsthal also mentioned the notion of the *paysage de l'âme*. In his preface to the unimportant Karel Červinka's *Hledání samoty* (Seeking aloneness) the important Jiří Karásek attributes the ability to realise Amiel's *paysage de l'âme* to the generation of poets who had immediately preceded the Decadents (the so-called Realists, Machar and Sova). Decadent literature, the new literature, must do more than that. The echo of Hofmannsthal here is probably coincidental; the new school has as its principle '*náladovost a suggestivnost umění*' (art based on mood and suggestion).[14]

Amiel may have expressed a fluid, Protean self, like the Decadents, but neither he nor they denied the possibility of some unity to hold together that dissipated self, some binding force or boundary to its fluidity. Indeed, precisely because they found the self so fluid, the Decadents often magnified the self to a degree that it went far beyond the sentient 'I' which was and perhaps, is generally accepted as somehow or other existing. Stirner was an exponent of the magnified self, long before Nietzsche claimed the self as the only true measure of things. In an essay published before *Der Einzige und sein Eigentum*, 'Das unwahre Princip unserer Erziehung oder Der Humanismus und Realismus' (The untrue principle of our education or Humanism and Realism, 1842), he aligns freedom with whole-selfness or personness:

Freedom lies only in *abstraction*: the only free man is he who has overcome the given and has himself brought together what he has lured out of himself by questions into the unity of his own ego. ... thus the final goal of education can no longer be *knowledge*, but the *will* that is born of knowledge, and eloquent expression of what education should aim for is: the *individual* or *free human being*.[15]

Amiel's conception of the self, or at least of an ideal self, is remarkably close to Stirner's in his entry for 6 April 1851: 'Happy are those, says the apostle, who are in accord with themselves and who do not condemn themselves to the side they take. This inner identity, this unity of conviction is all the more difficult, the more the mind discerns, decomposes, foresees. Freedom has great trouble returning to the open, free unity of instinct'.[16] On the other hand, Amiel rejects solipsism or the grand form of subjectivity proposed by Stirner. He conceives of the self as a prison, if one is not able to project oneself into any number of points of view (the Decadent ideal preached by Breisky). That leads him, however, to conceive of

himself as divided, for though he can be intellectually objective, he cannot prevent himself from being emotionally subjective. Because he lacks will, he cannot
achieve the ideal whole self; he writes on 12 September 1876: 'your individuality
is to be impersonal and your anxiety to have to be individual. What is lacking lies
in will; the principle of your abstention lies in doubt ... In other words, you have
adapted ill to the human condition and you will die before you have even really
unpacked.' (Amiel, II, 202) Then, only a little longer than two months before his
death, he writes (18 February 1881): 'It is a fluid existence ... I watch my impressions, dreams, thoughts, memories pass by like a man who has given up
everything ... This contemplative immobility is related to what is attributed to
seraphim. It is not the individual self that interests it, but a specimen of the
monad, a sample of the general history of the mind,' (II, 311 ...). Ryle considers
such division of one's self into various states as mythological fabrication. It is not
various bits of one's mind that do the forgetting, inferring, smelling and hearing
'in the way in which my solicitor or chimney sweep or my electric oven do things
for me. I do things.'[17] Against the scepticism which later had a profound influence
on the anti-Positivist Decadents, at least in Janaway's interpretation, Kant had
suggested that the large number of mental states one can ascertain in oneself, and
then link, provided a subject which could apprehend an objective world. Kant, he
writes, states that the relation of a self's mental states to an object is the same as a
self's experience of the unity of his consciousness.[18] Through Schopenhauer, but
also Stirner and Nietzsche, the Decadents, though very few of them could be
called anything like profound thinkers,[19] rejected Kant. All they seemed to have to
replace the apparently stable, whole Kantian self was Amiel's fluid, fragmented
existence and an awareness that they should pursue some genuinely free, whole
self like Stirner's. Moreover, as the Decadent stridently defended himself, his
personness, against modern society's attacks on the self, so too he questioned the
health of the self that he conceived of as attacked. 'My self', writes Barrès, 'is as
jealous as an idol; it does not want me to forsake it. A lassitude and nervous disgust warned one as soon as I began to neglect myself in order to adore strangers.'[20] For Barrès, perhaps, the self was not *unrettbar*, though his ideology of
egotism boils down very much to the same thing as the Austrian (i.e. Austrian-
German and Czech) Decadents' and, indeed, Wilde's attempts to live life as art,
since, if the *Ich* was *unrettbar*, it was necessary to create an artificial *Ich*. They
appear to have been aware that the 'I' was irreducible, that its semantic boundaries were unique.[21] That irreducibility could as easily support solipsism or grand
egotism as it could the notion that the self is definitively fluid or unsalvageable.

Because self-conception lies at the centre of Decadent artistic thinking, no
student of the period can leave the matter untouched. One such student is Misao
Miyoshi. Apparently unaware that he had chosen for his book the same title as
R. D. Laing had previously given his study of schizophrenia, Miyoshi pursues a

critical method which is a little confusing. He alleges that three types of 'self-division' dominate what he labels Victorian literature. First, the 'dissociation of sensibility': the division of the self is manifested in 'the breakdown of formal unity' in the writer's work. Secondly, the division or, here, disintegration, of the self is projected by a highly self-aware writing through his creations of doppelgängers, Gothic villains or split personalities or by his philosophical constructions of 'symptoms of the self', which are then argued in his works. Thirdly, self-division is, Miyoshi claims, particularly 'severe' where, in the artist, the frontier between life and art is unclear or actually vanishes.[22]

Miyoshi, true to the time when he was writing, sees art in terms of identity crisis, and though his book is chaotic, it suggests ways of approaching the Decadent self, as long as one accepts its semi-Freudian path as viable. Because of the tendency of the Decadents to return to the Gothic villain (Wilde's *Dorian Gray*, Huysmans's *Là-bas*, Karásek's *Scarabaeus* or Meyrink's *Das grüne Gesicht*), Miyoshi's idea that the Romantics had created 'the myth of the infinite self' on the basis of Gothic novels is not empty: the vile 'other self' the Gothic novelists had, writes Miyoshi, embodied in the villain became with the Romantics 'a fugitive beauty, eternally attractive, forever unreachable' (cf. the chimeras of proto-Decadents like Julius Zeyer). Gothic and Romantic heroes constituted methods of exploring the 'unconscious and the irrational.'[23] His interpretation of the Romantics' predilection for incest as an expression of insecure identity encourages one to consider the great number of sexual ambiguities that the Decadents manipulate as constituting part of their concern with the self. Miyoshi's one probably original idea is that liberation could come in the disintegration of the self.[24] The irony in that for the Decadent lay in the fact that, if the self did disintegrate, there was a danger that Decadent man might become a social, indeed even a sociable, being.

In *The Autonomy of the Self* Garber maintains that the division of the self consists in a 'dialectic of aloofness and association'; in his history of European narration from Richardson and Rousseau to Huysmans, the Decadence is little more than an epilogue in a history of 'images of desire.'[25] Like Miyoshi, Garber, predictably, sees the self living life as if it were art, first in that further precursor of the Decadents, Poe, then in the Decadents themselves. Poe also altered, restructured Nature in attempts 'to build enclosed worlds of the self.' Garber points out that Poe's 'antinaturalism' is prefigured in Novalis and E. T. A. Hoffmann and that it precedes Baudelaire's, although, Garber maintains with naughty-boyish innocence that it is generally stated that Decadent 'antinaturalism stems from Baudelaire's disgust with "de stupides céréales" and, along with that, his love of an artifice which found its most delicate employment in the shadings of *maquillage.*' He then rationally links Baudelaire's 'terrible marriage of man with himself' with that version of self-sufficiency displayed by Huysmans's des Esseintes, who lived in his isolation from the world like a gorged animal settling down to hibernate. Garber suggests that the Decadent self's living off itself is somehow inferior to a notional 'productive relationship' of inner and outer selves. From a different angle, Garber accurately notes the role of frustration in the Decadents' creation of the self (here one thinks particularly of the Hlaváček's *Mstivá kantiléna* [Cantilena of revenge, 1898]); the failed or mediocre figure who populates so much Decadent literature in Austria[26] 'needs little from outside except a cause for frustration'; the failed intellectual has a self or personness whose continuity is based on 'the activity of self-consumption.'[27] (Hence, possibly, the ubiquity of the uroboros image in Decadent art.)

A far more lucid contribution to the understanding of the Decadent self is Janaway's *Self and World in Schopenhauer's Philosophy*, which, retaining Schopenhauer as central point of reference, describes the history of self-conceptions from Berkeley to the only apparently solipsist, near-Decadent Wittgenstein of the *Tractatus*. Although the Decadents turned mainly to Schopenhauer and Nietzsche and their understanding of the self, some did go back to Berkeley (notably Klíma). Schopenhauer distinguishes between the will and the intellect and conceives of the self as a combination of the two, although the intellect remains subsidiary to the will. Schopenhauer provides the bases for the Decadent cult of the mask and the Decadent treatment of the self as refuge, when he maintains that the self as knowing subject is unknowable, because the knowing subject cannot be the object of its own knowing: the subject is the knower.[28] One might also see there the potential for the mental aristocratism which so appealed to *fin-de-siècle* man. Schopenhauer does not maintain that there can be no self knowledge whatsoever, but that the self can know itself only as a willing being; his 'doctrine of the primacy of the will ... undermines any conception of the self as primarily or solely a non-worldly knowing intellect,' as Kant conceived of it.[29] Another aspect of Schopenhauer's perception of self which was generally taken over by *fin-de-siècle* writers was his contention that sexual desire constituted the fundament or essence of human being. Indeed the sociologist and philosopher of history, T. G. Masaryk, considered that contention or the manifestation of that contention to be the chief feature of a Decadent. And it is quite clear that the Decadents derived their cult of the aesthetic experience from Nietzsche's perception of the Dionysian. Janaway points out that Schopenhauer in the third book of *Die Welt als Wille und Vorstellung* sees the aesthetic experience 'as resulting from a qualitative change in both the experiencing subject and its object. We can be so taken up with an object we are contemplating that we cease to have desires, and cease to evaluate the object according to our own ends and needs .... In short ..., we cease to will.'[30] Janaway spends little time on Nietzsche and Wittgenstein, but he ties them with Schopenhauer and demonstrates how they arrived at their *fin-de-siècle* views on the basis of Schopenhauer. He sees Nietzsche's dissolution of 'the self into a multiplicity of essentially organic drives directed towards mastering the environment' and Wittgenstein's casting 'the individual body and soul into the realm of mere facts in the world' and his looking to 'the philosophical "I"' which mirrors the world from no point of view within it' as fundamentally interpretations of Schopenhauer's material.[31] In what is, perhaps, his most truly Decadent work, the self-ironic tirade, *Ecce Homo* (written 1888, published posthumously, 1908), Nietzsche, however, comes particularly close to Schopenhauer – though in his work he consistently reviles him. Still, instead of losing self when listening to music, instead of fusing with the Will, Nietzsche, claims to have discovered self in listening to Wagner, 'the absolute certainly about what I *am* projected itself into some changed reality – the truth about me spoke from a terrible depth.'[32] And, concerned with the fragmentation of his self, Nietzsche declares that he has found unity of self, 'My cleverness lies in my having been many things in many places in order to become *one* – in order to be able to arrive at *oneness*.'[33] Schopenhauer was not a solipsist, even if he sometimes appeared to be one.

Wittgenstein was, to a limited extent. Nagel summarizes the Wittgenstein of the *Tractatus* thus: 'solipsism coincides with pure realism. Everything in the world is equally real – from my sense impressions to the stars – but still the world is *my* world. This shows itself in the fact that however objectively I describe the world ... I can always add redundantly: "And it is I who am saying and thinking this."'[34] The notion that Wittgenstein was a solipsist and the extent to which that solipsism is compatible with realism is discussed by Peter Carruthers in his *The Metaphysics of the 'Tractatus'*. Carruthers considers that Wittgenstein has often been misread because his hyperboles have been taken literally – this very use of hyperbole links Wittgenstein with the Decadents. When Wittgenstein writes that good or bad employment of the will causes the world as a whole to wax or wane (Carruthers gives this as an example of hyperbole), he is using the Decadent rhetoric. Furthermore, within Schopenhaurian concepts, the notion is 'true', as it is in Decadent concepts. Carruthers argues that Wittgenstein is actually combining the Humean conception of the self with a notion of the metaphysical subject. Wittgenstein's apparently solipsistic statement that the world is 'my world', Carruthers continues, is true in that 'the set of metaphysical possibilities coincides with what it is possible for me to represent. And secondly, that the only way of finding a place for the metaphysical subject of thoughts and experiences is to identify it with the ineffable "myness" of the point of view from which these representations are formulated'.[35] Janaway pointed out that Schopenhauer considered the self unknowable because the knowing subject cannot be the object of the knower, but that the doctrine of the will subverts any notion of the self as a nonworldly knowing intellect. Carruthers interprets Wittgenstein's placing of the subject outside the world, in other words, outside what is thinkable, thus: if there were a 'complete objective description of the world and its contents', it would include 'mention of that body which is in fact my own, together with a description of those thoughts and experiences which are in fact mine'. On reading that description one would, Carruthers continues, experience a 'shock of recognition', that these thoughts and experiences are 'mine'. It is in this 'my' perspective, Carruthers interprets, that Wittgenstein sees 'the truth to be found in solipsism' (p.82). In his summary Carruthers puts his point convincingly: 'Wittgenstein's endorsement of solipsism gives little evidence of solipsism'; Wittgenstein is actually saying that 'there is no distinction between what can be represented in my thoughts and what is possible in reality' (One thinks of des Esseintes's 'visit' to London or the mental worlds of Karásek's 'melancholy prince' or the 'imaginary lives' of Breisky's *Triumf zla* (Triumph of evil, 1910), and that 'the "myness" of the point of view from which I describe the world is an unsayable aspect of it (a "limit")'; that is 'equally consistent with realism.'[36]

Some other conceptions of selfness

Because of their eclecticism, their Roman Catholic cultural roots and their highly literary culture it is unlikely that the Austrian Decadents did not directly or indirectly know St Augustine's attitude to the Manichaeans and his conception of self. His conception of the self in *The Confessions* is perhaps not original, and yet it summarizes the European conception from the beginning of the Middle Ages to the Enlightenment. In Book VIII section [IX] 21, he summarizes the fundamentals of a view of the intellect and the will, a summary which Schopenhauer was also reacting to. If there is a dichotomy between body and intellect, it derives from degrees of obedience (the subject of irresolution fascinated the Decadents and the following might be read as an analysis of the character of Rojko in Zeyer's *Dům "U tonoucí hvězdy"* (House at the sign of the sinking star, 1897):

The mind commands the body, and it obeys instantly; the mind commands itself, and is resisted ... The mind commands the mind, its own self, to will, and yet it doth not ... It commands itself, I say, to will, and would not command, unless it willed, and what it commands is not done. But it willeth not entirely: therefore doth it not command entirely. For so far forth it commandeth, as it willeth: and, so far forth is the thing commanded, not done, as it willeth not. For the will commandeth that there be a will; not another, but itself. But it doth not command entirely, therefore what it commandeth is not. For were the will entire, it would not even command it to be, because it would already be.

Augustine's conception of memory also looks forward to Decadent conceptions of the place of the self in history. Augustine perceives a unity between past, present and future just as the Decadent often perceived his self as an expression of the history of his nation or of the human race as a whole (in Czech literature, particularly Otokar Březina, but also Zeyer and, spasmodically, Karásek).

Augustine asks in Book XI, Part [XXXVIII] 37:

Who therefore denieth, that things to come are not as yet? and yet, there is in the mind an expectation of things to come. And who denies past things to be now no longer? and yet is there still in the mind a memory of things past. And who denieth that the present time hath no space, because it passeth away in a moment? and yet our consideration continueth, though that which shall be present proceedeth to become absent.

As irresolution may be seen as a Decadent intermediate state, so may be this manner of conceiving of time, history or memory. Augustine's well-attested hatred of the Manichaeans is important for us here because of the Decadent tendency to see life in terms of good and evil forces (for example, Karásek or Šlejhar), and because of the frequent interpretation of nineteenth-century intellectuals' 'inner conflicts' as essentially Manichaean (compare Miyoshi). The Manichees are seducers of the soul, 'who observing that in deliberating there were two wills, affirm that there are two minds in us of two kinds, one good, the other evil' (Book VI, Part [IX] 21).

Hume likewise rejects the Manichaean manner of thinking. 'It has been proved', he writes, 'that even the passions commonly esteemed selfish carry the mind beyond self directly to the object; that though the satisfaction of these passions gives us enjoyment, yet the prospect of enjoyment is not the cause of the passion, but, on the contrary, the passion is antecedent to the enjoyment ... the case is precisely the same with the passions denominated benevolent.'[37] Hume conceives of the self as a bundle of perceptions, much as Decadent authors will conceive of the self, especially in their cycles of verse and short stories (for example, Schnitzler, Kamínek, Hlaváček). The self or soul or mind is 'nothing but a system or train of different perceptions – those of heat and cold, love and anger, thoughts and sensations – all united together but without any perfect simplicity or identity.'[38]

The Augustinian triad of the human mind reflects the Holy Trinity: we are, know that we are, and love to be and to know it. Amiel, who does not have an utterly consistent conception of the self, but who normally comes close to Hume and the Decadents, also has a triad of conception of the self in his entry for 30 August 1869; here his thoughts are inspired by his own contemplation of Schopenhauer. He imagines that his beloved philosopher has confused nature, character and individuality. Amiel's distinctions here very vaguely presage the Freud triad of the I, the It and the Super-I. One notices the author's customary courtesy towards himself: 'I am inclined to think that individuality is fatal and primitive, the *naturel* very old but alterable, and character more recent and susceptible to voluntary or involuntary modification. Individuality is a matter of psychology, the *naturel* a matter of aesthetics, and only character a matter of morality' (Amiel II, 67). In the conclusion to *The Renaissance,* Pater, who had an enormous impact on the Czech late Decadent, Miloš Marten, conveys a sense of self embraces Hume and, probably coincidentally, Schopenhauer (including Schopenhauer's conception of aesthetic experience). Pater's picture has a chance similarity with parts of Amiel's depictions of the fluid self and certainly demonstrates or prefigures the Decadent cult of the moment; it also manifests more than a hint of solipsism:

If we continue to dwell in thought on this world, not of objects in the solidity with which language invests them but of impressions, unstable, flickering, inconsistent, which burn and are extinguished with our consciousness of them, it contracts still further: the whole scope of observation is dwarfed into the narrow chamber of the individual mind. Experience, already reduced to a group of impressions, is ringed round for each of us by that thick wall of personality through which no real voice has ever pierced on its way to us, or from us to that which we can only conjecture to be without. Every one of those impressions is the impression of the individual in his isolation, each mind keeping as a solitary prisoner its own dream of a world. Analysis goes a step further still, and assures us that those impressions of the individual mind to which, for each one of us, experience dwindles down, are in perpetual flight; that each of them is limited by time, and that as time is infinitely divisible, each of them is infinitely divisible also; all that is actual in it being a single moment, gone while we try to apprehend it, of which it may ever be more truly said that it has ceased to be than that it is.[39]

Individualism, memory, social being

In the Conclusion to *The Renaissance* Pater also speaks against habit in our appreciation of art (one remembers how Augustine inveighed against habits), and Pater believes that forming habits prevents us from noticing every moment of the splendid experience of life, and its brevity. Burning with gemlike flame means avoiding all habit and practising ecstatic individualism.

Individualism means conscious differentness (non-submission to the habits of the surroundings) together with the view that 'society is constituted of autonomous, equal, units, namely separate individuals, and that such individuals are more important, ultimately than any larger constituent group.'[40] In the Bohemian Lands individualism in an artist meant breaking with the artist's traditional identification with the national ideology, ceasing to act as mouthpiece for the interests which were supposed to bind together a social or national unit.[41] In both the Austrian and the Bohemian Lands, *fin-de-siècle* individualism also involved rejecting the emergent populist nationalism. Moreover, Broch saw stylistic individualism as a more or less inevitable reaction to the *Un-Stil* of turn-of-the-century Vienna: 'in an epoch of non-style [*des Un-Stiles*], of style-vacuum, stylelessness there is only personal style and that is a frightening and almost debilitating freedom for the person who is conscious of it'.[42]

The Decadents feared all isms as habits or conventions which would constitute part of the *Un-Stil* which oppressed them. All the leading Czech Decadents denied at some time or other that they were or had been Decadents, that is: adherents of an ism. The fear of such *Un-Stil*, together with the propagation of the individual, forms a necessary part of the anarchist Stirner's doctrine of the self. In 'Das unwahre Princip unserer Erziehung', he asks sarcastically: 'Dualism, materialism, spiritualism, naturalism, pantheism, realism, idealism, supernaturalism, rationalism, mysticism and whatever all the abstrusisms of overstrained speculations and feelings are called: what blessings have they brought for the State, the Church, the arts, the national culture [*Volkskultur*]?' (Stirner, 14) It is not just coincidence that a key-passage of the manifesto of the Czech *Moderne* (1895) expresses similar sentiments:

We want an art which is not a luxury article and which is not subject to the changing whims of literary fashion. What we mean by modern is not what happens to be *à la mode*: the day before yesterday Realism, yesterday Naturalism, today Symbolism, Decadence, tomorrow Satanism, occultism, those ephemeral slogans which for a few months give bland uniformity to a whole series of literary works, and which literary gigolos then ape. Artist, impregnate your work with your blood, your brain, your self.[43]

My other inspirer of Austrian Decadents, Amiel, clearly a man of individual ideas, at least in his private diary, was perhaps suspicious of individualism as a doctrine. On Schleiermacher's individualism, really: ideological egotism, Amiel sees individualism and egocentricity expanding to become a system wherein one acknowledges nothing alien to oneself; nor does one accept any limits to one's powers; the result is that Schleiermacher promulgates prophetic security and immortal youth for the self. Amiel links Schleiermacher's conception of absolute freedom with Emerson. In the latter, man becomes almost God because he has learned how to take refuge in a personal conscience. The danger of such conceptions as Schleiermacher's and Emerson's are, maintains Amiel, that their elimination of humility threatens man with a further fall: if man is to become his own master again, as the Decadents also claimed he must, he will again resemble the Elohim or fall. The first danger of individualism is, then, for Amiel, hubris; the second is a weakness which results in solitariness and asceticism; this Amiel sees in Vinet, whom he characterizes thus (Amiel I, 62): 'Casuistry of conscience and casuistry of grammar, eternal suspicion of the self, perpetual moral examination, these explicate his talent and his limits.' Such casuistry is what the Decadents despised in the Protestants and in those who espoused 'Protestant ethics.'

The notion of individualism was particularly linked with Protestant cultures, but extreme egotism was common to Protestant and Roman Catholic cultures. A notion which could support both individualism and extreme egotism, but which could also suggest immense spiritual, even mystical humility, was the notion of the historical self. The self contains history in the present. First one might take an exaggerated statement of that from a French Decadent Boulangiste, Barrès:

My pride, my plenitude is to conceive of them *sub specie aeternitatis*. My being enchants me when I catch a glimpse of it spreading out over the centuries, developing through a long sequence of bodies … The soul which inhabits my self today is made up of particles which have survived thousands of deaths … I am nothing but an instant in the long development of my Being; in the same way, the Venice of this age is but an instant of the Venetian Soul. My Being and the Being of Venice are without limits.[44]

Amiel has a sense of a built-in or natural morality (essentially his conception is Kantian), which may be compared either to the common Decadent, and now common genetic engineer's, notion of the historical self or to a notion of metabiological memory. In the expression of his notion Amiel, however, does evince a thoroughly Decadent scepticism towards the idea of a 'fact': 'It is not history that teaches the conscience honesty, but conscience that teaches history. The fact is corrupting; it is we who correct it in persisting in our ideal. The soul moralizes the past lest it be demoralized by the past' (Amiel I, 32). Hofmannsthal understands the attitude of the Swiss to the fact, to the objective world altogether, perceptively: Amiel deplores the world as a system of deception to which he feels bound both out of a sense of duty and because he bears affection for the wretched place.[45] Whether the perception of an historical self rests on a moral memory (as in Amiel or, say, Rádl) or on the sense that layers of history going back to the beginnings of mankind, indeed even to man's animal prehistory (as in Barrès or Březina) exist in one, the notion 'historical self' can easily lead to mysticising interpretations embodied in *karma* or the idea that the individual soul is merely an emanation from the great primal Soul. The mystical way of thinking could lead to an arrogant (nearly dandyesque) form of moral relativism. Thus Meyrink's Swammerdam says of the base ruffian sailors of Amsterdam: 'In reality these men are far better than one thinks: they have just got lost in the primal forests of their souls and, in their present state, they resemble clawing, tearing animals.'[46]

The notion of the historical self may also draw our attention to memory itself, that is: to what we remember of the existence we have inhabited since our mothers bore us. One may say that a self, or an instance of the self, is largely a collection of memories (its own and others') at a particular moment.[47] The nature of memory had some fascination for the Decadents because individual memories could be intermediate states: memory is the making present of the past. What further interested them was the apparent variation in character contained in remembered episodes of a single self's life. Memory, therefore, contributes to the sense of an unstable or fragmentary self. If one's mental self consists largely in memory, including the memory of one's own reaction to events and indeed one's reinterpretation of events (which may change individual memories or aspects thereof), one may become utterly convinced that there is no fixed self. The individual's grasp of his or her own story – indeed, of the stories of anyone and anything else – depends on two kinds of editing, as Glover suggests: abridgement and endorsement or non-endorsement. Fantasizing and self-deception may help us in our abridging or censoring of our memory of the past. Endorsement means that we assume attitudes (often affective attitudes) to episodes in our past, identify ourselves with some and not with others, interpret many *ex post* to our advantage or detriment. Furthermore, for the Decadents with their particular interest in ecstasy and in the artificial paradises engendered by toxic stimulants, the mind or body seemed consciously to expunge some episodes without the knowledge of the self and also to emphasize others in moments of ecstasy, so that certain episodes became distorted without the self's having consciously interfered to distort. Cases of these sorts illustrate 'the inadequacy of identifying *me* with my actions or with the desires that prevail in them.'[48] Furthermore, the very idea of ecstasy involves a standing outside one's self, and therefore implies the body as an essential part of the self.

Solipsism, Decadent aristocratism and Stirner

If we conceive of ourselves as consisting primarily of memories, we might well be inclined to a solipsist view of life, the belief that only my experiences are real or that self-existence is the only certainty. That amounts to the complete egocentricity of Stirner of the 'ludibrionism' or 'ego-solipsism' of Ladislav Klíma, which is expressed in the introduction to *Der Einzige und sein Egentum* (1845). If self-existence is the only certainty, the self must be its own amoral creator (Stirner, 37):

I am [not] nothingness in the sense of emptiness, but the creative nothingness, the nothingness out of which I myself as creator create Everything. Away, then, with every thing which is not entirely My thing! ... Indeed, I am myself My thing and I am neither good nor evil. Neither of those concepts has any meaning for Me ... My thing ... is not universal, but is unique, as I am unique. Nothing matters to me more than I!

Stirner has, then, gone further than Fichte, for whom the self determines the self, but he identifies the object in self-consciousness with the subject, while simultaneously saying that they are distinct.[49] In contrast to Fichte, Stirner founds his notion of self on the transience of the self, that is, not on its absoluteness; Stirner's notion prefigures all Decadent notions of the present self. 'When Fichte says,

'The self is everything', he seems to be perfectly in harmony with my tenets. Except: not the self *is* everything, but the self *destroys* everything, and only the self-dissolving self, the never existing self, the final self is really the self. Fichte speaks of the "absolute self". But I speak of My Self, the transient self' (Stirner, 124). Stirner has to admit that there are other selves beyond his self, for he has empirical evidence that there are other human beings, but he knows only his self and can only use the word 'I' for himself; thus other individuals are for him incomplete. His is the only being who can really exist for him and the only being of whom he can maintain that he is unique. Amiel's account of Édouard Claparède's philosophy of the self combines Stirner with Schopenhauer. Claparède's thought is also completely compatible with Decadent notions (Amiel II, 13).

Only the self exists and the universe is only a projection of my self, a phantasmagoria that we create without doubting its existence, believing ourselves to be its contemplators. Our noumenon objectivizes itself into a phenomenon. The self would be a radiating force which, modified without knowing the modifier, imagines it by virtue of the principle of causality, in other words, gives birth to the great illusion of the objective world in order to explain itself to itself. Waking would only be a better connected dream. The self would, thus, be an unknown that gives birth to an infinity of unknowns through a fate of its nature.

Amiel dislikes absolute egoism or individualism. He declares it sheer foolishness, for, though we may sometimes find ourselves temporarily in total seclusion from the rest of mankind, generally all our thoughts are somewhere attached to or echoing humanity as a whole. Decadents might be suspicious of such a view; it apparently runs counter to their elitism. Arnošt Procházka, for example, could not countenance the notion that his thoughts could echo humanity as a whole; his thoughts could only be in symbiosis with those of other aristocrats of the soul.

More important for our understanding of the Decadents is Amiel's view on laughter and the self. The laugher, he claims, is normally a solipsist. In order to love, he writes, one has to believe in the reality of what one loves, and one has to become serious (that is, to learn to suffer, to give oneself and to forget oneself). Amiel's characterization of the eternal laugh provides an analysis of (and possibly an impulse to) the demonic laugh of the central character in Zeyer's *Dům "U tonoucí hvězdy"*, whose laugh is also eternal in that it expresses ultimate self-knowledge in death, fusing with his astral self: 'The eternal laugh is absolute isolation; it is the proclamation of perfect egoism' (Amiel II, 26). Those words constitute a distillation of an impassioned exposition of theoretical egoism uttered over ten years previously (Amiel I, 117–18); we notice that Zeyer's 'demon' enters here:

The self alone, and that is enough; the self through negation, through ugliness, through contortion and irony; I in my sovereignty; my self emancipation by laughter, free as a demon, exulting in spontaneity, self master of my self, my self for myself, an invincible monad, a being sufficient unto itself, at last for once living through itself and for itself. That is what is at the root of this joy; an echo of Satan, the temptation to make oneself the centre, to be the Elohim, the great revolt.

All-pervasive irony was a feature of the writings of most of the main pre-Decadents and Decadents, Baudelaire, Verlaine, early Thomas Mann, Gide, Hlaváček, Dyk, Wilde (most obviously). The demonic laugh of Zeyer's Rojko may also be generically linked with the sexual ecstasy experienced during combustion by the erotically obsessed heroes of Karásek's 'Genenda' (*Posvátné ohně,* Sacred fires, 1911) and Šlejhar's experimental novel, *Peklo* (Hell, 1905).

The eternal laugh can, according to Amiel, belong only to the solipsist. Stirner can be sarcastic, and ironic, but he is no laugher. His solipsism constitutes a serious, if wild, rejection of the contemporaneous growth of materialism. Amiel fears the unspirituality of solipsism, but Stirner's version is spiritual, or at least is not materialist, even if he does express his spirituality in proprietorial terms (Stirner, 43): 'Thoughts had become *corporate* for themselves, were phantoms, like God, Kaiser, Pope, *Vaterland* and so forth. If I destroy their corporeality, I retrieve them for my Mineness and say: I alone am corporeal. And now I take the world as what it is for Me, as Mine, as My property: I relate everything to Me.' Schopenhauer believes that such solipsism which holds all phenomena outside the individual self to be phantoms is a useful tool for the sceptic, but considers it unworthy as a belief. And, as Janaway comments, 'It is the very absurdity of solipsism which gives it its devastating edge when used polemically.'[50] Furthermore, solipsism is attractive to anyone who wishes to *épater le bourgeois,* a common pursuit of the middle-class Decadents. Stirner's solipsism is conscious; indeed, he condemns what he calls 'involuntary egoism', being out for oneself and pretending or trying not to be. The involuntary egoist is always looking for higher ideals than the self and in so doing he is simply manifesting the uncomprehended drive or instinct to self-dissolution (*Trieb nach Selbstauflösung*). Amiel sees what Stirner calls involuntary egoism as utilitarian materialism, the idolatry of the self and Mammon, which for him will be the likely by-products of any socialism (Amiel I, 26–7) – and the Decadents were as anti-socialist as Stirner and Amiel.

As, at least in Austria, the Decadents rejected liberalism or were born of the 'failure of liberalism', so Stirner considered that liberalism was an onslaught on the self. The proponents of liberalism had emphasized its rationality, its aim to create a rational ordering of society, a reasoned limited freedom. The liberal doctrine of political freedom is, states Stirner, just a second phase of Protestantism, and political freedom will not liberate the individual from the State, but bind him to it with rational laws. Where reason rules, however, the person, the self, is subjugated (Stirner, 79). Stirner seeks total liberation of the self. The liberated self is when only the *Ich* has power over the *Ich* – and here one thinks of dandyism of the Breisky brand. The free man lives in truth; that is: liberation from everything not part of the self and the regaining of naivety, the achievement of the self-suffi-ciency of the self. The liberated self is a self that does not measure itself against other selves, that is aware of its uniqueness, its incomparability with other human beings. The liberated self is in complete control of its thoughts and its sensuality. Again that looks forward to *fin-de-siècle* dandies, but also to the goal of mystical self-awareness that we find in some Decadent literature. It also looks forward to the Decadents' fear of losing their selves in sexuality and, thus, to their percep-tions of woman as sap-sucker or *vagina dentata*. Stirner writes of the liberated *Ich*'s self-cognition as existing 'if it is knowledge of and by itself, or ..., know-ledge of the idea, a self-awareness of the spirit' (Stirner, 20). It is almost as if Meyrink had recently read Stirner when he writes of his Hauberriser: 'But he stood watch before the door of his will and did not allow in [importunate thoughts]. Once again his old habit of observing himself was beginning to assume its rights.'[51]

Stirner's conception of the unique *Ich* only apparently prefigures Wittgen-stein's statements in the *Tractatus logico-philosophicus* (1921): 'I am my world' (5.63) and 'The subject does not belong to the world, but is a boundary of the world' (5.632). In Karásek's novel, *Scarabaeus*, a practical solipsism of a sort becomes a way of analysing one's sexual activities. The Decadent stood to lose his self in sexual passion, and so the analysis here may help to protect one against such a loss. 'When you experience the most fiery, most splendid passion, are you not pleased essentially by the confirmation of your own idea of passion rather than by that particular passion? In fact, what we love in people and things is only our own imagination'.[52] Sexual behaviour is social behaviour, and, ideally, the anarchist and the Decadent were antisocial or asocial.

The self versus nation and State

All collectives threaten the freedom of the unique *Ich*. According to Stirner, one has to grasp one's *Geist*, spirit or intellect, which one uses to fight against the world, that is: the rod of authority. In finding oneself by means of the spirit or intellect one becomes superior to the world: '*Geist* is the *first* finding of the self, the first undivining of the divine, that is, of the uncanny, the ghost, the "higher powers". Now nothing impresses our fresh sense of youth, this sense of self, any longer: the world is declared discredited, for We are above it; We are *Geist*' (Stirner, 30). Then one must complete, perfect, that *Geist*. One's only active con-tact with the world must be enjoying it; thus Stirner conceives of an anti-egalitar-ian hedonism, which again foreshadows the dandy strain of Decadence(192–3):

What is the point of my intercourse with the world? I want to enjoy it and, therefore, it must be My property, and therefore I must win it. I do not want freedom nor the equality of men; I want only My power over them, want to make them My property, that is: make them enjoyable … My intercourse with the world consists in My enjoying it and, thus, in my using it for the enjoyment of My self. Intercourse is world-enjoyment and belongs to My self-enjoyment.

Stirner satirizes the middle-class liberal view of State. Citizenship is constituted, he writes, by the notion that the State is the true man and that the human value of the individual lies in being a citizen of a State. Interests of State and service to the State become ideals; one is meant to cease serving one's self and instead serve the State. Indeed, the State has 'become the actual person, before whom the individual personality vanishes: it is not I who live, but it lives in Me'. (Stirner, 74). This liberal State, he maintains, does not in fact yet exist, but it is an ideal goal and it already has rights, for example, the right to demand that I be a human being. That assumes that I am not human and that the State could consider me inhuman. (This prefigures Václav Bělohradský's conception of the 'innocent might' of the State: the State is impersonal and 'impersonalizes' its subjects.) The world which man (the human spirit or intellect) creates is the State, but that is not the world of the *Ich*. Stirner denies the collectivising abstraction 'human', since one's actions are not human, but one's own. Each individual's actions are different from every other individual's (Stirner, 122).The State is objectionable also because it consists in an ordering of dependence. The State is necessarily the adversary of the individual, is always repressive: 'The State always has one goal, to restrict, restrain, subordinate the individual, to make him subject to some kind of common principle …. The State never aims at bringing about the free activity of the individual, but always activity bound to the *design of State*' (Stirner, 144). This repressiveness will eventually lead to the State's liquidation of the individual; the State necessarily becomes totalitarian. Indeed, the State decides what is good for it, and then does everything in its power to murder the sovereign individual (again, compare Bělohradský, and Havel as dissident). In other words, Stirner's anti-State political philosophy appears to be directed at all notions of 'progressive' politics and social 'progress'. In that he is at one with Decadents from Baudelaire onwards. The following words from *Mon Coeur mis à nu* link the Decadents more or less directly with Stirner's manner of thinking, except that Baudelaire, like Nietzsche, believes in the possibility of progress in the individual; Baudelaire, by the way, linked the Belgians with the herd mentality, massed bands of dulness:

The belief in progress is a doctrine of the lazy, a doctrine of Belgians. The individual
    who counts on his neighbours to do his job for him.
There can be no progress (true, that is to say, moral, progress) except in the individual
    and through the individual himself …

There are also people who cannot enjoy themselves otherwise than in a herd. The true hero enjoys himself quite alone.[53]

Progressiveness is linked as much with liberalism as with socialism, both of which involve the State and thus indented labour, offering no chance of a free self: 'the State rests on – *the slavery of work*. If *work* became *free*, the State would be lost' (Stirner, 87). In the Decadents, anarchism was sometimes linked with oc-cultism; one thinks of Karásek, but possibly most or all of the French, Paul Adam and Laurent Tailhade.[54] S. K. Neumann's so-called satanism was, in fact, vitalist luciferism, and the true Decadent occultist novelist, Emanuel z Lešehradu, really had nothing to do with anarchism. The State is virtually invisible in Lešehrad's *belles lettres*. Just as the State threatened individual political freedom, so it threat-ened individual spiritual freedom. The perceived 'failure of religion' in the sec-ond half of the nineteenth century was, indeed, largely inspired by faith in the State. It was, then, the State that was the general enemy of the Decadent self – and the State's servants, primarily the middle classes, but sometimes simply the masses (the herd, the mob, the philistines, and so forth – those to whom the Decadents considered themselves superior).

As the State was linked by the artistic avant-garde with middle-class thought, so was the nation. Though he devotes far less space to them than to the State, Stirner has little time for nations. Nations or peoples have no power. The self can have its own freedom when that freedom is its own power; the notion of national freedom is empty because peoples have no power. Any free self can overcome a nation, and one notes in the following grandiose statement that Stirner appears to have been as attracted to the personality of Nero as the Decadents: 'I blow peoples down with one breath of the living self, whether it is the breath of a Nero, an Emperor of China or a poor writer' (Stirner, 115). He mocks the idea of the nation's having taken over as the ruler in the French Revolution; in fact, the nation had been created as a greater autocrat than the previous monarch. Kings were nothing in comparison with the new 'sovereign nations'. One had had cer-tain rights to protect oneself against the king, but one has none to protect oneself against the nation (Stirner, 75–6). The sovereign nation is an abomination. One can easily see how, given the contemporary welter of nationalist and nationally conscious literature, the Czech Decadents would be highly suspicious of national(ist) ideologies, at least in their writing. Karel Hlaváček, for example, while a full-blown anational Decadent poet and art critic, was, however, also an enthusiastic member of the patriotic gymnastics movement, Sokol.

Amiel, while sharing many of Stirner's political views, because Amiel was an intelligent individualist, in his early forties still appears to be better disposed than Stirner to the nation. He declares a principle that nationality, unlike State, constitutes voluntary association, in an entry for 4 December 1863: 'if it is a matter of nationality, it is consent, if of State, it is constraint' (Amiel I, 177). For Amiel nation/nationality is a moral category. Thus the profound experience of a foreign nation may enrich one's own moral existence. When travelling abroad, he seeks to grasp the soul of alien things and, in his terms, the national soul which will be part of that soul. Travelling abroad will open for him a new moral *patrie* (Amiel I, 80). He is, then, still entrammelled in sentimentalized notions of objective nationality.[55] By the time he is in his fifties, Amiel has woken up to the hollowness of the concept 'nation'; his only chosen native country, he concurs with Mme de Staël, is the company of individuals he has elected to be with. Otherwise a nation is simply man, the ideal man. 'As far as national man is concerned, I tolerate him, study him, but I do not admire him' (Amiel II, 220). Together with all other group allegiances, Amiel rejects both patriotism and nationalism – though it is not quite clear that he distinguishes between the two terms (Amiel II, 221): 'the patriotic illusion, chauvinist, family or professional, does not exist for me. On the contrary, I feel more warmly towards the failings, blemishes and imperfections of the group to which I belong.'

Both Stirner and Amiel reject liberal rationalism – like the Decadents who read their works. For Amiel, and this is fundamental to grasping why Austrian *fin-de-siècle* writers found him so attractive, liberal ideology can never be successful in a Roman Catholic country: 'To preach liberalism to a population that has been Jesuitized by its education is like recommending dancing to a man with no legs' (Amiel II, 86). Continental liberalism's main failing is that it appears to believe in some abstract freedom without free individuals. Quite coincidentally, at the same time the Austrian Masaryk is pointing out the difficulty of evolution in Roman Catholic or Orthodox countries, which prefer as their means of social change revolution and venereal disease. As a liberal state is impossible where the local religion is illiberal, so, maintains Amiel (Masaryk would agree), it is almost impossible where there is no religion at all. Amiel compares the Germans (Germanic peoples?) favourably with the Slav and Romance peoples, those racial groups who are dominated by illiberal religion and who have a tendency to be collectivist rather than individualist. Collectivism is probably always illiberal; it represents for Amiel an uncivilised type of human behaviour (once more we think of Václav Havel). Austrian Decadents would have had difficulty agreeing with much of the following because of both the Czech, and in general, the serious Austrian German 1890s writers' mistrust or hatred of German nationalism; furthermore, the notion of the West being saved by the Slavs was not uncommon in *fin-de-siècle* France and that fact did have some impact on the Czech intelligentsia. Amiel (II, 230) goes almost as far as to suggest that to be a free self, one has to be Germanic:

Perhaps the need to think for oneself and to go back to principles is altogether peculiar only to the Germanic mind. The Slav and Romance peoples are ruled rather by collective wisdom, tradition, usage, prejudice, fashion; or, when they transgress these, it is as revolting slaves who do not of themselves perceive the law inherent in things, the true, unwritten, non-arbitrary, unimposed rule. The German wants to penetrate very Nature; the Frenchman, the Spaniard, the Russian stop at convention ... If the spirit is outside the things, it does not have to conform to them. If the spirit is lacking in truth, it has to be received from revealers of truth; this is the Romance world. This is thought despising Nature and subjugated to the Church.

It stands to reason that neither Stirner nor Amiel (nor the Decadents) has time for the political creed which aimed at obliterating the self, socialism or Communism. (They could not know Fascism; but, contrary to their 1890s anti-collectivism, after the Great war leading Decadents did become Fascists: Barrès, D'Annunzio, Procházka.) Amiel (II, 230) foresees either the destruction of mankind by foul Communism or the salvation of mankind by foul Americanization (Karásek interpreted Verlaine's *barbares blancs* as the Americans who would come to save decayed European civilization): 'I suspect that international Communism is only the sergeant of the old and the servile races, of Romance and Slav peoples; in this case it will be brutal individualism of the American type that will be the salvation of humanity.' Stirner is more vociferous. Socialism or Communism is for him simply despicable. His argument on the 'proletarian state', that 'Its ideal is the wretch; we should all become wretches' (Stirner 89), would have sounded like right-wing tub-thumping before the mass of the European intelligentsia actually began to realize what attempts at creating worker states resulted in. However much Stirner and Amiel suspected liberalism, they find the illiberalism of Communism a good deal more repugnant. Stirner (93) conceives of a future Communist society as of a system of coercion:

The idea that the Communist sees the man, his brother, in you, is only the Sunday-best side of Communism. His working-week side in no way considers you a man as such but as a human worker or working human being. The liberal principle lies in the first view; illiberalism is concealed in the second... The bourgeoisie had *freely laid out* intellectual and material goods and left it to everyone to reach for them if he felt a strong desire for them. Communism really does supply them to everyone, forces them on him and compels him to acquire them. It seriously demands that we, because only intellectual and material goods make us human, acquire these goods without arguing, so that we can be human. The bourgeoisie made acquisition free; Communism compels acquisition.

A little later, Stirner beleaguers both the liberal position, which is essentially *laboro, ergo sum,* and the Communist position, whereby everyone becomes a forced labourer (Stirner, 99). For Arnošt Procházka in his *Polemiky* (Polemics, 1913), a socialist revolution would constitute an inquisition in the name of progress and equality which would destroy by fire all dissenters.

Because of their attitudes to the individual self, Stirner and Amiel were profoundly anti-egalitarian. The abstraction 'equality' can have nothing in common with any solipsist, egotist or believer in the unique self, let alone observer of the fragmented self. The anti-liberal, anti-egalitarian, anti-socialist writing of Stirner, Amiel and the Austrian Decadent intelligentsia seemed finally to be invalidated by the left-wing interwar Avant Garde and Nazism, Fascism and so forth, but after World War II, and particularly since the end of the 1960s, their views on egalitarianism, like their views on self or personality, have begun to comport with contemporary political and philosophical views. Amiel, who is normally so restrained and kind, cannot be restrained and kind when he sees a political notion or the programme based on unrestraint and hatred (Amiel I, 177):

Egalitarianism, having erased conventional inequalities, arbitrary privileges, historical injustices, then rises up against inequalities of merit, capability, virtue: having been a just principle, it becomes an unjust principle. Inequality is as true and as just as equality; it is only a matter of understanding each other. But that is precisely what is not desired. Passions have a horror of light, and egalitarianism is a hatred which wants to pass itself off as love.

As we know, he regretfully sees the salvation of mankind (from socialist egalitarianism as well as from monarchic autocrats or bureaucratic oligarchs) in American mob democracy, manufacturers pandering to the appetites of an ochlocracy of consumers dedicated 'to the cult of Mammon and pleasure and adoring only strength'. The result of Americanization will not be quite the same as that of the destruction of the Roman Empire by the Barbarians. Americanization will not, avers Amiel, immediately undo all the achievements of high culture, but it will vulgarize and mutilate everything. For it is clear (Amiel I, 189–90):

That aesthetic tact, elegance, distinction, nobility, Atticism, urbanity, the suave and the exquisite, the refined and the delicate, everything that gives a select literature and an aristocratic culture its charm will vanish at one and the same time as the society which corresponds to it ... one can only say that the democratic spirit develops the mind greatly, since it has one believe in the quality of merits by virtue of the similarity of pretensions.

All these little egalitarians, he continues, that are busying themselves about the world are no more than a teeming heap of petty tyrants. Democracy may well be the legitimate heir to monarchy and aristocracy, but it has the congenital vice of dereliction of duty (duty is replaced by envy and arrogance); obedience and discipline disappear because they are incompatible with the false notion of equality (Amiel I, 192).. Again one thinks of Baudelaire's *Mon Coeur mis à nu*: 'There is no reasonable and safe government except an aristocratic one. Monarchies or republics based on democracy are equally absurd and weak.'[56]

In Amiel we may find pessimism founded on the sight of the workings of Nature, pessimism of the sort one associates with Baudelaire. His feelings about democracy comport with his nineteenth-century catastrophism (the hatred of mediocrity makes for one of the most urgent underlying themes of the works of such as Zeyer, Procházka, Karásek, Šlejhar, Vladimír Houdek, and Marten): 'The egalitarian age is the triumph of mediocrities. It is tiresome, but it is inevitable, and it is a revenge from the past ... Is not universal levelling the law of Nature and, when everything is on the same level, is not everything finished? After all, the world strains with all its might towards the destruction of what it has given birth to. Life is the blind pursuit of its own negation' (Amiel II, 31–2). Democracy constitutes a means by which one may give the masses the right to indulge the animal in them. It is, then, part of an impulse to uncivilization which humanity appears to bear within itself. The politicians' fostering of democratic ideals supported, indeed spurred on, the Decadents' catastrophism. The animal is what holds mankind together; what makes the unique self is the style with which the individual tames and decorates the animal within his or her self. Amiel appears to be approaching this Decadent view on the democratic trend (Amiel II, 113–14):

Democracy, having the masses rule, gives the leading role to instinct, to Nature, to the passions, that is to say, to blind impulse, elemental gravitation, generic fatality. A perpetual swinging between opposites becomes its single mode of progression because that is the infantile form of the narrow mind, which becomes infatuated and falls to pieces, adores and curses, always with the same haste. The succession of contradictory foolishnesses gives an impression of change which democracy identifies with improvement ... The only equal of the stupidity of Demos is its presumption. It is an adolescent who had the power, but cannot manage reason.

The idea of democracy rests on a legal fiction that the majority has the right as well as the might. This fiction is dangerous because it flatters the masses, and the masses will of necessity, Amiel continues, always be below average. When the democrats do what they are bound to do, he predicts, when they lower the age of majority and remove the barrier between the sexes, the democrats will arrive at the absurd situation where decisions, on the most important matters, will be made by the least capable people. Amiel is frightened by the ideal individualism, non-solidarity, propagated by the American democrats (so too, incidentally, was his near-contemporary, the popular Hungarian cultural critic Max Nordau);[57] he understands American greed as part of the general ugliness democratic ideas are preparing for the world. The enterprise mentality nurtured by the Americans is just as vulgar and unspiritual as biological theories about the survival of the fittest (Amiel II, 254):

Americanism destabilizes the moral substance of the individual who subordinates everything to himself and believes that the world, society, the State are made for him. This absence of gratitude, of spirit of deference and of solidarity instinct chills me. It is an ideal without beauty or nobility.

One consolation. Egalitarianism counterbalances Darwinism, as one wolf keeps itself at a respectful distance from another wolf. But both are strangers to duty. Egalitarianism affirms the right not to be eaten by one's neighbour; Darwinism states the fact that the large eat the small, and adds: so much the better. Neither of them knows love, fraternity, kindness, pity, voluntary submission, the giving of oneself.

That giving of oneself would not appeal to ideological Decadents, but, one has to repeat, however strong Amiel's influence on the Czech and Austrian German Decadents, not all his views were compatible with Decadent views.

The self-centredness of art and artist

According to Amiel, democracy is of itself hostile to art and artistic ideals. Democracy is vulgar, unserene, does not encourage the cultivation of the self, the spirit which produces high art. High art, claim the Decadents, is of its nature aristocratic (the product of an aristocratic mind, not of a social aristocracy). Art has nothing to do with the herds, the people.[58] Pessimistically, Amiel writes that 'the democratic age is gradually making the art of serenity impossible: the turbulent herd does not know the gods any more' (Amiel II, 12). The more democratic ideals become law, the more alienated the artist will become from society. Indeed, Amiel (II, 31) sees a direct relationship between democratization and the retrogression or debasing of art: 'Judicial progress, aesthetic recession. Consequently artists can see their *bête noire* multiplying: the bourgeois, the philistine, the presumptuous ignoramus, the ill-bred pedant who poses as an expert, the imbecile who considers himself the equal of the intelligent man.'

The Parnassian ideal of art for art's sake was a natural weapon for the Decadents against the overwhelming tide of bourgeoisie, the capitalists' more or less total assumption of the social roles (including the patronage of the arts) once played by aristocrats. Thus, in his preface to *The Picture of Dorian Gray*, Wilde took over from Gautier's *Mademoiselle de Maupin* the catchy notion that all art must be useless. In fact, the slogan, art for art's sake, as greatly despised by do-gooder social realists as by Socialist Realists, suggests that art should simply always strive to be art; high art is always for art's sake, even if the author is writing or painting for money. And, anyway, as rident Ryle writes: 'even to say that he is swimming for swimming's sake is to sell a verbal pass to the illusion that all things done on purpose must be done for some ulterior motive.'[59] And Broch, assuming a mystical understanding of art for art's sake in the *fin de siècle* period, says that every artist or, indeed, artisan of honour had always known what art for art's sake was, but that it had gained rationality as a notion in the course of the nineteenth century. Art for Art's sake is a marked feature of *Sozialgleichgültigkeit*, indifference to social affairs, and in that highly socially conscious century that involved resisting and, often, attacking the values of the middle classes, who

were in full command of taste and guilt at the latest by the 1880s (after the
Austro-Prussian War, the *Ausgleich*, the failure of Trialism, the financial crisis of
1873 – and after the Franco-Prussian War and the Commune): 'precisely the artist's resistance to society placed him inside its framework, just as a heretic can
perform a useful function only within the Church ... "Art for art's sake" and
"Business is business" are two branches of the same tree.'[60] Because he had appeared to be free, the artist had aroused envy and suspicion in the bourgeoisie;
furthermore – and here Broch pre-empts students of West European Decadence
like R. K. R. Thornton or Frederick Garber – the aesthetic and ethical appear to be
almost indistinguishable: 'artistic *l'art pour l'art* is simultaneously also ethical
l'art pour l'art, so that the development of art ... always simultaneously serves
ethical progress and participates in the mystical hope that ethical progress exists
and will in the end still overcome the world's ills [*Welten -Unheil*].'[61] And yet that
does not mean that their art is not self-centred. Self-centredness may itself be an
ethically laudable position – as it is in the Old and New Testaments where we are
instructed to love our neighbours as we love ourselves.

Vivian's words in Wilde's 'The Decay of Lying' demonstrate something of
the ethical realism of self-centredness in art; the artist's hedonism, for all his
bragging about selfishness, may improve the life of all society (one thinks of the
comingling of aestheticism and social *engagement* in the Arts and Crafts movement or in the Wiener Werkstätte). The indoor life that Vivian speaks of (Decadence was primarily the literature of studies and libraries – a literature born of
introspection combined with reading) stimulates the imagination; the artist's self
can transport itself into exotic sensuous and moral experiences. The healthy
unDecadent life led to all those nineteenth-century attempts to create a Positivist,
scientific system of living and of world development: 'Egotism itself, which is so
necessary to a proper sense of human dignity, is entirely the result of indoor life.
Out of doors one becomes abstract and impersonal.'[62] In one's study one is free;
outside, the vulgar rationality of enterprise culture, the market economy, assails
the artist's freedom. In one's study one may dream. The artist's dream is more
certain than reality in Barrès's *Un Homme libre* and, indeed, in Huysmans's, *A
Rebours* (one thinks, again, of des Esseintes's 'trip' to London). One recalls also
the Czech Karásek (see the dream-faith of the main characters in his *Legenda o
melancholickém princi* [Legend of the melancholy prince, 1896], or *Gotická
duše* [A Gothic soul, 1900]). In 'The Critic as Artist', Wilde writes, perhaps senti-
mentally, but with the ethical or mystical conviction – and irony – of the true
Decadent: 'a dreamer is one who can only find his way by moonlight, and his
punishment is that he sees the dawn before the rest of the world.'[63] Amiel worries
lest Fichte's solipsism be the real answer to reality, lest the world be only the
solitary dream of each individual self. In dreams he sees the only freedom that a
man can possess: 'At least in our dreams, except in nightmares, we give ourselves

ubiquity, omniscience and complete freedom.'

The Decadent artist's aesthetic and ethical selves fuse in his narcissism. For Broch, the artist comes nearest to the saint, for both live secluded from society and both live in dreams. Where the saint might devote himself entirely to the next world, the artist, in all his Decadent realism, devotes himself entirely to this world, however oneiric his version of this world might be. In the artist-hermit, then, according to Broch, duty and freedom merge and 'the artist is party to harsh mercy, but one which does not shatter his narcissism, merely submits it to discipline.'[64] It is clear how solipsism may engender narcissism or *vice versa*. The dreams of the narcissist may express the Decadent's only hope for the liberation of the self. So in Andrian's *Der Garten der Erkenntnis* (The garden of knowledge, 1895), in Schorske's words, the 'aesthetic aristocrat remained the devitalized Narcissus, hoping as a dying man that a dream might give him what life had failed to provide: contact with "the other."'[65]

Inspired by Theodor Herzl, Schorske sees the *feuilleton* as a manifestation of *fin-de-siècle* narcissism in Vienna. Devotion to art became fused with a preoccupation with one's own mind. In Prague, it was not the *feuilleton* that was the province of the older generation or of the Realists, but the literary and fine-arts review in avant-garde periodicals. The reviewers did little to try to be objective; indeed they programmatically sought to describe their own emotional reactions to the psychology of artists and their creations. What Schorske says of the Vienna *feuilletoniste*, applies equally to the Prague reviewer (in *Moderní revue*, *Niva* or *Literární listy*): he 'exemplified the cultural type to whom he addressed his columns: his characteristics were narcissism and introversion, passive receptivity toward outer reality, and, above all, sensitivity to psychic [i.e. mental] states.'[66] This narcissistic preoccupation with the self in art is typified by the young Vienna artists characterized in Hofmannsthal's lines in 'Prolog zu dem Buch "Anatol"' (1892): 'So we perform theatre, / perform our own plays, / precocious and tender and sad, / the comedy of our soul, / the today and yesterday of our feeling, / pretty formulae of evil things, / smooth words, colourful pictures, / secret, half perception, / agonies, episodes.'[67]

These lines are ironically echoed in the prose-interlude of Hlaváček's *Mstivá kantiléna*, in words referring to those young men or children who do not join in the games of others, the artist–hermits who have never been attracted to sheer ornament and live in permanent, painful introversion: 'you will meet there the alien, over-bitter gaze of two eyes which matured too early and which are not promised a long life, for they are redolent of the bitter mortal scent of hemlock.'[68]

It is all too easy to treat narcissism and introversion as synonyms, as, indeed, Schorske comes close to doing. Even in the case of Hlaváček, if one had the artistically irrelevant knowledge that the poet was lying on his death-bed as *Mstivá kantiléna* was being printed, one might see some macabre, ironic narcissism in the alienated hemlock-fragrant eyes. What one could, however, note is that it of-ten appears that Decadents identified themselves biologically as well as spiritu-ally with their writing. After all, as I wrote near the beginning of this section, Decadents often considered states of mind to be states of body. They usually tried not to be dualists.

Hlaváček's image constitutes a variation on the theme of the *maladie du siècle* which was introduced into literature as a term or designation by Musset in his *La Confession d'un enfant du siècle* (1836). Musset understood that sickness to be embodied, first, in the destruction of royal and, then, revolutionary authority (the Terror) in the Revolution and, secondly, in woman as a provider of sexual pleasure (after a certain financial investment on the man's part). Matthew Arnold saw the sickness of the nineteenth century as arising from modern man's passion for self-analysis.[69] Amiel finds the same sickness, but he blames it on the egali-tarian, utilitarian age where the useful has replaced the beautiful and industry replaced art: '*Ennui* will become the sickness of the egalitarian age' (Amiel I, 26). And the materialism of the age is preparing a universal moral depression and a morbid fear of anything that might diminish the stature of man. Amiel imagines modern man floundering in a sea of narcissism, which he considers spiritual cowardice: 'He wants to approve of himself, admire himself, congratulate himself and, consequently, he turns his eyes away from all the abysses which would remind him of his nothingness' (Amiel I, 207). This cowardly striving for self-admiration has become the modern morality (Amiel II, 104):

Eternal effort is the character of modern morality. This painful becoming has replaced harmony, equilibrium, joy, in other words, being. We are all fauns, satyrs, silenuses aspiring to become angels; we are unsightliness working at beautifying self, gross chrysalides laboriously giving birth to our own butterflies. The ideal is no longer the serene beauty of the soul, but the anguish of Laocoön struggling against the hydra of evil.[70]

The belief in (an inadequately delineated notion of) progress occasions modern man's sickness (Amiel I, 208), and faith in science and in the increase of human experience leads man to believe that the modern individual is more experienced than his forebears. Modern man does not know what to do with age, but the mod-ern adolescent, who may be more cultivated than his forebears when they were his age, is as fallible as they had been. Overweening self-confidence is too readily understood as self-awareness. Man's nature is not subject to any progress. Per-haps conditions have improved , but that is not progress in man. Man's faults change their forms, but such changes in form do not enrich the human moral ex-perience (Amiel II, 161).

For Amiel, modern man felt too secure for his own moral good. Conscious insecurity became one of the hallmarks of the human condition in *fin-de-siècle* art. That insecurity may, however, also be seen as a constituent of the period narcissism. The number of pictures men painted of women looking into mirrors or mirror-like pools[71] might also suggest that men depicted female narcissism (vanity) because of their own narcissism. Male narcissism (self-adoration) could be interpreted as deriving from sexual insecurity. It may have been the other way round; moreover, common representations of sexual insecurity like the diverse depictions of *femmes fatales* may have resulted largely from a fashionable pose.

The *femme fatale* was an emblem for a general Decadent notion that woman, particularly love for a woman, even more particularly loving sexual intercourse with a woman, sucked the strength out of a man. Loving a woman diminished a man's self and, finally, woman was capable of destroying, devouring, a man's self. Since the *femme fatale* was a vamp who played with men, and who normally, indeed, did not copulate with men whom she had bewitched, she could embody hyperbolically the insecure man's fear of erotic rejection. When considering this, however, one must not forget the Decadents' plain love of meaningful ornament and their delight in all forms of the erotic, including the sensuous exotic. On the other hand, one cannot forget the Decadents' bedfellow, Freud, in whose thinking infantile sexuality appears potentially to destroy adult sexual security. Reading Freud's cases and casebooks may, indeed, have encouraged sexual insecurity in the first years of the twentieth century, the last stages of the *fin-de-siècle* period. Glover is not being merely flippant when he asks, 'Did Freud's patients have unusually Freudian childhoods, or is it just that you had a very dull one?'[72]

This sexual insecurity is, in fact, an aspect of a far broader insecurity, an aspect which had a particularly strong impact on socially dislocated humanity after World War I. The imagined organic-tissue transplants found in Czech science fiction writings by Arbes or Čapek-Chod might also reflect *fin-de-siècle* insecurity. The former imagines a brain transplant, and in such an operation one does begin to wonder where the self has its location. Notions of soul and general emotional obstructions begin to disturb average non-materialist man's thought. If Salome's brain were transplanted into John the Baptist's head, John's into Salome's, one might well ask, which one is Salome now. Glover also mentions brain transplants as testifying to the 'elusiveness' of the self.[73]

The fluid, Protean self

The Decadents' and their precursors' consciousness of the elusiveness of the self stimulated their conceiving of the self as changeable, fluid. In his essay on Amiel, the young Hofmannsthal declares what he calls the gift of Proteus to be an essential talent for a poet. Thus he distorts the divine a little, and sees in the Protean the gift of empathy, a key notion in the nineteenth-century aesthetics: 'a waft of fragrance snatched from the air becomes for him plant and forest; he gains insights into the tenderest mood of the landscape and his perception enters the souls of things.'[74] One could say, wary of paradox, that what unifies the different shapes in the Decadent self is precisely Proteus, the artist.

But it seemed to these Austrian artists (and here I think particularly of the Czechs) that the Proteuses might have no unifying capacities. Politics, nationalities, classes, even schools and the bureaucracy were in a state of flux. The army-officer ethic seemed to be as hollow (Schnitzler, Hořica) as the Monarchy itself. The Emperor had became a bureaucrat and the colonies were in revolt. Some, like Nordau, in *Die conventionellen Lügen*, felt that the Monarchy might dissolve. The rise of political antisemitism and, say, the race riots in Prague in 1897 confirmed the existence of the fundamental problem which faced Hofmannsthal and Schnitzler as well as Zeyer and Hlaváček: 'the dissolution of the classical liberal view of man in the crucible of Austria's modern politics.'[75] The liberal view had more or less unified the body politic, but now nothing fulfilled that function. In 1907 Hofmannsthal writes: 'But the essence of our age is ambiguity and indefiniteness. Our age can rest only on something shifting and something that is aware that it is shifting, whereas other generations believed in the firm. A gentle chronic vertigo vibrates in our age. There is much in it that makes itself heard only to a few, and there is much not in it, that many believe is there.'[76]

Schorske imagines the serpent to represent this ambiguity and uncertainty, and that comports with Hofmannsthal's conception of the slipping, shifting basis to the *fin-de-siècle* period. The serpent, Schorske writes, in his critique of Klimt, constitutes 'the great dissolver of boundaries: between land and sea, man and woman, life and death.' He suggests that it is linked with the sexual ambiguity with which Praz is greatly concerned in *The Romantic Agony*, but, more important for this chapter Schorske states, perhaps a trifle melodramatically, 'Wherever dissolution of the ego was involved, whether in sexual union in guilt and death, the snake reared its head.' So in his *Hygeia* (in *Medicine* in the University ceiling painting), 'Klimt proclaims the unity of life and death, the interpenetration of instinctual vitality and personal dissolution.'[77]That reminds one of the late nineteenth-century conception of music – to which Pater says in his essay on style that all art aspires, an idea he shared with Mallarmé. The self could be totally dissolved in music, for in music no feature whatsoever of the creator's or the listener's self could be delineated or distinguished. Music was abstract in quite a different manner from contemporary science and morality. Heine, who had a considerable influence on the Decadents, conceived of the whole material world dissolving into welling music.[78] One remembers stories evoking that sensation by Karel Kamínek as well as Čapek-Chod.

Amiel's conception of the fragmented or fluid self is complex. In one version (Amiel I, 147), he perceives his self as split; he sees himself as too weak to become creatively fluid; he lacks the inner firmness to allow his self to be impressionable: 'The great contradiction of my being: a mind that wants to forget itself in things and a heart that wants to live in people. The unity of contrast lies in the need to abandon constraints, to cease willing, no longer to exist for oneself, to *impersonalize* oneself, destabilize oneself in love and contemplation. What is lacking is character, will, individuality.' He conceives of his indecisive self as a prison; the trouble is that one is not sure who is the warder of this prison, or who the designer: 'I love everything and only detest one thing: the irremediable imprisonment of my being in an arbitrary form … Inner freedom would, after all, be the most tenacious of my passions, perhaps my only passion' (Amiel II, 22). In another version (Amiel II, 288–9), the self is again potentially fluid, but distilled and then stripped of all accretions till it is a state which is spirit, the intense self which the Decadent dandies generally sought in vain:

I possess only myself in the state of monad and self, and I feel my faculties being resorbed in the substance which they individualised. All the benefits of animality are, so to speak, repudiated; likewise, all the products of study and culture are nullified; all crystallization is redissolved in its bath; the whole arch of Iris has withdrawn into the inside of a dew drop; the consequences return into the principle, the effects into the cause, the bird into the egg, the organism into the germ.

The interior of a drop of dew constitutes an image of the inner meanings which Decadents or Symbolists searched for, when they were critics. (And even in their novels they tended to act as critics, Huysmans in *A Rebours*, Wilde in *Dorian Gray*, Karásek in *Legenda o melancholickém princi*.) Corresponding to this second version, Amiel has a third, a variety of the second, where the self becomes totally fluid. This epitome of the Decadent fluid self looks like a self out of control, the Protean that has lost its Proteus (Amiel II, 63–4):

I am returning from myself to the fluid, vague, indeterminate state, as if all form were violence and disfigurement. All knowledge, ideas, maxims, habits are erased in me, like the ripples of a wave, like the folds in a cloud; my personality has the minimum possible amount of individuality. I am to most men what the circle is to rectilinear figures; I am at home everywhere because I no longer have a specific, named self … Being less a man, I am perhaps closer to man, perhaps a little more man. 63-4)

Hofmannsthal's tripartite poem, 'Terzinen', combines that type of the fluid self with the historical self, and then expresses the fusion of the self with material reality and with 'dreams' outside the material. Hofmannsthal may be superficial compared with Amiel, but he indicates the same direction of thought:

And since my own self, obstructed by nothing, slipped over to me out of a small child, strangely mute and alien, like a dog. Then, since I existed also a hundred years ago, and my ancestors, in their shrouds, are as related to me as my own hair, as much one with me as my own hair… Small girls who look very pale … and know life is now silently flowing from their sleep – drunk limbs into tree and grass, and, tiredly smiling, they strike attitudes like a saint shedding her blood … [Dreams are] in us and always have life. And three are One: a man, a thing, a dream.[79]

One does not then know what identity is. It is not far from that to the near-Humean self of Meyrink: 'life on Earth is … just a condition.'[80]

And that may be interpreted as a mood – just as the notion of a fluid self can be understood as a conception of life as of a series of moods. The Decadents culti-vate the mood in their writing (Hlaváček, Yeats), and moods may be understood as either: particularly expressive representations of consciousness sequences (self-perceptions), or: as clutches of consciousness which affect or indicate the self's perception of the external and internal and, thus, contribute to the creation of unique moments. Edelgard Hajek suggests that literature of the Decadent period was, in any case, concerned only with states of consciousness;[81] thus, perhaps, as Zeyer or Karásek would maintain, art really is essentially a matter of moods and impressions. For the Decadent writer, the self certainly appears to be either the product of his moods or simply the projection of his moods. And moods may themselves express the insecurity (or: instability) of the self. The mood may also be a mask.

Amiel, in April 1952, felt himself to be swinging between two types of mood, both of which form symptoms of the *maladie du siècle*: 'I oscillate between languor and *ennui*, dispersal in the infinitely small and nostalgia for the unknown and distant' (Amiel I, 40). The mood is also the moment which Decadent man so cultivated; Amiel's perception of the moment is as Decadent as his interior of a dew-drop: 'the ideal is the eternal moment of perishable things' (Amiel I, 194).

The transcendent self

To express something as the eternal moment of transient objects is to employ a *fin-de-siècle* oxymoron of mysticality. And one wonders whether the young Hofmannsthal had not been drawn to mysticism, had not derived especially the last line of his 'Terzinen' from works being peddled in contemporaneous Vienna. He may have already known Schopenhauer, who had a profound understanding of mysticism or mysticality. Schopenhauer plainly and simply distinguishes mysticism from quietism and asceticism: 'Quietism, that is the surrendering of all willing asceticism, that is the intentional destruction of self-will, and mysticism, that is the consciousness of the identity of one's own essence and with that of all things or with the nucleus of the world, are most precisely linked.'[82] The self is aware of the mystical, which is concerned with areas beyond cognition. Mysti-cism begins, 'where all cognition necessarily ceases … In the broadest sense, mysticism is everything that leads to the immediate awareness of that to which neither notion nor concept, that is no cognition whatsoever, extends'.[83] Mysticality is a significant element in the Decadent reaction to the malodorous industrial, banal nineteenth century. The last of the Viennese artists to be speaking seriously as a child of the Decadence, Ludwig Wittgenstein, writes, in his *Tractatus*: 'It is true, there is the inexpressible. This is *manifested*; it is the mystical' (6.522).

Amiel expresses a mystical self in accordance with the definition of his mentor, Schopenhauer: an awareness of one's identity with the essence of all other things. The following words follow on from Amiel's description of that state of selfness where the effects have returned to the cause, the bird into the egg:

This psychological *reinvolvement* is an anticipation of death; it represents life beyond the grave, the return to She'ol, vanishing among the phantoms, falling in to the region of *Meres* [cf. the Cabala etc.], or rather the simplification of the individual who, allowing all his accidents to evaporate, now exists only in an indivisible, pin-point state, the state of energy, the fertile zero. Is not that the definition of spirit?

The mystical conception of the self among Decadents usually fuses with their conception of the historical self. On the other hand, one will find serious Decadent writers who consider notions like the astral self. One thinks of Zeyer (especially *Dům "U tonoucí hvězdy"*) or Meyrink (especially *Der Golem*). Later, Meyrink arrived at a conception of the mystical self close to Schopenhauer's. Man forgets his beginning, and then, when he starts seeking his beginning, that inhibits him from finding it. In fact, every moment of our lives suggests to us that we should ask who we are, but we do not follow that suggestion and, thus, we do not find our beginnings. Naturally, that lies in what Schopenhauer calls the essence of all things, and what Meyrink calls the spirit into which we must again dissolve: 'we must dissolve in the spirit which was from the beginning if we wish to reach open sea.'[84] Romain Rolland wrote to Freud of the same sense of dissolution as the 'oceanic' sensation. Glover mentions this when he is writing of the mystical notion of the individual mind merging with the cosmic. 'Part of the appeal of this', he suggests, 'may be its echo of a common mystical feeling: many people sometimes feel that they themselves are limitless, in some way one with the world as a whole.'[85]

For Baudelaire, symbols themselves have their origin in the mystical sensation. And Baudelaire was one who spoke of the sorcery, the literal magic, of words. One will realise true symbols when one is in that mystical state of mind, where one's self awaits revelation (i.e. not that state where one is open to the search for 'true knowledge'): 'In certain, almost supernatural, states of the psyche, the whole profundity of life is revealed in the spectacle before one, however ordinary that spectacle is. It becomes the symbol of that profundity.'[86] Broch denies there was anything mystical about Baudelaire, especially about his relationship with language, but, playfully, he accepts that one could call him a mystes of his artistic technique – and, anyway, 'The fanatical pursuit of truth always has something mystical about it'.[87] Later Broch comes to the linguistic mysticism of Mallarmé and Joyce and in the course of his discussion he makes a statement which initially appears paradoxical, but in fact might serve to explain why so few Decadents surrendered themselves to mysticism, however attracted they were to mysticality: 'all true mysticism is rational, and linguistic mysticism is the mysticism of the medium.'[88] The Decadents were suspicious of the rational, and the Decadent self in all its fluidity was venerated for its glorious non-rationality, sometimes irrationality.

For Baudelaire, the self was also a vehicle for sincerity, sincerity as a weapon against that *Wert-Vakuum* Broch writes about. Baudelaire states this at the beginning of his 'Richard Wagner et Tannhäuser à Paris', which has a certain irony for us, since Broch condemned Wagner as the humourless affirmer of the *Wert-Vakuum*.[89] For Baudelaire, then, the irritating public self has moral value: 'This *I*, in many cases justly accused of impertinence, nevertheless implies a great modesty: it endorses the writer in the strictest limits of sincerity.'[90] Baudelaire saw in Wagner a mystic (as an infamous scion of the Viennese *fin-de-siècle* period, Adolf Hitler, would also see him): 'I fully conceived the idea of a soul moving in a luminous environment, of ancestors *made of sensual delight and of knowledge*, and floating above and very far from the natural world.'[91] There is no need to comment on the Wagneromania which assailed Paris, but also Vienna and London. And there is admiration in Beardsley's tauntingly salacious satirizings of Wagner. In his *Wagner and Literature*, Furness does not mention our pre-Decadent Amiel's reaction to Wagner. Not unlike Baudelaire, Amiel sees in Wagner an abdication from the self. But, not unlike Broch, he sees in Wagner's art socialist democratic music replacing subjective, aristocratic art. For Amiel, Wagner's is mob music, not individual music. Wagner's denial of the self, for all its Decadent sensuality, represents Freud's It; it opens up the pandemonium of the animal self and, thus, destroys the civilized self art had cultivated – that animal self-analytically displayed in some poems by such as Baudelaire and Karásek: Wagner's music represents the abdication of the self and the emancipation of all the forces previously conquered. It is a falling back into Spinozaism, the triumph of fatality. This music has its roots and fulcrum in two of the age's trends, materialism and socialism, both of which fail to recognize the value of the human personality and obliterate it in the totality of Nature or society (Amiel I, 112–13).

The landscape of the self

For the Decadents, the self appears often to have served as a refuge from the cultural ochlocracy, from the *Wert-Vakuum* and *Un-Stil*. The instability of the self (which includes the possibility of polypsychism) makes the self more exciting than the dull bourgeois vulgarity outside. As Barrès puts it in the 'Examen' to his trilogy: 'Our Self is the manner in which our organism reacts to the stimulations of the environment and against the opposition of the Barbarians.'[92] Escape into the self soon became preoccupation with the self. Two things are fashionable today, wrote Hofmannsthal in 1893, 'the analysis of life and flight from life.'[93] And preoccupation with the self resulted in Decadent painters and writers adopting a manner of depicting Nature, where every landscape (usually autumnal or sultrily aestival) became a landscape of the soul.

The term may be Amiel's and, in mainstream Decadence, he may well have inspired the numerous landscapes of the soul (even as a title of a poem, for example, as in Karásek), but Decadent landscapes of the soul predate the publication of his *Journal*. A perhaps banal example is Verlaine's 'Crépuscule du soir mystique' in *Poèmes saturniens*, which ends:

> Parmi la maladive exhalaison
> De parfums lourds et chauds, dort le poison
> – Dahlia, lys, tulipe et renoncule –
> Noyant mes sens, mon âme et ma raison,
> Mêle dans une immense pâmoison
> Le Souvenir avec la Crépuscule.[94]

The often quoted or misquoted passage in Amiel is from the diary for 31 October, 1852. After a pretty Decadent description of an autumn scene, he writes: 'Any sort of landscape is a state of the soul and anyone who reads in both marvels at finding similarities in every detail' (Amiel I, 55). Before that, he had written that 'in the garden of the soul, every feeling has its floral minute, that is: its unique moment of blossoming grace and radiant royalty' (Amiel I, 9). I take one example of that image, in Hlaváček's 'Praeludium' (1895): 'In the devastated flowerbeds of my soul smokes the fragrant breath of future springs – and from the distance softly tuned music seeps into the sleepy silence which longing has made tired.'[95]

The dandy

Dandyism is one of the most remembered masks that the Decadents employed to conceal the self or ironically grandly to emphasize the self, to offend against bourgeois decency. This mask was designed primarily by Barbey d'Aurevilly and

Baudelaire. I have written about Stirner as a precursor of the Decadents, but his interpretation of the dandy is the opposite of his contemporary, Barbey's, and hence of the Decadents'. In 'Das unwahre Prinzip unserer Erziehung', he sees the dandy not simply as having been vanquished by the capitalists' usurpation of society after Beau Brummell, but also as a worthless, ineffectual phenomenon (Stirner, 12):

To be sure, the empty elegance of the Humanist, the dandy, could not avoid defeat; but the victor glittered from the verdigris of materiality and was nothing more elevated than a *tasteless industrialist. Dandyism* and *industrialism* fight over the booty of charming boys and girls and often seductively exchange outfits, the dandy appearing in unpolished cynicism and the industrialist in white linen. It is true that the live wood of the industrial mace will smash the dry stick of dandyish saplessness; live or dead, wood remains wood, and if the fire of the intellect [des Geistes] is to shine, the wood must go up in flames.

In fact, most of the characteristics of Stirner's sovereign *Einziger* would apply to the dandy as the Decadents, and Baudelaire, imagined him.

For Baudelaire, the dandy was the opposite of the Belgian. And he was young. The Decadence was, in essence, something of a youth culture. That aspect of the Decadence is racily described by Weber:

Decadence was a phenomenon of youth. In its search for novelty, its hostility to repetition, its rejection of specialization for dilettantism, its quest for new relations, new experiences, new ideas, and the constant escalation of its stimulants, in its pursuit of whims and fads, even in its nostalgia for certain traditions that were meant to provide not structure but colour, the new ideology was a creation of idleness. Yet, however trivial, frivolous, and sometimes shallow, it was responsive to its times.[96]

Perhaps the whole Decadence was 'a creation of idleness' in France, though I doubt it. Certainly it was not Austria. The idea of the dandy was, a creation both *of* idleness and *for* one's own idling. It was also, however, an artistic, even aesthete, version of the *Übermensch*. The dandy is 'an affirmation of superiority, a moral prophylaxis which saves soul and intellect from contamination.'[97] Here is an attempt at Nietzsche's man of the future, his noonday bell which will liberate the Will, redeem man from the great repellency of modern life:

The *redeeming* man of great love and disdain, the creative spirit which over and over again drives his urgent strength out of everywhere that is at the side or on the other side, a man whose aloneness is misunderstood by the people as if it were an escape from reality ... this Antichrist and anti-nihilist, this conqueror of God and of the *nothingness – some time he must come...*[98]

The dandy embodied Decadent aristocratism of the soul: the elevation of the strong, sophisticated self above the herd, and above the animal in man. His freedom lies in his freedom from desire, and here one remembers Isaiah Berlin's comment on freedom: 'If I find that I am able to do little or nothing of what I wish, I need only contract or extinguish my wishes, and I am made free.'[99] In Baudelaire woman is natural, animal and, therefore, the opposite of the dandy. One might reasonably maintain that the Decadents' concentration on ecstasy, frustration or orgasmic death reflects their striving to be liberated from desire. When we think of Weber's connecting of the Decadence with a striving to be free of desire, we remember that ascetics tend to be young (or very old). The lover in Meyrink's *Das grüne Gesicht* is an exception, but his beloved is not. One may interpret Wilde's *Dorian Gray* as a picture of the inability of the self to survive if it submits to desires. Thus one may see the dandy also as an ethical category.

Amiel's aristocratism more or less comports with Decadent aristocratism. His exclusiveness also has a moral justification, since art is for him a matter of elitist aesthetics, as we see in his remarks on Wagner. After an unclear discussion of his own sickness, of the inconsistency of life and of a new type of man, who is better (rarer, more beautiful) than others, he makes a statement on the vulgar which could come from any Decadent: 'Vulgar men are still souls, except they are of no interest to anyone but the Creator' (Amiel II, 241). I do not think Amiel's 'man of genius' corresponds to the dandy, though he comes close to the version of the dandy given by Baudelaire and Breisky:[100] 'Men of genius bear the substance of history, whereas the crowds are only a necessary but passive critical filter, the limitation, slackening, negation of the ideas borne by the genius. Dynamically, foolishness is the indispensable counterweight of the spirit' (Amiel II, 212). The dandy of essence knows well the crass foolishness of those who surround him and he sets himself up in opposition to it. He embodies the desire to *épater le bourgeois* and, ideally, he embodies 'the most perfect type of manly Beauty,' that is: '*Satan* – in the manner of Milton.'[101] He is superior man, a non-specialist with leisure and a broad education; ideally he is rich and loves work.[102] Like Ludwig of Bavaria in Karásek's *Legenda o melancholickém princi*, he believes that the whim is one of the few genuine sensations in the world.

The dandy has no models, for he is entirely himself. He is a glorification of the self as master of all his surroundings. Thus the dandy admires in history figures like Apollonius of Tyana, Caligula, Tiberius, Heliogabalus, Cagliostro and, especially, Nero. (Even those just touching the fringes of the Decadence, like Stephen Phillips, wrote about Nero.) Karásek's Ludwig admires Caligula primarily because of the manner in which he used his luminous spirit as a shield against the vulgarities of the world.

The dandy's primary quality is style. And style is a visible incorporation of selfness. Not entirely uninfluenced by Pater, Schaukal writes of style: 'Style is a unity of the legitimate … it is a self-approving law…. It is not personality. Personality must be expressed in style. Style is unthinkable without personality…. But the essence of style is not personality but its colour.'[103] The dandy is essentially stable, the stable mask to conceal instability, the stable self to give artificial form to the fluid self.

Multiple personality and autostylization

Dandyism acts as a check on proteiformity, and in the twentieth century the psychologists have established a new sickness of the Protean, fluid self, the multiple personality. It may be only coincidence that the first clinical cases of multiple personality were described during the end of the Decadent period, Alfred Binet's *Les Altérations de la personalité* (1892) and Morton Prince's account of 'Miss Christine Beauchamp' from 1905. After all, the instances of demonic possession which occur, say, in the Bible, might today be described as multiple personality. What matters is not what is described, but how it is understood.

It was easy to see how an awareness of the fluidity of one's self might stimulate the notion that one had two or more different personalities or at least a series of subpersonalities which guided the actions of one's body alternately or consecutively (cf. Stevenson's Jekyll and Hyde). Nietzsche breaks down the self into a multiplicity of instincts or drives, and the self becomes fiction created by manifestations of the will to power.[104] He imagines a multiplicity of interacting subjects which together form the foundations of consciousness and thought. It does not matter whether we decide Nietzsche is speaking of potential multiple personality or of the fragmented self. The notion of fragmented self was common in and long before the period; it suggests alienation, where the notion of fluid self suggests insecurity or sensitivity.

Amiel's description of the multiple self is poetically persuasive; one notices that there is a unifying factor here, some unique force which heaves at the background somewhere behind this chameleon. Similarly, in a multiple personality there is a uniting body though, allegedly, that body may have sets of gestures which distinguish one personality from another. Amiel's multiple self is sensitive, but essentially passive, subjugated to existence itself (Amiel I, 228):

I feel a chameleon, a kaleidoscope, a Proteus, changeable and polarizable in all ways, fluid, a virtual and so a latent image, even in my manifestations, absent even in my representation. I am, so to speak, present in the molecular vortex that is called individual life; I perceive and am aware of this constant metamorphosis, this irresistible mutation of existence taking place within me; I feel all the particles of my being, all the drops of water in my river, all the effulgences of my individual strength fleeting, renewing themselves, modifying themselves.

That was written in December 1866; in January 1868 (Amiel II, 20–1) this conception of the multiple changing self has become clearer and more complex; again there is a unifier, this time the body:

It seems to me that I have lived many dozens, almost many hundreds of lives. Every individuality of character is moulded in me as an idea, or rather, forms me momentarily in its image, and I have only to observe myself living at this moment to understand this new manner of being in human nature. Thus I have been a mathematician, musician, scholar, monk, child, mother, and so on. In these states of universal sympathy, I have even been an animal and a plant ... This faculty of rising and falling metamorphosis, of *déplication* and *réimplication* ... is doubtless a result of my enormous aptitude for impersonal objectivization, which, in turn, makes for the difficulty I experience for my part in individualizing myself, in being merely a certain man, with his own number and label. Returning into my body has always seemed strange to me, something arbitrary and conventional. I thought of myself as a container of phenomena, a point of vision and perception, an impersonal person, a subject without determined individuality, as pure *determinability* and *formality*.

Every soul, every self, Amiel writes elsewhere (I, 67) has its own climate or is itself a climate and thus has its own meteorology within the general meteorology of souls. The soul is, however, essentially active (I, 68) and the activity we know about constitutes only a small part of the whole of our activity. Amiel conceives of the self as passive empathy, as a chameleon, but, at the same time, the self can be active, can be in control of its metamorphoses by controlling its imagination. In other words, Amiel abides by two sets of rules for Decadent selves, that which pertains to the sensitive, sickly noble who is the last of a long line, and that which pertains to the dandy. For the dandy, too, in Amiel's version, may have a multiplicity of selves, though he controls them, for he may manipulate his vision (Amiel I, 68–9):

Thus we ourselves produce our spiritual worlds, our monsters, our chimaeras and our angels; we objectivize what is fermenting in us. Everything is wondrous for the poet, everything divine for the saint, everything great for the hero, everything shabby, wretched, ugly, bad for the base and sordid soul. The evil man creates a pandemonium around him, the artist an Olympus, the chosen man a Paradise, and each of them sees it only himself. We are all visionaries and what we see in the objects around us is our souls.

The way *fin-de-siècle* literature consciously employs the notion of polypsychism might be epitomized by Proust's words: 'at every moment there was one more of those innumerable and humble "selves" that compose our personality which was still unaware of Albertine's departure and must be informed of it.'[105] And an amateur psychologist of today's America, Flora Rheta Schreiber, a university professor of English who writes with the elegance of a three-legged dromedary chasing a mosquito, unwittingly suggests that an artist exploits his own chameleon nature to create. She is writing about a woman sick with multiple personality: 'None of the paintings, of course, was Sybil's alone. Most were collaborative efforts of several of the selves.'[106]

There seems to be some link between the multiple personality and the recognized split personality which, for example, the quasi-Decadent philosopher Freud describes in the *Interpretation of Dreams* when the dream-experiencer's knowledge is divided between two selves; in the dream, the extraneous self corrects the real self. Freud maintains that this state is more or less the same as that continuously experienced by someone suffering from hallucinatory paranoia. This sort of split personality is a common literary device, because most of us know it from dreams. Glover points to the possibility of self-deception playing a role in the engendering of the condition of multiple personality. But, as he says, 'Self-deception presents the disturbing appearance of being both widespread and impossible.'[107] Self-deception is theoretically rejected by the lie. First, the Decadent (there were few, if any, female Decadents in Czech literature, though one could certainly make a strong case for some works by Růžena Jesenská and a few poems by Irma Geisslová) regards truth as a banal bourgeois imposition. Second, because one is necessarily enserfed by any truth one accepts, truth threatens one's individuality. Third, one cannot possess but only share truth, whereas one can possess a lie, exert power through a lie, be completely individual in a lie. Furthermore, the highest art consists in lying (see, for example, Karásek's Preface to his *Sodoma*). Lying is a form of 'Self'-control and, at least externally, a manipulation of memory.

A continuity of memory usually forms a self. As a writer, one may distort memory deliberately, and one may create a whole series of selves, especially if the age is such as Hofmannsthal describes. In such an age as this, one tends to indulge in what one might call artistic fugue:[108]

It is as if the whole task of this sensitive, eclectic century had consisted in instilling an uncanny life of its own into things from the past. Now they are flying around us, vampires, living corpses, animated broomsticks of the unfortunate sorcerer's apprentice! We have made the dead our idols ... we have conducted our best blood into their veins; we have girded these shades with a more elevated beauty and more miraculous power than life can tolerate: with the beauty of our longings and the power of our dreams... Nothing has remained for us except chilling life: bleak, insipid reality, drooping resignation. We have nothing but a sentimental memory, a crippled will and the uncanny gift of self-duplication.[109]

In literature, usually lyric verse, multiple personality has its parallel (or representation) in autostylization, where the lyric first person stylizes himself or herself as a figure of a different century, a different country, a different occupation, an alien psychology, and so forth. Autostylization may be used as an emotive device, as it is in the case of the committed Silesian poet, Petr Bezruč. Normally, however, it is used for the exploration of the self, for experimentation in sensitivity, or for irony. The whole *fin-de-siècle* quest for the self, perhaps even, attempt to reassert *seine Majestät das Ich*, is satirized by Meyrink in *Der Golem* in the words: 'waiting for one's own self to become king is waiting for the Messiah.'[110]

In Meyrink the only total unity of personality appears to be the individual soul's unity with the cosmic Soul. The sense of the failure of religion, especially in France and Austria, certainly made for the nineteenth-century growth of occultism, but probably also contributed to writers' determined study of their selves.

The split self of Baudelaire's 'L'Héautontimorouménos' is aptly described by Garber: 'The self-devourer of the poem ("je suis de mon coeur le vampire") sustains himself by living off himself, parodying the autonomy the author of the *Paradis artificiels* finds indispensable for the sustenance of the soul.'[110] Hlaváček's 'Upír' (Vampire [*Pozdě k ránu*, Early morning, 1896]) may be a dream poem and so describe the split self described in Freud's *Interpretation of Dreams*. Here the vampire flashes above the lyric narrator as he is walking through an unknown landscape. The vampire is on his way back from sucking blood from the breasts of his involuntary or chance, passionate, sickly mistresses. Then it turns out that the vampire is actually the *Ich*'s soul which leaves him at night to indulge in mystic orgies. In the early morning the vampire soul returns to him and wakes up a wretched parasite who will have to get down to everyday drudgery with him. So, as with Baudelaire, one self is a parasite on another. Furthermore, Hlaváček labels the vampire as the symbol the Decadence and a *barbare blanc*.[112] Thus he is identifying himself also with Verlaine's verse, for the autostylizing poem, which, probably gave the Decadent trend its name was Verlaine's 'Langueur' which begins:

> Je suis l'Empire à la fin de la décadence,
> Qui regarde passer les grands Barbares blancs
> En composant des acrostiches indolents
> D'un style d'or où la langueur du soleil danse.
>
> L'âme seulette a mal au coeur d'un ennui dense.[113]

Hlaváček may be declaring his allegiance to Baudelaire and Verlaine with 'Smutný večer' (Sad evening [*Pozdě k ránu*]), since he dedicates it to the memory of 'Karel' Verlaine – but he may have simply got the Christian name wrong. This poem, like most of *Pozdě k ránu*, is also founded on autostylization. The lyric narrator is a knight, last of a long line, whose fealty is due to Byzantium. Given Hlaváček's irony, this could allude to Vicaire and Beauclaire's *Les Déliquescences . Poèmes décadents d'Adoré Floupette*, which was published in 'Byzance', that is, Paris, in 1885.

Autostylization could be used to explore topoi of *fin-de-siècle* literature. This has nothing to do with split or multiple selves, but with empathy. So Le Gallienne, in his 'Beauty Accurst', examines the mind of the *femme fatale*; irony fuses with the straightforward. In the last stanza the irony is heavy-handed, when the *Ich* declares she is waiting for God to descend from His throne, so that she can take His place. Still the piece, by a poet who tried not to be a Decadent, contains some fine Decadent verse:

> I am so fair that whereso'er I wend
>> Men yearn with strange desire to kiss my face,
> Stretch out their hands to touch me as I pass
>> And women follow me from place to place.
> . . .
> Lo! when I walk along the woodland way
>> Strange creatures leer at me with uncouth love
> And from the grass reach upward to my breast,
>> and to my mouth lean from the boughs above.[114]

In the untitled introductory poem to his first collection of verse, *Zazděná okna* (Walled-up windows, 1894), Karásek gathers together a series of topoi in autostylizations. The *Ich* is an old flagellant scourging himself while he sings a sombre hymn, then an aged mariner who suddenly encounters the Devil, then a dour priest confessor, then a sex-sated woman and, finally, a morose poet whose work had tormented him to death.

One might consider that to be simply experimenting with metaphor rather than practising empathy, let alone the display of multiple personality. Still, on the face of it at least, we all pretend a multiple personality in normal social inter-course. We edit ourselves according to geographical situation and according to whom we are talking to. For all we know, we may be someone very different for A from who we are for B. So too, we must most of us lie, since sincerity is nor-mally coarse, or at least ungracious. And lying, as we have seen, formed part of the Decadents' code – for they were reacting to what they considered the false-hood of all that surrounded them. If we lie, apart from being polite, we shall often also be exhibiting, at least superficially, a slightly altered personality from the one we may be so bold as to state to ourselves that we have. Obsessive lying may well sometimes involve very much the same sort of 'doubling' as that performed by the master-torturer with his much-hugged daughter.

In any case, in the fluid self, non-rational sequences of consciousness, the distinctions of meaning between true and false may easily be or become nugatory. Furthermore, from the point of view of Decadent self-control and rejection of social environment, if one lies, one is in possession of one's meanings (or one believes one is), whereas if one tells the truth, one is possessed by someone else's meanings. Stirner (214–16) has an utterly Decadent approach to lying:

Truth is dead, a letter, a word, material that I can consume. All truth of itself is dead, a corpse; it is only living in the same way as my lung is living, namely, to the extent that I am living. Truths are material like herbs and weeds; the decision whether it is a herb or a weed lies with Me …Truth … is insubstantial because it has its value not *in itself*, but *in Me. Of itself* it is *valueless*. Truth is a – *creature*.

Amiel has little or nothing in common with Stirner or the Decadents as far as lying is concerned. For Amiel, truth is something for the aristocratic soul, something the masses fear, but still, very broadly, it is exclusive as in Stirner. Also, like the Decadents, he despises useful truth. He writes (Amiel II, 45–6), for example: 'What rules men is the fear of truth, unless truth is useful to them, which comes down to saying that self-interest is the principle of vulgar philosophy, or that truth is made for us, but we are not made for truth.' Elsewhere he advocates the cult of truth for the purification of all religions and sects; in that he shares a view with the anti-Decadent Masaryk. On critics, he says there is a way of killing the truth with truth, such as when a critic pedantically takes a work to pieces, studies details without seeing the whole.

The Decadent view on truth has two aspects. First, one has the rebellious Decadent who believes he has been brought up on falsehoods, spiritual, social and national. That aspect is well illustrated by Hlaváček's cycle, *Mstivá kantiléna*, which combines an element of the story of *Manon Lescaut* with elements from the history of the Gueux's uprising against Philip II of Spain and from the history of the Anabaptist 'state' in Münster, describing a rebellion which is itself mendacious. In *Mstivá kantiléna,* Nature lies (the fields are barren, like the Gueux women, like Manon Lescaut; the moon lies; the stock [i.e., the flower] lies; nothing in Nature has any warmth or fragrance); religion lies (the bell cannot ring; the *Kyrie eleison* is deceitful like everything in the church, from the candles to the pictures of the saints), like the hirsute brawler's fingers, but these fingers at least create beautiful music. Conventions lie, then: (i) Nature or the love of Nature, the Romantic and the rural sentimental traditions; (ii) the woman or the love of woman; (iii) religion, Catholic and Protestant alike; (iv) the conventional promoting of revolution by socialists and nationalists.

Hlaváček is rejecting the Czech tradition. In the same cycle, in its prose interlude, he also expresses the second aspect of the Decadent view on lying: that lying is the basis of art and ever new lying is necessary for the regeneration or preservation of high art. Wilde states this in 'The Decay of Lying':

Society sooner or later must return to its lost leader, the cultured and fascinating liar … For the aim of the liar is simply to charm, to delight, to give pleasure. His is the very basis of civilized society…

Nor will he be welcomed by society alone. Art, breaking from the prison-house of realism, will run to greet him, and will kiss his face, beautiful lips, knowing that he alone is in possession of the great secret of all her manifestations, the secret that Truth is entirely and absolutely a matter of style; while Life – poor, probably uninteresting human life – tired of repeating herself for the benefit of Mr Herbert Spencer, scientific historians, and the compilers of statistics in general, will follow meekly after him, and try to reproduce, in her own simple and untutored way, some of the marvels of which he talks.[115]

Where autostylization may be considered the artistic representation of the Decadent conception of self as a series or bundle of consciousnesses, lying must be considered a means towards new consciousness(es).

The Decadent self and Freud

Though he had the lucidity of style of the best Decadents and though his preoccupations were largely those of the Decadents, it would be facetious to call Freud a Decadent. Certainly he grew out of the Decadence, but that is far as one can go. When Marxists used to call him a Decadent, that was one ideology attacking another. To be sure, one may compare any two ideologies, especially two which, at certain points in history and geography, acquired the status of a religious cult. Northrop Frye, although his dismissal of the scientific contribution of Freud is unjust, puts the view of a student of letters with apodictic precision. Freud and Marx, he writes, both 'developed an encyclopaedic programme that they called scientific, and … nine-tenths of the science of both turns out to be applied mythology.'[116] Glover discusses briefly and dispassionately the reasons some regard Freudianism as a religion, and some as unscientific speculation of a brand similar to phrenology, since the defence, if anyone questions an aspect of his theories, is that 'the theory as a whole has proved its explanatory power elsewhere.'[117]

Freud was an anti-religious materialist who made a new Positivism putting a twisted snaffle and a martingale on the stallion of anti-Positivism which his *fin-de-siècle* fellows were riding bareback. In Freud the irrational can be rationalized or, perhaps, the border between rational and irrational ceases to be tangible, for there is a continuum between abnormal and normal behaviour. No doubt his social background did play a role in Freud's determination to be a great man. And Otto Weininger must have meant something when he wrote of the Jewish self: 'what is inaccessible to the genuine Jew in all eternity is *immediate being, the theory of divine right, the fanfare, the Siegfried motif, the oak-tree, the creation of his self, the words: I am!'*[118] Freud did attack the 'the sovereign intactness of "Ich"' and in that he showed himself to be very much a man of the *fin-de-siècle* period. He was a determinist, like most Decadents and Naturalists, although he gives the individual some control over the shaping of himself.[119] Glover finds this the most important aspect of Freud's theory of the self: 'It is the great contribution of his theory of the I that he gives us this active role without the metaphysics of the rational will, but as part of a determinist model, in which our actions are still caused by our desires.'[120] For Freud, the controlling centre of the individual is the *Ich* as against the *Es*, which comprises involuntary desires and thoughts; to put it vulgarly or Decadently: the animal in one. Because Freud was a *fin-de-siècle* man and *fin-de-siècle* men believed in synthesis as a panacea (in religion, sociology and literature), Freud distinguishes further between the *Ich* and the *Es* by stating that the *Ich* tends towards unification and synthesis, which the *Es* does not and cannot, for it is wild and primarily inhabited by the instincts and the desire for pleasure. The Decadents emphasized this side to the detriment of that part (or moment) of the self which is concerned with self-preservation, Freud's *Ich*; thus, Freud's *Ich* is normally not entirely conscious, even in its role as an intermediary between the *Es* and the world outside. That is a complex notion if one does without rational will, as, again, Glover points out: 'If the Freudian I is to avoid the problems of the rational will, its decisions have to be seen as motivated by desires. It has to restrain some desires in order to carry out plans motivated by others'.[121]

Freud acknowledged that the roots of his conception of the *Es* lay in Schopenhauer's notion of the instincts or drives as a distinct component of the self, different from the *Ich*. The Decadents took over the Schopenhauer notion (Schnitzler, Karásek), and sometimes identified it with the notion of Evil (Šlejhar), but generally the Decadents assumed that what Freud calls the *Es* was not only analysable by the self and thus trainable, but also that it was potentially totally controllable, domitable. The dandy as a type of the self was in sole charge of his *Es*, all his motives and affectations, all the distant, inaccessible parts of the human personality. The child and woman are for the dandy predominantly *Es*, for, like Freud, the Decadents appeared to believe that a personality began to develop on the basis of a chaotic unconscious; personality or personness is developed on the basis of a system of perception which lies on the surface of the unconscious; the unconscious is then refined by knowledge, awareness, the acquisition of self-control, what Freud calls consciousness. The Decadents have no conception of a preconscious that one can draw on at will.

The Decadents were determinedly anti-scientific, indeed were so perturbed by the advances of science that many of them cultivated an interest in alchemy, witchcraft and the Tarot. (Even the music-hall-fan Decadent Symons, the man of whom Wilde had said he was an egoist who had no ego, wrote a poem on the Tarot.)[122] Freud, on the other hand, was determinedly scientific. His holist, universalist mythology of the self may be compared with Schnitzler's mythology of decayed Vienna or of Jewishness or with Nietzsche's *Übermensch* mythology or even Miloš Marten's mythology of literary criteria. (I use the term mythology, as in the sections dealing with national myths, to mean a system through which a member of humanity or a particular society may interpret the origins of his, her or its behaviour). The difference is that Freud claimed too hard that he was being scientific; actually, he was primarily a man of great, if obsessive, imagination. He used his imagination in putting together his system rather than in producing grand new ideas. Furthermore, as Glover states, to read a book in the psychoanalytic tradition 'is often to be confronted with claims that seem authoritative. These claims are apparently based on a body of knowledge, but you never seem to be reading the book where the supporting evidence is given.'[123]

Freud's concern both with the self and with sexuality are of the period, and thus of the Decadence as well. His pansexualism, that is his notion that no group of ideas exists which cannot represent sexual desires and experience, may well correspond to Decadent pan-erethism and to the Decadent tendency to lend human sexual qualities to non-human objects. (I am not forgetting that the Decadents saw sexuality in non-human objects because for them true elitist humanity lay in the dominating of one's sexuality. Linked with that is the statement of the Decadent philosopher, Ladislav Klíma, that man has only two freedoms – which also distinguish him from animals – the freedom to kill himself and the freedom not to reproduce.) Freud's concern with infantile sexuality and puberty is matched by the Decadent concern with puberty. The Decadents' interest in puberty stemmed from the importance they assigned to intermediate states as metaphors for the age of transition in which they lived. Puberty is a period of ambiguity: the child is not quite child and not quite adult, and also is moving from a state of non-personness to personness. The Decadents employed as one of their ambiguous images of horror the *femme enfant*, the sweet little thing with malicious eyes and curves which foreshadowed her *femme*-fatality. Freud's invention or discovery of the Oedipus complex seems to correspond to the Decadents' unwitting predilection for parthenogenesis (when fathers appear at all, normally they are objects of hatred or contempt). Erich Heller has interpreted Freud's notion as reflecting Viennese young men's experience of having given their fathers a position of ultimate authority and then having experienced their failure. One thinks of the story in the *Interpretation of Dreams* where a Goy knocks the hat off Freud's father's head and of Freud's repeated assertion that the *potestas patris familias* was already invalid, out of date, at the time he was writing.

Freud shared his interest in dreams with the Decadents, and for both, dreams revealed a somehow liberated world or liberated self. As dreams are for Freud always egotistic, so for the Decadents they are expressions of the complete self unrestrained by the bourgeois. For Freud, the preconscious enters dreams, for the Decadent only the unconscious. Just as in Decadent art multiple personality is normally generated by autostylization, so in Freud's dreams a multiple *Ich* may appear as, according to his theory, autostylization. Freud's oneiric auto-styli-zations, however, result from censorship. He writes that in dreams where his *Ich* appears together with other people, after identification it transpires that these other people are also his *Ich*, but part of the *Ich* which had been subject to censorship. In many notions Freud comes close to the Decadence, but, at least in his work before the Great War, he was an optimist, a man with a cure. No Decadent may be an optimist. No Decadent has cures.

4

CONCLUSION:
CZECH SELF-DEFINITION
THROUGH MARTYRS

Introduction: Varieties of national self-definition

No Czech Decadent has cures, not even for his self-searching, and he might well find the reason for his particularly strong awareness of the surrounding decay in his Czechness. Villon, a poet much admired by the *fin-de-siècle* circle, had curiously stated the Czech Decadents' plight for them well over four hundred years previously in his 'Ballade (des menus propos)': 'Je congnois la faulte des Boesmes, / Je congnois le povoir de Romme, / Je congnois tout, fors que moy mesmes.'[1] The Decadents' awareness of the fluidity, inconstancy of the self was of itself a dead end, disintegration rather than manipulable proteiformity. The image that expressed this was the *danse macabre*. In Karásek's 'Smrt Salomina' (Salome's death, *Posvátné ohně*), the ageing Jewish princess flings herself into a wild dance before the young gazelle-hunter who will not love her; in this dance she regains all the beauty of her youth – of the self she considers hers – but afterwards her wrinkles twist her again; she returns home to her palace and sends the hunter her severed head on a silver salver. The luxuriant courtesan Tarsie, who loves the homosexual eponymous hero of the same writer's *Apollonius z Tyany* (Apollonius of Tyana, 1905), also suddenly aware of growing old, performs a similar dance, and then goes out of her mind. When Tarsie dances, however, she looks like a revived corpse. When Klára, in Karel Sezima's (1876–1949) *Passiflora* (1903), hears that the sadistic husband from whom she has run away is dead, she also dances, like an angered animal, liberated, but with the chain still jangling behind it; her *danse macabre* expresses both nostalgia and satisfied revenge. The liberation is, however, false, except in that it is a liberation from her illusion that there really were knights in shining armour. She achieves a spiritual sensuality of a kind, but soon becomes apathetic; she dies soon after the man who has been wooing her by her sick bed well-nigh rapes her. In Felix Tèver's (1852–1932) *Duše nezakotvené* (Souls adrift, 1908), a beautiful painter dances an ecstatic *csardás* shortly before hanging herself to prevent her brutish broad-nostrilled husband from having sexual intercourse with her. She preserves herself in death.

The Decadent Michal in Marten's *Nad městem* (Looking over the city, 1917), a work which endeavours to provide a solution to the national element in Czech Decadents' sense of decay, is described as 'an exile more in his inner self than in the world that he blames'.[2] In a programmatic introduction to his first collection of verse, which is more Decadent in its means of expression than anything else, Theer (1880–1917) declares that he wishes to overcome Decadence, indeed the *fin-de-siècle* writers altogether. For him all the writers of the main trends, 'try to be deeply immersed in themselves, want to depict their souls either in the calmly flowing current of everyday life or in the precious moments of ecstasy vibrating the deepest depths of seas; they want to make their soul tremble "laid bare, at the moment it is horrified by itself as its clothes fall off."'[3] Theer appears to have been aware of his failure to overcome Decadence, to cease to search for his soul in his writing, for he writes in the introductory 'letter' to his next collection, *Výpravy k já* (Expeditions to the self, 1900), 'I have been that futile horseman galloping in quest of the secret of his inner self. The uncertainty, searching and secret were both rapture and pain for me, both disappointment and hope ... Instead of the mystery I wanted to find the mechanism; I wanted to solve my self.'[4] And in the final poem of this collection, 'Transatlantic' (Ocean liner), in the first four lines he indulges in an autostylization which has its roots (the first four lines) in Decadence: 'I am like a dejected adventurer, bored by conquests, despairing at his inner self, exhausted by his mistresses,/I am horrified by my own soul, a necropolis of memories /where strange gamblers come to go wild with their pain.'[5]

In the Czech Decadents this historical self replaces what was for them the necropolis of their nation – and one remembers that this was at a time when, generally, Czech *belles lettres* were reflecting the political battles of the times, particularly patriotism. The Decadents rejected the National Revival, which meant, in the sense Macura uses the term, rejected 'Czech culture'. In fact, however, they did not reject all of it, Mácha, Neruda or Zeyer – though the last, at least in part, was one of them. Still, Macura's argument holds, as long as one then interprets the rejection of 'sweet' Bohemia as also involving replacing it with the Amielesque landscapes of their souls as well as strong foreign influences. Furthermore, they were willy-nilly also obeying the commands of their contemporaries who were telling Czech writers to be themselves – in order to be genuinely Czech. The moment at which 'Czech culture is emancipated from the Revival', writes Macura, is accompanied by the experience of the 'non-existence' of Czech culture. 'In these circumstances it is evident that the European Decadence would not find simply a passive recipient in Bohemia. Czech culture had to identify itself in the sensations of the Decadence; indeed, through them it discovered its real substance; with the aid of these very sensations it acknowledged its own physiognomy.'[6] (This cannot but remind one of Havel's – but also Ivan Vyskočil's and Josef Topol's – reception of the Theatre of the Absurd at the beginning of the 1960s, based on a repudiation of socialist culture.) It would be permissible to interpret Hlaváček's *Mstivá kantiléna* as describing the cultural wasteland of Bohemia and the futility of any rebellion against it together and as constituting a statement on the potential aesthetic qualities of that wasteland.

The artistic code of the Czech Decadent writer, indeed virtually any writer who belonged to 'Modernist' circles, included criticism of the contemporary state of Czech culture, often of Czechness. That belonged to the way they defined themselves as Czechs. Like more or less contemporary historians of the Pekař brand, among the Revivalist myths the Decadents most despised was the notion that the Czechs were a dove-like nation. Procházka accepts one Revival myth, Czech quarrelsomeness, but considers the peace myth a national curse: 'Czech pacifism, the Czech "dove-like nature", the Czechs' readiness to forgive wrongs and to forget any humiliation or injustice that they have suffered, together with the Czechs' factiousness in their own country, are hideous monsters that pose a horrifying threat to any national future.'[7] Czech doves lead to a weak-spined compromise in society and literary culture, suggests Karásek: 'the half-baked, compromising nature of Czech poetry runs parallel with the half-baked, compromising nature of the whole of Czech life, Czech society.'[8] In the same author's novel, *Bezcestí* (Lost, 1893), we find the statement: 'Our glorious Czech literature – which remains great only for as long as it is not so bold as to go abroad. What is there in our literature? Nothing, a vast nothing.'[9] At a time when neo-Revivalists are praising Czech strength (Alois Jirásek) or lauding the vitality of the Czech peasant tradition (Svatopluk Čech) and Masaryk is declaiming on the Czech national vocation, the Czech Decadents see Prague and Bohemia in a state of putrefaction. 'The *caput regni* is rotting; the whole *regnum* is rotting,' writes S. K. Neumann (1875–1947).[10] A character in Krupička's (1879–1951) comedy, *Velký stil* (The grand style, 1915, confiscated by police), says of the Czechs: 'You're rotting here. Like worms in a puddle, long forgotten by the whole of Europe, the whole world.'[11] For Karásek, the Czechs are 'a race incapable of action, crushed by their own paltriness.'[12] And Procházka maintains that the Czechs actually admire weakness: 'We are shallow and flabby. We love feebleness; we take pleasure in torpor; we protect and tend our feebleness and torpor like flowers in a greenhouse.'[13] Dyk (1877–1931) ironizes the Czechs as grovellers in one of the interpolated poems of his novel, *Prosinec* (December), 'A decent Czech always doffs his hat /when he sees something that is *k.u.k.*,[14]/and humbly bows/ before all who are up there at the top.'[15] A writer who pretty constantly attacked Czech Decadent circles, but who shared the Decadents' views on contemporary Bohemia, J. S. Machar (1864–1942) observed Czech society from Vienna, where he worked. In his poem, 'Boží bojovníci' (Warriors of God [*Golgatha*, 1901]), he describes the Czechs as servile cowards and in 'Monolog' (ibid.), he conceives of his nation as the concierge of the House of Austria who always runs about commenting over the cracks of that crumbling edifice. The Slovaks had no Decadent literature, but one poet, Ivan Krasko (1876–1958), manifests a considerable debt to the Decadent linguistic code, and, in his imagery and his use of the acoustics of Slovak, he echoes particularly Hlaváček. (He was living and working in Bohemia in the period during which he wrote his verse.) Nevertheless, he remained very much his own man in his displays of the moods of his grief-tormented self against a background of mist, rain, dark poplars, grave-yards, wayside crosses (*Nox et solitudo*, 1909). Not quite all the poems in the collection are, however, intimate. His is not, however, the irony or facetious sarcasm of his Czech contemporaries; 'Jehovah', the most powerful of his non-intimate poems, expresses angry despair at his fellow-countrymen as he calls the Wrath of God down upon them, and he is contemptuous of their Magyar over-lords. His second collection, *Verše* (1912), also contains poems like the pessi-mistic 'Askét' (The ascetic) where he fears he might succumb to the apathy that he so loathes in the Slovaks, or 'Otcova rol'a' (My father's field), a masochistic expression of nationalist despair, or 'Otrok' (The slave), which presents a well-nigh revolutionary desire for revenge on the overlords.

However wary one might be of attributing specific characteristics to mem-bers of individual nations, Czechs – particularly Bohemians – and Slovaks not only have different conventions of social behaviour but also regard their national-ity in a different manner. No doubt the reasons for that are mainly historical (Czechs under Germans, but Slovaks under Magyars; less likely, Czechs with a long tradition of independent statehood, Slovaks with practically none; Slovaks very largely an agrarian people for far longer than the Czechs, and so forth) and geographical (Slovaks mainly mountain and valley-dwellers, Czechs mainly plain-dwellers), but, anyway, any attempt to explain such differences, even on historical grounds, is likely to lead to pseudoscholarly mythopoeia. Slovaks are more vociferous in their nationalism than the Czechs. Whatever Western news-papers after 1989 liked to tell their readers, there is nothing new about this Slovak nationalism; just some forms of it, nostalgia for praise of the war-time puppet Slovak State would not have been permitted to appear in print in socialist Czechoslovakia, but they did, with a vengeance, in émigré periodicals in Ger-many and Canada. In Bratislava pubs, even in the Communist Writers' Union bar such nostalgia and praise could frequently be heard. Recent suggestions that – since there is no Slovak saint – the president of the Slovak State, the priest, Jozef Tiso, who was sentenced to death as a war criminal on 15 April 1947, should be canonized as a martyr are essentially spoofs[16] – only dangerous when the naive take them seriously. Since the Herderian creation of the mythic nation, the Slovaks have had to struggle enormously hard to have themselves recognized. Before Štúr succeeded, 1843–44, in creating a workable Slovak literary language, the means of patriotic literary communication had been Czech – otherwise, German, Latin or Hungarian. It took some years before the small Slovak intelligentsia were all persuaded to reject Kollár's 'Czechoslovak' ideas and accept Štúr's, and during the second half of the nineteenth century the forces of Magyarization expanded. The fact that Magyarization was largely inspired by Hungarian liberals who wanted to make sure that all the 'nationalities' of Hungary had an equal chance to enter state service and so forth was, quite naturally, unpersuasive for a Slovak. Although the Slovaks had been promised some autonomy in the new state, when the creation of Czecho-Slovakia (it became Czechoslovakia a little later) was declared, it was met with nothing like the enthusiasm that was seen in parts of the Bohemian Lands. Slovak became an official state language, but the Slovak intelligentsia was small, and so a large number of teachers at all levels was imported from the Bohemian Lands. Much of the industry that had been built up by Hungary in Slovakia failed during the First Republic because it could not compete with the advanced industry of the Czech areas. It is, then, not surprising that many Slovaks began to feel that all the republic meant for them was that Czech overlords had replaced the Hungarian. That feeling was not so visible among the intellectuals, who tended to do their studies in Prague anyway. During the War, although the Germans sustained it for some time, the Slovak economy suffered immensely on account of the government's keen implementation of anti-Jewish laws. Unrest grew and the 1944 Slovak National Uprising was the second (after the Warsaw Uprising) largest mass resistance effort against the Germans during the whole of World War II. After the War, the Slovaks, unlike the Czechs, did not vote for the Communists, and so again the Slovaks had a government imposed on them. Nevertheless, although leading Slovak Communists were condemned as 'bourgeois nationalists' in the show-trials of the 1950s, Slovak nationalism was condoned, sometimes even encouraged, by the socialist state, especially in the wake of the 1964 anniversary of the Uprising. The most evident and pervasive expression of this was linguistic. Even more or less scholarly editions of any Slovak book published before the War was heavily de-bohemicized; this applied not only to grammar but also to vocabulary. Scholarly editions of Slovak writers from the nineteenth-century National Awakening certainly contained the poems or essays they had written in Czech, but a good deal more often than not they appeared in these editions only in Slovak. This practice continued throughout socialism except, normally, in the case of texts from the eighteenth century and before. In an area where the linguocentricity of its nationalism was emphasized because of the closeness of Czech and Slovak, such editions amounted to the falsification of history. At the same time, while the Slovaks read Czech literature, very few Czechs apart from intellectuals with a literary interest (among them, Havel and his fellow dissident, Ludvík Vaculík) read Slovak literature. Czechs would claim that they could not understand the language, although they eagerly read Slovak translations of Western literature. After the Soviet occupation in 1968, the repression of Slovak writers was minimal in comparison with that of Czech. One result of this was that Slovak literature developed (one thinks especially of Johanides, Ballek and Vilikovský, but also the grand old man of Slovak literature, Bednár), where Czech literature, sanctioned (i.e. published in state publishing houses) or unsanctioned (i.e. 'dissident' and exile), tended, at least until the latter half of the 1980s to remain in something like a time-warp, either returning more or less to the 1950s in style or structure (Party writers like Kozák, Houba or Nohejl) or remaining in the 1960s (for example, Havel's plays, Škvorecký, Páral). Naturally, one will find serious Czech writers who did develop (say, Milan Kundera). The different circumstances in Slovak cultural life in the 1970s may well also have contributed to the fact that so few Slovak writers joined Charter 77. All these matters increased the Slovaks' sense of a distinct national identity. How far the apparently Czech leadership of the events of November 1989 further encouraged a Slovak nationalism, based on a sense of being left out once again – however successful the Slovak VPN (Public Against Violence) initially was – I am not in a position to say. My main points are that Slovak nationalism is far from new and that, given history and the economic weakness of the Slovaks in comparison with the Czechs, it is understandable that, after 1989, nationalism soon became the strongest political force in Slovakia, however small a proportion of the population might consider itself nationalist.

The Slovaks appear to have a self-confidence about what a Slovak is which one might compare with that of the English, Scottish or Welsh. They do not appear to need the endless self-defining 'philosophies' of national history that the Czechs have. Fundamentally, Štúr (with a little help from Šafařík) had defined Slovaks and that was enough. Štefan Polakovič, a hard-line nationalist of the old school, author of *K základom slovenského štátu* (On the foundations of the Slovak state, 1939), who emigrated to Argentina in 1947 and was nearly eighty when he joined the new campaign for a separate Slovak state, is speaking for most Slovaks when he claims; 'No Slovak Question has ever existed for the Slovaks, for our nation has never questioned its existence as an independent, individual, specific identity … It was the Czech founders of "Czecho-Slovakia" who questioned the existence of Slovaks as a nation.'[17] Macura makes a similar point. Czechs, he writes, 'often' feel insecure about their 'conscious identity'; 'we are not Czechs because we exist … our closest neighbours, the Slovaks, with whom we shared a state for three quarters of a century, have no problems with their identity: they are Slovaks because they are Slovaks.'[18] Havel introduces a mythic distinction between Czechs and Slovaks in a New Year's Day address (1 January 1991), when describing his vision of the federal state. Like characters in a medieval dispute, the Slovaks represent Emotion and the Czechs Reason: the Slovak Republic 'will be a republic of love and pride for all its citizens', but the Czech Republic 'will be a republic of wisdom and tolerance for all its citizens.'[19] One cannot doubt that Havel is expressing a version of a general Czech perception here, one that is coincidentally supported by Macura, albeit with some self-irony:

There is something perceptibly female in the Czechs' image of Slovakia. In contrast to the Czech world which appears almost severely 'rational', almost 'calculating', 'combative', the Slovak world appears to be linked with roots, Nature, irrationality, feelings, spontaneity. Slovakia is loved for her 'beauty', 'charms', 'sweet songfulness', 'virtue', 'honour', 'naturalness', but one also speaks of Slovak 'volatility' and 'capriciousness'.[20]

Needless to say, the Slovaks' perception of themselves is of manlier creatures. I take just a sample of the key characteristics which Štúr lent the Slovaks. His starting point is that the Slovaks are Slavs and thus share the Slav vocation. That vocation had been to supply the brawn (where the West's had been to supply the brains) in the foundation of modern European civilization. The West had had their crusades, but, from the time that the Ottomans had started expanding, it had been the 'Slavs' calling to serve the budding civilization of the Christian West as a wall against the onslaught of Eastern barbarism.'[21] The Slovaks themselves had in their historical role primarily been civilizers. They had had to teach the Magyars how to plough and how to build houses; Štúr's Czech style is biblical, for he is writing the Scriptures of Slovakhood:

And it was difficult for the Magyars to become accustomed to tilling the fields and exposing themselves to the burden of summer heat, and the desire overcame them to set off plundering once more, but the Slovaks restrained them from pillage and showed what they had gained from the womb of the land by their toil, telling them that they would do this well if they become accustomed to work, and thus by their example did they give them courage.

Finally, the Magyars began to work and, seeing that the soil brought them corn and that their toil was rewarded, they bent to it and became accustomed to work. The Slovaks rejoiced that the Magyars were beginning to work, for they knew well that thus they would relinquish their old savagery and that they would be able to live peacefully with them in one country.

And hitherto the Magyars had not had permanent dwellings or houses, but had led a nomadic life; they had had only wretched quickly-built cottages and shacks in which filth resided and where there were no implements; and the Slovaks taught them to build clean, airy dwelling-places and showed them how to make various implements for domestic use.[22]

By the twentieth century, some Slovak writers had begun dismantling the Štúrian myth of fine farming Slovaks. Timrava (1867–1951) creates quite a different type in her *Ťapákovci* (The Ťapáks, 1914): the desultory, if not downright bone-idle, Slovak peasant; Martin Kukučín (1860–1928) has his drunkards, his money-minded peasants – and, in *Dies irae* (1893), his Slovak miser. The very structure of rural society is threatened by money-mindedness in Jozef Gregor-Tajovský's *Statky-zmätky* (Money-muddle, 1909). Then, between the wars, writers like Milo Urban (1904–82) and J. C. Hronský (1896–1960) introduce sheer coarseness, backwardness and violence into depictions of Slovak village life. Nevertheless, the Štúrian myth of Slovak farmers and builders was by no means dead at the end of the 1980s; for example, in the Marxified nationalist novels of Habaj, with ironic whimsy, in Šikula's *Majstri* (The master-carpenters, 1976). Jaroš's immensely popular and slightly sleezy *Tisícročná včela* (Thousand-year-old bee, 1979) depicts the Slovaks as a nation of builders, a mythic interpretation of Slovak social origins greatly fostered by Vojtech Mihálik in the 1950s and by the master Socialist Realist, Mináč, in the 1970s and 1980s. The latter writes in an essay: 'The Slovaks are a nation of constructors, builders, not only in the metaphorical, but also the literal sense of the term.'[23]

Štúr's mythic picture of the Slovak nation does not end with farming and building. Having taught them to build houses, the Slovaks began converting the Magyar common people to the Christian faith and, eventually, when their ruler, Géza, saw that Christianity was spreading among his people, in 980 he sent for the Czech Archbishop of Prague, St Adalbert[24] to do missionary work in Hungary and to baptize his son, Stephen. When in Hungary, Adalbert and the Czech priests in his retinue spoke Slovak.[25] This part of Štúr's myth, the Slovaks as the apostles of Hungary, might be said still to be alive in the politicized Roman Catholicism of Slovak nationalists since the 1930s, and is certainly alive in the St Adalbert Association (founded 1870), which organizes the publishing of Roman Catholic literature and scholarship, by virtue of the association's very name. From the time of Adalbert, Magyars and Slovaks lived together in peace and concord, according to the Štúr myth, until the beginning of the nineteenth century, when Magyarization began; within the passionate account of this period Štúr also establishes another mythic element (actually, also a form of active atavism), the Hungarians' false hospitality in accepting foreigners as inhabitants of Slovak territory (one might interpret the novelist Ballek's depictions of Slovakia as constituted by a vivid mixture of different nations as a faint echo of this part of Štúr's complex myth):

The councillors continued and said: 'Since the Magyar nation conquered this land and assumed the government of her, it is meet and right that this nation's language should rule over all her nations and expand, and that the languages of the other, servile, nations should bow before it and, with the passing of time, be eradicated, for it is good and needful that only one language should rule in the country, that only one should be spoken and that this should rightly be the language of the rulers.'

At these words the council chamber was filled with a persistent purring, for the men of vanity realized that, henceforth, they would not have to learn languages, but would be able to abide by one.

And the councillors continued and said: 'Since the Slovaks are subjugated, let them learn the lords' language; once they learn it, they will abandon and forget their language.

The same must be done by the Germans, whom we received into our houses when they were wandering far from their country and to whom we gave everything good, without which they would have perished in hunger and poverty. And all the other nations in Hungary must do the same. So, to achieve this goal, let us issue strict laws and start our work.'[26]

One aspect of this episode did not enter the myth, for Štúr adds that a great number of Slovaks had been at this council meeting. They had, however, all been either cowards or lickspittles or pompous braggarts. The last group, and there is little doubt that Štúr means the Slovak petty nobility, are the worst, since they now start behaving as if they were the true lords of the land. The view that the Slovak gentry were all Magyarized, that they had betrayed their nation, is that espoused by the nationalists of the Polakovič type.[27]

An essential element in the myth by which Slovaks tend to define themselves is the notion of the Slovaks as a nation of drinkers. Štúr played his role in this too; he founded temperance groups in several Slovak villages. Amongst Štúr's followers, Ján Kalinčiak (1822–71) uses drink largely for comic effect when he describes its role during elections in his affectionately ironic depiction of the petty nobility, *Reštavrácia* (Deputy-sheriff elections, 1860), whereas M. Š. Ferienčík (1825–81) goes to war against drink in his *Jedlovský učiteľ'* (The schoolmaster, 1862). The conflict of this *novella* consists in true Slovaks set against Magyars, renegade Slovaks and the Jewish village publican, that target for hatred in Slovak writing from the Awakening to this day, the stock figure used as an excuse for antisemitism among nationalists.[28] In recent literature, the mythic quality of Slovak drinking habits is satirized by Mitana when the main character of his *Koniec hry* (The end of a game) has gone on the water-wagon: 'Money and success came, but his old friends went away. Before, they had liked him; now, they respected him, and nothing more. No, they did not start to despise him, but all naturalness had vanished from these friendships, and, what was even worse, they had started avoiding him. With regret he had discovered that a sober Slovak is condemned to solitude.'[29] Drink also forms part of the Czech self-image and two Czech leaders followed Štúr's example. Masaryk became a total abstainer at the beginning of the twentieth century and began lecturing and writing on alcoholism in Bohemia and, once, in 1905, at the Grand Lodge of the Second Order of Good Templars in Danzig. His disciple and successor to the Czechoslovak presidency, Edvard Beneš, published in 1915 a work on the economics of alcohol production and the sociology of consumption, whose main aim is to discuss how some form of prohibition could be instituted.[30] In the twentieth century, beer-drinking formed a salient part of the Czech national identity myth. After World War II, this was supported by the literary legend of the beer-drinking Švejk and his beer-drinking author, Hašek (1883–1923). According to Masaryk, however, at least from the beginning of the nineteenth century 'hard liquor became the national drink' and, from the middle of that century, 'beer became the second national drink.'[31] The Czech beer-drinker, he informs us, is 'very frequently from the educated classes.'[32] Here, if Masaryk is right, Czech literature is misleading; certainly, we see students and lawyers drinking beer in pubs, at least from Neruda's (1834–91) time, and wine was more common in Klicpera's (1792–1859), but at least from the 1880s pubs seem to be full of petty bourgeois and workers drinking beer (for example, Herrmann [1854–1935] or Čapek Chod [1860–1927]), though, to be sure, Šlejhar's (1864–1914) workers tend to be slaves to spirits.

In trying to describe what might distinguish Czechs from Slovaks, one can actually fall back on little except history and, through the use of a model to describe differences of evolution that might help account for the two peoples' senses of their own differentness. Not only is a description of different drinking habits of little more than passing anthropological interest, but to concentrate on language as the determinant of nationality tends towards the specious. The difference between the Czech and Slovak languages is probably smaller than that between standard English[33] and Lallans. Still, Lallans is a dialect of English, but, from an epistemological point of view, it would be difficult to find any grounds for calling Slovak a dialect of Czech, as was common in the nineteenth and early twentieth centuries. That before Štúr's codification the Slavs of Upper Hungary generally wrote in Czech, German or Latin is immaterial. Štúr, after false starts primarily by Anton Bernolák (1762–1813), simply converted a vernacular into a written form. Because French was established as a vernacular before Italian, Italian is not a dialect of French and neither is it in any useful sense a dialect of Latin. Nevertheless, it is still far easier to say what a Czech is on the basis of history than to say what a Slovak is. The composition of 'national' histories takes more inventiveness in the case of some peoples than of others.

The model I take to make the historical distinctions between the creation of the Czech and Slovak nations is Anthony Smith's.[34] In Smith's model for the creation of nations, a people goes through four periods and may take one of two routes, and two types of ethnie may be distinguished (there is a third ethnie, taken to create modern American and Australasian emigrant-colonist based nations that does not concern us). The first period is when tribes 'coalesce' and is linked with ancestry and foundation myths. The second period is that of 'ethnic consolidation', often linked with a blossoming of culture, military heroes, saints. The third period is of division; 'often seen as decline. The old order hardens around the upper classes; the community ossifies and decays, and is sometimes conquered and exiled.' Within this period nationalist movements appear, breaking with the past, rewriting history and so forth. The fourth period, when the people finally becomes a modern nation, is associated with the drawing up of a constitution, the provision of social welfare and economic reforms. The two types of ethnie are the 'aristocratic', where culture is in the hands of the upper classes though most of the peasantry will belong to the same linguistic community. The second is 'demotic', where the culture is in the hands of the whole community, and 'barriers to marriage with outsiders are higher' than in the aristocratic ethnie. The first of the two routes 'proceeds through bureaucratic incorporation consequent on an economic and administrative revolution and based on an ... aristocratic ethnie; the second through a cultural revolution, vernacular mobilisation and the politicisation of culture.' On the basis of this model it appears at first sight clear that one may see the Czechs as an aristocratic ethnie which took the bureaucratic route (Smith's example is the French) and the Slovaks as a demotic ethnie which took the cultural revolutionary route (Smith's example is the Greeks).

If one accepted that, however, one would first have adequately to dismiss or explain elements in interpretations of both Czech and Slovak history. In the case of the Slovaks, one would have to say that the Slovaks' belief that the Great Moravian Empire (c.833–900s) is part of Slovak history is as ill-founded as the modern Greeks' popular beliefs that they are the descendants of the Ancient Greeks. In the case of the Czechs, one would be dismissing out of hand Patočka's explicit and Macura's implicit view that the Czech 'nation' created in the nineteenth century had nothing but an artificially cultivated literary language in common with the medieval Czech 'nation'. They would, no doubt, argue that the modern Czechs had followed the demotic route, like the Slovaks.

In attempting to trace the evolution of the Slovaks into a modern nation according to Smith's model, the first and second periods present difficulties, and deciding when the third period begins depends on whether or not one accepts Štúr's and modern Slovak historians' accounts of ninth-century activity on the territory of today's Slovakia as accounts of Slovak activity. Smith accepts that his periods may overlap and that individual periods may last for centuries, but may also last for a few decades. In the cultural revolution which transforms demotic ethnies into nations, 'the intellectuals [in our case, mainly Štúr and the Štúrians] seek to resolve their own identity crises by reappropriating the history and culture of their community or ['and' in the Slovak case] by reconstructing a defective ethno-historical record.' The 'civic nations' which arise out of the aristocratic-bureaucratic route base their national ideology on 'territorial citizenship' rather than on 'collective ties of descent', regarding themselves as descendants of the original, or founding, community like the 'ethnic nations'. For the latter, a 'myth of common origins and descent has been elevated into the defining criterion of the nation itself.' Slovak historians' approach to Great Moravia is fundamentally a territorial approach, although their tendency to call at least the inhabitants of the eastern part of the territory Slovaks adds a genealogical element to it; that genealogical element is enhanced if they use for that part of the territory the label invented in the nineteenth century, Slovakia. For, at least at that time, 'Slovakia' suggested the 'natural' dwelling place of the Slovaks who had once had their own state. 'Slovakia' remained an ethnic rather than a territorial denominator until the founding of Czecho-Slovakia. That the Slovak government of today considers the Slovaks an ethnic nation and Slovak as essentially designating the Slovaks' birthright is clear from the Preamble to the Slovak Constitution:

WE, THE SLOVAK NATION, mindful of our ancestors' political and cultural legacy and of centuries' experience of struggles for national existence and our own statehood, / in accordance with the Cyrilo-Methodian spiritual legacy and the historical heritage of Great Moravia, / on the basis of the natural right of nations to self-determination, / together with members of national minorities and ethnic groups living on the territory of the Slovak Republic, / in the interests of permanent peaceful cooperation with other democratic states, / in the endeavour to implement a democratic form of government, guarantees of a free life, the development of spiritual culture and economic prosperity, / *we, the citizens of the Slovak Republic* / *resolve* ...

These words of national self-definition also comprise statements relating to all four periods in Smith's model. One notes that national minorities have more or less the same status as foreign powers; this emphasizes the desire of the politicians to make Slovakia an ethnic, not civic, nation-state.[35]

    The first period in the national evolution of the Slovaks, not mentioned in the Preamble, though 'ancestors' and, indeed, 'struggles' (notice the plural) could cover it, may or may not include migration, according to individual writer's interpretation. If it does, the myth will refer to Slavs, not Slovaks, coming into the area which had previously been abandoned by Germanic tribes, and previous to that, Celtic tribes (late fifth and early sixth centuries). Mention may well be made of Roman civilization in 'Slovakia' reaching as far as Trenčín, and of pre-Slavonic Christian communities in South West 'Slovakia'.[36] The foundation myth concerns the Frankish merchant, probably arms-dealer, Samo (claimed also by the Slovenes, and once by the Czechs, who now call him simply the organizer of the first West Slavonic association of tribes). He probably wielded power over what was to become the Habsburg Monarchy, 623–58, had twelve Slav wives who bore him fifteen daughters and twenty-two sons. The Slavs elected him 'king' because they needed his help in fighting the Avars. Two hundred years after its conception, the Herder myth of the Slavs helps the modern historian to explain why the Slavs should take a Frank as their leader: 'The peaceful farmers were at an evident disadvantage, faced with the Avar professional warriors.'[37] The fact that the Slavs 'chose' Samo (according to the chronicle of so-called Fredegar), demonstrates that the Slavs are by nature democrats.[38] Furthermore, Samo was not only an ordinary merchant, but belonged in an 'ancient minority', for his name clearly betrays that he was a Celt.[39] When Samo's Slav realm was becoming too strong, Dagobert I invaded in 631, and the Slavs defeated the Franks at Samo's fortress of Wogastisburg. For Czech historians this fortress was probably in Bohemia and was not Samo's power-centre;[40] apparently, the most generally accepted theory is that the fortress stood on Rubín Hill in Western Bohemia and Samo's power-centre was in Southern Moravia.[41] Kučera, however, demonstrates another theory – which supports the foundation myth. He takes a dozen other theories into consideration, but after examination of documents, archaeological finds and geography, he is convinced that Wogastisburg lay in today's Bratislava and that this area was his power-centre.[42] It is to the period of Samo's empire that 'the deep foundations of today's Slovakia and Slovaks stretch.'[43]

The second stage according to Smith's model comprises the Great Moravian Empire and the arrival of the Greek brothers, Cyril (Constantine the Philosopher) and Methodius. The period between Samo and Mojmír I of Moravia is virtually entirely undocumented for the Bohemian Lands, as for 'Slovakia'. We do know of eighth-century Frankish and Irish missions to parts of today's Slovakia and of Alcuin of York's interest in them[44] – but that is of no interest to Kučera who glosses the nigh-on two hundred years with the following: 'The ambitious Frankish merchant left the historical scene, but the no less ambitious Slovak people remained there; they established their settlements in the region between the Danube and the Tatras, cut their ploughs into the soil, drove their livestock onto the hillsides. They had found a "promised land" – their new home-country, and set down roots there that none of the subsequent gales of history managed to tear up.'[45] Conceptually that is the same as Štúr's description of the pre-Christian Slovaks (at this stage, Štúr is ignorant of Samo, but that makes little difference); the essence of national myths cannot change:

Your fathers moved into this land in times immemorial, about which even the folk tales have perished, and they found it thorny and overgrown. But, having settled, they slowly began to cultivate the soil; they cleared thorn and thistle and ploughed the land in the sweat of their brows, and sowed and planted so that it bore corn and fruit. And the soil produced abundant corn and brought forth sweet fruit, and your fathers were much pleased at their work … And they cut through the dense forests and in the clearings they built houses in which they dwelt with their families, and they enjoyed living there and rejoiced at their work.[46]

This second period functions in the Slovak myth exactly as Smith maintains that it should. His flowering of ethnic culture is represented primarily by SS Cyril and Methodius and the translations and original work which they are said to have composed in Great Moravia. Since archaeologists started work on the area, the churches and adornments of the period have been added to the myth. The military exploits consist in the wars with 'Germans' and, just before the eradication of the state, their repulsion of the Magyars in 902. The heroes are the princes of Moravia and Nitra, especially Pribina,[47] Rastislav (*reg.* 846–70) and Svatopluk (*reg.* 870?–94). True to Smith's model, Great Moravia has been recalled as the 'golden age' of the Slovaks since the beginnings of time the National Awakening. The two main works by the one writer of merit to use Bernolák Slovak, Ján Hollý (1785–1849), concerned this age, *Svatopluk* (1833) and *Cirillo-Metodiada* (1835). For Štúr, Great Moravia was the Slovaks' 'one great moment.'[48] For Kučera it is important that by 833 the Slovaks and Moravians clearly had some stable state organization when the Bohemians to the West were still split into clans.[49] He does not mention the likelihood that the West Slavonic ruling classes in the area were acquiring their great wealth through slave-trading, as Czech writers assert.[50] I am not suggesting that Kučera is not a serious historian but merely a mythopoet. His work manifests sound, often original, research. His general approach is, however, national mythic, and thus provides a fine example of demotic-genealogical national treatment of history. Kučera does not unthinkingly accept the Kollár–Štúr variety of the myth. For example, the theoretically just about tenable view I mentioned in the section on Kollár and Šafařík that, if the Magyars had not driven a wedge between them, the Slavs might have remained one 'nation' is implicitly considered Romantic panslavism by Kučera. On the other hand, he uses the same idea to suggest an explanation for the fact that the Slovaks were not Orthodox Christians. During Samo's reign, the Avars had driven a wedge between the 'Slovaks' and Byzantium and subsequently the Magyars had done the same. Since he evidently considers the arrival of SS Cyril and Methodius the zenith of the golden age, one concludes that he imagines that, without these wedges, 'Slovakia' might have remained the centre of Slavonic culture.

Štúr will have known the sketchy outline history of Great Moravia from the Latin chronicle of Cosmas Pragensis (*c.*1045–1125) and the Czech verse chronicle by the so-called 'Dalimil' (*c.*1314); he will have known Hájek's (d.1553) *Česká kronika* (1541), though, generally speaking this work gives no history of the Empire, only detailed accounts of certain events in Moravia, especially those that affected Bohemia.[51] Štúr will, however, also have known local Hungarian (Latin) accounts. His account of the founding and first rulers of Great Moravia is mythopoeic, emphasizes Slav democracy, wisdom, valour and piety. He begins by telling us that the Slovaks had elected a ruler because they had needed to organize themselves against the incursions of marauder nations (historically, though that is unimportant for this chapter, the Avars). Initially, he appears to be forgetting Pribina and Nitra and certainly to be avoiding explaining what territories Great Moravia comprised. Štúr's history is, however, consciously a literary work, intended to inspire national pride and devotion, not only to instruct Slovaks in their past; Great Moravia is in essence Slovak:

Who is that, staff in hand, enveloped in a thin, shabby cloak, climbing up onto a lone rock in an empty field, and what is that multitude gazing respectfully at the sturdy figure on the rock? It is their elected ruler, who must remember whence he had come and that he may go if he does not rule his people justly. And the rulers ruled the people justly and the people lauded and honoured their rulers.

In AD 816 King Mojmír ruled over Great Moravia. The annals inform us that he was the first to occupy the Great Moravian throne. He had already been baptized and many of his people willingly followed his example. A caring and wise king, he ruled his people as a good family father his house. He also drew his sword to protect the country from destruction. But the German emperor disliked his valiant deeds as well as the growing might of the Slovaks and, therefore, he invaded the country with an army and unthroned King Mojmír. And the nation grieved at its dishonour and at the overthrowing of its good king and lamented at its loss.

And after him, his nephew Rastislav ascended to the Great Moravian throne, and the nephew excelled the uncle, for he surpassed him in wise counsel and heroic valour. He waged cruel wars against the Germans and liberated his country from the vassalage which the Germans sought to impose on the land of your fathers. But he was not occupied only in wars, for he was also concerned for the salvation of his people, and he summoned to his land two brothers from Greece, Cyril and Methodius, to go about his country teaching the people the divine Word of Christ. And, going about, they taught and the people listened to their words about great matters and God's miracles, and the people tore down all idols and bowed down before the Lord. And the Lord took great pleasure in this people, for He multiplied them and extended the frontiers of their country. But the Satan of the Germans drove the God-loving king to destruction and ensured that he was dogged by treachery and that he fell into the hands of his enemies.[52]

Štúr, from his mid-nineteenth century priestly point of view imagines that all the pious (in Herder's myth) Slavs would immediately accept Christianity. Kučera knows that that was not so and that Slav paganism survived, though perhaps patchily, for over two centuries after Cyril and Methodius' mission, but he found the need to adapt the old myth by employing the method of Marxist mythopoeic historiography. His words echo the Czechoslovak Marxists' panslav appropriation of the mission in the 1950s:

It would be an entirely understandable social and class phenomenon if the simple serf population resisted the new religion. After all, in Slovakia Christianity spread 'downwards' from the ruling classes as a component of government and as a product or attribute of princely power and violence. For this reason, in many Slav lands Christianization was accompanied by a series of uprisings, rebellions, and one cannot discount the possibility that such rebellions also took place in Great Moravia, even though we do not have any concrete data on them.[53]

Kučera's analysis of the warrior ruler Svatopluk's character and reign is unimpeachable. Svatopluk had been a difficult character for Slovak and Czech writers and historians because, for all his military prowess, his numerous defeats of the

Germans, he was a thoroughly devious character, employed a great deal of that 'heroic cunning' that was later acceptable in medieval romances, but detestable in life. Hence the annalist of Fulda's description of Svatopluk as 'a vessel [*vagina*] full of perfidy'.[54] Štúr, predictably sings his praises as the wisest and boldest of rulers – because he had wrought so much damage on the Germans, and had defeated the Magyars.

The missionary activity of Cyril and Methodius was, finally, as important for the Czechs as for the Slovaks. Kučera does his best to make the two saints Slavs, although there is no concrete evidence whatsoever to suggest that Cyril had not learnt Slavonic just as he learnt Latin, Hebrew, Syriac and Arabic. It is, however, likely that both brothers had learned Slavonic in their native Salonica, given that Slavs and Albanians had overrun most of Greece. Kučera's cautious account of their childhood serves to support the Slovak and Czech national myth that Slav literacy and learning spread from Great Moravia to the Slav world (it is, in fact, probable that Cyril and Methodius spent a very brief time in Bulgaria before they went to Great Moravia, and there is no doubt whatsoever that the language Cyril had learned and in which he wrote was the Bulgarian or Macedonian dialect of Old Slavonic. Much Slav learning spread to Kievan Rus' from Bulgaria rather than from Moravia and the Czech Sázava Monastery): 'Both boys knew Slavonic from childhood, and we were able to speak it. That was the Byzantine emperor, Michael III's, argument when he sent them to Great Moravia. Some scholars have interpreted that as indicating that their father was a Slav. And, they say, if their father was not, then certainly their mother (her name was Mary) inculcated Slavonic in her children as their mother tongue.'[55] Cyril and Methodius did found a seminary and a literary school in Moravia, and their disciples, when they were banished, certainly went to the South Slav lands and Bohemia to continue their work. Pekař's view that accounts of St Wenceslas's education in the early legends demonstrate a strong Byzantine influence in Bohemia is clearly correct. On the other hand, Chaloupecký's notion that the work of the Slav Apostles' disciples determined which West Slav groups should remain linguistically independent of the Germans constitutes mythopoeia: 'they created basic linguistic education not only for the Bohemians, Moravians and Slovaks, but also the Poles, Sorbs and other Slav tribes. It was, indisputably, above all Slavonic Christianity that enabled these Slavs, as against their Polabian fellows, to retain their national individuality and not to submit to Germanization.'[56]

In the course of the nineteenth century, the foundations were laid for the status Cyril and Methodius had attained by the mid-twentieth century, that of national saints of Slovakia.[57] Initially as a vehicle for the Slav idea, then also to propagate the uniting of Slovak Roman Catholic and Lutheran forces, a Slovak periodical called *Cyrill a Method* was published, 1850–1 in Czech, 1852–3 in Slovak, 1853–6 again in Czech, and then from 1857 to 1870, when it collapsed, in

Slovak again.[58] Also in 1850, Moravian clerical men of letters founded the Heritage of SS Cyril and Methodius for the publication of Catholic literature; that resulted from a Moravian cult of the saints which had been fostered since the 1820s to offset the growing renewed Czech cult of Jan Hus. This cult reached its peak with the 1863 jubilee celebrations in Velehrad and Brno which glorified 'Cyrillo-Methodian Christian panslavism.'[59] This Moravian cult showed no knowledge of Irish and German missionaries prior to the Slav mission and bore none of the baggage involved in Kollárian panslavism, whereby the Slavs had always lived in idyllic peace and ploughing, long before Christianity. As we learn from one of the leaders of the Moravian Catholic literary movement, before Cyril and Methodius come with their 'bright light', 'dark clouds' had covered Moravia, and 'the rule of evil'.[60] A secular version of the same conception is to be found in an 1880 article by the Slovak Realist, Vajanský (1847–1916), where the saints 'disperse the dark clouds of inertia and blindness from the towns [*sic*] and settlements of our forebears'.[61] The ecumenical Cyrillo-Methodian Idea survived a Slovak periodical. In 1891, the Czech priest, Antonín Cyril Stojan (1851–1923), later Archbishop of Olomouc, founded the Apostolate of SS Cyril and Methodius which fostered the reunification of the Roman and Orthodox Churches, under whose auspices international congresses were held to promote the cause (1907–22). When the Czechoslovak Republic was founded, the Czechs imposed the 'traditions of St Wenceslas and Hus' on the Slovaks, but this same Stojan, together with the Slovak politician Milan Hodža, persuaded Prague that the 'Cyrillo-Methodian tradition' should be incorporated in the republican ideology.[62] Finally, when the Communists took control of Roman Catholic theology faculties in 1950 and restricted their numbers to one in Prague and one in Bratislava, in the spirit of Stalinist panslavism, they were both given the name 'Roman Catholic Cyrillo-Methodian Theological Faculty.'

The third period according to Anthony Smith's model, the period 'often seen as decline', was, indeed, a period of decline for the Slavs of what, after the Magyar destruction of Great Moravia, became Upper Hungary. This third period (decline, division, development) lasted from the beginning of the tenth century until 1918; some nationalists would say, until 1939, others, until 1 January 1969 (federation), and, the Slovak Constitution says, until 1 January 1993. It has two stages, the first from the fall of Great Moravia to the National Awakening, and the second from the Awakening to some time in the twentieth century; the date one chooses will depend on one's interpretation of the national myth and on the extent to which one can accept 'Czechoslovak' as embodying 'Czech and Slovak' rather than 'Czech-cum-Slovak'.

Štúr's version of the first stage of the third period is conciliatory because that comports (i) with his perception of the Slovaks as the civilizers of the Magyars and (ii) with the Herderian vision of the Slav character. On the other hand, it is a literary device to emphasize the unwarranted aggression constituted by nine-teenth-century Magyarization. The Slovaks had lived, worked and fought side by side with the Magyars for centuries. While leading his audience up to the peripeteia, he lends the Magyars the standard psychological motivation for their altered behaviour (standard because this is traditionally the chief characteristic of Satan or Lucifer):

See, my fellow-countrymen, how much our fathers died for the land we live in, how many sacrifices they offered up for Hungary! And who would be able to count or, indeed, remember them all? I do not want to spend the time it would take to name them; actually they are innumerable, because, in all ages, the Slovaks have been re-nowned for their diligence, valour and great mental refinement, so that if you started to list the men of Hungary who are famed for their wisdom, you would find that, with a few exceptions, they were by race Slovaks, your men.

And the Magyars were pleased that in their country they had a nation like this, on whom they could depend and rely for everything, and they lived with them in peace, for they recognized what they had done for the land which sustained also Hungarians.

But because the Slovaks excelled the Magyars thus and had gained greater riches than they through their industry, envy began to awaken in Magyars who were angry that they were unable to equal the Slovaks in intellect or property. And these envious people began to invent all manner of calumny on the Slovaks and to consider how they could excel the Slovaks; when nothing occurred to them, their hatred grew and in-creased.[63]

Kučera's version of this long stage in the national myth displays even more pa-thos. Romantic psychology is replaced by Marxist political science and for Kučera all problems have been solved by socialism. Nevertheless, the core of the myth remains intact and the Slovaks remain Slovaks, have an uninterrupted his-tory as they do in Štúr:

A state which had for nearly a hundred years formed and informed the history of central Europe perished without politicians and intellectuals showing any interest [sic]. Some older historians interpreted this as a national catastrophe that meant the interruption of [the nation's] life. It is impossible to agree with that. Today we know that Slovakia and the Slovaks simply reached the threshold of a new life, a new age which, however, was not so favourably disposed towards them. They became a com-ponent of the multinational Hungarian state which, on the one hand, preserved many of the economic achievements and the state organization of Great Moravian society, but, on the other, gradually annihilated the political and cultural representation of the Slovaks, which severely obstructed the Slovaks' emergent nation-forming process. At the time when 'nation'-states were being created all over Europe and the historical foundations of modern nations were being laid, the Slovaks were unable to become involved in this natural historical process; they were falling behind. That is why their path to national independence and freedom was so slow, complicated and, frequently, thorny. How true that is becomes graphically clear if we compare our fortunes with those of the fraternal Czech nation which made Moravia itself an integral part of its political unit and was able to form a strong central European state very shortly after the break-up of Great Moravia. Centuries had to pass before our two nations met again in a common state, before we found ourselves on the same path in a battle for national freedom and, after a hard class struggle, also in a battle for a social freedom worthy of the human race and its struggles for historical progress.

All this could come to pass only because the Slovak plains and valleys were not abandoned after the fall of Great Moravia. Once more the peasant cut his plough into the soil; the scythe swished on the meadow; songs could be heard on the hillside and a child's tears in the cradle. Life and work, the two constants of history preserved Slovak society from extinction.[64]

The second stage in the third period began with the late Enlightenment, a few scattered intellectuals who began to promote the Slovak cause. Bernolák was the most influential figure, a philologist whose attempt to codify a literary language on the basis of Western Slovak was ultimately a failure, but whose lexicographical work was, however, of lasting value. Independently of Bernolák and much to the latter's annoyance, Jozef Ignác Bajza (1755–1836) invented his own literary Slovak for his novel in two very tenuously linked parts, *René mláď enca príhodi a skusenosti* (1785). The first part is an anti-Islamic adventure novel, an ill-considered attempt at imitating Voltaire and expressing notions of natural law in fiction. It never rises above *Trivialliteratur*. The second part, which Bajza did not know how to finish and evidently simply stopped writing and published, is largely a satire on the Upper Hungarian clergy, particularly monastic orders. The Preface to the first part is important for its statements on the necessity of a Slovak literary language. Bajza's concern is for the Slovaks to have a civilization of their own; history and the present social situation are of little interest to him. The Slovaks, he claims, are feckless and idle: they had not even attempted to protect their language, let alone use it for *belles lettres*. The result had been a myriad of dialects, whereby not only the vocabulary but even 'word-endings' vary from village to village. Bajza ends his Preface by stating that it was solely the Slovaks' own fault that their language was the last in Europe. Czech interest in the Slovaks and Slovak culture at the beginning of the nineteenth century, together with Kollár's influential 'Czechoslovakism' probably hindered the fulfilling of Bajza's hopes. It took a charismatic teacher like Štúr, a man who led his pupils not only to adopt his codification, but also to follow him into an uprising in 1948–9. The first poet to write in Štúr Slovak, Janko Kráľ (1822–76), remains the most original and enigmatic of all Slovak poets, even if he did write some tediously enthusiastic ditties expressing Slav messianism. Another poet, however, Andrej Sládkovič (1820–72), had a more immediate impact, however turgid to the point of incomprehensibility he can be. Every Slovak schoolchild still today knows by heart the opening lines of one or both of his two narrative cycles, *Marína* (1846) and *Detvan* (A Detva man, 1853). The latter made a contribution to the national myth, for it attempted to explain the popularity of Matthias Corvinus (*reg.* 1458–90) in Slovak folksongs, by having Slovak peasants as members of the king's elite Black Guard. Such tales apparently helped to fill the 'gap' in Slovak history between Great Moravia and the Awakening. That function was also performed by the literary works written on Mati Csák, a Magyar baron who rebelled (1301–16) against the election of Charles Robert of Anjou as Hungarian king in favour of the Bohemian crown prince Wenceslas (Ladislaus V in Hungary). Csák amassed, often by violence, huge estates; and at one time most of what is now Slovakia was under his sway. As a rebel twice placed under an interdict by the Church, Csák appealed to the Romantics. Štúr himself wrote a long epic poem on him, 'Matúš z Trenčína' (Mati of Trenčín, *Spevy a piesne* [Songs and chants, 1853]), where Mati is freedom-fighter whose army is willingly joined by fine young Slovaks from all counties. Štúr's propaganda intention is clear when at one point he has a minstrel sing of the glories of Great Moravia. Viliam Pauliny-Tóth (1826–77) contrives a similar link in the Introduction to his novel *Trenčiansky Matúš* (Mati of Trenčín, 1868), where the hero is perhaps even more of a Romantic bandit than he had been in Štúr. Pauliny-Tóth explicitly states that Mati had no choice but to be a bandit because he sought the independence of the Slovak nation.

In Anthony Smith's fourth period, whenever one decides that the Slovaks gained their independence and started becoming a 'modern nation', events of the third period took on a mythic character. Polakovič's volume provides a wealth of such mythicized events that are usually to be found only individually in a given work – or at a given wine-cellar table. One would perhaps expect a rationalist of Polakovič's stamp to consider Kollár a treacherous villain, but other nationalists would retain him in the Slovak 'pantheon' for cultural economic reasons: Kollár is deemed a great poet and one cannot afford to squander such national assets.[65] Polakovič writes that Kollár 'sold his soul to Czech. Without Štúr's intervention the biological essence of the [Slovak] nation would have passed partly into Czech and partly into Magyar waters, where it would have dissolved without leaving a trace.'[66] The Hungarians' closing of the three Slovak grammar schools in 1874 constitutes part of the nation myth even for non-nationalists, like the closing down of the Slovak cultural organization, Matica slovenská in 1875. The Matica, according to its constitution, belonged to the 'Slovak nation', and this is what Polakovič is alluding to in phrases like 'we did not exist for the Hungarians.'[67] On 15 December, 1875, the Serbian MP, Svetozar Miletić asked the Hungarian prime minister and minister of the interior, Kálmán Tisza, whether it was true that he would be administering the assets of the Matica slovenská. Tisza replied that he had been going into the matter of these assets, had been studying the documents, and had discovered that, according to the statutes, the Matica belonged to the *szláv nemzet* (Slovak nation).[68] He would, he said, dearly like to find the owner of the Matica, and he had been looking all over Hungary, but he had been unable to find a legal body called *szláv nemzet*.[69] The leaders of the Czechoslovak First Republic become as great demons as Tisza. For example, Polakovič writes:

In 'Czechoslovakia' Masaryk and Beneš saw a renewal of the Czech state which was territorially expanded by Slovakia, and they saw in the Slovak population (they did not even consider this population a nation) simply a biological amplification of the Czech nation. It is well known [that favourite phrase of mythopoets] that these Czech thoughts even found their expression in a Czech encyclopaedia where the Czechs were informed that Slovakia was a Czech colony, and that Czech officials behaved like colonizers in Slovakia and, like colonial officials, they had salaries which were higher than in the Bohemian Lands.[70]

The same mythic conception of the Slovaks as victims of the Czechs is expressed by Polakovič's repeated use of the terms 'Czechomarxist' or 'Czechocommunist' for the post-1948 regime.

Nationalisms need enemies. In the Slovak Awakening, the Czechs were 'our brothers'; for obvious reasons, it was the Magyars who were demonized, a manner of perception that was by no means dead as late as the 1980s, in the novels of Ivan Habaj. While some Awakeners, like Kráľ or Kalinčiak, were mainly concerned with the Magyars' recognizing the independence of Slovak culture (and Kalinčiak is typical in that he was both a Hungarian patriot and a Slovak patriot), Štúr introduced the myth, adumbrated by Kollár, of the Magyars as the barbarian Asiatic hordes. That myth was also propagated by Czech Slovakophil writers like Julius Zeyer as late as the 1890s.[71] Štúr's conception of the Magyars as barbarians is the precondition of his conception of the Slovaks as civilizers. The Magyars had been encouraged to enter Slovak land by the Germans during the reign of Svatopluk:

At that time some wandering brigands called Magyars reached Transylvania; they were afraid of other nations since they had slipped out of their own mother-country near the Urals to evade subjugation, and they lived off pillage and horse-meat. So the Germans said to them, 'Come and attack the land of the Slovaks with us, for neither you nor we could achieve anything, if we attacked this warlike people alone, but if we assail them together, we shall conquer them. You will have a beautiful, fertile country to live in and we shall be rid of a terrible enemy.' And the nomads took their advice, for they had nowhere to camp and to graze their horses.[72]

The perception that the Magyars and Germans were joint oppressors was common during the Awakening; one thinks of Ján Botto's *Smrť Jánošíkova* (The death of Jánošík, 1862); the term 'German' usually meant the inhabitants of the German towns in Upper Hungary or the Germans of Austria proper, particularly Vienna; Štúr's use of the label 'German' instead of 'Frank' or even 'Bavarian' serves, as was usual in the Slovak Awakening (or, indeed, the Czech Revival), to make a mythic link between the 'Germans' of the ninth century with those of the nineteenth. A continuum of oppression by the same enemy serves the national myth.

Still, it is the Magyars who are the 'savage Asiatic nation',[73] and with that savagery comes a dulness of mind. That is why the Slovaks were able to survive the disintegration of Great Moravia; although they had fallen into servitude, the Magyars were not such as could 'penetrate them with their spirit and paralyse them.'[74] Dulness of mind had made the Magyars accept Calvinism, a confession Štúr abhors because the notion of predestination would make the adherence to any moral standards futile: 'since they are a Finnic nation, prosaic, unawakened by the spirit, this faith containing the idea of predestination is the most fitting for them.'[75]

The chief villains for the Czechs, their enslavers, are the Germans. In the National Revival, František (Franz) Palacký (1798–1876) made that perception into a national ideology, particularly in his *Dějiny národu českého v Čechách i v Moravě* (History of the Czech nation in Bohemia and Moravia, 1836–67). This work acquired the status of a national epic[76] or as the Slovak Kučera puts it, a trifle ironically, 'the catechism of Czech national historicism'.[77] Palacký's representation of Czech history as a constant battle of the Czechs against the Germans is reflected in the anti-German feeling which was a persistent motif – albeit with varying degrees of intensity – in Czech literature from the beginnings of secular literature written in Czech (the verse Alexander romance, *c.*1290) to the 1960s, and even later in Establishment writing; for 'anti-fascist' writing was often little more than a socialistically *engagé* variation on old anti-German sentiments. Generally, however, in the twentieth century Teutonophobia lies in the province of popular literature. The Decadents, generally convinced that the Czechs belonged to the West, usually avoided political statements in their writing. When, however, they do make statements on German–Czech relations, their attitude tends to be ambivalent. That is nowhere clearer than in Arnošt Procházka, who is rarely consistent anyway, at least before World War I. For example, in *Cesta krásy* (Path of beauty, 1906), he maintains that the Czechs are Westerners through and through and that everything Slavonic is alien to them, whereas in *Literární silhouety a studie* (Literary silhouettes and studies, 1912) he conceives of the Czechs as tossed between two mutually hostile currents, the German and the struggling Slav, though he suspects that very few Czechs have Slav blood in them that is not mixed with at least some German. In contrast to that Procházka can write, in the spirit of extremist neo-Revivalism, 'We are not racially related to the Germans. On the contrary, we are enemies.'[78] Generally, Decadents were indifferent to matters of nationality because such questions were of such great interest to those authors who were not in the elite *Moderní revue* circle.[79] The view of Pekař, an historian with whom the Decadents later identified themselves, is sober: Bohemia had been under the Western cultural sphere of influence. From the beginning of their national history, the Czechs had been dependent on the Germans. The German inhabitants of Bohemia had usually shared the fate of the Czechs. Even in the expulsions after the Battle of the White Mountain (1620), Germans as well as Czechs had had to leave the Bohemian Lands, contrary to what adherents of the national myth believe. If the Czechs are more developed than other Eastern nations (*národové východní*), that is thanks to the Germans. In Bohemia, 'The Germans had in part been bohemicized linguistically, and we have been Germanized in our character traits and our capabilities.'[80] For Rádl, there is no more a question about the German element in the Czechs than about the Magyar element in the Slovaks: 'As the Czech has an affinity with everything German, so the Slovak has an affinity with everything Hungarian.'[81] What concerns Rádl most at the time is that the Czechs have assumed the German mystical conception of the State; he derives the roots of that conception from Herder, Fichte, Kollár, Jungmann, Pangermanism, Panslavism and 'national consciousness.' Leading figures in Czech culture, with the exception of Masaryk and Beneš, had expressed this mystical conception at the founding of the Czechoslovak Republic, for example Jirásek, Holeček and Zdeněk Nejedlý. Contemporary central European nationalism was based on a mystical conception of the people and thus of the State: 'An organic or transpersonal conception assumes that the people and the State are an "organism" for which individuals are the "organ"; the individual fulfils the meaning of his life only if he or she embraces the spirit of the State. The State, people, nation are the fruit of a natural course of events; as a tribe necessarily grows out of a family and a nation out of a tribe, so the State grows out of the nation.'[82] In fact, then, the State becomes a myth, like the nation.

The creation of the Czech nation conforms more easily with Anthony Smith's model than that of the Slovak, though the third period will demand more radical, if briefer, scrutiny than was the case with the Slovak nation; at this stage, I shall deny Patočka's argument whereby, if we followed Smith's model, there would be two Czech ethnies, an aristocratic which disappeared in the seventeenth century and a demotic whose foundation myths would include elements from most of Czech history up to the end of the eighteenth century. The first period is concerned with a series of myths registered from the earliest chronicles. Forefather Čech comes to the land of Bohemia where he decides to settle having climbed a mountain (Říp) like Moses and seen the milk and honey spreading out before him. Then comes Krok and his three Parcae-like daughters; one of them, Libuše (Libussa), the prophetess and judge, rules the land. The men begin to grumble that the land needs a firmer hand and that Libuše should have her a husband; Libuše agrees and a magic horse is sent to find the chosen man; he is found ploughing a field; he is Přemysl, the founder of the dynasty that was to govern Bohemia till the beginning of the fourteenth century. Before he leaves the field he sticks his share-cleaning rod in the soil and it sprouts three sprigs (five in another version), like the branch from Eden planted at the head of Adam's grave in the Rood-Tree apocryphon. Soon, the women of Bohemia rebel against Přemysl, and the men win the war only with considerable difficulty. This war of the Bohemian Amazons has often been interpreted as representing the transformation of the Western Slavs from a matriarchal into a patriarchal society. That is superficial. The name Přemysl, literally, 'meditator', no doubt represents Wisdom; the name of the women's leader, Vlasta, means 'power', 'governor'. The name of her fortress, Děvín, probably has nothing whatsoever to do with women,[83] but with 'wonder' (*div*), thus with gods, magic. Thus the war may consist in a metaphor for a war between two cults. On the other hand, it might reflect nothing more than a power struggle between two clans, perhaps one Slav, the other Germanic – and such a struggle might well have had some religious dimension. Whatever the background, the main weight lies on the victory of Wisdom, which certainly pertains to the foundation myth. The coalescence of clans follows the foundation of the dynasty, predominantly through wars, but is not completed until after the beginning of the second period (chiefly 970s).

The second period begins with the growing influence of Christianity in the ninth century, though it could be argued that it begins in the eighth when the Bohemian Slavs first pay tribute to the Franks, but that is an historical interpretation. The baptism of Prince (Duke) Bořivoj in Great Moravia (870s or 880s), which is generally believed to have taken place under compulsion, might be considered the beginning, especially since his wife Ludmila presumably converted to Christianity soon afterwards; Ludmila became the Czech protomartyr (strangled 921?). Pitha provides a somewhat sentimentalised mythic interpretation of Ludmila, which is admissible, since she may be understood as the replacement for some fertility goddess. Grandmother of St Wenceslas, she appears to have replaced his mother, Drahomíra, for whom he, apparently, harboured little affection. Pitha's point that 'grandmothers are the chief bearers of tradition and play a greater role in the preservation of continuity than mothers'[84] may be expanded. Not only could she ensure that Wenceslas was educated in the Eastern Church tradition, but, as a former heathen (Drahomíra shared that quality with her but she was not Bohemian), she could instruct him on his future people's religion and customs. She also, considered from the point of view of hagiography, provided him with the example of martyrdom. Ludmila comprises the end of the old tradition and the beginning of the new; she had acquired and may transmit the wisdom of both. Pitha does not suggest that Ludmila represents a fertility goddess; he goes further: as grandmother she 'is the prototypical mother …, representative of Mother Earth, from whom we are born and to whom we return on death.'[85] She is also, however, the progenetrix of Christian Bohemia. St Wenceslas appears to have been not only an ascetic, but also doughty warrior and an accomplished politician. His fratricidal brother, Boleslav, who succeeded him to the throne, became, however great his sin, one of the great military heroes of Czech history. (Achieving the status of hero in the Czech national myth normally involves killing a large number of Germans – as Boleslav did – unless that hero is an 'heroic martyr', in which case he or she will often be killed by Germans. In the legends, the names of Ludmila's two assassins are Germanic.) In 975, a Saxon became the first bishop of Prague, Thietmar; the second bishop, the Czech Adalbert, died a martyr's death at the hands of the heathen Prussians (997).

For all the international and civil wars (mainly around the hapless Prince Jaromír) Bohemia's strength grew in the eleventh century. Vratislav II (*reg.* 1061–92) was given the personal title of king by Henry VI in 1065 for services to the Holy Roman Empire, of which Bohemia was a part.

Vladislav II (*reg.* 1140–72) was accorded the same honour in the subsequent century (1158) by Frederick Barbarossa, especially for a special place in the Czech national myth since the Czech knights proved themselves such efficient warriors that they were rumoured among the Italians to be paedophagous. A part of the ethnic myth concerning this campaign that survived into the fourteenth century was that the Czech knights made the effeminate Milanese whom they had defeated swallow horse turds as their mounts coked. Bohemia finally became a kingdom in 1198 under Přemysl I (*reg.* 1197–1230; the royal title not acknowledged by the Pope until 1212, when the Sicilian Golden Bull established the hereditary nature of the title). Under Přemysl and his son Wenceslas I (*reg.* 1230–53) the economy thrived, but that involved introducing large numbers of German colonists, especially to run and work in the new silver mines. The royal court and the upper nobility became ever more Germanized. This process increased under the most extravagant of Bohemian kings, Přemysl II Otakar (*reg.* 1253–78), under whom, briefly, the Bohemian realm stretched virtually from the Baltic to the Adriatic. In the Czech national myth, this imperious man on the one hand became the Czech Alexander the Great (in other words, fell on account of his hubris); on the other hand, he was a symbolic victim of treacherous nobles, and, most of all, of the Habsburgs, since he was defeated by Rudolph of Habsburg at the Battle of the Marchfeld (1278). They had already humiliated him in 1274 by taking Carniola from him and in 1276 by forcing him to take the Bohemian Lands in fief and surrender Egerland and Austria. Přemysl Otakar was particularly unpopular with the lower nobility for the power he had given Germans; according to the folklore of the contemporary gentry, the king had said that one soon would be able to hear only German spoken on the bridge in Prague. Rádl observes in the nationality friction that arose at this time, during the reigns of the last Přemy-slides, the emergence of a dominant anti-spiritual force among the Czechs – and however he might criticize Palacký elsewhere, his view might be understood as simply contributing a psychological version of Palacký, without Palacký's nationalist intention: 'In Bohemia, racial antipathies, i.e. essentially *biological forces*, became the driving force of history when the people should have been following an *ideal*'.[86] The Přemyslide dynasty died out on the sword side with the assassination of Wenceslas III (1306). According to contemporary folklore, and, subsequently, the national myth, his assassin was a Thuringian.

The civil strife under Henry of Carinthia (*reg.* 1306, 1307–10) and Rudolph I Habsburg (*reg.* as usurper 1306–7) contributed to the national myth on account of the growth of the power of the nobility who in effect formed an oligarchy during much of the reign of the first of the Luxembourg kings, John (*reg.* 1310–46), son of the Holy Roman Emperor, Henry VII. John lived outside Bohemia for much of his reign because his concerns were those of a warrior; he won back various lands for the Bohemian Crown, but found his place in the myth mainly for his blindness and his riding blind into battle against the English at Cressy. (There is little to support the English legend that the crest and motto of the Princes of Wales were taken from John of Luxembourg, although the three horizontal emblematic rivers which sometimes formed one of the Bohemian royal coat of arms could, just, have been transformed into the three plumes.) John's reign did, however, introduce the influence of French culture on the Czech court and his son Wenceslas (later Charles IV, *reg.* 1346–78, from 1355 Holy Roman Emperor) was educated at the French court.

With Charles IV came the 'golden age' that Smith demands of this period. Charles expanded the lands of the Bohemian Crown, largely by useful marriages and the power of his purse, but also undertook major building enterprises, particularly the Prague New Town, one of the first all-stone planned towns in Europe, specifically for Czech burghers. While young he had won his military and spiritual spurs in northern Italy where, as he informs us in his autobiography, he had overcome lust with the help of a vision of a lecherous noble whose penis was amputated by an angel. Charles greatly supported the clergy, who in turn supported his well-nigh obsessive collecting of relics of saints. In the national myth Charles had a constructive concern for the poor, which turned into unkingly consorting with burghers with his son, Wenceslas IV (*reg.* 1378–1419, unthroned as Holy Roman Emperor 1400), who progressed to incognito drinking in pubs. Although Charles had invited the first reformist preachers to Prague, under Wenceslas IV the Czech Church Reform movement grew to such proportions that it went out of control and led to war, iconoclasm, the destruction of books, the impoverishment of the countryside (the peasantry had been particularly prosperous under Charles IV and in the first two decades of Wenceslas's reign) and to the debilitation of Prague University, founded by his father in 1348.

Perhaps no Czech king has been the subject of such mythopoeia as Wenceslas IV. Interpretations of him vary from depictions of something of a folk hero whose desires to do well by his people were thwarted by priests and wicked barons to demonization, where he is a drunken, lascivious, undignified sadist who attended and joined in torturing sessions and had his first wife torn to pieces by his hunting dogs. As a folk hero, he was slowly poisoned by his enemies; in the tyrant version, he died as a result of his dissolute living. The names he retained in history books were Wenceslas the Lazy or Wenceslas the Inebriate. He was a weak, well-meaning king, subject to violent outbursts of temper, indifferent to the morality of his favourites, and something of a depressive.

The Hussite Wars when the Bohemian Lands stood against the rest of Europe, may be interpreted as the beginning of the end of the second period or, as many would claim with Palacký, the glorious culmination of the 'golden age', the first expression of the true Renaissance spirit of questioning authority (Palacký) and, very much part of the national myth, a great demonstration of the Czechs' natural inclination to 'democracy'. The wars produced a popular hero in that great strategist, the Hussite general, Jan Žižka, whom Fate made comparable with John of Luxembourg because he lost one eye and, eventually, probably was entirely blind. The Hussite hymns became part of the nation's cultural mythology, but, on the whole, the Hussite period was culturally limiting. Certainly, theological or generally religious literature continued developing, but *belles lettres* were restricted largely to adaptations of Latin medieval texts. The son of the so-called Hussite king, George of Poděbrady (*reg.* 1458–71), Hynek z Poděbrad (1452–92), wrote some slightly bawdy narrative verse that was still based on the courtly tradition, though his prose, including his adaptation of Boccaccio tales, perhaps showed something of the Italian Renaissance spirit. George did succeed in pacifying Czech society, though in the national myth he is best known for his proposition that something like a league of nations or holy alliance be established in Europe.

Palacký ends his history of the Czechs with 1526, the Battle of Mohács and the subsequent ascent of the Habsburgs to the Bohemian throne. And, if we apply Smith's model, 1526 is certainly a more defensible date for the beginning of the third stage in the development of the Czech nation, the period 'of development and division often seen as decline', than the Battle of the White Mountain which the Revivalists and most later nationalist intellectuals (including the Communists) considered the disaster introducing decline. The removal of practically all the towns' privileges, some privileges of the nobility and the beginnings of the growth in power of the magnates, which the Counter-Reformation simply served to confirm, took place in 1547–8. During the sixteenth century most of Prague was 'Protestant', mainly Utraquist, Lutheran and Bohemian Brethren (the Unity still thriving, though often oppressed, e.g. at the 1508 St James's Diet, i.e. before the Habsburgs), and most other towns and a large proportion of the countryside in Bohemia and Moravia showed a similar pattern of confessional allegiances. Even taking into consideration Maximilian II's (*reg.* 1564–76) limited tolerance of Protestants, Rudolph II's (*reg.* 1576–1611) decree guaranteeing religious freedom, and the 1615 language decree imposing financial sanctions on those not taught Czech, the vitality of Czech culture and institutions was diminishing fast.

From the point of view of the national myth, the irony lies in the fact that this period was considered a golden age of Czech culture. The Revivalists adopted so-called Veleslavín Czech, the form of Czech used by the Prague publisher and minor author, Daniel Adam z Veleslavína (1546–99), as their model for 'revived' literary Czech. By so doing, they greatly impoverished the Czech literary language through politico-linguistic purism, and so the Czech literary language had to begin to develop naturally again during the nineteenth century. The Revivalists' reason for the choice was ideological; for them, language had necessarily degenerated with the Czech nation after the White Mountain; the language of the Brethren's Kralice Bible (1579–88) expressed the highest linguistic cultural level. For the most part, the literature of the so-called Renaissance period was unoriginal. Serious verse became the domain of the Humanists, and verse in Czech constituted for the most part the composition of unimaginative, frequently occasional, jingles. Prose consisted almost entirely of moral and religious tracts written in a medieval spirit; medieval *exampla* were revived almost unaltered by writers like Šimon Lomnický z Budče (1552–?1623) and Václav Dobřenský (d.1595). Authors like the erudite satirist Vavřinec Leander Rvačovský (1525–after 1590) or the courtier, military leader, musician and scholarly travel-writer Kryštof Harant z Polžic a Bezdružic (1564–1621) are exceptions. Where Czech writing did develop was in law and politics, in other words, writing concerned with threatened institutions. On no account, then, was it a 'golden age' compared with the fourteenth century.

The rebellion of the disgruntled Czech Estates (1618) was finally put down at the Battle of the White Mountain (1620), which led to the executions on the Prague Old Town Square of three lords (including Kryštof Harant), seven knights and seventeen burghers (including the vice-chancellor of Prague University, Jan Jesenský/Ioannes Iessenius a Iessen [b.1566]), the confiscation of rebels' estates, and the exiling or driving to emigrate of thousands of Czechs and Germans who either had refused to convert to Roman Catholicism or had been debased to penury by the war and taxes. All these events quickly acquired mythic status through emigré writers like Jan Rosacius Hořovský (d. after 1637), Adam Hartman (d.1691) and most of all the philosopher, allegorist and educationist, Jan Amos Komenský (Comenius, 1592–1670). In the myth, the re-Catholicization of the Bohemian Lands consisted in horrendous national oppression led by the Jesuits and foreign nobles come to take over the confiscated lands of true Czechs. There is no doubt whatsoever that the Habsburg administrators tended to be anti-Czech and that the Czech language was considered the language of heretics. A remark written to one Catholic noble by another in 1665 about the appointment of Jan z Lobkovic as earl marshal is telling; Jan z Lobkovic was a Czech 'and that is like being afflicted by an hereditary sin'.[87] Pekař maintains that the White Mountain changed Czech thinking a good deal less profoundly than the godless developments induced by the Enlightenment or coming to fruition in the socialist programmes of the technological age.[88] He does, however, see a major change, one that had begun to take effect in educated circles with Renaissance Humanism, the marginalization of Czech vernacular thinking by European Latin thinking (the use of the term 'democratic' instead of 'popular' reflects the period of his writing):

We shall understand the true extent of [the White Mountain's] significance best *if we compare it with the Hussite period*. In so doing, we see the victory of the principle of *authority* over the principle of *freedom*, the victory of a predominantly *aristocratic* ideal over a strongly *democratically* tinted ideal, of a *European* culture over the striving for a specific *national* culture, of a *universal* Church over a *national territorial* Church. One could put that briefly thus: the victory of the *Romance age* over the *Gothic age*.[89]

Two Decadents in particular, Karásek and Marten, share Pekař's ideas, though they take them a little further. Pekař speaks variously of the western inspiration of Hus and of the extent to which, later, Lutheranism had started a Germanization process from below in Bohemia and, particularly, Moravia. Karásek perceives the Counter-Reformation as the Czechs' return to the Latin West which they had gradually abandoned after the reign of Charles IV. Protestantism had extinguished their 'innate vitality' and capacity for 'mystical subjectivism'; the White Mountain is, however, no less a national disaster for him:

Pre-White Mountain Czech history is a psychological process of racial decay where Czechness was a mere substratum which Lutheran ideas put to its own use and where the emotiveness of national self-manifestation was replaced by the reproduction of foreign ideas. Czech post-White-Mountain history showed that very clearly. The Czechs were no longer capable of fighting and regaining their independence; they were racially totally passive. They were able to die heroically, as the executions on Old Town Square witness, but they were unable to live heroically. Foreign ideas so tyrannized the nation's natural resistance that the Czechs left their country and then, abroad, for the sake of those same ideas, abandoned their nationality and fused forever with alien elements.[90]

The foreigner, Allan, of Marten's *Nad městem* perceives Bohemia's Western purtenance in the architecture of Prague as it reaches its zenith in the Baroque St Nicholas's Church and the Baroque addition to St Vitus'; Prague architecture incorporates the turmoils of the West: 'the whole drama of the Latin spirit enchanted in a beauty which rises from the gay garden of the three churches at the end of the Charles Bridge, along its avenue of statues, up to the enormous green rose of St Nicholas's, and with its proud brow of tangled palazzi creates harmony for the great contour of the castle with its cathedral, on which some delectable caprice had placed the upturned emerald goblet of a copper dome, like a beacon of victorious light.'[91] Bohemia had been the site for 'the great spiritual war of the West that had been unleashed by the Northern devil of negation and scepticism'.[92] The Counter-Reformation had represented the victory of spiritual strength over

Germanic materialism that breeds despair. Just as for Karásek the White Mountain constituted a means to national rejuvenation: 'the whole nation had to be trampled underfoot so that defiled shrines could ring out again with pious hymns and prayers,'[93] so for Marten it was a purgative catastrophe, 'whose lava burnt up the poisoned vegetation of life'.[94] To speak of the White Mountain as the fall of the Czech nation represents self-pitying prejudice and superstition: 'it is necessary ... to extricate oneself from the black magic of that word, *fall*.'[95] Rádl clearly concurs, for what he sees defeated at the White Mountain is a Bohemia 'living on local squabbles between a backward nobility and backward towns'.[96]

The subsequent Baroque period was far from a period of 'darkness' culturally. Quite apart from the magnificent architecture and statuary, Czech literature at home and abroad had writers like Comenius or Bedřich (Fridrich) Bridel (1619–80) who, in their own *genres*, outshone anyone in the 'golden age' of the Renaissance. Furthermore, the Baroque period contained the germs of National Revival patriotism. In the year which saw the beginning of the Estates' rebellion, 1618, the historian Pavel Stránský wrote the first little work in the sub-*genre*, 'defence of the Czech language' (*obrana jazyka českého*), *Okřik* (Hullabaloo). However ungraceful its latinate Czech, it expresses with passion a conception of Bohemia embroiled in a linguistic war such as one will find for much of the nineteenth century. Stránský describes German linguistic expansionism as 'transgression of natural law'.[97] Like a Kollár, he emphasizes the antiquity of the Czech languages and of Slav culture and bewails the Germans' virtual annihilation of the Polabian Slavs and 'their excellent princes, leaders, lords, laws, customs and manners' chiefly because 'their fertile ..., healthy and commercially advantageous land was a sharp thorn in the Germans' side.'[98] Echoing Dalimil and foreshadowing Palacký, Stránský conceives of Czech history as the history of the German threat to the Czechs.[99] Whereas *Okřik* was not published until 1910, the Jesuit Bohuslav Balbín's (1621–88) *Dissertatio apologetica pro lingua Slavonica, praecipue Bohemica* (1672) was published in the beginnings of the Revival proper (1775). Balbín writes of the anti-Slav feeling prevalent in Bohemia and has found proof of that in a tract he had acquired which was 'brimming over with contumely against the Slavonic tongue, minced meat greased with the oil of lies and manifold errors.'[100] Vienna is bleeding Bohemia of her riches to delight her own insatiable gullet and Bohemia is an old house falling into decay. Chiefly, he demands due respect for Slavonic, not only because it was one of the seventy-two languages that had issued from the Tower of Babel or because St Jerome had translated the Bible into Slavonic as well as Latin, but also because it was the court language of the Ottomans – hardly persuasive defences of Czech by 1775.

Balbín was an historian, but his vision of Czech history had little lasting impact on the Czechs' self-definition during the nineteenth century. Palacký did that for them and to no Czech historian (except Dalimil in the fourteenth century) can

Hobsbawm's statement better apply: 'historians are to nationalism what poppy-growers in Pakistan are to heroine-addicts: [they] supply the essential raw material for the market.'[101] In the Preface to the first volume of his *Dějiny národu českého*, Palacký states that his aim is to serve his nation with a faithful picture of its past, in which he would recognize himself. Thus he endeavours to combine his own relationship to his Czechness with scholarly precision, subjectivity with objectivity. Born a Protestant in Moravia and therefore educated in Hungary rather than strictly Catholic Austria, his history's glorification of the Hussites (on whom he had been working for years before he started his *chef d'oeuvre*) exemplifies that combination of the subjective and objective; he regrets that contemporary Czechs lack the patriotic enthusiasm they had demonstrated in the fifteenth century. The subjective also occasionally arises in anachronistic emotionality, for example, when he writes of the coronation of Prince Vratislav II that it had been an affair of such unheard-of splendour that it had moved all patriotic hearts and made the beloved prince even dearer to his subjects. His contention that the roots of the present animosity between Czechs and Germans lie in pre-history evinces a certain 'active atavism'. In his intention to defend the Czechs, or the Slavs in general, against the Germans and to depict the Germans as the Slavs' permanent enemy he sometimes indulges in Herderian sentimental anthropology. That is particularly true of his assessment of the early history of the Czechs. He compares German aggressiveness with the Slavs' love of peace and extols the Slavs for their simplicity, piety, and sensitivity. He also states repeatedly that the Slavs constituted just as noble, if not a nobler, nation as the Germans. Although he is proud of his nation and tries to instil that pride in his readers, he does criticize the Czechs, particularly for their love of things foreign (a motif in Czech historiography since Dalimil), their obstinacy, perfervour and, above all, religious quarrelsomeness. These qualities then represent standard attributes in nineteenth-century Czechs' self-definition. Not quite so standard until the chief literary codifier of Palacký's conception of history, Alois Jirásek, is Palacký's reasonable contention that, at least until their incorporation in the Austrian Empire, the Germanization of the Bohemian Lands was to be blamed largely on the Czech Estates.

Palacký has a Carlylean concern for those he considers the great figures of Czech history. He is defensive about Přemysl II Otakar in whom he sees strong anti-democratic forces at work. He admires the king for his success in increasing trade and industry in Bohemia, for giving the towns political rights, and for his chivalry, but he reprehends Otakar for his Germanophilia and the resulting feudalization of his country. Palacký considers the king's fall to have resulted from faithless friends, fickle foes and envious Germans more than from his own arrogance. As we would expect, Palacký perceives Charles IV as one of the greatest figures in all Czech and German history. He greatly admires one of Charles's chief characteristics: a love of order and a desire to impose order on everything in his political and personal life. However many virtues he finds in Charles, Palacký still looks for failings, which he considers to have been primarily pride and occasional dishonesty. That same attempt at balance is manifest in his treatment of Charles's son, Wenceslas IV, the weakling king who had suffered, says Palacký, because Charles spoiled him and his other sons exploited him. Wenceslas had a great redeeming feature, an utter lack of selfishness. That Palacký contrasts with the character of his brother, Sigismund of Hungary,[102] whom, in spite of all his labours towards the healing of the Church Schism, Palacký loathes.

That loathing largely derives from Palacký's emotional reaction to the role Sigismund played in the trial of Jan Hus at Constance and in the organization of the crusade against the Hussites. Nevertheless, Palacký's view of Sigismund has dominated Czech writers and cultural historians ever since. Palacký goes into far greater detail in the treatment of Hus and the Hussites than any other figure or period in Czech history. His national pride wells over in his admiration for the courage and honesty of Hus or Jerome of Prague (burnt at the stake, 1416) or even the Calixtine Jan Rokycana (before 1397–1471), and for the Hussite military prowess epitomized by Žižka and Prokop the Great. Although Palacký perceives the growth of Hussitism, its 'democratic ideals', and its militant defence of conscience as the greatest moment in Czech history, he does not hesitate to castigate the Bohemians for fanaticism and theological fractiousness and for their cruelty in war (at one point, he accuses the anti-Hussite crusaders of being even more brutal than the Bohemians). In Palacký's view, the central problems of the whole Hussite period, that is proto-Protestantism, lay in (i) the conflict between those in authority and those subjugated to this authority, and (ii) nationality (*národnost*). Concerning the first, Palacký conceives of the Hussites' (and the Lollards') activities as Christendom's first attempt to liberate itself from spiritual servility to its leaders. Freedom, however, had brought disunity. Even the freest society needs authority. The authority of family, parish or state is inadequate; only religion and *národnost* can supply such authority. Palacký's ideas on the role of *národnost* in Hussitism have a greater mythopoeic quality than his notion of the democratic principle at work in Hussitism; the latter resulted simply from the appropriation of the contemporary terminology of revolution. The former, however, expresses his desire to make Hussitism comport with ideas similar to Kollár and Šafařík's and his own conception of the 'meaning' of Czech history. Palacký saw the notion of *národnost* providing the Hussite period with two distinct features: (i) an intensification of the Czech–German conflict (the Germans representing authority), and (ii) the first inklings of Panslavism in the Hussite Czechs' various alliances with Poles, Russians, Ruthenians and the Hungarian Slavs (Slovaks).

Palacký imagines George of Poděbrady to embody everything positive that came out of the Hussite Wars. Again, Palacký's vision of George informed literary depictions of the man for the subsequent hundred years. George was the first great representative of the modern age and could become the first independent, constructive Renaissance ruler because he combined new Renaissance authority with old medieval authority by being both a Hussite and an elector of the Holy Roman Empire. Under him Bohemia had become the first lay state in Europe. Palacký sees him as a brilliant diplomat and political tactician, even though he had not been particularly well educated. He had been able, in the first part of his reign, to fulfil the Czechs' wishes for religious independence and to support their love for their language and country. Later, the peaceful unity of his lands had been shaken by papal hatred, the Czech Roman Catholic baronial league, and the double-dealing of his former protégé, Matthias Corvinus. Then most of Europe turned against him, where, once, most of Europe had turned to him, for advice. On his death he had been mourned by Roman Catholics and Hussites alike, for, having been born from the womb of the nation, he had never become alienated from it, but had always been a wise, caring father to the Czechs.

The two weak Jagellon rulers of Bohemia, Vladislav II (*reg.* 1471–1516) and Lewis (*reg.* 1516–26), had simply paved the way for the final fall of Czech democracy, the confirmation of the feudal omnipotence of the largely Germanized nobility and the diminution of the Czech king's power to something like that of a nineteenth-century constitutional monarch; Czech history became parochialized. For Palacký, the Czechs, indeed the Slavs altogether, were innately democratic. This myth of Czech democracy persisted until after the Changes of 1989, hence Havel's words on the abiding Czechoslovak 'humanist and democratic traditions' in his presidential address of 1 January 1990.[103] The virtues attributed by Palacký to the Czechs were automatically transferred to Masaryk's First Republic, a state that was democratic in comparison with its immediate neighbours, but which indulged in severe political censorship of the press, and where police violence was normal. In *Válka Čechů s Němci* (The Czechs' war with the Germans), Rádl points out just one law that manifests a far from democratic way of thinking: that of 14 April 1920, whereby the police were permitted to confiscate and read private letters, and another law which manifested a particularly petty-minded understanding of democracy: the law of 10 December 1918, whereby the nobility was abolished and the use of a noble title could be punished by twenty-four hours' to fourteen days' imprisonment or a fine of between fifty and 15,000 crowns.

Another myth derived from Palacký's *Dějiny* was the notion of Bohemia and Moravia as a bridge between East and West. Palacký perceived the Bohemian Lands to be geographically and historically predestined to act as this bridge, essentially a bridge between the Germans and the Slavs. According to him, this bridge was no idealistic dream, but a tangible result of Czech religious, and thus, to a great degree, political, dependence on the German Holy Roman Empire. The Communists abhorred this notion. Thus, in his Stalinist days, the Slovak Mináč wrote in a sarcastic attack on R. W. Seton-Watson: 'Doddery old Seton-Watson spoke for the fiftieth time about Czechoslovakia's key position between the East and the West.'[104] Macura associates the late 1940s and 1950s' abandonment of Palacký's bridge notion with the conception of the 'new' world of socialism with its 'new man': 'The concepts of ... a land at the crossroads and of Czechoslovakia as ... a synthesis of East and West, concepts which repeated the old Revivalist ideogram, disappeared.'[105] As he points out, the Czech or Czechoslovak self-conception as a bridge corresponds to the Russians' 'window on Europe', the Bulgarian 'gateway to Europe' – and one might add that the Hungarians have the bridge cliché and the Macedonians the self-conception as a crossroads of Europe. He perceives a transcendental dimension in the Czech self-conception:

The Czech national identity was never satisfied with statements of the type 'we exist', but needed a declaration of identity of a different kind: 'we exist because we have a metaphysical task.'
   To be a bridge seemed to be an adequate justification; it lent significance to the nation and its culture. ... This symbol also gave a supranational dimension to the inner, nation-liberating impulse for the emergence of modern Czech culture. We exist because we are an intermediary in the meeting of two cultures, two worlds. We are even, perhaps, the basis, or at least the precondition, of the future synthesis of these two value spheres.[106]

The bridge metaphor, however, creates another semantic possibility that Macura does not mention. A bridge is something that links A and B, but belongs neither to A nor to B; it may, then, constitute a metaphysical no-man's-land.
   Palacký himself became something of a cult figure in the nineteenth century. The centenary of his birth presented an occasion for patriotic adulation. Two quotations from Křen's little book on the historian, published 'For the benefit of the Palacký Fund of the Sokol organization for the establishment of *public libraries* and reading rooms in Moravian towns under the Yoke' (i.e. of the Habsburgs), will adequately demonstrate the cult: 'we must pause in humility and reverence before this immense work, for elsewhere, among other nations, a whole series of men achieved what a single human life [i.e. Palacký] achieved here by virtue of untiring industry.' And 'Not only did Palacký arouse and revive the Czech nation with his *Dějiny*, but, on the basis of historical information he also set the nation a *clear, definite goal.*'[107]
   The most important of these venerators of Palacký for the self-definition of the Czechs was Masaryk. Primarily a socialist and, in the broadest sense of the word, a politician, Masaryk extracted from Palacký his own variant of Czech history and of the Czech national mission. Masaryk did, indeed, as Patočka states, by refurbishing Palacký's conception of Czech history, simply create 'a new myth'.[108] Masaryk had given Palacký's philosophy of history 'a more ambitious stamp', but both men's interpretations are fantasies more than anything else, for the problems they present 'permit no purely theoretical treatment'.[109]

Jan Hus. Naše obrození a naše reformace (Jan Hus. The Czech Revival and the Czech Reformation, 1896) and *Česká otázka. Snahy a tužby národního obrození* (The Czech question. The endeavours and desires of the National Revival, 1895) provide the essence of Masaryk's conception of Czech history, though aspects of it are evident in his first book, his *Habilitation* dissertation, *Der Selbstmord als sociale Massenerscheinung der modernen Civilisation* (Suicide as a mass social phenomenon of modern civilization, 1881). Masaryk dislikes the automatic anti-clericalism of the Austrian liberals and finds a solution to that in the admiration of the Bohemian Brethren, in other words, will not take the liberal path of 'free-thinking', but has to find a spiritual line of thought. He cannot accept Roman Catholic thinking because he associates that with the Counter-Reformation (a period he considers typically 'liberal'), that is: the debasement of the Czech nation, and so he has to choose Protestantism as the vehicle of the true Czech spirit. This choice leads to well-nigh sophistic, selective mythopoeia. The main bearers of the 'humanitist' (Masaryk's neologism to describe his not entirely fathomable ideology) line are Hus, Chelčický, Comenius, to some degree the Roman Catholic Josef Dobrovský (1753–1820), Kollár, Palacký, and the anti-clerical Catholic, Karel Havlíček (1821–56). In other words Masaryk perceives, through a process that approaches Kollár and Šafařík's active atavism, a continuum of his own ideological precepts among the Czechs, but this continuum essentially ignores everything between Chelčický and Comenius and between Comenius and the National Revival. Masaryk defends that by interpreting the National Revival as a reassumption of the Hussite Reformation, of which Comenius would then be, so to speak, a late scion, as the last bishop of the Bohemian Brethren. This defence, however, compels him to render the Revival a far more overtly Christian matter than it was; Masaryk explicitly states that the Czech question was a religious question. Czechness lies in the idea of the Brethren, and the contemporary Cyrillo-Methodian Idea, creating a connection between the Great Moravian mission and the contemporary national mission: the mission of today's Church was unCzech, anti-Revivalist and anti-humanitist.

Hus had founded that democratic Protestantism which was finally expressed in the Unity of Brethren. Hus had been no nationalist; his aim had been to reform the international Church, and the brotherly Hussites' violence had been sparked off not by Hussite doctrine, but by the violence of Hus's opponents. The brotherliness of the Brethren was epitomized by the patriotic cosmopolitan, Comenius. The White Mountain, which drove Comenius out of Bohemia, had taken place because of a lack of unity among the morally unsound nobles, but the common people had been the chief sufferers in the subsequent Counter-Reformation. Dobrovský had despised the Counter-Reformation, as had Kollár after him, and Palacký and Havlíček had subscribed to the ideals of the Reformation.

For the theme of his book, Masaryk's treatment of Kollár constitutes the most instructive aspect of *Česká otázka*. Masaryk states that he agrees with Kollár that the history of nation was not fortuitous, that a definite plan of Providence was revealed in it, and that it was the task of thinkers to discover that plan and its role in the world. Czech history had a meaning. Masaryk avowed anti-mysticism, particularly in his study of Russian literature and thought,[110] but this conception of national history is mystical. He understands Kollár's idea of Slav Reciprocity as a weapon against national pettiness (*malost*), as a means to bolster the Slavs' culture and self-confidence, but also as a means of encouraging European reciprocity. Masaryk clearly had not noticed the venom and the parochial prejudices that recur in Kollár, though he does acknowledge that, in his racist nationalism, Kollár had deviated from the humanist ideal with *Slávy dcera*.

Masaryk led the Czechs into Smith's fourth period of nation-building with the creation of Czechoslovakia. The chief theoretical opponent of Masaryk's philosophy of Czech history in this fourth period was an historian who had written substantial works before 1918, and had published his first attack on Masaryk's conception of the meaning of Czech history in 1912, Josef Pekař.[111] Pekař rejects the implication of Palacký's historiography, that, up to the seventeenth century, the Czech nation had been the bearer of a single programme, that of democracy. And, although he by no means makes light of Czech hostility towards the Germans, he does not accept Palacký's depiction of Czech history consisting of a battle between Czechs and Germans. The Germans, usually as mediators of Western ideals, had made an enormous contribution to Czech culture; indeed, he goes as far as to say that all Czech civilization had come from abroad. Naturally enough, he also rejects Palacký and his contempories' view that the Slavs had a dove-like disposition; nothing suggests that the Czechs had been great peace-lovers and from the earliest times of the Bohemian state their military organization had been similar to the German. As far as Masaryk and his 'meaning of Czech history' is concerned, Pekař, in agreement with Zdeněk Nejedlý, more of less accuses Masaryk of active atavism; 'Masaryk seeks to authenticate, support, justify his doubtless noble educative aim by means of the imagined agreement of past generations.'[112] Masaryk's evaluation of history with its 'desire, so to speak, to clear the last veil off the secret of life' is permeated 'by a mystical-teleological view' that inevitably leads to high-flown metaphysics or a 'religious solution'.[113] Pekař rejects the pattern Masaryk imposes on Czech history and eventually comes up with his own 'meaning', however, averse as he has hitherto been to seeking 'meanings' at all. Pekař actually attributes two 'meanings', one to contradict Masaryk's, the other to make a moral statement on nationalist self-importance. It would be difficult to deny the first 'meaning' in general terms, however emotional Pekař becomes and however semantically dubious the content of terms like 'incomparably':

The German threat cultivated the great strength of Czech national consciousness from the Gothic period onwards; it was incomparably stronger than in other nations because the threat was greater and the nation had a strong spiritual constitution (certainly, the position of St Wenceslas as patron also played its role in this) … one bond … represents uninterrupted continuity of life and will, over the centuries, and that is *national consciousness*. … Only the consciousness that we are limbs of the same tribal body, the same national family … is the immutable basis that permeates and actually bears our history … The national idea is the precondition of [Czech history], its cause, the blood that pulsates in its living heart.[114]

Pekař's other 'meaning' does not contradict the mythic first 'meaning', but either suggests some Czech national immaturity, again a mythic concept, or simply results from Pekař's frustration or pique at the history of the Czechs as he understands it:

A great deal is being written now about the meaning of our history. If I were to try also to contribute some stirringly mentorial interpretation of our history to improve the Czechs' present, I should probably say: the 'meaning' of Czech history is that, whenever they achieved a high level of freedom and independence, the Czechs immediately subverted both by lacking reasoned restraint – in both political and spiritual matters.[115]

That approaches Palacký's criticism of Czechs' perfervour.

Pekař far from disparages the Hussites, but he approaches them without Palacký's nationalism. The Hussites were a Gothic phenomenon. The ideas and moral endeavour of the Hussites may have been developed in western Europe, but by digesting and adopting them, the Czechs had become so Europeanized that they had a sensation of cultural might and wanted to give direction to the rest of Europe. The Czechness of Hussitism lay in its applying to imported ideas a specifically Czech conception of what Christian living consisted in.[116] There was nothing of the Renaissance in the Hussites as Palacký believed. 'The medievalism of Hussitism lies in the fact that it was a *fruit* of the medieval mentality and sensitivity of the thirteenth to fourteenth centuries, an expression, manifestation, deed of the *Gothic Middle Ages*.'[117] Hussitism had not brought the Middle Ages to an end in Bohemia, but, rather, prolonged them.[118] Pekař also denies Palacký's assertion that the Taborites had demonstrated a democratic world-view. Neither in Taborite nor Hussite theory or practice does one find the idea that ordinary people, the serfs, should have political rights or 'be considered free Czechs in the medieval sense, like lords, knights and the burghers of royal towns. The Hussite revolution only gave firm foundations to the political power of the free towns and embedded them in feudal society; that is as far as the revolution's democratic interests went and this was in accord with examples abroad and with the spirit of the times.'[119] Palacký and Masaryk considered the Battle of Lipany (1434), where the Taborites were defeated by the moderate Hussites (and Catholics), a national disaster. Pekař, however, considers it to have benefited the vast majority of the population. Pekař's view had no impact on this element of the national myth; in the popular transmission of history, Lipany remained a national disaster second only to the White Mountain.

The rebellion of the Estates that led to the White Mountain was, asserts Pekař in *Smysl českých dějin*, little but the exploit of a few German or German-inspired cavaliers predisposed to political intrigues. Of course, in the national myth the rebels symbolized the Czech democratic spirit rising up against Habsburg and Jesuit tyranny. Connected with this myth was the tradition that the lot of the peasants became intolerable after the White Mountain. Pekař demythicizes that as well: the peasants' lot had begun to worsen during the Hussite Wars; as the political and social significance of the nobility 'became far greater in the Renaissance and Baroque periods, so the subject peasant's position became lower and lower on the social scale.'[120] The devastation of the Bohemian Lands during the Thirty Years' War had affected the landowners just as ruinously as it had the peasants. Pekař further assails the national myth by asserting that the Baroque era was one of cultural light, not darkness: 'it was the period when not only the Prague Towns came alive with the remarkable beauty of the Baroque, but also when the whole nation, down to the last village, the last hovel, the last lace pattern and the last folksong melody was filled with the vital joy of Baroque culture, that was penetrating, creating, building a new society, a new nation, that very nation from which our National Revival arose.'[121]

That statement already suggests the most recent 'philosophy of Czech history', that of Patočka. This dissenting philosopher conceived of a 'great history' and a 'small history' for the Czechs, and the small history began at the end of the Baroque with the National Revival. Patočka shares Pekař's view on the role of the Germans in Czech history; he considers the whole so-called *Drang nach Osten* to have constituted a positive contribution to European culture in that the Germans had civilized the Slavs. In the period of 'great Czech history', which had lasted for approximately a century and a half in the Late Middle Ages, the Czechs had been great because of the ambition of their rulers: the last Přemyslides had wanted the German imperial crown. In addition, this period saw Bohemia becoming the base for the organization of central and eastern Europe on the Western model. Bohemia had remained an outpost (*Vorposten*) of Western civilization well into the Reformation. She had retained 'greatness' for as long as Czechness remained *unthematisch*, in other words, had not become an issue.[122] She had lost any chance of greatness, Patočka maintains conventionally, with the White Mountain. The seventeenth century had not, however, meant 'the demise of the Bohemian state, but it had meant the Czechs' divorce from world responsibilities, the provincialization of Bohemia and an end to its greatness.'[123] The chief effect of the White Mountain had been spiritual and intellectual. The nobility had become alienated from the country and, although the state had in many respects become stronger, burghers and farmers had entirely 'concentrated on the Counter-Reformation'. Somewhat hyperbolically and more or less following Palacký and Masaryk's conception, he writes that the 'germs of bourgeois intellectual life, particularly literature in Czech, were constricted [Patočka's mixed metaphor], if not stifled'. The social and spiritual developments of the Counter-Reformation 'crippled the Czech-speaking population intellectually for the future, for at the time when the Enlightenment was setting in throughout Europe, the Czechs were mercilessly and uncritically driven in the opposite direction.'[124] On the other hand, and this is Patočka's attempt at a contribution to that section of the national myth that concerns the Baroque, the period had inculcated in the Czechs 'a remarkable piety ... which lives in some corner of every Czech's mind, as long as he is not Enlightenment-sceptical through and through'.[125]

The National Revival was anti-Enlightenment, the Enlightenment being embodied for Patočka in centralization and Germanization. Indeed, 'Czechness was the bearer of an opposite principle.' Because the Revival ran against the general trends of the time 'it gave Bohemian Germans the unique opportunity, by associating themselves with the Enlightenment, to take almost a third of Bohemia into their possession.'[126] The Revivalists' anti-Enlightenment affiliation was a mark of their 'smallness', signalled the fatal beginning of Czech 'small history'. Patočka sees four points by which Revival nationalists expanded on Herder in their programme. First, they clearly separated nation from state and held that a nation continues to exist after the loss of its own state. Secondly, they defined a nation by its character and its character by its language, and thus they defined nation by language. Thirdly, they considered the nation as something given by Nature. Fourthly, they saw the distinctions between family, nation and national tribe simply as distinctions of quantity.[127] Here Patočka compares the chief creator of the Czechs' linguocentric programme, Josef Jungmann (1773–1847) with Bolzano. Bolzano's doctrine of nation is not directed to the past like Jungmann's, but is Utopian, and national problems are social problems for Bolzano. For Jungmann, language is absolutized, whereas for the rationalist Bolzano, it is only instrumental.[128] Furthermore, Revivalists of the Jungmann school, notably Kollár and Palacký, had perverted Herder's notion of humanity: 'under the impact of nationality [národnost], humanity becomes Slav messianism.'[129] All this is, incidentally, borne out in the Slovak Awakening by Štúr's messianism and his linguocentric nationalism, which approaches the sanctification of language:

Every nation is most ardently coupled with its language. The nation is reflected in it as the first product of its theoretical spirit; language is, then, the surest sign of the essence and individuality of every nation. Just like an individual human being, the nation reveals its deepest inner self through language; it, so to speak, embodies its spirit in language; this external form corresponds exactly with the inner self of the nation at all stages of its development; the spirit of the nation develops in and with the language in the form most appropriate to it: they are interdependent, and so one cannot exist without the other.[130]

Linguocentrism had split Bohemian society into the Germans and the Czechs, and modern 'small' Czechness had arisen from this split. Since very few members of the upper classes had retained Czech, the new Czech society was 'essentially constructed "from below"', and 'small Czech history' consists of the history of that society's 'struggle for advancement and equality'.[131] Modern Czechness is, asserts Patočka, inseparably associated with the rise of the lower classes and the levelling down of European society that had been taking place since the end of the eighteenth century. 'The foundations of the Czech nation are an oppressed class without rights ..., the peasant class subsequently liberated,' and this class 'in part remains on the land, in part becomes a social element approaching the petty bourgeoisie, attached to private property.'[132] He claims that Czech society is the first European society where the lower classes have risen to the position of sole rulership. Thus he can re-create the Palacký–Masaryk myth of Czech natural democraticness on a sociological rather than religious basis. The 'elemental democratism' of modern Czech society's development is 'derived from the essentially lower-class composition of our society' and, thus 'the lower-class intellectuals' that form 'the ruling class do not detach themselves from the broad masses, but remain intimately bound up with them.'[133] This democratic tradition, however, carries within it its own weakness, which can be called 'the tragic form of a society constructed "from below". At the moment when the hand is stretching out for its longed-for goals, the *inner* strength reveals itself to be inadequate.'[134] 'Small Czechness' lacks just that : inner strength: 'While great [Czechness] could think about the problems of Europe and realize itself or waste itself in the service or tension of those problems, from the very beginning, small [Czechness] had to concentrate on itself, on maintaining its own existence.'[135] These new Czechs were a people of freed serfs, defined by their mother tongue. The trouble is and was that they had not freed themselves, but had been freed by their ruler's decrees, were themselves far less radically inclined than their ruler, remained fundamentally conservative and concerned primarily with any advantages that might accrue to them.[136]

As far as the Czechs after the dissolution of the Habsburg Monarchy are concerned, in *O smysl dneška* (Towards the meaning of today), Patočka simply abides by the myth. The First Republic was democratic and had been accompanied by enormous intellectual vitality. Although Stalinism had 'inflicted deep wounds on the moral unity of the nation', it had made the nation meditate on how to return to the liberating meaning of socialism, socialism as 'the starting-point of the national programme'.[137] (The latter, of course, does not belong to today's Czech national myth.) Later, Patočka shows more courage. Beneš embodies 'small Czechness'. The Munich Agreement was no *Diktat*, for no one could dictate submission to anyone unless that person or country acceded to submission. 'Beneš surrendered and, in so doing, broke the moral backbone of our society, which was ready to fight; he did not break it just for that moment, but for a long time to come.' Patočka's contempt for Beneš is muted only by despair: 'Beneš ... was a weak man, good at being a secretary, but nothing else. And the right to decide on the future moral profile of the Czech people was conferred on a man like that.'[138] In the early 1970s when Patočka was writing that, these words constituted an attack on the sentimental mythicization of everything to do with pre-socialist Czechoslovakia. Furthermore, his words manifest the courage to come close to the standard Communist interpretation of Beneš's demobilizing the Czechoslovak Army, albeit the Communists had different grounds for that interpretation, including the necessity to camouflage the ambivalent reaction to Munich of their brother Russians.

The West was to be blamed for Munich,[139] for the capitalist West threatened the Slav socialist paradise after World War II as the West had brought disaster on Eastern Europe at Munich. Border-guards were the much besung defenders of that paradise.[140] The Communist view on the West was foreshadowed in the nationalism of the first half of the nineteenth century, and not only in Kollár's racism. Štúr develops Kollár: avid materialism in the West, spiritual values in the East, selfishness versus unselfishness, just as in 1950s socialist propaganda:

Look at Europe, and in the West you will see ill humour: one group casts doubt on everything; another calls out for help, and yet another immerses itself in the material; from the West you hear only the shouting and despair that comes from those who expect great misfortune. In the West we see this preoccupation with the material, personal interest, as if that were the fulfilment of everything, not just an aid or means to life ... In contrast to that, we see among the nations of Eastern Europe stimulation to higher concerns, spiritual concerns.[141]

So too, Štúr claims, the subject of Slavonic poetry is the purely spiritual, not the suffering of the individual as in the Romantic West. The Slavs are natural collectivists: 'Among the Slavs, the individual as individual cannot love only for himself, but he serves the true commonality.'[142] Macura points out how Nejedlý linked Slav socialist collectivism with the defeat of Nazism, saw this defeat as part of the Slavs' age-old battle against Western ideas incorporated in the Germans. Nejedlý returns to early Jungmannian Revivalist ideology, 'to the ideal of the great Slav nation: "We Slavs, a great power that not only is party to decisions, but, in a certain measure, determines the situation in Europe." Naturally, he looks at the circumstances of postwar Europe through this lens, too, i.e. as a solution of the historical struggle between "German barbarism" and "the Slav world led by the USSR."'[143] Any obstacle that stood in the way of creating a socialist regime in Czechoslovakia was unSlavonic. The renewal of the Kollárian panslav idea in pro-Soviet propaganda was rendered acceptable by a pretty general pro-Russian sensitivity among the Czechs. The Soviet occupation of 1968 marked the end of that sensitivity. Miloš Horanský's popular, unremarkable and emotionally over-charged reaction in verse to the Warsaw Pact Intervention includes, with reference to Kollár's sonnet cycle, *Slávy dcera* (Daughter of Sláva), a melodramatic declaration of the ending of the Slav idea: 'Oh, Kollár, / The Daughter of Sláva forgot your words, / She became a whore of Judas, / Oh, Kollár, / The Russian circus. The ringmaster is the son of Sláva / And our blood drips into the sawdust.'[144]

Special qualities attributed to the Slavs by Štúr became the special qualities of socialists in the 1950s. The first is obedience, a precondition for entry into the Slav paradise: 'Anyone who wishes to be a Slav must learn obedience – like our national heroes. Otherwise, he will be bewitched and will never enter the Slav realm, never see our glass castle – the Slav world.'[145] Štúr makes that one of the three essential qualities needed to create pleasure and peace; the other two are qualities attributed to the Slavs by Herder, diligence and piety. Štúr's choice of obedience has two origins. First, obedience constituted a key virtue in Renaissance popular literature and thus in the didactic literature of the Enlightenment and early Revival in Czech; it was a burgher virtue, thus understood at the time to be 'progressive'. Secondly, Štúr was thinking as an organizer; obedience among his followers was necessary for the assertion of Slovak culture. Obedience is a military virtue. In the 1950s obedience was seen in terms of Party discipline, but especially discipline in the Youth Movement. Obedience to the kind Komsomol brings joy in work and can even repair a broken marriage, as Pavel Kohout demonstrates to his audience in *Dobrá píseň* (Good song, 1952).

That same play contrasts the upright moral behaviour of young socialists with the immorality of those tainted by the West, like the actor who has lived for a while in Paris. In *Dobrá píseň* smoking is a sign of frail morals, a weakness that excludes one from the socialist paradise. Kohout's Katka is unsocialist in her marital infidelity, but that is also unSlav in Štúr's conception: 'We know about the fidelity and fine morals in Slav women's behaviour to their husbands from old writers – and when that chastity falls, the morality which characterises Slavs falls also.'[146] The Slav woman is like Věra in Milan Kundera's 'Láska a život' (Love and life) who says to her man: 'I will go with you through mud and stones / where gales blow most violently! / If there is too little Bolshevik blood in your heart, / top up your veins from mine.'[147]

Love is de-eroticized among true Slavs as among true socialists. Štúr compares Slav love with Germanic romantic love:

Among Germanic peoples a family comes into existence when two human beings fall in love; and their goal is self-satisfaction; when these two people attain inner satisfaction, they leave their families and found a new one. This is quite different from the way Slav families are founded: among our peoples the oldest member of the family has the power to betrothe ... sexual love among our peoples is quite different from romantic love. What is romantic love? The satisfaction of the excited inner self when one person has found in another of the opposite sex something that corresponds to his or her inner self – their souls fuse so completely that no one can tear them asunder; but for that reason, they find contentment only in themselves, derive pleasure from nothing else. Slav love is quite another thing; it is *contentment in the family circle*, in that natural moral bond. Not one person's satisfaction in another person, but in the family … In Germanic peoples suicide for love exists, for example, Romeo and Juliet; that does not exist among the Slavs – no one throws himself or herself into rivers; no one takes poison, and so forth.[148]

Slavonic lyric verse is furthest developed among the Slovaks because Slovaks' love 'is not for individuals, but is inclined towards the family'.[149] The chronicler of ideal South Bohemian life, Josef Holeček (1853–1929), describes his peasants as having a natural godliness and spirituality which constitutes the opposite of the erotic, which is always selfish, for 'The body is always unfree; only the spirit is capable of freedom.'[150] Thus, also, no such thing as despair exists in South Bohemia. 'In South Bohemia the word "love" is not used in sexual relationships. That word belongs in the Bible, has nothing whatsoever to do with everyday life … Publicly these people never admit to more than that they like so and so, and in private they will not say more than: "I am fond of you."'[151] Once a South Bohemian man has his own sweetheart, he will not even look at other girls. If South Bohemians are inadequate lovers, they are excellent spouses and parents and, though marriages may be contracted on economic grounds, that can be no bad thing, for claims Holeček, suicide does not exist in South Bohemia. Similarly, Božena Viková-Kunětická (1862–1934) observes among the North Bohemian mountaineers 'a love as cold as steel, but also equally hard and unchanging'; she has never seen anyone kiss or adopt a tender tone of voice, even newly married couples.[152] Macura notices this de-eroticization in socialist writing and links it with a definite programme, whereby if a woman is 'too much a component of the private space of home … she is condemned.' The ideal woman of the 1950s is a 'woman fellow-fighter, a comrade wife … and even her beauty results naturally from the fact that she leaves the home surroundings to work in public.'[153] In Kohout's play the audience learns that the Communists have a monopoly of human love. Love is a public moral principle. Thus the young soldier, the perfect fighter for peace Slávek declares, 'anyone who can calmly betray their love / could then equally well betray their country!'[154] The erotic is consigned to traitors, in other words, typically to the Communist and other political figures who had been or were being tried when Kohout's play was put on. The erotic was dirty, had no place in socialist society: 'It is no coincidence that all those who have been revealed to be malefactors and parasites led a repulsive personal life. Their treachery was, naturally, closely linked with their impaired morality.'[155] On the other hand, the armed forces constitute the guardians of love; 'I raise my glass on behalf of the Army', declares the young officer Slávek, 'on behalf of the lads in helmets. Yes,

them. / To whom is love more precious than to us? / We received our weapons in
love's name, / so that love could create immortal deeds / and never have to suffer
again.'[156] The husband in Kundera's 'To není láska' (This is not love) bewails his
wife's petty bourgeois tenderness and her playing the role of housewife:

> Fair hair, blue eyes: That is his nice wife.
> The schoolmaster's daughter. With a little love and a little dowry
> she settled into love like a kid-goat into an easy chair
> to warm her tiny feet by the family stove.

> He gazed at her sadly until sorrow clogged his throat:
>   'I am breaking, cracking
> under the weight of the times.
> And you, not noticing the outside world, knit away
> at your life by the stove as if it were a long stocking.
> But this is not love!
> Do you hear?
> This is not love!'
> This is how he spoke to her in his mind, sitting silently over his plate,
> on which a piece of meat with a little rice lay untouched.
> Seeing him sitting there so sadly, his nice wife said:
> 'I know, I know. I am sorry. I put too much salt in the rice'.[157]

The trouble with her had been that she had not asked how his Bolshevik fighting
had gone that day and whether he had triumphed.

It goes without saying that elements discovered in the Slav nation by Herder
and embroidered on by others curiously comported with socialist mythology. The
conception of Slavs as a peace-loving nation recurs in the socialist fighting for
peace, peace campaigns, soldiers for peace. The notion that Slavs had never
armed but to defend themselves finds its parallel in the depiction of the belligerent imperialist West as threatening the socialist paradise, thus in the Soviet Bloc
interpretation of the arms race. Even the ancient Slavonic religion in the course of
whose rituals the Slavs 'surrendered themselves to festivals of joy and filled the
forests with delectable singing,'[158] prefigures the joy of living youthfully in the
socialist paradise.

Masaryk and the Czech 'martyr complex'

Perhaps Masaryk's only contribution to assessing Czechness was his observation
in Česká otázka that Czechs had a predisposition to martyrdom and to the veneration of martyrs. Masaryk had avowedly been inspired to the idea by Ernest Denis.
He writes about what in intellectual discourse has come to be labelled the 'Czech
martyr complex'[159] in the context of what he perceives as a Czech national passivity. He bases his argument that this martyr cult exists on the fact that the most

glorious period of Czech history had begun and ended with martyrdom, that of St Wenceslas and of Jan Hus. He further points out that it is remarkable that Hus was burnt at the stake whereas Wyclif and Luther were not. His anticlericalism and contemporary fashion lead him to label St John Nepomucene a pseudomartyr, but he sets up that cult as a deterrent for those Czechs who, he claims, are far too fond of exhibiting their suppurating national wounds to their audiences at home and abroad.

The cult does demonstrably exist, at least in the popular consciousness, and, in general terms only, it may be linked with the nationalist myth of the suffering Slavs. But, at the same time one must try to explain how the cult of martyrs tallies emotionally with the cult of leaders. The latter occurs, however, predominantly in the twentieth century among the Czechs, parallel to new martyr cults.

The Slav idea in Kollár or his precursor, Antonín Marek, derived in part from a perceived need to put an end to Slav suffering, subjugation. With the great free Slav people, the Russians, by their side in the greater Slav nation, there would no longer be any need for self-pity. Marek saw the true 'spirit of Slavia' breathing in Russia thus: 'So what if the Teuton presses on us from one side / and on the other there is a wretched life among the Ottomans? That the gallant arm of the fighting Serbs fell / and that King Svatopluk's empire is in ruins? / After all, Rurik's sceptre has not been wrested from us; / it will no longer be a disgrace to be called Czechs / and our beauties will become Slav women.'[160] Štúr is more militant. The Slavs had had their mission to defend Christendom from the Asiatic hordes; still their geographical circumstances had played a role in this. The Slavs might appear culturally backward today, but if they had inhabited the lands the French and Germans had, their cultural position would be quite different. Štúr expresses himself more assertively than Marek: in ancient times the Slavs had had as 'neighbours on one side the still savage Germanic peoples and, on the other, wild Asiatic nations, and so they had not had the opportunity to learn anything human.' Furthermore, their fight to save Christendom, which had, Štúr claims, lasted from the fourth to the fifteenth century, denied them the chance of advancing themselves intellectually. Almost all Slavs had been involved in this fight, 'Russians, Poles, Czechs, Slovaks, Croatians, Serbs and Bulgarians', and they had had to defend western Europe from 'Huns, Khazars, Avars, Pechenegs, Kumans, Mongols, Tatars and Turks.' The Czechs and Poles had succeeded in cultivating scholarship at various points since the fourteenth century, but after their golden ages, 'new storms rained down upon the Slavs … to knock off the first Slav buds and blossoms'. The Slavs had then remained in darkness virtually until the French Revolution and the Napoleonic Wars.[161] Štúr considers that unfortunate, but his interpretation evinces not a tint of self-pity. His view on Hus, expressed in a letter (7 May 1843) to the Czech Revivalist physician and anatomist, Josef Václav Staněk (1804–71), attributes to Hus the heroic qualities one links with the Slovak bandit

Jánošík, while simultaneously associating Hus with a specifically Slav attitude, which Štúr unwittingly bases on the Czech emblemization of the concept Truth; his statement thus contrasts tellingly with Masaryk's (of literary historical importance is the fact that he dismisses the greatest Czech poet of the nineteenth century as unSlav – for only the unSlav can fail to move Štúr):

In the romantic world we can see people jumping from towers, throwing themselves into rivers and lakes, flying off to battle, and so on, because of unhappy love; you can see nothing of that in the Slav world. In none of our tales will you find suicides; no, a Slav determinedly suffers death in the service of the truth of the spirit, like your Hus and so forth ... The opposite is true of the Germanic world. During the Reformation, the greatest chain of events in the world, no one feels like sacrificing himself; in the beginning even Luther is undecisive at [the Diet of] Worms, but Hus goes calmly singing to the stake.[162]

When Štúr does admit that the Slavs are suffering or have suffered, he maintains that it is their fault and that it is up to them to remove this suffering: 'It is certain that we shall succeed in lifting this spell from ourselves – but not before we start working, with the greatest humility ... My heart bursts when I recall the causes of our fall: that we undermined ourselves and the Germans took over a large part of our land.'[163]

The Decadent Procházka, alluding mainly to such as Kollár and Štúr, writes of a Slavonic mythic masochism: 'Slavs have the well-nigh pathological desire to see Slavs everywhere; they indulge themselves with the idea that they had been the autochthons of all central and southern Europe and see an exceptional claim to fame in the fact that they had been eradicated, suppressed, deslavicized almost everywhere.'[164] Depending on whether they took the beginning to be 1526 or 1620, Czech Revivalists bewailed their 200 or 300 years' suffering; Czechs on the declaration of the Republic, their 300 or 400 years' suffering under the Habsburg Yoke. Slovaks have written for more than a century of their thousand-year subjection to Magyar rule – an aspect of Slovak nationalism which is wittily satirized in Pavel Vilikovský's *Večne je zelený...* (Ever green is ..., 1989), but which can lead to feral *faux pas*. Štefan Polakovič writes: 'The Slovak saying "birds of a feather flock together, like will to like" contains a great deal of sociological wisdom, distilled from our thousand-year life experience.'[165] And other Slavs do, indeed, bewail their suffering in a similar manner; for example, the Bulgarians speak of the Turkish Yoke and of their five centuries under the Turks (usually forgetting the two centuries under Byzantium). Communists assumed this mythopoeic numerology for their own purposes. Thus Kundera asserts that 'there are keys in Communism / with which thousand-year-old cages are opened, / from these cages free human souls / fly up into unimagined regions'[166] – in other words, the socialist paradise. Then, in the post-Communist era, socialism itself becomes a suffering myth. Macura points that out succinctly: 'In the last century "two hundred years' suffering" was spoken of; from the beginning of the twentieth century "We have been groaning under the Yoke for three hundred years" was the cry; since November 1989, speculation has been fostered on half a century's oppression by two forms of totalitarianism.'[167] Suffering may serve as an excuse: Havel emotionally states that 'human creativity has disappeared from our lands thanks to the totalitarian system.'[168] None the less, Macura writes that all Czechoslovaks had shared in creating the 'semiotic construct called the world of socialism',[169] which reminds us of Štúr's words on the Slavs' bringing their suffering upon themselves.

The Czechs' leader cults seem unrelated to Štúr's transformations of suffering into a mission. The leader-cults seem to be fimicolous, leadership bred on and rising above the dirt of suffering. They appear, thus, to be based on self-made men, thus even, possibly, to pertain to the belief in innate Czech democracy. If one follows Palacký, the striving for, or demonstration of, democracy might, indeed, be understood as a mission. In his recounting the legend of Oldřich, Prince of Bohemia, taking the peasant Božena for his wife, 'Dalimil' considers the benefits of social mobility and emphasizes the fact that the founder of the Bohemian royal dynasty had been a farmer. Since we are concerned with Czech self-definition, it is of little interest that St Stephen's crown fell from heaven on to his head while he was having lunch by his plough, that the Polish Piast foundation myth also concerns the founder being called from the plough, and that similar legends exist for Romans (Cincinnatus) and Goths.[170] Patočka's interpretation of the legend, whereby the prophetess princess Libuše decided to marry Přemysl the Ploughman to introduce a new age, Přemysl founds agriculture, and the Czechs are driven out of paradise 'into the hard world of soldiering and working on the land',[171] might also be linked with the Masarykian work ethic, and the whole nineteenth-century mythology surrounding the idea that 'Czech hands are made of gold'. In 1841 a monument was set up to Přemysl on the spot where he had allegedly received his call from Libuše, and under Communism the nineteenth-century conception of Přemysl as representative of the democratic spirit was hyperbolized by Konstantin Biebl (1898–1951). This poet has Přemysl the Ploughman serve at the steering-wheel in an army of tractors.[172]

Vítězslav Nezval (1900–58) had the 'first worker president', Klement Gottwald as a modern Přemysl, albeit called from his carpenter's bench, not his plough.[173] Generally 'Gottwald's arrival in the Presidential Palace was not depicted simply as a revolutionary change' by 1950s writers, 'but as the fulfilment of the meaning of Czech history'.[174] This mythicization of Gottwald represented not only a reflection of the Stalin personality cult, but also an attempt to replace the Masaryk cult. Masaryk was of humble origins.[175] And Masaryk, too, had been eulogized as the fulfilment of the meaning of Czech history. Masaryk had been sent to the Czechs by the Spirit of History in Jan Rokyta's (1864–1952) ode for the president's seventieth birthday. Rokyta maintains that he embodies Hus, Žižka, George of Poděbrady and Comenius, in other words the tradition that Masaryk himself interpreted as the true tradition of Czech history. He is the 'Great Man'[176] who had fulfilled Comenius's prophecy[177] of eventual salvation for the Czechs. Since the White Mountain the Czechs had been in the wilderness, led there by the 'cursed hand' of the Habsburgs; the new Republic is the Promised Land. The window in Hradčany shines as he works and looks over his nation, just as it would under Gottwald; Masaryk is the 'lighthouse keeper' of Czechness.[178]

Since Havel has not yet achieved cult status, though he came close to it during the first year or so after the fall of socialism, and though in some Czech circles it is counted as blasphemy to criticize him, the most recent leader cult is that of Dubček. His background, though lower-class, was not exactly humble since he had an elite Party education, but newspapers and television made him the humble man in 1968 and the victim in 1969. The inept slogan associated with him, 'socialism with a human face', very soon acquired the meaning 'socialism with Dubček's smiling face' or the politically irrational 'liberal Communism'. Ironically, since he became a mainstay of Normalization, the Slovak poet, Mihálik was the first to publish a cult work on Dubček, the cycle *Rekviem*. This cycle of liturgical verse expresses despair at the Soviet intervention, the destruction of Dubček's reform Communism and the author's own illusions about the USSR. Dubček becomes Christ and the Soviets with their ritual kisses at Čierna and in Moscow become Judas in the poem, 'Sanctus': 'You modern Christ, what has remained / for you from the empty kisses? / On the Mount of Olives Dubček / sweats blood.' [179] Dubček embodied a myth and, as Macura has pointed out, history fuelled the myth further in his death. On the occasion of his funeral, his former Party colleague, Čestmír Císař, stated that Dubček had a messianic charisma like Christ or Hus (*sic*). On the day after his eventually fatal motoring accident, the newspaper headlines (2 September 1992) concerned first the Slovak National Council's acceptance of the new Slovak Constitution and then the ardent federalist Slovak Dubček's crash. To cap that, Dubček died on the anniversary of the October Revolution (7 October 1992).[180] For some time after that, the kilometre marker-post near Humpolec where the crash had taken place became something of a motorists' shrine.

Various spots in and around Constance were just such a shrine for Czech nineteenth-century travellers, as the statue of St Wenceslas was after August 1968, but especially after Palach's death in January 1969, though Dubček is not considered a martyr, however many inevitable rumours there were at the time suggesting that his accident was the work of Slovak nationalists. The Czech martyr complex, however, certainly survived Czechoslovakia's entry into the modern world of market-economy atavism.

In the same year as Masaryk published his *Česká otázka* in book form, 1895,

Julius Zeyer published his *Tři legendy o krucifixu* (Three legends about cruci-fixes). Two of those stories pertain to my subject. The third of them, 'Samko pták' (Samko, the bird), expresses on the basis of a retarded Slovak the true Christian devotion of Slavs, the potential of Slav meekness and goodness achieving salva-tion for others; in fact, suggests the Slavonic passivity that concerned Masaryk. The first story, 'Inultus', however, expresses Czech masochistic nationalism. A destitute poet, some twenty years after the White Mountain, models Christ for a statue that is being sculpted by a representative of the invading forces, the Milanese Donna Flavia. She is the sadist of *Trivialliteratur* depictions of the ram-paging Counter-Reformation Jesuits. She tightens ever more firmly the ropes binding the poet to the cross, as she falls further and further into love with him. He experiences a combination of intense masochistic sexual pleasure as she torments him, and a growing conviction that he is being martyred for the Czech nation. She eventually kills him and herself. The resultant statue is, however, miraculous, and excites veneration from a crowd of ragged Czechs, the poor who are now the only true Czechs. Inultus' messianism is founded on passivity. An admirer of Zeyer, Karásek, perhaps reacting to Masaryk, states that the Czechs are 'a nation condemned to passivity'.[181] A character in Dyk's *Prosinec* wryly re-marks, 'Anyway, a Czech is only good for martyrdom.'[182] And the attractive drinking, gambling Bukovina Jew Bartlmé in a work by the popular *fin-de-siècle* novelist, Emil Tréval (1859–1929), says of the Czechs: 'You Czechs are flagellants. Indeed, born suicides. If someone blames you for something, you bend your heads and accept the blame.'[183]

Macura notes the survival of the Czech martyr complex today: 'It is truly striking how much strange masochism there tends to be in Czechs' self-evalua-tion.' He characterizes the mythic memory of Lipany and the White Mountain as inherently masochistic, and notes that Czech 'heroes' tend to be 'tragic heroes', figures who 'could easily be stylized into the role of martyr'.[184]

In considering the six main Czech martyrs (one of whom, Švec, is now al-most forgotten), I treat them as mythic figures and the authors of their legends as mythopoets (in the case of Fučík, the editors of his legend). Nothing I write con-stitutes a critical comment on their characters in real life. All six are symbols and I introduce elements of their biographies only to shed light on some aspect of the legends. I have omitted Milada Horáková, however many streets have been named after her since the fall of socialism, because I have not been able to trace any literary treatment of that extraordinarily brave woman, someone who had the truly heroic qualities that many of my six probably lacked. Another, more impor-tant, reason for omitting her is that no cult has arisen around her.[185] Still, in Czech official terminology, she was a martyr, not simply a victim. In an address given on 25 February 1990, the anniversary of the Communist take-over, Havel employed the language of the Czech martyr complex: 'Today we have publicly remembered the martyr's death of the priest Toufar and the monitory self-sacrifice of Jan Zajíc. May these two, like the thousands of others, from Milada Horáková to Jan Palach, from the tragic figure of Rudolf Slánský to the hero of rights, Pavel Wonka, continue to remind us anew that we ourselves, and by no means always honourably, survived the great work of destruction, and that now it is for us to do something decent for our country and to sacrifice something for that endeavour.'[186] The same conception of heroism manifests itself in the name I noticed in the little town of Veselí nad Moravou, National Martyrs' Street.

St Wenceslas

Very little indeed is known about Wenceslas except what can be derived from the Old Slavonic and Latin legends. Debates ran on whether he was killed in 929 or 935, but now the latter date is generally accepted. He was in his early twenties when he died, may have become Duke or Prince of Bohemia in the 920s, but was too young, so that his grandmother, Ludmila became regent, possibly much to the distress of his mother Drahomíra. He is the good King Wenceslas of the English carol, which J. M. Neale adapted from a German poem by the Czech Revivalist, Václav Alois Svoboda (1791–1849).[187]

The two versions of the early legend[188] that I use mainly are the First Old Slavonic and the legend of the monk Christianus, *Vita et passio sancti Venceslai et sanctae Ludmilae aviae eius* (990s?). There is no doubt that the First Old Slavonic Legend was composed in Bohemia, but the date of its composition is not certain. It does appear that it was written at sometime between 940 and 1000, in other words either as altogether the first legend or as a legend based partly on the early legends and partly on local oral tradition.[189] The Wenceslas legend has two serious political purposes at its inception: first, to reassert the primacy of the Přemyslide family in contemporary Bohemia which was still suffering clan conflict, thus also to elevate the Přemyslide dynasty; secondly, to give Bohemia its proper place in Christendom through producing a princely martyr as potential patron (the patron saint of St Wenceslas, thus of most of Bohemia was St Vitus, who was also the patron saint of the Saxons; he was an Italian); the international political propaganda is clear from the fact that in *Crescente fide*, perhaps the earliest, one of Wenceslas's posthumous miracles takes place in the land of the Franks.

Wenceslas had a sound education in Latin, Greek and Slavonic and from childhood was particularly pious. He wore a hair-shirt under his princely garb, cared for the poor, grew grapes and corn to make wine and bread for the Sacrament, disapproved of the death penalty and always left the court if such a penalty had to be carried out, so that he did not have to look at such violence. On the other hand, he was a successful warrior. Either he never married, or he married, had a child, and then gave his wife away (that depends on which legend one reads). The page of the English carol, Podiven, appears to have been something of a missionary. Wenceslas longed for martyrdom, and since he had from youth had the gift of prophecy, he knew what was going to happen when his brother, Boleslav, invited him to visit him. That is different in the First Slavonic Legend, where, when he is at his brother's, his servants inform him that Boleslav intends killing him and he, passively, puts his faith in God. The next morning, as Wenceslas is going to Mass, Boleslav stops him in the doorway of the church. In the Slavonic, Boleslav strikes him, and Wenceslas turns round and knocks him to the ground, and then two of Boleslav's confederates, Česta and Tira, kill him in the doorway. In Christianus, evil counsellors persuade Boleslav to rid himself of his brother, and at dinner on the first day the assassins decide to commit their deed, but rise from table and are restrained by some force three times; the next morning, Boleslav does strike the first blow, at Wenceslas's head, but 'hardly any blood came'; Wenceslas grabs the sword with his bare hands, but returns it to Boleslav when he sees he is determined on fratricide. Then Boleslav calls his confederates and they kill him. For this study, it is important that Wenceslas's physical strength and courage are emphasized just as much as his piety and wisdom: he is, then, heroic.

Nevertheless the beginnings of the stock five-stage martyr story of the Czech myths are here: (i) Wenceslas goes voluntarily into an dangerous situation and (ii) is betrayed by someone close to him (in some versions his mother is involved, but in the First Slavonic and Christianus, Drahomíra has maternal affection for him), but stage (iii) is omitted, and we come to (iv) where he is mocked, or his piety is mocked, in that his is killed at the church door, and (v) he is killed.

As the cult grew, so did the legend, which achieved its complete cultic form during the Counter-Reformation with Jan Tanner's (1623–94) *Trophaea sancti Wenceslai Bohemiae regis ac martyris* (1661; Czech version by Felix Kadlinský [1613–75, 1669), which combines scholarship with literary imagination. The dynastic element remains strong, for Tanner demonstrates that the Habsburgs are descended from this great 'duke, king and martyr and holy patriot'.[190] Tanner greatly embellishes the legend with miraculous events. For example, one of the saint's assassins, Hněvsa, becomes a lunatic for one month every year and is eventually driven to suicide. Another, Štyrsa, contracts a particularly malodorous and painful affliction of the legs, which one day drives him to blaspheme against God and Wenceslas, whereupon he is swallowed up by the earth together with his dog, horse and sparrow-hawk. In 1619, when the Calvinists desecrated St Vitus' cathedral – an event which is, incidentally also important for the John Nepomucene legend – St Wenceslas and other patrons had called out that they were leaving and from that moment the Estates' rebellion began to fare badly.

Patočka appears to believe in nothing of the legend, believes that Wenceslas lived, but that the oral tradition had created in him a 'mythological figure', wherein his conflict with his brother emblemized 'the conflict between the spiritual and the secular'.[191] As an emblem, certainly the conflict is between the Christian and the pagan. This is not, however, what at times made the figure of Wenceslas problematic for nationalists, and exploitable by latterday believers in Bohemia as an appurtenance of Germany. Wenceslas was considered the ruler who had compromised with the Germans. Pekař maintains that there is no reason for believing that he feared German military might and therefore surrendered Bohemia's sovereignty, for the legal dependence of Bohemia on the Germans had been firmly in place before Wenceslas ascended to the throne. Palacký's statement that Wenceslas had agreed to pay an annual tribute to the emperor of 500 talents of silver and 120 oxen was, according to Pekař, a product of Palacký's Romantic imagination,[192] but Pekař's assertion has not dissuaded historians from repeating Palacký.[193] In Pekař's view, Wenceslas's pious life (and death) had made it possible for Bohemia to become a 'full member of the community of Western nations'.[194]

The cult of St Wenceslas is still alive, though it became secularized in the nineteenth century. For example, Charles IV wrote his own version of a *vita*; the moderate Hussites sang the Wenceslas chorale at the Battle of Lipany; the Baroque translation of the Bible was called the St Wenceslas Bible, and the first Wenceslas statue on the Horse Market (now Wenceslas Place) was erected in 1678 (the present statue is from the late nineteenth century). The Mass before the statue on the Horse Market in 1848 marked the beginning of the Whitsun Storms, the mild Czech contribution to the Year of Revolutions. In 1968 the new statue became the symbolic centre of Czech resistance against the Soviet occupation and by 1988 students began meeting there regularly first in small, barely noticed protests, but from January 1989 onwards to considerable effect, until the statue became the shrine it is now after the fall of socialism. Today St Wenceslas has become a symbol of freedom and resistance to tyranny, as Jan Hus had been, especially in the fifteenth and nineteenth centuries.

Jan Hus

Masaryk's choice of St Wenceslas as marking the beginning of the Czech martyr tradition and thus of the gradual formation of the Czech martyr complex is unconvincing for three reasons. First, fraternal jealousy plays too large a role in the story. Secondly, Wenceslas is an heroic figure – his ardent desire for martyrdom certainly appears in versions of the legend, but that may be understood either as a topos of legends (see St Amadus, for example) or as the reflection of the ascetic and bloody idealism of the times. And thirdly, Czech martyr cults inevitably contain the idea of the martyr's having died defending some truth before a tyrant or some matter of national honour; Wenceslas certainly dies a Christian, a victim of his devil-inspired brother, but he dies defending little except his own piety. One might make a fourth point: Wenceslas, however much he is portrayed as a people's monarch, has the wrong family background to make a Czech martyr, for the Czech martyr complex belongs to what Patočka calls 'little Czech history', whereas Wenceslas belongs to 'great Czech history', however much Patočka might doubt his historical authenticity.

Hus may belong to a period when, according to Patočka, 'great Czech history' was far from dead, but Hus was very much of the people and with his Czech sermons and devotional writings, was even something of a populist. Patočka perceives him as an inspired leader of a movement whereby 'laymen were beginning to emancipate themselves [from the aristocratic Church] and to claim for themselves the care of the spiritual content of life, of the Church and piety, of Christian morality.'[195]

My chief source of knowledge on Hus's trials and burning at the stake at the Council of Constance in 1415 is the eye-witness Peter of Mladoňovice's (c.1390–1451) *Relatio de Magistro Johannis Hus causa in Constantinensi consilio acta* (1415–16). The five stages of what would become the model Czech martyrdom are laid out in Peter's account. Hus goes voluntarily into a dangerous situation (Constance), is betrayed by his friends or disciples (Štěpán Páleč and Michal de Causis), writes letters to friends in Bohemia (often smuggled letters), is mocked (by prelates and doctors), and then is killed.

In the Wenceslas legend that first stage is linked with the prince's desire to become a martyr. In Hus's case fact provides a variant of the topos. Although he had a safe-conduct from King Sigismund, it is clear that Hus knew that he might be going to his death. Just before he leaves for Constance, he writes to his friend and fellow-preacher in the Bethlehem Chapel in Prague, Martin z Volyně, 'that he should not open it [the letter] before he is certain that he [Hus] has met some or other kind of death.'[196] One could argue that Hus was wary of bandits, but the group that set out with him was numerous and armed. Furthermore a passage in another letter he sent before he left, to the people of Prague, also contains a passage suggesting he could expect death in Constance: '[The Lord God] also suffered, and why should we not suffer? After all, our suffering in grace is the purging of our sins and riddance of eternal torment, and death is our victory.'[197] In Constance, Hus also says or writes phrases indicating his premonition – words which express his steadfastness, but also humility, and, most important, phrases that make for mythicizing. The clearest example runs thus: 'and if they ask me something, I hope I shall choose death rather than deny the Truth that I have from the Scriptures or have learned elsewhere.'[198]

Although Peter admires Hus, he also shows compassion for his physical and mental suffering, though he never allows that to interfere with the documentary nature of his account. In showing this compassion, however, Peter willynilly lays emphasis on Hus's ordinariness, as especially nineteenth and twentieth-century exploiters of the myth will demand. A description of his pallor during a hearing will serve as one example: 'he was now very pale, for, as those who were informed said, he had not slept the whole previous night because he had tooth-ache and a head-ache, and a fever was beginning to shake him.' The following constitutes a more vivid example: 'a bad fever and constipation came upon him with the result that there were doubts as to whether he would survive, and Pope John XXIII sent him his physicians, who administered a rectal enema in his cell.'[199]

Other passages in Peter's account could be employed by mythopoets to present Hus as a warrior against tyranny. He informs his reader twice about the security measures in and around the refectory where the hearings took place. Soldiers with swords, long-bows, axes and spears surround it. The detail into which Peter goes in describing Hus's execution and the subsequent treatment of his remains serves to contrast Hus's Christian meekness with the ecclesiastical authorities' unChristian brutality, and thus to demonstrate Hus's adherence to Truth and the authorities' to infernal lying:

Then, having tied his hands behind him to a sort of pillar, they stripped off his clothes and bound him to the aforesaid pillar with a rope. Now he was facing the East, and some of those standing around said, 'Do not let him point East, for he is a heretic. Turn him towards the West.' And that is what happened. Then, when they were attaching his neck [to the pillar] with some smoke-blackened chain, having taken a look at it, he smiled and said, 'The Lord Jesus Christ, my Saviour and Redeemer, was fettered with a harsher and heavier chain; wretch that I am, I am not ashamed to bear this one for the sake of His Name.' The stake resembled a thick plank about half a yard in breadth. Having sharpened it at one end, they knocked it into the earth of the aforesaid meadow. Then two faggots mixed with straw were placed around his body right up to his chin ... one could see him moving before he breathed his last for as long as it would take to say quickly two or, at most, three Lord's Prayers ... the henchmen knocked the corpse together with the stake onto the ground and, having fed the fire with a third barrow-load of wood, burnt it and crushed the bones with cudgels to accelerate its turning into ashes. And, having found the head, they smashed it into little pieces and threw it into the fire. Then, when they found the heart among the innards, they sharpened a staff and stuck it through the heart and roasted it.[200]

An emended and somewhat livelier Czech version of Peter of Mladoňovice's account was published in an incunabular passionary (1495, reprinted 1515). Two changes in the account are significant for the development of the Hus cult, for they indicate the adapter's intention of appealing to the broad masses. The first, though no doubt true to life, involves symbolism, which may suggest magic ritual, but could also constitute a intratextual symbol. Seven ropes are used to tie Hus to the stake which could correspond to the seven bishops presiding over the tribunal (naturally, one may not exclude the possibility that seven is used in accordance with medieval numerology to indicate a complete life-span): 'one rope over the top of the feet (or at the ankles), a second below the knees, a third above the knees, a fourth through the crotch, a fifth round the loins, a sixth round the midriff, and a seventh through the armpits.' The second change creates an emblematic link between the lowest classes and Hus in death. Where the chain round Hus's neck is simply 'smoke-blackened' in Peter, in the passionary we have 'a black and sooty chain, on which a poorman had hung his pot over a fire there.'[201]

The Hus cult grew during the fifteenth century, was upheld especially by the Utraquists during the sixteenth, but as far as it survived during the Counter-Reformation, it was an underground cult. The National Revival roused it again; Palacký gave it apparent intellectual justification, as did Masaryk, which meant that it survived among patriots and in schoolbooks during the First Republic. In the 1950s the cult was politicized and Hus became the inspirer of the great Czech medieval bourgeois revolution, an embodiment of the dearness of revolution to the Czech national soul.

St John Nepomucene

John Nepomucene (John of Nepomuk, Jan z Pomuka, Jan z Nepomuku), Masaryk's pseudomartyr, was a dull ecclesiastical bureaucrat, probably a Bohemian German, who was indeed a martyr to the extent that Thomas à Becket was a martyr. He died for obediently supporting the interests of the Church against the interests of the State (King Wenceslas IV). John Nepomucene represented no revolution, but the superiority of spiritual rules over secular. And where St Wenceslas and Hus became major cult figures soon or immediately after their deaths, John Nepomucene enjoyed only minor cult status until the seventeenth century and became the major cult figure, often outshining even Wenceslas, after his beatification (1721) and canonization (1729). Though Vlnas argues that the Counter-Reformation cultivated Nepomucene to displace, then replace the Hus cult, one is not entirely persuaded. He points out that Hus is frequently mentioned in Baroque writings and depicted in paintings, but that does not support his argument. What Vlnas has clearly noticed, but failed to express, is that Hus became a representative of the diabolical work of heresy and Nepomucene of the divine work of clerical obedience to the laws of God and the Church. The cult of John Nepomucene did, however, have as potent a political motivation as that of Wenceslas. The Czechs had a bad name in Europe as heretics and therefore were politically unreliable; the Bohemian clergy fostered the cult of Nepomucene and laboured relentlessly to have Rome acknowledge his sanctity because the new Czech Catholicism needed to be demonstrated to the rest of the world to ensure the Czechs' reception back into the 'civilized' Roman Catholic Europe.

The Bohemian Church in their pride in Nepomucene desired to provide the Czechs with 'support *against the contempt* in which the victorious Roman Catholic world held the Bohemian nation of heretics and rebels, to return self-confidence to the nation and to reinstate the respect for the Czechs abroad; the use of Nepomucene as a weapon against heretical echoes of the Hussite period was only a secondary element.'[202]

As far as Wenceslas is concerned, the only historical reality we can accept has to be taken from the tenth-century legends; it is certain that there was some sort of putsch in Bohemia and that one leader was Christian and pro-Western (the idea that Wenceslas was baptized by St Methodius constitutes a propagandistic accretion) and another leader who was not pro-Western, but may not have been pagan. Whether or not the Christian leader was the Wenceslas we know from the legends is unimportant. Hus's life is so well documented that the circumstances and causes of his martyrdom pose virtually no problems. The case of Nepomucene differs entirely from those of both Wenceslas and Hus. The historical Jan z Pomuka and the legendary Jan z Nepomuku are so tenuously connected that they amount to two quite distinct personalities; from the point of view of cultural history, the two figures are equally real.

The historical John was the son of Wölflin, mayor of the tiny market town of Pomuk in south-western Bohemia, which belonged to the nearby Cistercian monastery. František Stejskal has suggested that the discrepancy in name between the historical and legendary John derives from the fact that the monastery was Pomuk and its subject village Ne-Pomuk, the basis of the distinction lying in the verb *pomukávat*, 'to communicate by sounds which do not constitute speech' – the Cistercians as a silent order needed some code while going about their daily work. These sounds were used in Pomuk, but not in the little town, hence the name, non-Pomuk.[203] The little town was named both Pomuk and Nepomuk in contemporary documents. Jan (Johánek) z Pomuka became a notary public in the vicar-general's office of the Prague Archbishop, Jan Očko z Vlašimě. In 1373, he was involved in the tribunal investigating the activities of the so-called precursor of Hus, Jan Milíč. By 1380, his ecclesiastic career began to take off. He was appointed altar-chaplain for the side-chapel of SS Erhard and Otylia (before which he was later reburied) in St Vitus' Cathedral and was ordained soon afterwards, in 1380, when he became rector of St Gall's. In 1381, he receive his Ll.B. and, shortly afterwards, went to Padua to continue his studies; in 1386 became Vice-chancellor for ultramontane students there, in 1387 was awarded his doctorate in canon law, and then returned to Prague. In Bohemia he took three livings – two canonries and one archdeaconry. At the time that did not legally constitute pluralism, which is important since nineteenth-century patriots levelled against John not only the charge of being a German, but also a pluralist and, incidentally, a usurer – nothing supports the last, since he is known to have extended loans, but not to have charged any interest. In 1389, John became Archbishop Jan z Jenštejna's vicar-general and, at the end of 1392 or the very beginning of 1393, one of Wenceslas IV's favourites, Sigismund Huler had two clerics executed in Prague; John and another bureaucrat, Mikuláš Puchník, sent Huler a summons because he had taken legal action against clerics, who were not subject to secular law. Huler's action appears to have been part of Wenceslas's attempts to diminish the power of the archbishop. At this time the king was attempting to create another archbishopric in Western Bohemia, whose financial basis would be provided by Kladruby Abbey; the monks there, however, elected a new abbot, thus thwarting the king's plans and this election was confirmed by John on the archbishop's orders. The archbishop escaped the king's wrath, but four of his officials were arrested, including John and Puchník; three of them were then tortured and the king appears to have taken part in the torturing. When the king ordered the torturing to stop, he demanded a vow of silence from the victims. John could not swear, since he was unconscious and soon died, in the torture chamber; so the king ordered that his corpse be thrown into the river.

From this moment a legend began to grow, for Jan z Jenštejna went to Rome in the same year, 1393, where he composed an onslaught on King Wenceslas to present to the Pope; in this report he writes of his vicar-general as a 'holy martyr'.[204] Other words were soon written mentioning the martyrdom and the oral tradition was established by the time Pavel Žídek (1413–71) was writing his mirror for princes-cum-history book, *Jiří Spravovna* (Rule-book for George [of Poděbrady], completed 1471), that Jan z Pomuka had been the queen's confessor and had been martyred for refusing to reveal to the king secrets of the confessional. In the fifteenth-century *Staré letopisy české* (Old Czech annals), under the year 1392 (*sic*), although the reason for John's martyrdom remains the historically correct one, two further elements of the legend are present: John was drowned in the Vltava and his tombstone at St Vitus's has miraculous qualities: 'his name is engraved in the stone, on which there is also a cross; to this day no one can step on this cross.'[205] Finally, the date given for John's death in the bull of canonization is 1383. This mistake arose because, in his Czech chronicle (1541) Hájek found no way of making various accounts tally, and so came to the conclusion that two different Johns had been martyred by Wenceslas, one in 1383 for abiding by the secrecy of the confessional, another in 1393 for confirming the Kladruby abbacy.

The canonical *vita* of John Nepomucene was written by Bohuslav Balbín (1621–88), who lifted practically all his material from a manuscript *vita* by Jan Ignác Dlouhoveský (1638–1701).[206] Balbín published it in 1680 in the Bollandistes' *Acta sanctorum* and, in a slightly revised version, in his *Bohemia sancta* (1682). I take my account from the Czech version which was published in 1698, and then again, with small changes, in 1710.[207] Four of the five stages in the narration of the martyrdom are clearly present: (i) John goes voluntarily into a dangerous situation (facing the king's rage fearlessly twice; we note that previously the king had behaved towards him with respect, but suddenly changed his manner, because of evil advisers: the topos that we saw in the Wenceslas legend); (ii) John is not betrayed by anyone close to him, unless we interpret the king's change of heart as betrayal, certainly a tenable interpretation, for in an anonymous eighteenth-century play, known simply as *Hra o svatém Janu Nepomuckém* (Play about St John Nepomucene), the king and John are made former fellow-topers; the author appears to be consciously drawing a parallel with Thomas à Becket when he has Wenceslas say to John: 'And this is the John who used to drink wine with me, / who today pours me a cup of gall';[208] (iii) the equivalent of Hus's letter writing is John's sermon fierily preached after the king has him released from torture. History gives us no information suggesting that John was a preacher; this element in Balbín's *vita* constitutes a politically motivated element designed to make John eclipse precursors of Hus like Conrad Waldhauser. In his sermon, 'being full of the spirit of prophecy, weeping abundantly ... he described how heresy would rise up from Hell, so that there would be no distinction between the temporal and the spiritual; all churches and monasteries would be burnt down ... the almost complete destruction of the Church in Bohemia was nigh.'[209] (iv) John's mockery had taken place mainly before stage (iii), in the torture-chamber and at the king's residence, when he had had his cook roasted before John for serving an undercooked capon, though this mockery does continue when the king summons him as John is returning from a visit to the sacred Czech 'ninth-century' icon in Stará Boleslav, whither John had gone on a pilgrimage after his prophetic sermon. (v) John is killed by drowning, 'at night for fear of public uproar.' Balbín does not mention the five stars which, traditionally, flew up from the Vltava when John was thrown in and which form an essential element in his statues, but mentions 'an innumerable number of very bright lights, as if fire and water had merged'.[210] The eighteenth-century play does, however, at least allude to the stars, when Providence speaks of the 'five stones' linked with 'the man of the tongue'.[211]

The most intense period of the John Nepomucene cult covered the first half of the eighteenth century.[212] In the course of the beatification commission's enquiries, John's body was exhumed (1719). Inside his skull a large fleshy red lump was found and adjudged by clerics and leading physicians to be John's tongue; this miracle contributed a great deal to the Czech clerics' request for John's canonization. The faithful were permitted to kiss this tongue until 1866, when the authorities decided that the relic was deteriorating. The tongue was actually a clump of brain tissue which had been preserved for reasons which are apparently more or less explicable scientifically; the last scientific investigation, which conclusively demonstrated that it was brain tissue, took place in 1973.[213]

Colonel Švec

In the last stages of the National Revival, the Czechs appear to have felt the need to find a martyr linked with the Year of Revolutions. They chose the political journalist, Karel Havlíček, who had, indeed, been exiled to the South Tyrol (arrest December 1851, return, 1855), but died in Prague (1856). It is not at all clear whether there is even any truth in the conventional assertion that his exile in the Tyrol undermined his health; he lived there in considerable physical comfort, though he did suffer depressions because he was cut off from his friends and relations. He was frequently called a martyr, to which Masaryk objected more than once. Not until the twentieth century did the Czech 'martyr complex' again have any success in creating legends that had popular appeal.

The first was short-lived because world affairs did not allow it to survive the 1930s and, certainly, the Communists did not allow it to be revived; anyway, they had their own martyr. The subject of this first twentieth-century martyr cult was the Moravian Josef Jiří Švec (1883–1918). Švec became, in 1903, a master in a council school in Třebíč, where he rose to be the deputy-commander of the local branch of the Sokol patriotic gymnastics movement. In 1911 he was sent by the central office of Sokol to Russia to teach physical training in secondary schools, and in September 1914 he joined the Czech unit which eventually became the Czecho-Slovak Legion in Russia. He was promoted to colonel in August 1918, became commander of the First Division on 17 October, shot himself on 25 October and was buried in Chelyabinsk on 28 October, the day of the foundation of the First Republic – another case of history promoting myth. His remains were eventually brought to Prague, where they were interred on 1 October 1933; the next day another gymnast, Konrad Henlein published his declaration on the formation of the Sudetendeutsche Heimatsfront; thus Švec's second burial also acquired through history symbolic import.

At the time when Švec took command of the First Division, the Czecho-Slovak Legion was in disarray. Initially, the Allies had given it great support and its successes with the pre-revolutionary Russian Army against the Central Powers had made it a useful tool in negotiations with the Allies concerning the dissolution of the Habsburg Monarchy and the establishment of a Czecho-Slovak state. When the war was coming to a close, the Allies lost interest, and the few Allied troops there were in Russia made no attempt to make contact with the Legion. Even before he became commander, Švec wrote in a letter of 10 October:

In all this mire the Czech sections were left alone. The disruption of the Russian forces demoralized our soldiers terribly and had the effect that their fighting capacity sank to nil … when our men could see that the nation did not want to defend this country, they became firmly persuaded that they were fighting other people's causes;

that is why they are in such a hurry to leave this place.[214]

Švec was apparently 'the most popular of the legionary officers', but he had lied to his men, with the best of intentions, telling them that Allied aid was certainly on its way; still, when they refused to obey him, he was 'crushed', and, in Peroutka's version of the legend, 'It seemed to him that he could purge himself only in death … A little cynicism would have permitted him to go on living.'[215] Švec's men, however, were so shocked by his suicide that they went to the front, obeying his orders after his death.

Švec, like John Nepomucene and, indeed, the other two twentieth-century martyrs, represented the views of the intellectual elite that created his cult.

The most significant literary document of the Švec cult was a particularly tedious drama by the ex-legionary Rudolf Medek, which, naturally, received the State Prize for Literature. The pattern of Švec's martyrdom in Medek's version is consistent with that of my earlier examples. (i) Švec goes voluntarily into a dangerous situation (the Legion altogether, but mainly the defence of Kazan' and his risky retreat). (ii) He is betrayed by friends (first, by the Allies and the Whites, and then by his own men). (iii) He does not write letters home, which was impossible in the circumstances, but, instead he spends much of his time remembering South Bohemia and his sweetheart there. (iv) He is mocked (by his own men, but mainly by the Marxist Martyška). (v) He dies, or is, so to speak, killed by his men's mutiny; in the play, he commits suicide with the intention of convincing his men that they must go into battle.

When they are thus convinced, the representative of the socialists who had undermined the effectiveness of the Legion, Martyška, disappears. The all too stentorian argument of Medek's play is, however, not directed only against the cowardly Social Democrats, but also against Tolstoyan humanitarian pacifism (represented by the legionary Janda), and against Russians altogether. The one Slovak legionary is a mere caricature, but still Medek's aim is to demonstrate with his essayistic dialogues that the Czechoslovaks are Westerners and have nothing in common with Russians; traditional Czech Russophilia could affect the new Czechoslovakia only destructively, for the Czechs were, unfortunately, Slavs, and too much contact with the Russians could re-awaken that Slavness: 'We all have it in us. It's something wild, of the steppes, Asiatic and it has been slumbering at the bottom of our souls! Slav confusion, Slav indiscipline!'[216]

The messianic element of the Czech martyr complex is particularly evident in Medek's Švec legend. Švec perceives his own task in the world as to resist evil wherever and whenever it is to be found. He also declares that no sacrifice, even a human life, is too much to achieve the goal of making Czechoslovaks true men; although Medek is unaware of it, this is a version of the topos which entails the true martyr's expressing his burning desire to become a martyr. Švec's martyrdom does not have as many parallels with Christ's Passion as do Hus's and even

Wenceslas's, but, at least symbolically, his burial after three days is also his resurrection, for Švec is intended to represent the very spirit of the Czechoslovak Republic.

Julius Fučík

The Communist cult of the journalist and literary critic Julius Fučík (1903–43) was based largely on the account of the prelude to his martyrdom that he composed himself on paper that was smuggled out of the Pankrác prison where the Germans had interned him. The scraps of paper were collated and made into a book by his common-law wife, Gusta, and the Stalinist critic, Ladislav Štoll (1902–81), and entitled *Reportáž psaná na oprátce* (Report written on the noose, 1945). Gusta lived off the cult, becoming president of the Communist Women's Union, and publishing three books on Fučík; the last appeared at the beginning of the Normalization, that is, when urgent attempts were being made to re-invigorate the cult, *Život s Juliem Fučíkem* (Life with Julius Fučík, 1971). The cult was imposed with such force in the 1940s and 1950s that intellectuals suspected that Fučík's prison memoirs were a forgery (to a very limited degree, they were), that Fučík had been a coward and traitor and that he had not been executed by the Germans but had found luxurious refuge in South America. The seriousness with which the Communists treated the cult is eloquently transmitted by Jaromír Lang's virtually incoherent fury at 1960s scepticism:

In the second half of the 1960s they wanted to silence him, wipe his name from the memory of the people, silence this man who was so brave when faced by death, so great in his thought and work that his existence gives his death extra meaning, renders it greater in the ranks of glorious friends and comrades. They dared spit on his lifelong heroism. That great journalist of Havlíček and Neruda's ilk. These paltry creatures writing in *Reportér, Literární listy, Student* and, in the spring of 1968, many others, suddenly belittled his art, but what was worse, also his character as a man and a journalist ... In the 1950s many wrote theses about him. In the 1960s they were silent.[217]

Reportáž psaná na oprátce is a narcissistic work where the narrator projects himself as a naive boy proud at having survived terrible torture when the prison doctors had said he would die, a naive boy proud of his Communism and proud of having founded a Communist gymnastics organization (we notice the near parallel with Švec) and, finally, proud that he had revealed no secrets under torture. The Fučík legend also keeps to our martyrdom model. Fučík goes voluntarily into a dangerous situation (underground anti-German activity); he is betrayed by friends (mainly Mirek); he writes letters home (in this case the text of his memoirs); and he is killed. It is, however, difficult to claim that he is mocked, though he is, indeed, in Milan Kundera's version of the legend, the sentimental epic, *Poslední máj* (The last May, 1955).

Like Wenceslas, Nepomucene, Hus and Švec, the Fučík of the *Reportáž* narration believes that by suffering he is fighting for a truth that will outlive him, hence phrases like 'I press firmly the hands of all comrades who survive this last battle and who will come after us.' The last words of the *Reportáž* quickly became part of the Communist liturgy and were used as an inspiration for all manner of political hysteria: 'People, I loved you. Be on your guard!'

Kundera may have been inspired to a degree by Kohout's *Dobrá píseň*, for here, too, Fučík is Christ-like, albeit like Christ after the Resurrection. Like Wenceslas and John Nepomucene in their posthumous miracles, Fučík has the qualities of a revenant: 'When in the evening snow is falling on Prague / … Fučík walks through our city / inspecting the day's work'; 'He will be always amongst us / in the peace blossom of the apple trees/ in the happy eyes of young mothers / bending down to their children. / He builds factories and bridges with us, / he is always the same, straightforward and merry.'[218] In *Poslední máj*, Fučík combines the features of Christ with those of the Slovak bandit hero, Jánošík, but the Christ element dominates. The Gospel allusions are clear. The Gestapo man Böhm leads Fučík up the Petřín Hill in Prague, as Satan led Jesus to tempt him. Kundera's Fučík is a man of light like Christ, and, more important, a man of love like Christ: 'And Fučík smiles tenderly: / "Dead is he who lives without love."'[219] The satanic Böhm represents everything that destroys light and love, just like the richly clad prelates in the Hus legend or the anarchist, undisciplined Russians in Medek's Švec legend. And we are strongly reminded of Švec when Kundera has Fučík declaim: 'Communists will never be traitors, / to save their own lives. / They will not betray those for whom they lived. / After all, without them, a preserved life / would in their hands change / into mere vegetating, an empty dying / a river-bed where there is no river.'[220]

The cult of Fučík, directed mainly at youth, the new people of the socialist paradise, was centrally organized on a grand scale. The government awarded Fučík the posthumous title National Hero; Young Pioneer troops, local Komsomol organizations, schools, streets, mines and a huge park in Prague were named after him. The cultural award given by the Czechoslovak Komsomol was called the Fučík Badge (the awarding of these badges was wittily satirized by Škvorecký in *Tankový prapor* [The tank battalion, 1971]). *Reportáž*, as Macura remarks, 'was understood as a canonical text conserving the supreme truth.'[221] He also points out that the Fučík myth comported with ancient mythic cultures, and one presumes he is also thinking of Christ as a solar deity and of the Green Man: 'The Fučík myth manifests clear features of solar and calendar myths; its storyline concerns the death of a young god and his resurrection; the motifs of "youth", "the smile", "joy", "beauty" evidently correspond with an ancient archetype. The close link of the Fučík cult with spring corresponds with the same archetype.'[222]

Jan Palach

The Palach myth shares some of those features. He is also a solar deity of a kind. His self-immolation, the rays of his burning body in Wenceslas Place, represent the sun's self-consumption; his resurrection is embodied in the 'Palach Week' demonstrations of January 1989 and, particularly, in the Prague students' demonstrations of 17 November 1989 that started the 'Velvet Revolution'. And during the twenty years between Palach's suicide and the January demonstrations the memory remained alive like the memory of Christ in the disciples between Good Friday and Easter Day: 'Face to face with truncheons people felt still more duty-bound to Jan Palach, who with his death had wanted to warn people against violence ... As became clear in January, not only had people not forgotten over the twenty years, but young people who had not yet been born in 1969, adopted the memory of Jan Palach as their own.'[223]

The Palach cult began in January 1969, immediately after the young student had set himself on fire. Its beginnings were popular, very much like those of the 'patriot saints' and 'martyrs for liberty' during the French Revolution.[224] Even the renaming of the square in front of the Arts Faculty of Prague University, hitherto Red Soldiers' Square, 'Jan Palach Square' resulted from popular feeling; and, after its old name was returned, for a few months some tram-drivers still publicly called it Jan Palach Square. The cult did not become an official cult until 1989. The novelist Lenka Procházková published her emotional documentary account, *Jan Palach* (1990), as part of the new regime's series of commemorative political coffee-table books. And the pages are unnumbered as in some bibliophile edition (cf. Mihálik's *Rekviem*).

In the popular cult Palach's setting fire to himself as a demonstration against the Soviet occupation was immediately associated with the burning of Hus at the stake. In fact Palach's demands were modest (historically speaking, so were Hus's), the abolition of censorship and a ban on the propaganda paper, *Zprávy*. In the model for martyrological texts I have used in this section, the first stage is missing. Palach does not voluntarily enter a dangerous situation like Hus – before he sets fire to himself; the 'dangerous situation' of the occupation had been imposed on him. The second stage is present; he is betrayed, so to speak, by the woman who sees him set alight: '"For God's sake, young man, what have you done?" shouted some woman. "What are you young people doing to us?"'[225] The third stage is also present in that, previously to his suicide, he writes a letter (a note signed 'Torch No.1'). The mockery stage takes place after his death (particularly the police desecration of his grave; a bronze relief was attached to his tombstone in July 1970; on 18 July the police removed it and melted it down;

in October 1973 the police exhumed him, cremated his remains and sent his ashes to his mother who had to wait many months before she was permitted to bury them in Všetety). It takes Palach three days to die (another occasion on which fact promotes a myth), and while on his death-bed, he declares, 'I am not a suicide', a statement which may be said to be analogous to Wenceslas's desire to be a martyr, or Švec's. The words of a Czech student at the memorial ceremony for Palach (25 January 1969) coincidentally echo the words of one of Švec's fellow officers in Medek's play. The student proclaims that 'Jan Palach's act was not that of a desperate man ... It was a conscious protest and heroic deed, carried out on behalf of life. He did not sacrifice himself only for his generation, but for everyone in this country, for the whole world.' Thus, for his contemporaries, too, Palach, like Fučík, dies to save mankind.

In a sense, then, one might say that the Czech martyr complex itself represents an expression of that collectivism the Revivalists saw in the Slavs. The national martyr obliterates his personal identity for the sake of the nation's identity.

NOTES

1. Introduction: questions of identity and responsibility

1 References to Havel's works will be given in parentheses by a date, thus:

1963   (with Věra Poláčková), *Josef Čapek*, Prague, 1963.

1964   *Zahradní slavnost. Hra o čtyřech dějstvích* (The garden party, A play in four acts), Prague, 1964.

1966   *Protokoly* (Protocols), Prague, 1966.

1968   *Ztížená možnost soustředění* (The increased difficulty of concentration), supplement to the periodical *Divadlo*, May 1968 (appeared as book, 1969).

1977   *Hry 1970-1976* (Plays, 1970–76), Toronto, 1977.

1984   *O lidskou identitu* (Towards human identity), London, 1984.

1985a   *Dopisy Olze (červen 1979-září 1982)* (Letters to Olga, June 1979–September 1982), Toronto, 1985.

1985b   *Largo desolato. Hra o sedmi obrazech* (Largo desolato. A play in seven scenes), Munich, 1985.

1986   *Pokoušení. Hra o deseti obrazech* (Temptation. A play in ten scenes), Munich, 1986.

1988a   *Dálkový výslech (Rozhovor s Karlem Hvížďalou)* (Long-Distance Interrogation. A conversation with Karel Hvížďala), 2nd ed., London, n.d. [1988?] (Published in English as *Disturbing the Peace*).

1988b   *Asanace. Hra o pěti jednáních* (Redevelopment. A play in five acts), Munich, 1988.

1989   *Do různých stran. Eseje a články z let 1983-1989* (In various directions. Essays and articles, 1983–1989), Scheinfeld-Schwarzenberg, 1989.

1990   *Projevy. Leden-červen 1990* (Speeches, January–June, 1990), Prague, 1990.

1991   *Letní přemítání* (Summer meditations), Prague, 1991.

1992a   *Hry. Soubor her z let 1963-1988* (Plays. Collected plays, 1963–88), Prague, 1992.

1992b   *Vážení občané, (Projevy červenec 1990-červenec 1992)* (Dear citizens. Speeches, July 1990–July 1992), Prague, 1992.

2 The first Czech writer to express Slav consciousness was Daniel Adam z Veleslavína (1546–99), but awareness of the linguistic affinities of Czechs to Poles or Russians or Serbs is occasionally expressed by Czech writers from the fourteenth century onwards, for example by Martin Kabátník (d.1503), who came across a Serbian mameluke in Cairo. The term 'panslavism' was first used by a Slovak, Johan Herkel, in his *Elementa*

universalis linguae Slavicae (1826). See also Albert Pražák, 'The Slovak Sources of Kollár's Pan-Slavism', *Slavonic and East European Review*, 6, (1927–28), pp.579–92.

3 T. G. Masaryk, *Česká otázka,* 7th ed., Prague, 1969, pp.7–9.

4 See, for example, Marcuse's remarks in the 'Political Preface 1966' to his *Eros and Civilization: A Philosophical Inquiry into Freud* [1955], Boston, 1974, p.xxi.

5 Jan Patočka, *O smysl dneška*, 2nd ed., London, 1987, p.10. Most of the first edition (Prague, 1969) was destroyed by the authorities. When in the early days Havel broke taboos as president, he did have some direction. Rushing about the corridors of the presidential palace on a scooter or throwing the National Day diplomatic party at the Castle open to virtually all comers, or inviting his advisers to a business lunch and insisting that everyone paid for him or herself, was intended to serve, first, to dismantle the socialist regime's granite wall around leaders and, secondly, to fulfil a new democracy, a more thorough democracy than that of the First Republic.

6 It is, however, at least of passing interest that three of the most popular Czech writers of the twentieth century, Jaroslav Hašek (1883–1923), Karel Čapek (1890–1938) and Havel himself, have an unsexed approach to women in their *belles lettres*.

7 As we learn from Eda Kriseová's generally infantile biography of Havel, there was a literary streak in his family. His maternal grandfather, Hugo Vavrečka, was the author of the extremely popular play, *Lelíček ve službách Sherlocka Holmese*, and his paternal grandfather, Václav Havel, produced and wrote cabaret with the poet and dramatist, Jaroslav Kvapil (1868–1950) and the novelist Ignát Herrmann (1854–1935). *Václav Havel. Životopis*, Brno, 1991, pp.28 and 33.

8 See V. Havel, 'Poslední rozhovor' in Adolf Müller (ed.), *Jan Patočka - Osobnost a dílo*, Cologne, Index, 1980, p.107.

9 In a book of political journalism, where he uses quotations from Havel's plays – particularly *Zahradní slavnost* and *Asanace* – essays and speeches to attack his politics especially on the splitting of Czechoslovakia, Slavomír Ravik, sees this zeal as 'traditional Czech messianism', *Zahradní slavnost pro 15 miliónů*, Prague, 1993, p.10.

10 Bernard Bolzano, *Über das Verhältniss der beiden Volkstämme in Böhmen. Drei Vorträge im Jahre 1816 an der Hochschule zu Prag gehalten,* Vienna, 1849, p.37.

11 Ibid., p.36.

12 T. G. Masaryk, *Otázka sociální. Základy marxismu filosofické a sociologické* [1898], 3rd rev. ed. reprinted, Prague, Čin, 1946, vol.II, pp.230–33.

13 Patočka, *O smysl dneška*, p.146.

14 Havel himself disliked the appellation 'dissident'. In Czech the word has been used at least since the beginning of the seventeenth century to mean a (religious) dissenter. Those in opposition to the Communist government, though not necessarily to socialism itself, liked to be known as 'independent thinkers'.

15 The dates I give to Havel's plays are those of the first Czech printing in book-form in Czechoslovakia or abroad. *Samizdat* and foreign-language editions are not taken into consideration. Typescript *samizdat* editions are not publications and foreign-language editions are not the author's text. One play I mention, *Protest*, appeared only in *Hry* (1992), see note 1.

16 Havel may have been slightly indebted to Václav Bělohradský (born 1944), who had written about the way, ultimately through Machiavelli, the state had become divorced from conscience and personal responsibility: for the state had to accept only the rational

(the objective) and dismissed personal moral values as 'pure subjectivism' (*Krize eschatalogie neosobnosti*, London, 1982, passim).

17 Masaryk, *Otázka sociální*, vol.II, p.238.

18 Jan Patočka, *Kačířské eseje o filozofii dějin*, Munich, 1980, pp.96–7. These essays began circulating in a *samizdat* edition in 1975, which is significant for Havel's perception of the link between identity and responsibility.

19 This play had its first stage performance in Vienna in 1976. It was first published in book-form in *Hry 1970-1976*.

20 Patočka, *O smysl dneška*, p.13.

21 Bělohradský, *Krize eschatologie neosobnosti*, p.29.

22 Patočka, *Kacířské eseje*, p.133.

23 Jan Patočka, 'Proč nemá Charta 77 být zveřejňována...' (1977) in Müller, *Jan Patočka – Osobnost a dílo*, p.89.

24 Masaryk, *Česká otázka*, p.220.

25 T. G. Masaryk, *Naše nynější krise. Pád strany staročeské a počátkové směrů nových*, 2nd ed., Prague, 1908, p.240.

26 Masaryk, *Otázka sociální*, vol.I, p.406.

27 T. G. Masaryk, *Sur le Bolchévisme*, Geneva, p.19.

28 Masaryk, *Česká otázka*, p.155.

29 Masaryk, *Naše nynější krise*, p.241.

30 Ibid., p.355.

31 T. G. Masaryk, *Karel Havlíček - Snahy a tužby politického probuzení*, 2nd rev. ed., Prague, 1904, p.519.

32 Patočka, *Kacířské eseje*, pp.19 and 33.

33 Masaryk, *Naše nynější krise*, p.314.

34 Masaryk, *Otázka sociální*, vol., II, p.23.

35 Havel uses the term 'posttotalitarian' differently from the way it has been used in English over the last few years. In English it means 'postsocialist' or 'postcommunist'; Havel's is analogous to Marcuse's use of the term 'postindustrial': it means a socialist society in which ideology has assumed an entirely ritual function, where the ritual no longer has any relationship to any set of beliefs.

36 Patočka, *Kacířské eseje*, p.50.

37 Ibid., p.81.

38 Ibid., p.105.

39 Masaryk, *Naše nynější krise*, pp.217–18.

40 Masaryk, *Otázka sociální*, vol.I, p.8.

41 Masaryk, *Sur le Bolchévisme*, p.7.

42 Emanuel Rádl, *Krise inteligence*, Prague, 1928, p.33.

43 Emanuel Rádl, *O čtení děl básnických*, Prague, 1934 (colophon; title page: 1935), for example, p.6.

44 Before the Communist Party introduced the term 'normalization' to denote 'Brezhnevization', it had used 'consolidation'.

45 Masaryk, *Naše nynější krise*, p.207.

46 Masaryk, *Otázka sociální*, vol.I. p.113.

47 Patočka, *Kacířské eseje*, p.115.

48 Masaryk, *Světová revoluce. Za války a ve válce 1914-1918*, Prague, 1925, p.210.

49 Bolzano,*Über das Verhältniss...*, p.38.
50 T. G. Masaryk, *Ideály humanitní (Několik kapitol)* [1901]. Here *Ideály humanitní. Problém malého národa. Demokratism v politice*, Prague, Melantrich, 1968, p.15.
51 The performing of this play in 1963 was a landmark in the post-Stalinist era in Czech culture. The sight and sound of the dourly dressed, depressed audience in almost sustained laughter, becoming normal human beings, during the play's first run was extraordinary.
52 Masaryk, *Otázka sociální*, vol.I, p.299.
53 Ibid., p.300.
54 I am aware of the difficulty of defining cliché and of deciding at what stage a word or phrase becomes a cliché. I am also aware that clichés can be used to express one's identification with a past age, as for example in the Czech Decadent poet, Karásek's collection of verse, *Sodoma* (1895, confiscated; 2nd ed. 1905). Here, however, I use 'cliché', within the conceptual framework of Havel's writing.
55 Rádl, *Krise inteligence*, p.x.
56 Patočka, *Kacířské eseje*, p.104.
57 Ibid., p.76.
58 Psychotronics was a specialist study of the military and political application of the occult which was taken very seriously by Warsaw Pact countries. That had its own ironies. While, for example, the Bulgarian secret police had its own special department for the tracking down of religious, mystical and occultist groups, the Bulgarian intelligence services actively recruited occultists and people rumoured to be psychic. The term has now come into use in a non-political sense covering anything from 'alternative religion' to 'alternative medicine' or telepathy.

2. The Myth of Slavness: Pavel Josef Šafařík and Jan Kollár

1 Cf. Northrop Frye, *The Great Code. The Bible and Literature*, San Diego, New York, London, 1983, p.50.
2 Eric Dardel, 'The Mythic', in Alan Dundes (ed.), *Sacred Narrative. Readings in the Theory of Myth*, Berkeley, Los Angeles, London, p.226.
3 Frye, *The Great Code*, p.37.
4 Leszek Kołakowski, *The Presence of Myth* [1972], translated by Adam Czerniawski, Chicago and London, 1989, p.2.
5 Bronislaw Malinowski, 'The Role of Myth in Life', in Dundes, *Sacred Narrative*, p.199.
6 In this book I use 'Hungarian' to mean someone living in the Lands of the Crown of St Stephen and 'Magyar' for someone whose native language was Hungarian or who considered himself to belong to the Magyar race.
7 Cf. Elie Kedourie, *Nationalism*, revised edition, London, Melbourne, 1985.
8 Leslie Spencer, 'Elites, Nationalism, and Régime Legitimacy – Czechoslovakia and Yugoslavia', *Slovo: A Journal of Contemporary Soviet & East European Affairs*, 1, 1 (May, 1988), p.37.
9 Ernest Gellner, *Nations and Nationalism*, Oxford, 1983, p.7.
10 Kedourie, *Nationalism*, p.9.

11 Miroslav Hroch, *Social Preconditions of National Revival in Europe: A Comparative Analysis of the Social Composition of Patriotic Groups among the Smaller European Nations*, translated by Ben Fowkes, Cambridge, London, 1985, pp.3 and 5.

12 Ideology or metaphysic may contain or be based on myths and myths may help to form or may grow out of ideology. I am not trying to fudge the issue.

13 John Plamenatz, 'Two Types of Nationalism', in Eugene Kamenka (ed.), *Nationalism. The Nature and Evolution of an Idea*, London, 1976, pp.23–4.

14 Gellner, *Nations and Nationalism*, p.33.

15 Kedourie, *Nationalism*, pp.73–4.

16 Peter Brock, *The Slovak National Awakening. An Essay in the Intellectual History of East Central Europe*, Toronto and Buffalo, 1976, p.24. Brock's account of Šafařík and Kollár's careers is reliable in general, but occasionally not in detail.

17 Stanislav Šmatlák, *Dejiny slovenskej literatúry od stredoveku po súčasnosť*, Bratislava, 1988, p.285.

18 František Palacký, *Spisy drobné*, III, *Spisy aesthetické a literární*, ed. Leander Čech, Prague, n.d., p.520.

19 Pavel Josef Šafařík, *Dejiny slovanského jazyka a literatúry všetkých nárečí*, translated by Valéria Beťákova and Rudolf Beťák, Bratislava, 1963, p.238. Šafařík's surname is a problem; he published under the variants, semi-Hungarian name Safáry, German Schaffarik and Czech, Šaffařík. As far as I know he never used the Slovak form Šafárik which has now been adopted by Slovak scholars. This work will henceforth be called *Geschichte* in my text; references will be G and page number.

20 See Jaroslav Vlček, 'Šafařík na slovanském jihu', in Josef Hanuš *et al.*, *Literatura česká devatenáctého století*, II, *Od M. Zd. Poláka ke K. J. Erbenovi*, 1930, pp.571-72, and Jan Jakubec, *Dějiny literatury české*, II, *Od osvícenství po družinu Máje*, Prague, 1934, p.520. Jakubec's long essay on Šafařík here is more rewarding for the student than the much more recent, but tedious, *Pavel Josef Šafařík* by Karel Paul (Prague, 1961), though the latter has a useful bibliography.

21 *Über die literarische Wechselseitigkeit zwischen den verschiedenen Stämmen und Mundarten der slawischen Nation* [Pest, 1837; 2nd corrected ed., Leipzig, 1844], Miloš Weingart (ed.), Jan Kollár, *Rozpravy o slovanské vzájemnosti*, Prague, 1929, p.63. This essay will henceforth be called *Wechselseitigkeit* in my text; references will be W and page number.

22 Pavel Josef Šafařík, *Slovanské starožitnosti. Oddíl dějepisný. Okres druhý. Od l. 476 před* [i.e. *po*] *Kr. až do l. 988 po Kr.*, Prague, 1863, p.666. Henceforth references as SSII and page number.

23 Jakubec, *Dějiny*, p.524.

24 Lubor Niederle, 'Šafaříkovy "Slovanské starožitnosti"', in Hanuš *et al.*, *Literatura česká*, p.594.

25 Ibid., pp.595–7.

26 Jakubec, *Dějiny*, p.526.

27 Niederle, 'Šafaříkovy "Slovanské starožitnosti"', p.589.

28 The germ of *Slávy dcera* lies in Kollár's first book of verse, *Básně* (Poems, 1821), which contains eighty-six sonnets. The first *Slávy dcera*, called by the author 'second edition' was published in 1824 and had 151 sonnets; the next version, 1832, had 615, and by the fourth version of 1852 there were 645.

29 Šmatlák, *Dejiny*, p.289.

30 Cf. Felix Vodička, *Cesty a cíle obrozenské literatury*, Prague, 1958, p.160.

31 Jan Jakubec, 'Kollár básník a buditel', in Hanuš, *Literatura česká*, p.218.

32 Jakubec, *Dějiny*, pp.520-21.

33 The whole of the Polish Romantic's assessment is published in František Bačkovský, *Zevrubné dějiny českého písemnictví doby nové*, Prague, 1886, pp.542–5.

34 Jan Kollár, *Paměti z mladších let života* (Memoirs of my youth), Prague, 1863, p.203. References to this work henceforth as P and page number.

35 Jan Kollár, *Cestopis obsahující cestu do Horní Itálie a odtud přes Tyrolsko a Bavorsko se zvláštním ohledem na slavjanské živly roku 1841 konanou* (A travel journal containing a journey made in 1841 to Upper Italy and thence through the Tyrol and Bavaria with special attention paid to Slavonic elements), Prague, 1862, p.110. This work will henceforth be called *Cestopis* in my text; references will be C and page number.

36 Jan Kollár, *Nábožný pohled na tu krajinu, která jest matka evanjelickej víry. Kázeň při návratu odtud (Vypracována na utěšenej plavbě Dunajskej mezi Řeznem a Vídňou).* (A pious look at the land which is the mother of the Lutheran faith. A sermon given on returning from there, written on a pleasant cruise on the Danube between Ratisbon and Vienna), Pest, 1835, p.5. This work will henceforth be called *Nábožný pohled* in my text; references will be N and page number.

37 Cf. Kedourie, *Nationalism*, pp.37–8.

38 This extract is from a volume of essays, letters, polemics, extracts, initiated and edited by Kollár in reaction to Štúr's codification of a Slovak literary language. Kollár was the author of most of the volume although some parts which he clearly either wrote or for which he told the writer what to write are published under the name of minor Slovak clerics and schoolmasters: *Hlasové o potřebě jednoty spisovného jazyka pro Čechy, Moravany a Slováky* (Voices or: Votes for the need of a unified literary language for Bohemians, Moravians and Slovaks), Prague, 1846, p.176. This volume will henceforth be called *Hlasové* in my text; references will be H and page number.

39 Johann Gottfried Herder, *Ideen zur Philosophie der Geschichte der Menschheit*, Wiesbaden, 1985, p.433.

40 Jan Kollár, *Dobré vlastnosti národu slovanského* (The good qualities of the Slav nation), in the Weingart edition (see note 21), p.8. This sermon will henceforth be called *Dobré vlastnosti* in my text; references will be D and page number.

41 Anton Štefánek, *Kollárov nacionalizmus (Homoetnologická štúdia)*, Prague, 1937, pp.6–7.

42 Jaroslav Vlček, *Dějiny české literatury*, II, Prague, 1960, p.331.

43 Jiří Krystýnek, *Z dějin polsko-českých literárních vztahů: Vlivy polské literatury a její recepce v českých zemích v letech 1914-1939*, Brno, 1966, pp.17–18.

44 See Jiří Krystýnek, 'Slovanská idea u Antonína Marka', Artur Závodský (ed.), *Franku Wollmanovi k sedmdesátinám. Sborník prací*, Prague, 1958, p.107.

45 The article is printed *in toto* in Bačkovský's *Zevrubné dejiny*, pp.562-3.

46 Jan Kollár, 'O literárnej vzájemnosti mezi kmeny a nárečími slávskými', in Weingart edition (see note 21), p.130. This essay will henceforth be called 'O literárnej vzájemnosti'; references will be LV and page number.

47 Jan Kollár, *Básně*, Prague, 1952, p.351.

48 The section from the *Rozpravy o jménech* ... which deals with Slav Reciprocity is

included in the Weingart edition (see note 21); I quote here from p.29. This section will henceforth be called *Rozpravy o jménech* in my text.

49   Felix Vodička, 'Jan Kollár', in Felix Vodička (ed.), *Dějiny české literatury, II, Literatura národního obrození*, Prague, 1960, p.265.

50   Kollár, *Básně*, p.361.

51   Gershon Scholem, *Major Trends in Jewish Mysticism*, Jerusalem, 1941, p.92.

52   Pavel Josef Šafařík, *Slovanské starožitnosti. Oddíl dějepisný Okres první. Od l. 456 před Kr. až do l. 469-76 po Kr.*, Prague, 1862, pp.279 and 488. Henceforth references as SSI and page number.

53   Jan Kollár, *Výklad čili Přímětky a vysvětlivky ku Slávy dceře* (Explication or Remarks and explanations to *Slávy dcera*), Pest, 1832, p.250. This book will henceforth be called *Výklad*; page references will be V and page number.

54   Palacký, *Spisy drobné*, p.737.

55   Vodička, *Cesty a cíle*, p.158.

56   Šmatlák, *Dejiny*, p.285.

57   In the Herderian sense.

58   Jaroslav Purš and Miroslav Kropilák (eds), *Přehled dějin Československa, I/1 (do roku 1526)*, Prague, 1980, pp.37–53. This account has not been questioned in post-socialist times, see Ivan Rada *et al.*, *Dějiny zemí koruny české*, I, Prague, 1992, p.24.

59   Francis Dvornik, *The Slavs and Their Early History and Civilization*, Boston, 1956, p.13. Dvornik is also strongly, blindly, in favour of a Moravian origin for Slav literary culture; Bulgaria and Greece take very much second place.

60   Niederle, 'Šafaříkovy "Slovanské starožitnosti"', p.599.

61   Jan Kollár, *Cestopis druhý* (Second travel journal), Prague, 1863, p.31. References to this work will henceforth be CD and page number.

62   The Czech historian, Pavel Stránský ze Zapské Stránky (1583–1657), refers in his pamphlet, *Okřik* (Hullabaloo, written 1618, but not published until the early 20th century), to the derivation, Slav–*sláva*. He also writes of 'Slovak' and 'Slav' as synonyms.

63   Herder, *Ideen zur Philosophie der Geschichte*, p.434.

64   Ibid., pp.433–5.

65   In Czech there is a pun. Kollár rarely has games with sacred language. 'Já se obávám, aby Čechové své vlastenectví a svou národnost naposledy sami, v nejvlastnějším smyslu toho slova, neprohráli a nepromuzikovali.'

66   He uses the word *Řeč* which could refer to a grand national language, to *jazyk*, or to what our authors call a dialect, *nářečí*.

67   Bee-keeping is at present considered historically a particularly Slovak occupation largely as a result of Peter Jaroš's turgid mythopoeic novel, *Tisícročná včela* (The thousand-year-old bee, 1977).

68   Frye, *The Great Code*, p.48.

69   Kollár, *Básně*, p.50.

70   Vladimír Macura, *Znamení zrodu: České obrození jako kulturní typ*, Prague, 1983, p.104. Incidentally, the oak frequently represents the female principle in the sense that it often represented the mother goddess in Indo-European religion. It is clear that Kollár was unaware that the Bohemians were reputed in the Middle Ages to go into battle with a linden branch on their banner. George T. Gillespie, *A Catalogue of Persons*

Named in German Heroic Literature (700-1600), Oxford, 1973, pp.9–10.
71 For details see Jakubec, 'Kollár básník a buditel', p.184.
72 Raffaele Pettazzoni, 'The Truth of Myth'; Dundes, *Sacred Narrative*, p.102.
73 Kołakowski, *The Presence of Myth*, p.82.
74 Macura, *Znamení zrodu*, p.107.
75 Kedourie, *Nationalism*, p.87.
76 Kołakowski, *The Presence of Myth*, p.32.
77 As far as I know, Kollár's is the first use of the word 'modernism' in Czech literature.

3. The Decadent Self

1 Cf. Tom Cribbs, paraphrasing L. L. Whyte, 'only after Descartes' drastic separation of the self-aware subject from that which it is aware of did it become necessary to invent an unconscious. Previously, men had got by with a loosely held, holistic set of assumptions about the mind.' In Peter Collier and Judy Davies (eds), *Modernism and the European Unconscious*, Cambridge, 1990, p.72.
2 Bernard Shaw, 'The Sanity of Art' [1895, rev. ed., 1908], in *Major Critical Essays*, ed. Michael Holroyd, Harmondsworth, 1986, p.353.
3 'Eigentlichen Untergangszentrum', Hermann Broch, *Hofmannsthal und seine Zeit. Eine Studie* [1948], *Schriften zur Literatur, 1, Kritik*, Frankfurt on Main, 1975, pp.265 and 271.
4 Carl E. Schorske, *Fin-de-siècle Vienna. Politics and Culture*, New York, 1981, p.4.
5 Tomáš Vlček, *Sen, ideál a skutečnost*, Pilsen, 1987, p.6.
6 Viktor Dyk, interpolated poem in 'Privilegium, Akta působnosti "Čertova Kopyta", Episoda Tacitova', *Hučí jez a jiné prosy* [1901], *Spisy Viktoria Dyka*, II, *Počátky, Prósy mladosti*, Prague, 1919, pp.113–14.
7 James Joll, *The Anarchists*, 2nd ed., London, 1979, p.154.
8 Cf. Joan Ungersma Halperin, *Félix Fénéon, Aesthete and Anarchist in Fin-de-siècle Paris*, New Haven and London, 1988, p.265.
9 Gustave Lanson, *Histoire de la littérature française* [1894], 18th ed., Paris, 1924, p.1093.
10 F. X. Šalda, *Kritické projevy I*, Prague, 1949, p.11.
11 Walter Pater, 'Amiel's "Journal Intime"', *Essays from 'The Guardian'* [1901], Library Edition, 1910, pp.24–5.
12 Hugo von Hofmannsthal, *Ausgewählte Werke in zwei Bänden*, II, *Erzählungen und Aufsätze*, Berlin, Darmstadt, Vienna, n.d., p.271.
13 Ibid., pp. 277 and 278.
14 Karel Červinka, *Hledání samoty*, Prague, 1897, pages unnumbered.
15 Max Stirner, *Der Einzige und sein Eigenum und andere Schriften*, edited by Hans G. Helms, Munich, 1968, pp.16–17. Henceforth references given in brackets in text as 'Stirner' and page number.
16 Henri-Frédéric Amiel, *Fragments d'un journal intime*, edited by Edmond Scherer, Vienne, n.d., v.I, p.19. Henceforth references given in brackets in text as 'Amiel', volume and page number.
17 Gilbert Ryle, *On Thinking*, Oxford, 1979, p.52.

18 Cf. Christopher Janaway, *Self and World in Schopenhauer's Philosophy*, Oxford, 1989, pp.43–4.

19 Though one not infrequently hears Nietzsche called a Decadent, probably the one philosoper to arise from within the decadent trend was the Czech, Ladislav Klíma.

20 Maurice Barrès, *Un Homme libre* in *Le Culte du Moi* [1888-91], Paris, 1966, p. 218.

21 Cf. Jonathan Glover, *I; The Philosophy and Psychology of Personal Identity*, Harmondsworth, 1988, pp. 66–7.

22 Masao Miyoshi, *The Divided Self. A Perspective on the Literature of the Victorians*, New York and London, 1969, p.x.

23 Ibid., p.xv.

24 Ibid., p.335.

25 Frederick Garber, *The Autonomy of the Self from Richardson to Huysmans*, Princeton and Guildford, 1982, pp.ix–x.

26 When I use Austria in this chapter, I include the Bohemian Lands.

27 Garber, *The Autonomy of the Self*, pp.269, 292, 274, 142. Examples of such self-consuming failures are Schnitzler's Gustl and Zeyer's Jan Maria Plojhar or Rojko.

28 Cf. Janaway, *Self and World*, pp.7 and 122.

29 Cf. ibid., pp.7 and 122.

30 Ibid., pp.269–70.

31 Ibid., p.8.

32 Friedrich Nietzsche, *Der Antichrist. Ecce Homo. Dionysus-Dithyramben*, Munich, 1978, p.140.

33 Ibid.

34 Thomas Nagel, 'The Egocentric Predicament', *London Review of Books*, 11, 10 (18 May 1989), p.7.

35 Peter Carruthers, *The Metaphysics of the 'Tractatus'*, Cambridge, 1990, p.83.

36 Ibid., p.84.

37 David Hume, *An Inquiry Concerning Human Understanding* with a supplement *An Abstract of a Treatise of Human Nature*, edited by Charles W. Hendel, Indianapolis, 1977, p.23n.

38 *An Abstract*, ibid., p.194.

39 Walter Pater, *The Renaissance, Studies in Art and Poetry* [1873], Shilling Edition, London, 1912, pp.248–9.

40 Alan Macfarlane, *The Origins of English Individualism*, corrected ed., Oxford, 1979, p.5.

41 See, for example, Bohumil Svozil (ed.), *Česká básnická moderna. Poezie z konce 19. století*, Prague, 1987, p.20.

42 Broch, *Hofmannsthal und seine Zeit*, p.215.

43 F. V. Krejčí *et al.*, 'Česká Moderna', *Rozhledy sociální, politické a literární*, 1895–96, p.1.

44 *Un Homme libre*, p.239.

45 Cf. *Ausgewählte Werke*, p.276.

46 Gustav Meyrink, *Das grüne Gesicht. Ein okkulter Schlüsselroman* [1916], Munich, 1987, p.140.

47 An informative discussion of the role of memory as criterial of personal identity is to be found in the pieces by Richard Wollheim and A. J. Ayer in G. F. Macdonald (ed.),

Perception and Identity. Essays Presented to A. J. Ayer with His Replies to Them, London and Basingstoke, 1979, pp.186–233 and 318–24.

48 Cf. Glover, *I*, pp.149–50.

49 Janaway, *Self and World*, p.131

50 Ibid., p.149.

51 *Das grüne Gesicht*, p.164.

52 Jiří Karásek ze Lvovic, *Scarabaeus*, Prague, 1908, p.41.

53 Charles Baudelaire, *Journaux intimes*, ed. Jacques Crépet and Georges Blin, Paris, 1949, p.60.

54 Cf., for example, Renee Winegarten, *Writers and Revolution. The Fatal Lure of Action*, New York, 1974, p.223.

55 The notion of objective nationality and of 'foreign things' has been commented on by Roger Collins: 'Despite the persistent efforts of scholars to believe the contrary, artefacts are not necessarily ethnospecific: a fibula or belt-buckle is only as "Ostrogothic" or "Frankish" as its owner felt him or herself to be.' 'Reinventing the Germans', *Times Literary Supplement* No.4492 (5–11 May, 1989), p.492.

56 Baudelaire, *Journaux intimes*, p.64.

57 Max Nordau, *Die conventionellen Lügen der Kulturmenschheit*, Leipzig, 1883.

58 Cf. Robert B. Pynsent, 'The Decadent Nation: The Politics of Arnošt Procházka and Jiří Karásek ze Lvovic', László Péter and Robert B. Pynsent (eds), *Intellectuals and the Future in the Habsburg Monarchy, 1890-1914*, London, 1988, pp.74–7.

59 Ryle, *On Thinking*, p.39.

60 Broch, *Hofmannsthal und seine Zeit*, p.124.

61 Ibid., p.275.

62 Oscar Wilde, *The Works*, London and Glasgow, 1948, p.909.

63 Ibid., p.898.

64 Broch, *Hofmannsthal und seine Zeit*, p.192.

65 Schorske, *Fin-de-siècle Vienna*, p.310.

66 Ibid., p.9.

67 Hugo von Hofmannsthal, *Die Gedichte und kleinen Dramen*, 2nd ed., Leipzig, 1912, p.78. My translation is coldly literal, makes no attempt at rendering the author's almost facetious elegance.

68 Karel Hlaváček, *Básně* (*Dílo*, II), Prague, 1930, p.59.

69 Matthew Arnold, 'On the Modern Element in Literature', *Essays*, London, Edinburgh, etc., 1914, p.468. Cf. also Hofmannsthal, in 'Gabriele d'Annunzio': 'Man treibt Anatomie des eignen Seelenlebens, oder man träumt. Reflexion oder Phantasie, Spiegelbild oder Traumbild,' *Ausgewählte Werke*, II, p.293.

70 This passage may have inspired F. X. Šalda in his one novel, *Loutky i dělníci boží* (Puppets and workers of God, 1917), where he satirizes the old men in 1890s Vienna as 'aged Fauns, Satyrs and Silenuses' trying to make themselves look better and more beautiful than they are, 3rd ed., Prague, 1920, vol.II, pp.35–6.

71 Bram Dijkstra, *Idols of Perversity*, New York, 1986.

72 Glover, *I*, p.122.

73 Ibid., p.64.

74 Hofmannsthal, *Ausgewählte Werke*, II, p.277.

75 Schorske, *Fin-de-Siècle Vienna*, p.22.

76 'Der Dichter und diese Zeit. Ein Vortrag', *Ausgewählte Werke*, II, pp.445.
77 Schorske, *Fin-de-Siècle Vienna*, p.242.
78 Cf. Raymond Furness, *Wagner and Literature*, Manchester and New York, 1982, p.2.
79 Hofmannsthal, *Die Gedichte und kleinen Dramen*, pp.14–5.
80 Meyrink, *Das grüne Gesicht*, p.164.
81 Edelgard Hajek, *Literatrischer Jungendstil. Vergleichende Studien zur Dichtung und Malerei um 1900*, Düsseldorf, 1971, p.80.
82 Arthur Schopenhauer, *Die Welt als Wille und Vorstellung, II/2*, Zurich, 1977, p.717.
83 Ibid., p.715.
84 Meyrink, *Das grüne Gesicht*, p.164.
85 Glover, *I*, p.57.
86 Baudelaire, *Journaux intimes*, p.24.
87 Broch, *Hofmannsthal und seine Zeit*, p.123.
88 Ibid., p.130.
89 Ibid., pp.141 and 219. One is reminded of Nietzsche: 'What have I never forgiven Wagner? That he *descended* to the level of the Germans – that he became *reichsdeutsch* … As far as Germany reaches, she ruins culture.' *Ecce Homo*, p.117.
90 Charles Baudelaire, *L'Art romantique. Littérature et musique*, ed. James Austin, Paris, 1968, p.267.
91 Ibid., p.272.
92 Barrès, *Le Culte du Moi*, p.16.
93 'Gabriele d'Annunzio', *Ausgewählte Werke*, II, p.293.
94 Paul Verlaine, *Choix de poésies*, 14th thousand, Paris, 1898, p.22.
95 Hlaváček, *Básně*, p.88.
96 Eugen Weber, *France Fin-de-Siècle*, Cambridge, Mass., and London, 1986, p.149.
97 A. E. Carter, *The Idea of Decadence in French Literature 1830-1900*, Toronto, 1958, p.84.
98 Friedrich Nietzsche, *Zur Genealogie der Moral. Eine Streitschrift* [1887], Munich, 1983, p.84 (final ellipsis in original).
99 Quoted by Janaway, *Self and World*, p.231.
100 I have given an account of the version of the dandy produced by the Czech Arthur Breisky and the Austrian German Richard von Schaukal in my 'Conclusory Essay', Robert B. Pynsent (ed.), *Decadence and Innovation*, London, 1989, pp.172–8. I do not wish to repeat myself here.
101 Baudelaire, *Journaux intimes*, p.22.
102 Ibid., p.73.
103 Richard Schaukal, *Vom Geschmack. Zeitgemässe Laienpredigten über das Thema Kultur*, Munich, 1910, p.189. Compare Nietzsche's 'Every style is *good* which truly communicates an inner state,' *Ecce Homo*, p.130.
104 Janaway, *Self and World*, pp.354–5.
105 Kathleen V. Wilkes, *Real People. Personal Identity without Thought Experiments*, Oxford, 1988, p.145.
106 Flora Rheta Schreiber, *Sybil. The True Story of a Woman Possessed by Sixteen Separate Personalities*, Harmondsworth, 1975, p.99.
107 Glover, *I*, p.28.
108 Fugue in the psychiatric sense: when one person (A) for no apparent reason becomes

'someone else' (B) where A has no memory of B's life or vice versa.
109 Hofmannsthal, 'Gabriele d'Annunzio', *Ausgewählte Werke*, II, p.292.
110 Gustav Meyrink, *Der Golem. Roman*. [1915], Munich, 1970, p.192. The other, esoteric, meaning of this sentence – which refers to the possible eternal series of Messiahs, and to the human arrogance of expecting a Messiah, is irrelevant to the study of the Decadent self. Probably.
111 Garber, *The Autonomy of the Self*, p.275.
112 Hlaváček, *Básně*, p.46.
113 Verlaine, *Choix de poésies*, p.253.
114 Richard Le Gallienne, *English Poems* [1894], 4th ed., London and New York, 1900, p.85. John M. Munro takes this poem too seriously, because he takes it in isolation from the rest of the collection and the rest of the poet's works: *The Decadent Poetry of the Eighteen-Nineties*, Beirut, 1970, p.24.
115 Wilde, *The Works*, p.920.
116 Northrop Frye, *The Stubborn Structure. Essays on Criticism and Society*, London and New York, 1970, p.54.
117 Glover, *I*, p.118.
118 Quoted from *Geschlecht und Charakter* by Furness, in *Wagner and Literature*, p.107.
119 Martin Swales in Péter and Pynsent, *Intellectuals and the Future*, p.17.
120 Glover, *I*, p.129.
121 Ibid., p.125.
122 Arthur Symons, 'The Tarot Cards', *Knave of Hearts, 1894-1908*, London, 1913, p.53.
123 Glover, *I*, p.110.
124 Sigmund Freud, *The Interpretation of Dreams*, Harmondsworth, 1976, pp. 214f. and 417–18.

4. Conclusion: Czech self-definition through martyrs

1 'I knew the error of the Czechs, / I knew the power of Rome, / I knew everything except myself.' By 'the Czechs' he, naturally, meant the Hussites. See François Villon, *The Complete Works/Uevres complettes*, ed. Anthony Bonner, New York, 1964, p.136.
2 Miloš Marten, *Nad městem. Dialog*, Vinohrady, 1917, p.29.
3 Otakar Theer, *Háje, kde se tančí* (1897) in *Básnické spisy*, Prague, 1930, p.250.
4 Ibid., pp.11–12.
5 Ibid., p.36.
6 Vladimír Macura, *Šťastný věk. Symboly, emblémy a mýty 1948-1989*, Prague, 1992, pp.106–7.
7 Arnošt Procházka, *Na okraj doby*, Prague, 1919, p.112.
8 Jiří Karásek, *Ideje zítřku*, Prague, 1898, p.47.
9 Jiří Karásek, *Bezcestí*, Velké Meziříčí, 1893, p.116.
10 S. K. Neumann, *Apostrofy hrdé a vášnivé* [1896], *Básně*, I, Prague, 1962, p.127.
11 Rudolf Krupička, *Velký stil*, 2nd ed., Prague, pp.61–2.
12 Jiří Karásek ze Lvovic, *Impressionisté a ironikové. Dokumenty k psychologii literární. Kritické studie*, Prague, 1903, p.123.
13 Arnošt Procházka, *Meditace*, Prague, 1912, p.122.

14   I.e. *kaislerlich und königlich*, imperial and royal, something that is part of the Austro-Hungarian imperial state structure.

15   Viktor Dyk, *Prosinec*, Prague, 1906, p.15.

16   See Ferdinand Mojš, *Slovensko pôjde do neba. Od naivity k realite, s.l.* [Bratislava?], 1992, p.16. This work constitutes reams of crackbrained blether. (The title of Mojš's squib alluding to the song *Gipsies go to Heaven*.) Vital reading for the Church's attitude to Tiso is Ivan Kamenec, Vilém Prečan and Stanislav Škvoránek (eds), *Vatikán a Slovenská republika (1939-1945). Dokumenty*, Bratislava, 1992; many of these documents has been previously published in P. Blet *et al.* (eds), *Actes et documents du Saint Siège relatifs à la Seconde guerre mondiale*, Vatican, 1965–81. Of Tiso we read in a note sent to Rome by the Vatican chargé d'affaires in Bratislava, Giuseppe Burzio, on 5 September 1940: 'And the good Slovak people try to understand, but do not succeed and, embarrassed, they listen to the oratorial acrobatics of their beloved President Tiso, who draws on every source of his sacred profane rhetoric to explain the necessity of building a 'Populist' (or Hlinkaite) Slovakia in the rhythm of National Socialism and, using more or less appropriate quotations from the Gospel, he calls upon the Slovaks to renew themselves in the water and spirit of National Socialism' (*Vatikán a Slovenská republika*, pp.48–9).

17   Štefan Polakovič, *Obnova národa duchom Štúra*, Bratislava, n.d. [1991?], p.11.

18   Vladimír Macura, *Masarykovy boty a jiné semi(o)fejetony*, Prague, 1993, p.11.

19   Havel, *Vážení občané*, p.64.

20   Macura, *Masarykovy boty*, pp.40–1.

21   Ľudovít Štúr, 'Zásluhy Slovanů o evropejskou civilisaci' (1840), in D*ielo*, II, *Slovania, bratia!*, ed. Jozef Ambruš, Bratislava, 1956, p.164.

22   Ľudovít Štúr, *Starý i nový věk Slováků* (manuscript from end of 1841, first publ. in book form, 1935), ibid., p.80.

23   Vladimír Mináč, *Tu žije národ*, Bratislava, 1982, p.63.

24   St Adalbert (Vojtěch) was elected bishop of Prague in 982. (Prague did not have an archbishop until 1344.) Adalbert baptized (or had baptized) Prince Géza shortly before his own death (997); the Prague bishop did, indeed, baptize Géza's son, St Stephen, the first king of Hungary. In fact, the Bavarian dioceses, not the 'Slovaks' or Bohemians, were the first to put pressure on Géza to become a Christian.

25   Štúr, *Starý i nový věk Slováků*, p.81.

26   Ibid., p.85.

27   There is no room here to consider the role of the gentry as subjects or authors of Slovak literature. Suffice it to say that the Slovak gentry were evident enough in rural Slovak life for Hviezdoslav (1849–1921), himself from the gentry, to write about the need for the gentry to intermarry with the Slovak peasantry, to improve their genes and accept more 'modern' social values (see *Ežo Vlkolinský*, 1890). One of the most influential literary and political figures in Slovakia between the wars, Janko Jesenský (1874–1945), came from a particularly distinguished gentry family. The term 'gentry', in the context of Hungarian history, refers to the lowest level of nobility, has nothing to do with wealth. Indeed, the 'sandalled gentry' with their wooden swords, were often a butt of satire in Slovak and Hungarian writing. Also, at least traditionally, the Slovak gentry ensured the acceptance of Štúr Slovak, see Peter Sýkora, *Boj s drakom*, Bratislava, 1992, pp.76–104, *passim*.

28 At least in their cups, one has heard Slovaks state that the Jews had been lackeys of the Magyars, had kept the Slovak villager in the bondage of debt and so helped repress the Slovak underdogs. Though antisemitism is not at all common amongst the Slovak intelligentsia, that there is a problem was clear when the VPN was splitting into liberal and left-wing-cum-nationalist factions and the liberal was nicknamed the 'Jewish faction' because of three leading figures in it, Fedor Gál, who is Jewish, the literary scholar, Peter Zajac, who is half-Jewish, and the sociologist and fiction-writer, Martin Bútora, who is not Jewish at all.

29 Dušan Mitana, *Koniec hry*, Bratislava, 1984, p.201.

30 The second edition of Beneš's *Problém alkoholové výroby a abstinence*, published, Prague, 1947, by the Czechoslovak Temperence Assocation, will interest the cultural historian of things Czech for the one major revision apart from the updated statistical tables. After an account of the massive quantity of alcohol produced in Russia (last statistic, 1913), Beneš has inserted a lengthy passage on how the Communists have changed things there. One may interpret the following as a reflection of post-1945 worship of the liberators, or of the growing power of the Communist Party in Czechoslovakia immediately after the war, or of a weak-spinedness of the kind Patočka saw in Beneš. In spite of its intolerable style, and though the choice of words may well not have been Beneš's, I quote the passage (pp. 20–1) *in toto* for its documentary value: 'Today in the USSR, it is taken as self-evident that alcohol is detrimental to efficiency and safety at work, and for this reason, there is practically never any drinking at work anywhere. Transgressions of the rule are punished by fines and public reprimands, and the most distressing punishment is the communal contempt a citizen receives for "irresponsibly attaining a state of insanity during working hours." / And representatives of labour or of public life, whether in the highest governmental and official posts or in regional or local soviets, consider it their automatic duty to set an example in the organization of their time and energy and in spending their free time sensibly, healthily and purposefully. That is why the people's confidence in their superiors and respect for and recognition of their work are growing. That is also the source of the vast majority of the population's incontravertable ambition in work and culture, for examples draw followers and good experience is persuasive. / Thus, it is a great mistake or deliberate slander to spread the idea that alcoholism is still rampant in the Soviet Union, as it had been in Tsarist times, or as it sometimes develops in revolutions or wars.'.

31 T. G. Masaryk, *O alkoholismu* [1906], 6th ed., Brno, 1938, p.11.

32 Ibid., p.21.

33 This term is doubtless no longer politically correct. What I mean is that form of 'received pronunciation' and grammar which used to be called the King's English or BBC English or Oxford English, roughly speaking that English spoken by products of major public schools and, indeed, until recently (1970s), educated people as a whole in the South of England, Inverness and Southern Eire.

34 The neatly distilled version presented in his lecture, 'Origin of Nation', *Times Higher Education Supplement*, 8 January 1993, pp.15–16.

35 Referring to the Hungarians in Slovakia as a national minority has the same connotations as referring to the Scots and Welsh as national minorities in the United Kingdom. A French national may be a Breton or Basque; a Slovak national may be only a Slovak,

though a Hungarian may be a citizen of the Slovak Republic. See also Ján Dekan's statement: 'A nation is an historically evolving social organism. Its integrative basis is the ethnolinguistic identity of society at various levels of socioeconomical development. This identity is supported by a consciousness of historical continuity, but also ideological discontinuity, in individual periods. … one may accept the thesis that the historical consciousness of the nation forms the ineluctable base-line of its modern socialist consciousness' (Introduction to Matúš Kučera, *Postavy veľkomoravskej histórie*, Martin, 1986, p.5).

36 See Anton Bagin, *Apoštoli Slovanov. Cyril a Metod a Veľká Morava*, Bratislava, 1987, pp.15–24.

37 Kučera, *Postavy veľkomoravskej histórie*, p.21.

38 Ibid., p.25.

39 Ibid., p.19.

40 Jaroslav Purš and Miroslav Kropilák (eds), *Přehled dějin Československa I/1 (do roku 1526)*, Prague, 1980, pp.57–8.

41 Petr Čornej, Ivana Čornejová, Ivan Rada and Vratislav Vaníček, *Dějiny zemí Koruny české. I. Od příchodu Slovanů do roku 1740*, Prague, 1992, p.25.

42 Kučera, *Postavy veľkomoravskej histórie*, pp.39–44.

43 Ibid., p.50.

44 See Bagin, *Apoštoli Slovanov*, pp.35–9.

45 Kučera, *Postavy veľkomoravskej histórie*, p.50. He does mention Alcuin in another context, for his identification of the *imperium Francorum* with the *imperium Christianum*, p.121.

46 Štúr, *Starý a nový vek Slováků*, p.74.

47 It is not known when Pribina became prince of Nitra, i.e. the first 'Slovak' prince, but *c*.833 his lands were annexed by Mojmír I of Moravia, and thus begins the Great Moravian Empire. He fled to the Franks and the East Frankish King, Lewis the German, gave him sanctuary and had him baptized. In 840 he became a Frankish magnate when Lewis gave him an hereditary fief in Lower Pannonia; he established his seat at Blatengrad (Mosaburg, today's Zalavár) by Lake Balaton. It is thought that the Nitra principality probably covered virtually all of today's Slovakia except the South East.

48 Ľudovít Štúr, *O poézii slovanskej* (a series of lectures Štúr gave in his flat after having lost his post at the Lutheran lyceum in Pressburg; they survive only in the notes taken by three of his pupils), ed., Pavol Vongrej, Martin, 1987, p.80.

49 Kučera, *Postavy veľkomoravskej histórie*, p.73.

50 Josef Pekař, *Z duchovních dějin českých*, ed., Josef Klik, Prague, 1941, p.15; Jan Patočka, *Was sind die Tschechen? Kleiner Tatsachenbericht und Erklärungsversuch*, 2nd ed. (with parallel Czech translation, 1st ed.), Prague, 1992, p.124. In the following account I leave Kučera's label 'Slovak' without commentary.

51 This work is important for the semantic content of the word, 'Slovak', which appears simply to have meant Slavs east of Bohemia and Moravia, excluding Russia. Describing Cyril and Methodius pleading in Rome for Slavs to be allowed to conduct divine services in Slavonic, Hájek z Libočan, *Kronika česká*, ed. V. Flajšhans, vol.I, Prague, 1918, p.361, uses 'Slovak' to mean Slav. In the margin note concerning Methodius' taking papal bulls to the Bulgarians and Croatians allowing them to celebrate Mass in Slavonic, Hájek writes 'The Pope permits the Slovaks.' Ibid., p.363.

52 Štúr, *Starý a nový věk Slováků*, p.75. Štúr's date for Mojmír's accession (?) has no historical basis. The Moravians are first mentioned in an historical document in 822, among a list of mainly Slav nations who had come to Frankfurt on Main to pay tribute to the emperor. Mojmír is first mentioned as Rastislav's uncle in 846. Kučera, *Postavy veľkomoravskej histórie*, pp.80 and 89.

53 Ibid., p.127.

54 Quoted by Kučera, ibid., p.168.

55 Ibid., p.132. Bagin is far less enthusiastic: 'Some scholars hold the opinion that she [Mary] came from a Slav family' (*Apoštoli Slovanov*, p.65).

56 Quoted by Bagin, ibid., p.122.

57 They have that status also in Bulgaria, a land which has, unlike Slovakia, many saints of its own. The Bulgarian National Day is the feast of SS Cyril and Methodius (24 May). Under socialism it was called the Day of the Slavonic Alphabet.

58 It did not appear 1866–8.

59 See Jan Jakubec, *Dějiny literatury české, II, Od osvícenství po družinu Máje*, Prague, 1934, p.635.

60 František Sušil, 'Sv. Cyrill a Method', *Básně*, Brno, 1847, p.156.

61 Svetozar Hurban Vajanský, 'Azbuka', *Literatúra a národ. Kritiky a články*, I, Bratislava, 1989, p.110.

62 See Bagin, *Apoštoli Slovanov*, p.198.

63 Štúr, *Starý a nový věk Slováků*, pp.83–4.

64 Kučera, *Postavy veľkomoravskej histórie*, p.234.

65 He is now also *Ján* Kollár instead of *Jan* Kollár as he called himself. So too Kalinčák is Kalinčiak. Authors of the period when Slovaks wrote in Czech go through greater transformations. The Polish priest, Jerzy Trzanowski (1592–1637), wrote in Latin and Czech; the Czech version of his name which he normally used was Jiřík Třanovský, but Slovak critics normally refer to him as Juraj Tranovský; he did work in Upper Hungary from 1629 till his death, because as a Protestant he was driven to flee the Bohemian Lands. Such name changing constitutes something like a legitimization of ownership. It is analogous to the mixed territorial and ethnic criteria used to judge what historical personages are Slovak. One is often told that the leader of the Hungarian War of Independence, Lajos Kossuth, was a Slovak or a half-Slovak: his father was Magyar and his mother German, but he came from Upper Hungary. A Slovak born and living in, say, the Vojvodina, however, remains a Slovak, is not called a Serb. This all sounds bizarre, but it has become simply a national custom. Its original inspiration may have been radically nationalist, but the custom has completely smothered the inspiration.

66 Polakovič, *Obnova národa duchom Štúra*, p.19.

67 Ibid., p.11.

68 The word *szláv*, literally 'Slav', looks more ambiguous than it is. For example, in the 1861 report of the Committee on the Nationality Question, the nationalities listed are Magyar, *szláv*, Romanian, German, Serbian and Ruthenian, so that it was quite clear that *szláv* meant Slovak. Tisza may well, however, be using it ironically, given the flippancy of his whole answer, because *nemzet* itself, though by 1875 it certainly generally meant 'nation', still had undertones of the meaning *natio*, i.e. more or less the nobility.

69 See Gábor Kemény (ed.), *Iratok a nemzetiségi kérdés történetehez Magyarországon a dualizmus korában*, vol.I, Budapest, 1952, p.516.

70 Polakovič, *Obnova národa duchom Štúra*, p.37.

71 The establishment of the Dual Monarchy in 1867 had stimulated anti-Magyar feeling among the Czechs straightaway. Through the *Ausgleich* the Magyars had become an 'oppressor nation' *de jure*, whereas they had previously been such only *de facto*; furthermore, before 1867 it had been at least possible to perceive the Magyars as fellow draymen under the Habsburg yoke.

72 Štúr, *Starý a nový věk Slováků*, p.76.

73 Štúr, *O poézii slovanskej*, p.92.

74 Ibid., p.80.

75 Ibid., p.62.

76 Macura, *Znamení zrodu*, p.22.

77 Kučera, *Postavy veľkomoravskej histórie*, p.12.

78 Arnošt Procházka, *České kritiky*, Prague, 1912, p.260.

79 Some writers on the fringe of the circle were from time to time passionately concerned about the Germans, for example, Antonín Sova (1864–1928) and Viktor Dyk.

80 Josef Pekař, *Smysl českých dějin. O nový názor na české dějiny*, 2nd, rev., ed., Prague, 1929, p.16.

81 Emanuel Rádl, *Válka Čechů s Němci*, Prague, 1928, p.140.

82 Ibid., p.95.

83 This is the automatic asociation: *Děvín* from *dievka*, *děva*, 'girl'; the Czechs call or called Magdeburg 'Děvín', and a formerly Roman fortress on the outskirts of Bratislava is Devín.

84 Petr Piťha, *Dvě tváře českého vychovatelství. Ludmila Přemyslovna a Jan Amos Komenský*, Prague, 1992, p.27.

85 Ibid., p.28. Piťha is here also echoing Mácha's *Máj*.

86 Rádl, *Válka Čechů s Němci*, p.60. The lack of ideal in Czech culture recurs as a theme of Rádl's writing. See, for example, his words on post-World War I Czechoslovakia: 'Let us not be led astray by our demagogical age accustomed as it is only to caricature ideas.' *O čtení děl básnických*, Prague, 1935 [colophon: 1934], p.33.

87 Quoted by Josef Pekař in *Bílá hora* [1922], reprint, Purley, 1986, p.74.

88 Pekař, *Smysl českých dějin*, p.14.

89 Pekař, *Bílá hora*, p.105.

90 Jiří Karásek ze Lvovic, *Tvůrcové a epigoni*, Prague, 1927, p.124.

91 Marten, *Nad městem*, p.13.

92 Ibid., p.15.

93 Jiří Karásek ze Lvovic, *Legenda o ctih. Marii Elektě z Ježíše*, Prague, 1922, p.30.

94 Marten, *Nad městem*, p.18.

95 Ibid., p.19.

96 Rádl, *Válka Čechů s Němci*, p.81.

97 Pavel Stránský ze Zapské Stránky, *Český stát. Okřik*, ed. Bohumil Ryba, Prague, 1953, p.365.

98 Ibid., pp.371–2.

99 Ibid., p.373.

100 Bohuslav Balbín, *Obrana jazyka slovanského zvláště českého*, ed. and trans. Josef

Dostál, Prague, 1923, p.8.

101 E. J. Hobsbawm, 'Ethnicity and Nationalism in Europe Today', *Anthropology Today*, 8, 1 (February 1992), p.3.

102 Sigismund was King of Hungary, 1387–1437, was crowned King of Bohemia in 1420 but did not rule during the Hussite Wars, and so ruled Bohemia effectively only 1436–8. He became Holy Roman Emperor in 1433, though had been German king since 1410.

103 Havel, *Projevy*, p.14.

104 Vladimír Mináč, *Zvony zvonia na deň* (1961), third part of a trilogy published in one volume as *Generácia*, Bratislava, 1979, p.543.

105 Macura, *Šťastný věk*, p.13.

106 Macura, *Masarykovy boty*, pp.23–4.

107 J. Křen, *František Palacký*, 2nd, corrected ed., Valašské Meziříčí, 1898, pp.7 and 9.

108 Patočka, *Was sind die Tschechen?*, p.208.

109 Ibid., p.119.

110 T. G. Masaryk, *Zur russichen Geschichts-und Religionsphilosophie. Sociologische Skizzen*, normally known as *Russland und Europa* (1913).

111 Pekař had started lecturing on Austrian history at Prague University in 1897, and his first substantial work, on Wallenstein, had been published in 1895. The 1912 attack on Masaryk was *Masarykova česká filosofie*, of which an expanded edition appeared in 1927. I do not intend to discuss Pekař's disagreements with Masaryk except in a few details. For an analysis of the whole matter, see Karel Brušák, 'The Meaning of Czech History: Pekař versus Masaryk' in László Péter and Robert B. Pynsent (eds), *Intellectuals and the Future in the Habsburg Monarchy*, London, 1988, pp.92–106.

112 Pekař, *Smysl českých dějin*, p.5.

113 Ibid., pp.6–7.

114 Pekař, *Smysl českých dějin*, pp.19–20.

115 Pekař, *Z duchovních dějin českých*, p.79.

116 See Pekař, *Smysl českých dějin*, pp.10 and 18.

117 Ibid., p.26.

118 See ibid., p.28.

119 Ibid., p.30.

120 Ibid., p.57.

121 Pekař, *Z duchovních dějin českých*, p.144.

122 Patočka, *Was sind die Tschechen?*, p.118.

123 Ibid., p.115.

124 Ibid., p.168.

125 Ibid., pp.177–8.

126 Ibid., p.178.

127 Patočka, *O smysl dneška*, pp.92–3.

128 Ibid., p.98.

129 Ibid., p.101.

130 Ľudovít Štúr, *Die Beschwerden und Klagen der Slaven in Ungarn über die gesetzwidrigen Übergriffe der Magyaren* (Leipzig, 1843), in *Dielo*, II, pp.116–17.

131 Patočka, *Was sind die Tschechen?*, p.115. After this Patočka speaks of Czech Revival literature as literature for the common people, which may be true of some of it, perhaps

especially in drama, but was certainly not true of the elitist products of the mainstream (in drama, Turinský). Altogether, Patočka's remarks on literature tend to be invalid, whether it be writing of Bridel that his best known verse work constituted simply a catechism in verse, or the confusing of Chelčický with Štítný, or the repeated statement that Palacký was a Hungarian. Most frequently, Patočka simply quotes uncritically and without comment from Arne Novák (1880–1939). He would have done better to omit the literary side altogether and keep to his more or less sociological approach.

132 Patočka, *O smysl dneška*, p.106.

133 Ibid., p.146.

134 Patočka, *Was sind die Tschechen?*, p.210.

135 Ibid., p.183.

136 See ibid., p.189.

137 Patočka, *O smysl dneška*, p.149.

138 Patočka, *Was sind die Tschechen?*, pp.219 and 221.

139 However much blame one might attach to Edvard Beneš, I have few doubts that most of the blame should be borne by the British.

140 See Macura, *Šťastný věk*, p.16.

141 Štúr, *O poézii slovanskej*, p.23.

142 Ibid., p.45. Compare this with Milan Kundera's words in *Člověk zahrada širá* (Man, a great garden), Prague, 1953: 'Now I know that it is treachery / to live alone and for oneself', p.11 and 'Let him who wishes to live / alone, without his people, burn up in grief', p.43.

143 Macura, *Šťastný věk*, p.62.

144 Published under the pseudonym, Jan David, *Ruce Goliášovy. Verše 21. VIII-2.X.1968*, Prague, 1990, pp.14–17. The text was to be broadcast in Czechoslovakia by Radio Free Europe from Munich in part or as a whole on various occasions over the twenty years of Normalization.

145 Štúr, *O poézii slovanskej*, p.86.

146 Ibid., p.68.

147 Kundera, *Člověk zahrada širá*, p.37.

148 Štúr, *O poézii slovanskej*, pp.69–70.

149 Ibid., p.93.

150 Josef Holeček, *Jak u nás žijou a umírají* [1898], Prague, 1949, p.12.

151 Ibid., p.97.

152 Božena Viková-Kunětická, *Z cest. Obrázky a studie, 1894-1912*, Prague, 1919, p.23.

153 Macura, *Šťastný věk*, pp.37–8.

154 Pavel Kohout, *Dobrá píseň. Veršovaná lyrická veselohra o mládeži naší doby ve 3 jednáních (9 obrazech)*, Prague, 1952, p.143.

155 Ibid., p.7.

156 Ibid., pp.55–6.

157 Kundera, *Člověk zahrada širá*, pp.30–1.

158 Štúr, *Starý i nový věk Slováků*, p.74.

159 See, for example, Vít Vlnas, *Jan Nepomucký, česká legenda*, Prague, 1993, p.69.

160 Antonín Marek, 'Marek Jungmannovi' (1814) in Karel Polák (ed.), *Počátky novočeského básnictví*, Prague, 1950, pp.120–1.

161 Ľudovít Štúr, 'Panslavism a naša krajina' (1847), in *Dielo*, II, pp.240–5.

162 *Listy Ľudovíta Štúra*, I, ed. Jozef Ambruš, Bratislava, 1954, p.351.
163 Štúr, *O poézii slovanskej*, p.87.
164 Arnošt Procházka, *Diář literární a umělecký*, Prague, 1919, p.338.
165 Polakovič, *Obnova národa duchom Štúra*, p.47. The Slovak for 'birds of a feather' is *vrana k vrane sadá*, cf. 'Jackdaw to jackdaw' in Aristotle's *Ethics*; 'like will to like' is used by Homer, but best known as quoted by Cicero: *'pares cum paribus*. Polakovič also writes of the 'more than a thousand-year-old soul of the nation' p.75.
166 Kundera, *Člověk zahrada širá*, p.49.
167 Macura, *Masarykovy boty*, p.76.
168 Havel, *Vážení občané*, p.17.
169 Macura, *Šťastný věk,*, p.7.
170 See Vladimir Karbusicky, *Anfänge der historischen Überlieferung in Böhmen*, Cologne and Vienna, 1980, pp.80–1.
171 Patočka, *Was sind die Tschechen?*, p.127.
172 See Macura, *Masarykovy boty*, p.36.
173 See ibid., p.37.
174 Macura, *Šťastný věk*, p.52.
175 Even if he was Redlich's bastard, as persistent tittle-tattle maintains, his home background was certainly humble.
176 Jan Rokyta, *President Masaryk. Báseň k jeho sedmdesátým narozeninám*, Prague, 1920, pages unnumbered.
177 This refers to paragraphs 19 and 20 of Comenius's *Kšaft umírající matky Jednoty bratrské* (1650).
178 For a few other examples of the Masaryk cult, see the Introduction to Robert B. Pynsent (ed.), *T. G. Masaryk (1850-1937), 2, Thinker and Critic*, London, 1989, pp.1–9.
179 Vojtech Mihálik, *Rekviem*, Banská Bystrica, 1968, pages unnumbered.
180 Macura, *Masarykovy boty*, p.71.
181 Jiří Karásek ze Lvovic, *Renaissanční touhy v umění* [1902], 2nd ed., Prague, 1926, p.90.
182 Dyk, *Prosinec*, p.276.
183 Emil Tréval, *Na prahu Kanaanu. Román z dob současných*, Prague, 1919, p.266.
184 Macura, *Masarykovy boty*, p.76.
185 For the same reason the priest Toufar who was tortured to death and whose lot forms the *leitmotiv* of Škvorecký's *Mirákl* (1974), the vile but greatly pitied Communist boss, Slánský, executed in the 1950s, or the dissident Wonka, who died in prison, or Jan Zajíc, who followed Palach's example, have no place (at the moment) in a Czech literary martyrology. But nor does Wenceslas' grandmother, St Ludmila, whose cult grew later than Wenceslas's, but has left no lasting mark on Czech culture. One notes that she was strangled, thus did not achieve the dignity of true bloody martyrdom normally reserved for men in the western Church at that time. The Baroque cult of the Moravian Jan Sarkander never really took off. Jerome of Prague was as heroic as Horáková and a brilliant intellectual, but for some reason he did not appeal to the Czech popular imagination.
186 Havel, *Projevy*, pp.65–6.
187 Vlnas, *Jan Nepomucký*, p.226. This carol was greatly disapproved of by hymnologists who considered it 'doggerel', as 'poor and commonplace to the last degree' and hoped

that it 'might gradually pass into disuse' (Percy Dearmer, R. Vaughan Williams, Martin Shaw, *The Oxford Book of Carols*, London, 1928, p.271).

188 Those who support the pre-eminence of the Latin legends consider the oldest to be *Crescente fide* (970s) and the slightly later *vita* of Bishop Gumpold of Mantua.

189 For the dating, see the excellently annotated edition, A. I. Rogov, E. Bláhová and V. Konzal (eds), *Staroslověnské legendy českého původu. Nejstarší kapitoly z dějin česko-ruských kulturních vztahů*, Prague, 1976, pp.57–8. For the Slavonic I have used this edition and for Christianus, Oldřich Králík (ed.), *Nejstarší legendy přemyslovských Čech*, Prague, 1969.

190 Zdeněk Kalista (ed.), *Život a sláva sv. Václava*, Prague, 1941, pp.42 and 129.

191 Patočka, *Wer sind die Tschechen?*, p.125.

192 Pekař, *Z duchovních dějin českých*, p.46.

193 See Čornej *et al.*, *Dějiny zemí Koruny české*, I, p.35.

194 Pekař, *Z duchovních dějin českých*, p.48.

195 Patočka, *Wer sind die Tschechen?*, p.159.

196 Petr z Maldoňovic, *Zpráva o mistru Janu Husovi v Kostnici*, ed., Zdeněk Fiala, trans. František Heřmanský, Prague, 1965, p.73.

197 Ibid., p.75.

198 Ibid., p.85.

199 Ibid., pp.162 and 88.

200 Ibid., pp.173–4.

201 Václav Flajšhans (ed.), *O mučenicích českých knihy patery*, Prague, 1917, pp.41–3.

202 Pekař, *Z duchovních dějin českých*, p.145. Patočka shares this view: *Was sind die Tschechen?*, p.177.

203 Cited by Vlnas in *Jan Nepomucký*, p.8.

204 Quoted ibid., p.31.

205 František Šimek (ed.), *Staré letopisy české z Vratislavského rukopisu novočeským pravopisem*, Prague, 1937, p.2.

206 Vlnas, *Jan Nepomucký*, p.84.

207 The Czech title was *Život svatého Jana Nepomuckého, hlavního kostela sv. Víta kanovníka, kollegiálního u Všech svatých na Hradě Pražském děkana, v kostele nejblahoslavenější Panny před Tejnem kazatele, pro nevyjevení svaté zpovědi uvrženého do řeky Vltavy, kterýžto opatrovník a obhájce jest těch všech, ježto se světské hanby strachují.*

208 *Hra o svatém Janu Nepomuckém* in Zdeněk Kalista (ed.) *Selské čili sousedské hry českého baroka*, Prague, 1942, p.125.

209 Bohuslav Balbín, *Život svatého Jana ...* in Zdeněk Kalista (ed.), *České baroko*, Prague, 1941, p.157.

210 Ibid.

211 Kalista (ed.), *Selské čili sousedské hry*, p.117.

212 For details of the cult and the development of John's simple stone-slab tombstone into the silver monstrosity of a shrine, see Vlnas, *Jan Nepomucký*, pp.97–186.

213 Ibid., p.142.

214 Quoted by Ferdinand Peroutka, *Budování státu. Československá politika v letech 1917-1923*, vol.I, 2nd ed., New York, 1974, p.105.

215 Ibid., p.215.

216 Rudolf Medek, *Plukovník Švec. Drama o třech dějstvích* [1928], 7th ed., Prague, 1930, p.127.

217 Jaromír Lang, 'Julius Fučík 1903–71' in Jaromír Lang (ed.), *Kulturně historický sborník University 17. listopadu*, vol.I, Prague, 1974, p.225.

218 Kohout, *Dobrá píseň*, pp.111 and 113.

219 Milan Kundera, *Poslední máj*, Prague, 1955, p.26.

220 Ibid., p.28.

221 Macura, *Šťastný věk*, p.39.

222 Ibid., p.44.

223 Eda Kriseová, *Václav Havel. Životopis*, Brno, 1991, p.141.

224 See Albert Soboul, 'Religious Feeling and Popular Cults During the French Revolution' in Stephen Wilson (ed.), *Saints and their Cults. Studies in Religious Sociology, Folklore and History*, Cambridge, 1983, pp.217–32.

225 Lenka Procházková, *Jan Palach*, Prague, 1990, pages unnumbered.

INDEX